CWe1329581

Oundle's War

Memories of a Northamptonshire Town

1939-1945

Michael Downes

Foreword by
His Royal Highness the Duke of Gloucester G.C.V.O.

The Nene Press
Oundle

Oundle's War
Memories of a Northamptonshire Town 1939-1945
© Michael Downes 1995

All taxable profits from the sale of this book will go to The Royal British Legion
Registered Charity Number 219279

First published in Great Britain in 1995 by The Nene Press

All rights reserved. No part of this publication may be reproduced, stored in a retrieval system or transmitted in any form by any means, electrical, mechanical or otherwise without permission in writing from the copyright owner and the publisher.

ISBN   0-9526714-0-9
British Library Cataloguing in Publication Data.
A catalogue record for this book is available from the British Library.

Typeset by Brenda Durndell
Photo origination by TypeStart Digital Pre-Press
Printed and bound in Great Britain by Clays, St Ives plc for
The Nene Press, The Bursar's Office, Church Street, Oundle, Peterborough PE8 4EE

FOREWORD

by

HIS ROYAL HIGHNESS THE DUKE OF GLOUCESTER G.C.V.O.

KENSINGTON PALACE, LONDON W8

History is usually taught as a bare outline of facts. The Second World War was won by the Allies and in retrospect this is so fundamental to the history of the 20th Century that it is difficult to feel that the outcome could ever have been doubted. But at the time - particularly when Great Britain only had their Imperial Allies - the outcome was very much in doubt. It was only the sense of national unity which made so many people share the feeling that the fundamental rightness of the British way of life was well worth some personal sacrifice, to prevent its extinction by a very alien sense of values.

Inevitably such a complicated struggle could only produce the necessary victory if more mundane ambitions were put aside, or delayed, to benefit the whole community effort.

The contribution of Oundle was only crucial to the outcome in the sense that like other towns it shared a feeling with all other communities similarly committed to the prevailing of our national will to overcome another by whatever means came to hand.

Hopefully this book will demonstrate how the war affected various members of the Oundle community and how their efforts and sacrifices contributed in their own way to the ultimate victory.

January 1995.

To my family, in memory of the generation who fought for the right of families everywhere to live in peace.

CONTENTS

Illustrations	ix
Acknowledgements	xiii

Chapter One — Beginnings — 1
- Crusaders and Debaters — 3
- The Hitler Youth in Oundle — 4
- A Few Tables from the Führer — 6
- Witnesses to Persecution — 8
- Fears for the Future — 9
- An Education for War — 12

Chapter Two — Oundle in Wartime — 17
- First Changes — 17
- Evacuees — 21
- Blackout — 25
- Rationing — 25
- Food Production — 28
- The Women's Land Army — 28
- Schoolboy Farmers — 31
- A Farm Camp at Achurch — 34
- Growing Your Own — 35
- Ingenuity — 36
- Black Market — 36
- Scrap Metal — 37
- Comforts for the Troops — 37
- The Oundle Maids' Club — 39
- The Women's Voluntary Service — 40
- Fund-raising — 41
- Red Cross Fund-raising — 44
- Defending the Realm — 46
- The Observer Corps — 51
- Fire-watching — 52
- The Home Guard — 54
- A Comic Opera? — 60
- Spy Mania — 62

Life at the Manor	63
Oundle School	64
Schoolboy War Workers	65
A Schoolmaster's Memories	68
Oundle's War Poets	70
An Interest in the Enemy	72
Wartime Morale	76
Postwar Changes	76

Chapter Three — Active Service — 79

~ 1939 ~

Call-up	79
The Phoney War	83
The War at Sea	83
Waiting for the Weapons	84

~ 1940 ~

The Overrunning of Norway	85
Keeping the Sea Routes Clear	86
The Battle for France	89
The Evacuation from Dunkirk	92
Italy Enters the War: the Defence of Malta	95
The War in the Air: the Battle of Britain	97
A Blenheim Pilot Remembers	102

~ 1941 ~

The Mediterranean: the Malta Convoys	103
The War at Sea	105
War in the Western Desert: the Arrival of Rommel	106
Operation 'Crusader'	109
The War in the Air	111
Flying an Inferno	112
Working with the SAS: a Tragedy in the Desert	114

~ 1942 ~

The Fall of the Far East	115
The Fall of Java	116
Retreat to India	117
Life in the Sub-continent	118
The Battle for Malta	118

North Africa	124
El Alamein and the Turn of the Tide	125
Operation 'Torch': the Capture of Casablanca	127
The Battle of the Atlantic: a Merchant Navy Man's Tales	128
The Submarine War	131
The War on the Surface	134
The War in the Air	135
The Allied Counter-offensive in the Far East	137

~ 1943 ~

The Far East: the Arakan Offensive	138
Clearing Up in North Africa	139
The Battle of the Atlantic: Closing the Gap	141
The Attack on the *Tirpitz*	141
The Invasion of Italy: Delivering 'Major Martin'	150
The Assault on Italy	154
A Hero of the SAS	154
The Aegean Campaign	156
The War in the Air: Bomber Command at Work	161
An Oundle Airman	161
Busting the Dams	167
A Hero's Death in the Pyrenees	167

~ 1944 ~

The War in the Far East	168
Burma: the Arakan and Kohima	168
Oundelian Chindits	174
The Liberation of France: D-Day	176
Planning 'Overlord'	177
The Battle for the Beaches	179
The Battle of Normandy	180
The Secret War	187
Pushing Into Europe	190
The Disaster of Arnhem	190
The Fatherland Under Threat	194
New Enemies	196
Palestine	196
The Crisis in Greece	198
The War in the Air: the Bombing Intensifies	202
The Doodlebug Menace	208

~ 1945 ~

The Final Advance	208
The Bombing Goes On	210
Discovering the Death Camps	211
Victory in Europe	211
The Collapse of Japan: the Capture of Burma and Borneo	212
The Arrival of the Atom Bomb	214

Chapter Four — Friends and Allies 221
The Yanks	221
First Impressions	222
Hollywood in Polebrook	222
Fun with the Yanks	228
Mementoes	232
GIs' Girls	236
Chewing Gum Kids	238
Bombing Hitler's Germany	239
A Dangerous Job	242
Tragedies	244
The Tragedy of 'Ten Horsepower'	246
Enduring Links	250
New Bikes for Polebrook	252
The Poles	257

Chapter Five — Captives in a Distant Land 261
Prisoners in Europe	261
An Epic Tale: the Wooden Horse from Oundle	264
Prisoners in Asia	273
Prisoners in Britain	290

Chapter Six — The End 295
Celebrations	295
Oundle's Gratitude	296
Picking up the Pieces	300
Post-War Problems	301
Feelings for the Enemy	302
The Lessons of War	305
Postscript	309

Text and Picture Credits	311
Selected Bibliography	313
Index of Names	315

ILLUSTRATIONS

		Page
1:	Ashton's Miriam Rothschild: 'I had no doubt there was going to be a war.'	3
2:	Dr Ben Grantham: 'We were bitterly opposed to Fascism and Nazism.'	4
3:	Robin Miller with his diary of pre-war memories	7
4:	Elizabeth Berridge: 'I was absolutely terrified of Hitler.'	9
5:	One of Oundle School's air-raid shelters, at the top of Blackpot Lane	11
6:	Gerald Touch in 1935, hero of the technological war against the Nazis	13
7:	Gerald Touch celebrating his golden wedding with his wife Phyllis	14
8:	Speech Day tea at Oundle School, 25 June 1938	15
9:	Oundle's Drill Hall on Benefield Road	17
10:	19-year old June Gaunt and Ella Formby in 1943	18
11:	Cobthorne, on West Street, a wartime ATS base	19
12:	Oundle's Victoria Hall on West Street	21
13:	Military airfields in the Oundle area during World War II	22
14:	A children's Christmas party for evacuees in the Victoria Hall, 1939	23
15:	Oundle's Isolation Hospital on Stoke Doyle Road	24
16:	Wartime austerity: schoolboys outside an Oundle sweet-shop	26
17:	Cheerful smiles from a Women's Land Army group in November 1940	29
18:	Former Land Girl and Cotterstock resident Gladys Ashby in WLA uniform	30
19:	Gladys Ashby and friends at the Measures' farm, Hemington, in 1941	30
20:	A Women's Land Army reunion at the Royal Albert Hall in London	31
21:	Schoolboys at work attaching a pitch-pole cultivator to the school tractor	32
22:	Oundle School boys hoe between the rows of a fine crop of cabbages	33
23:	A farm horse being shod by a 16-year old schoolboy in 1941	34
24:	A group of Barnwell residents at work on socks for soldiers	38
25:	HRH The Duchess of Gloucester visits the WI Headquarters on South Road	39
26:	The British School, the wartime base of Oundle's Maids' Club	40
27:	Crown Court, facing north: The Assembly Rooms	40
28:	Ashton's 'Conker King' Vic Owen, with the author's daughter Rosie Downes	41
29:	War Weapons Week, July 1941: The band leads a march along West Street	42
30:	War Weapons Week, July 1941: Nurses at the tail-end of the march	43
31:	A plaque presented by the Admiralty to mark the adoption of HMS *Nene*	43
32:	Mrs Lottie Mason, MBE, one of Oundle's champion wartime fund-raisers	45
33:	HRH Princess Alice visits the Oundle Ambulance Division unit in 1942	45
34:	16-year old Peggy Wade, now Mrs Gidley, in Civil Defence uniform	46
35:	The old ARP post: Oundle's defensive nerve centre against Nazi bombs	47
36:	Oundle School staff experiment with a gas mask	48
37:	Oundle's Royal Observer Corps post	52
38:	Oundle Fire Brigade 1938-39	53
39:	Members of Oundle School fire-fighting squad at work in 1941	54
40:	Lt. Col. F. R. Berridge, DSO, MC, JP, inspecting a soup kitchen	55

		Page
41:	A member of Oundle School's JTC instructing the local Home Guard	58
42:	Oundle Rectory: wartime base of the Royal Army Service Corps	59
43:	The access to the Royal Army Service Corps base for 'other ranks'	60
44:	Oundle School boys working at the model lathes in the Metal Workshops	66
45:	Oundle School boys using oxy-acetylene equipment at the Workshops	68
46:	Oundle School history master Dudley Heesom	69
47:	Oundle School master Rolf Barber	73
48:	Dr Kenneth Fisher, Oundle's wartime headmaster	75
49:	Tanks in Oundle Market Place during a recruiting drive	79
50:	Flight Lieutenant Bill Monk, alongside a Halifax of Coastal Command	80
51:	Commodore Kenneth Gadd CBE, DSC	86
52:	A German 'Oboe' mine exploding a little too close for comfort!	88
53:	HMS *Clinton*, a Fleet Minesweeper built in 1943	89
54:	Major Patrick Hunter-Gordon, MC	90
55:	Lieutenant Gordon Potts, killed in action, 21 May 1940	91
56:	Captain Michael Potts, killed in action, 21 May 1940	91
57:	Oundle's most amusing ex-schoolboy: Lt Col Arthur Marshall MBE	93
58:	Flight Lieutenant George Rex Shepley, DFC	94
59:	Lucy Fallace with VAD friend Mara Marks in Malta 1940	96
60:	Oundle School's ATC working on the School's aeroplane engine	98
61:	Cecil Lewis, wearing his RFC Wings and MC in 1916	99
62:	Air Commodore Ian Brodie OBE	99
63:	Pilot Officer Douglas Shepley	100
64:	Air Marshal Sir Richard Atcherley KBE, SC, CB, AFC	101
65:	Sub-Lieutenant John Heron Rogers	106
66:	Bombardier Avery John Stooke Burdett	108
67:	An RAF victim of the battle for Tobruk: Flying Officer John Kelham	124
68:	Oundle School's future Second Master, H. J. Matthews	125
69:	Captain Norman Jewell, MBE, DSC in 1943	127
70:	A Merchant Navy DEMS man: George Bristow in 1942	129
71:	George Bristow today, in happier times	130
72:	A wartime picture of Rear Admiral Ben Bryant, DSO, DSC	133
73:	Wing Commander Lucian Ercolani, DSO, DFC with fellow aircrew	136
74:	Sergeant Pilot Alfred Taney	137
75:	Gunner James Roughton	138
76:	Captain B. Guy Measures	140
77:	Robert Aitken in 1941, wearing an Ordinary Seaman's uniform	142
78:	Robert Aitken in 1942	143
79:	Robert Aitken DSO, standing alongside the bow of X7 at Duxford	146
80:	A survivor of Operation 'Source': Robert Aitken in 1995	148
81:	Rear Admiral Godfrey Place, VC, CB, CVO, DSC in 1968	149
82:	Captain Norman Jewell, MBE, DSC, on a visit to Oundle in 1995	153
83:	Captain Patrick Laurence Dudgeon	155
84:	Lt Col Robert Butler MBE, MC, hero of the Battle for Leros	156
85:	Sergeant John Marlow, killed in action on 16 April 1944	162
86:	A telegram like many thousands of others arrives at 48, East Road, Oundle	162
87:	A mother's anguish: 'No news has yet reached us about him.'	164
88:	John Marlow's commemorative scroll of honour	166

ILLUSTRATIONS

		Page
89:	A message from the King to John Marlow's family	167
90:	Ex-Burma veteran Major Denis Eadie, MC, with his two sons	169
91:	Captain Edward Maslen-Jones, MC, DFC	170
92:	The Certificate of Gallantry received by Captain Edward Maslen-Jones	171
93:	Lucian Ercolani DSO, DFC, on a return visit to Oundle in 1995	173
94:	Former Oundle GP Dr Michael Lewis, an officer in the RAMC in 1944	180
95:	Normandy veteran Dr Michael Lewis, in his garden on East Road	181
96:	Colonel Sir Alastair Graesser DSO, MC	186
97:	Veteran of the ill-fated Arnhem operation, Albert Spring	191
98:	Albert Spring with two former wartime comrades at Kesteren, Holland	194
99:	Turnhout, Belgium 1944: Oundle churchwarden Tony Hayward	195
100:	Lt Col Robert Butler MBE, MC, on a return visit to Oundle in 1995	197
101:	Flight Sergeant Edward Brown, killed on his 28th mission	202
102:	The Memorial Window in Lincoln Cathedral	203
103:	Wing Commander Michael Trentham Maw, DFC	204
104:	Pilot Officer John Mason, pictured with his DFC and service medals	206
105:	Flight Sergeant John Horsford, DFM	207
106:	The grave of Flight Sergeant John Horsford, DFM, in Genoa, Italy	207
107:	Lt Richard Berridge, Scots Guards, killed in action on 9 April 1945	209
108:	Planning a low level attack at No. 2 Group HQ, 2nd Tactical Air Force	210
109:	Flight Lieutenant Robin Miller working on the score of *Crescendo*	216
110:	Phil Coombs, an Oundle friend for USAAF personnel	221
111:	Clark Gable as a B17 air-gunner	223
112:	Captain Clark Gable with USAAF colleagues at Polebrook, 6 June 1943	224
113:	Captain Clark Gable signing autographs at Oundle	225
114:	Hollywood star Clark Gable chats to Oundle School master Frank Spragg	226
115:	Clark Gable with local girls Delma Northen and Mavis Pollard	227
116:	Lorna Sloan's diary record of a meeting with Clark Gable	228
117:	Stars at Polebrook: The Red Cross Club, Polebrook, 5 July 1943	229
118:	The Chequered Skipper at Ashton	230
119:	Sgt Joe Smith's postcard to friends at Oundle's Rose and Crown	231
120:	19-year old June Gaunt outside the cycle shop in St Osyth's Lane, Oundle	232
121:	Corporal Philip Doucett's cartoon presented to Jean Mabelson	233
122:	Flying Ducks, World War II Disney-style	234
123:	'Sperry Turrets', drawn for his Oundle friends by US airman Lester Reinke	235
124:	Jean Mabelson, and her sister Margaret Hawkins	236
125:	Pauline Ashby and Lorna Sloan revive memories of wartime Oundle	237
126:	Members of the USAAF aircrew on Stewart Laxton's Yeovil flight	238
127:	Ex-USAAF navigator Whitney Miller on a return visit to Oundle in 1994	240
128:	B-17G (43-38465 TU-A) 'Favorite Lady' of the 510th Bomb Squadron	241
129:	USAAF officers Lt Col LeDoux, Col Romig, Lt Col Bowles	247
130:	David Poole's painting of the tragic episode of 'Ten Horsepower'	248
131:	USAAF personnel being welcomed at Barnwell Manor	249
132:	USAAF aircraft lined up for Operation 'Home Run'	250
133:	The USAAF memorial at Polebrook Airfield	251
134:	David Clark's memorial to 'Ten Horsepower' in Polebrook Church	252
135:	Peter Brookes' cartoon from *The Times* of 2 July 1992	253
136:	Eight-year old Jodie Richardson thanks ex-USAAF Major Johnson	256

		Page
137:	A wartime exile in Oundle: John Czwortek	258
138:	Emil Skiba outside his West Street shop	260
139:	Lovel Garrett, in happier times after his years as a POW in Oflag VIIB	261
140:	Elliott Viney, DSO, MBE, TD, on a return visit to Oundle in 1995	263
141:	Ralph Leigh, a Lance-Bombardier with the Royal Artillery	267
142:	Oundle veteran Ralph Leigh: 'a complete pacifist' after Dresden	271
143:	James Bradley MBE, a survivor of Japanese cruelty	279
144:	Oundle resident Aubrey Clarke, a prisoner of the Japanese	284
145:	Karl 'Charlie' Schoenrock, one of Oundle's former German POWs	292
146:	VE Day outside The Nag's Head in West Street	296
147:	Remembrance Sunday, 1994, at Oundle's War Memorial	297
148:	The Heron Rogers Wood Memorial to WWII's Old Oundelians	299
149:	The children of the Keens family who served during WWII	299
150:	The hero of El Alamein at Oundle in 1947	303
151:	Group Captain Douglas Bader on a 1961 visit to Oundle	304
152:	Hiroshi Abe, James Bradley and Douglas Weir in Yokohama	305
153:	Gerald Touch's widow Phyllis in Laxton School Cloisters	307
154:	Some of the heroes of *Oundle's War* with its author	308
155:	Oundle War Memorial, a drawing by local artist Diana Leigh	310

ACKNOWLEDGEMENTS

The production of *Oundle's War* has been facilitated by the participation of the following individuals and companies. I am most grateful to them for their encouragement in this project as well as for their generosity and goodwill in making it viable.

- Barclay's Bank, Oundle
- Ian Bishop, Manager, Oundle School Bookshop
- Quentin Bland, Grafton Underwood
- Melvyn Chapman, Titchmarsh
- Hilary Clack, Oundle Museum
- Andrew Clay, Clay's Ltd, London
- Brenda Durndell and Andrew Marlow, Titchmarsh
- Roger Eames
- Diana Leigh
- David Marsden, Wadenhoe, Strata Design, Oundle
- Michael Mills
- The staff of Oundle School Library
- Oundle Tourist Information Centre
- Ron Sismey, Weldon
- J. F. (Bing) Swain
- David Webb, Bulley Davey Accountants, Oundle

I would also like to thank the following pupils from various schools in the Oundle area who helped me gather material for *Oundle's War* by interviewing veterans and others.

- Caroline Barker
- James Bonney
- Gary Bosworth
- Nicholas Briggs
- John Burton
- Andrew Coulthurst
- Alix Delany
- Simeon Downes
- Christopher Emmott
- Andrew Gartside
- Thurstan Guthrie-Brown
- Penny Grewcock
- Adrian Hilton
- Matthew Joyce
- James Kilner
- Przemek Kordos
- Nicola Lancaster
- Tom Pickford
- Tim Robey
- Ben Shearon-Johnson
- Matthew Thornton
- Matthew Woods

Finally, of course, I am grateful to the many people who co-operated with me on this project by agreeing to share their experiences of World War Two. It was fascinating and frequently humbling to hear and read about their memories.

CHAPTER ONE

Beginnings

I'll always remember the moment I heard that war had started... it's so clear in my mind.... I was riding a pony when they told me... It frightened me so much I daren't ride the pony.
  Jessie Duffin, Bulwick (Nine-year old farmer's daughter Jessie Northen, living in Warmington in 1939)

I was at home in Benefield Road and I was going to school at Laxton School. I can remember push biking from home down to my father's shop, which is now Owen & Hartley's, and as I was cycling along I thought... 'War, war, war... What on earth is it going to be like?' You know...? And you just didn't know.
  Bevil Allen, St Anne's Court, Oundle (11-year old schoolboy)

As Big Ben finished striking eleven and Mr Chamberlain made the announcement that we were at war with Germany, without speaking, my mother and I walked to the front door and at the same time Mrs Roskelly next door did the same. Perhaps we wanted to look at our village, Stoke Doyle, wondering what was to happen in the years ahead. I noticed that Mrs Roskelly was crying and my mother's eyes filled with tears. They were thinking of families lost in the Great War, and dreading the same happening again.
  Ruth Keens, Herne Road, Oundle (15-year old Ruth Moisey, of Stoke Doyle)

I was finishing my Summer holiday as I was still at school. At the time we were fog bound in the port of Ostend waiting for a break in the weather. I am not precisely certain of the timing, but we ended up sailing across the North Sea, fog or not. And I can vividly recall coming into a sudden clear patch, and all around us were merchant ships heading like hell for home, very frightening! Then the fog came down again, blotting everything out other than the noise of fog horns, until we were very close to the East coast and found ourselves sailing for Yarmouth inside a destroyer screen, for which we were most grateful.
  Dr Ben Grantham, Mill Road, Oundle (17-year old schoolboy)

I was sitting on a troop ship in Clyde waiting to go out to the Middle East as reinforcements. It's difficult to remember my immediate reaction. I think probably relief as we had seen the build-up of the situation with lots of evacuees on the train up to Clyde. It was a nasty feeling and then relief as we knew the worst and we were not on tenterhooks any more.
  Major Charles Tod, South Road, Oundle (24-year old Army officer)

It's said that there's a legendary clarity with which our memory of a momentous event is preserved. Generations of Europeans were to remember where they were and what they were doing at that fateful moment on 3 September 1939, like some of their parents, who on 28 June 1914 had heard the news from Sarajevo heralding the start of the First World War. Almost half a century later, people in many parts of the world would remember what they were doing on 22 November 1963, at the moment of hearing the news from Dallas, Texas.

Unlike the assassinations of the Archduke Franz Ferdinand and President Kennedy, the start of World War II did not take Europe unawares. People throughout Britain had been following events in Nazi Germany closely, and Oundle was no exception. Yet up to the last moment most were hoping for peace.

John Hinman, a pupil at Laxton School in 1939, expressed a fairly typical view of the townspeople's attitude to Germany and the Germans. 'Everybody was hoping that there wouldn't be a war. It wasn't really anti-German at the time, it was anti-Hitler more than anything. They were hoping that the Germans would rebel against what Hitler was doing and stop it all.'

Those who were in the armed services in 1939 had a rather different view. Commodore Kenneth Gadd, who moved to Oundle from Hampshire in 1983, spent most of his career in the Navy on board minesweepers, and was already serving as First Lieutenant on the minesweeper HMS *Ross* in the Mediterranean when war broke out. 'We knew the war was coming for a year beforehand. You see, a lot of us were called up early because they knew it was coming — we all knew the war was coming. It was just a question of the date. We were quite prepared.' It was the politicians, in his view, who were less realistic. 'Since 1938 we knew there was going to be a war. It was quite clear but we dilly-dallied. The politicians couldn't make up their minds and we didn't have the ships or the war planes, so we were really caught napping there.'

For Vic Thorington, of Glapthorn Road, serving with the Army since 1932, war was also a foregone conclusion in his view and that of his fellow-soldiers in India, where he was stationed. Hitler's intentions were obvious.

> When I was on leave in this country, people were asking me if I thought there was going to be a war. I said, 'You're not wondering about that, are you? Of course there's going to be a war.' Out there, nobody hesitated a thought. They were just waiting for the day. Chamberlain, that chap who came running in at the end, waving his flag, saying 'Peace in our time' — what peace was he talking about? Anyway, we were fully aware that there was going to be a scrap. You have to look at it this way: they were armed to the teeth, they had spent their last penny on an army, a navy and an air force — invincible! He's not doing that for nothing: he wants a bit more space! We were reading about this out East, and over here they were still discussing what seaside they were going to go to for their holidays!

The naturalist, Miriam Rothschild, better known locally as Mrs George Lane, who often travelled in Europe and had close relatives in Austria and Hungary, had been alerted to the Nazi menace. She remarked: 'This country was so sleepy compared to the continent; they knew a war was coming. Even in neutral Switzerland, where we had a holiday home in the mountains, every single person in the village had a gun in their house. It was like a sort of dreamland in England. On the continent the Germans were seen as a terrible and inevitable threat to peace in Europe.'

The Swiss were ready for them but they knew they would not have much chance. On one occasion German mountaineers climbed the north face of the Eiger and they were first to get to the top, which of course was a tremendous achievement. When they came down the Swiss gave them a party in the hotel to celebrate and everyone got slightly tipsy. The Germans all stood up, waved their beer mugs and said, 'Take a good look round these mountains, because not only the Eiger but the whole of Switzerland will soon be ours'; they were nearly lynched as a result of this outburst. But that was the general feeling, and the Swiss were positive there was going to be a war, and I agreed with them.

1: Ashton's Miriam Rothschild: 'I had no doubt there was going to be a war.'

Crusaders and Debaters

Some of the younger generation were politically and passionately aware of the issues, in a way which might be considered surprising by many today. Former Oundle GP Ben Grantham remembered how he and his schoolfellows at Repton School in Derbyshire were kept well informed as to what was going on in Europe.

> Furthermore we were of the generation whose immediate seniors in the school had gone off when they could, to fight in the Spanish Civil War, and so we were bitterly opposed to Fascism and Nazism. We considered this a crusade — there was very little doubt about it at all. We thought this was a frightfully worthwhile thing, and had we been of an age to do so, we'd have all gone. We'd have all fought as Communists without the slightest hesitation. There was a tremendous amount of feeling about this.

Hitler's expansionist policy in the pre-war years had made Germany even more hateful than Spain for many of the future doctor's generation.

> There was this continual petty niggling, and this seizing of this and seizing of that, which we considered the most frightful wrongdoing. We were very anti-German, firstly because we considered their aggressions wrong, secondly because we nearly all of us knew Jews or Jewish families involved in their purges. Thirdly, for me personally, my feelings were influenced by members of my family who had been involved in the First World War, and we still believed the stories of the atrocities that the 'Huns' were said to have committed. I can remember at the Dragon School we were actually provided with old German machine-guns and things to play with. The myths and the legends went with them. We hated the Germans with a passionate hatred.

2: Dr Ben Grantham: 'We were bitterly opposed to Fascism and Nazism.'

For the young Ben Grantham the threat of Fascism in England had been dangerously real in the person of Oswald Mosley, the founder of the British Union of Fascists, known as the Blackshirts in the pre-war years. 'He had a hell of a following in the East End of London. Luckily everybody saw sense, but it was touch and go at one stage as to whether he would have been able to turn things round a bit. He was there; he was part of our background.'

Oundle School's pupils were apparently more diverse in their expression of political opinions, ranging from Fascists to Socialists and including some pacifists, according to history teacher Dudley Heesom.

> Almost every point of view had its supporters. There was even a small group of boys before the war who appeared in the Market Place wearing black shirts to mock the highly distinguished Professor Laski who, as his name ended in 'ski' must clearly have been a Communist! One of these boys was invited by the *Daily Mail* to go to Germany to write up Nazism. Later his contract was cancelled as the newspaper found that its support of Nazism was bringing about a disastrous fall in circulation. This boy was killed by the Germans in North Africa while fighting as a Captain in a British infantry regiment.
>
> The supporters of Labour were caught in the dilemma — 'War is evil' yet 'Hitler must be stopped!' The largest group who would not fight were however those who objected on religious grounds. In nearly every case at some stage they became combatant and at least two had distinguished war records.[1]

The Hitler Youth in Oundle

As early as 1936 the School's pupils had come into contact with the 'new' Germany, represented by a group of Hitler Youth who visited Oundle on 30 November with the aim of giving English people some idea of the cultural side of German life.

The group consisted of twelve girls belonging to the 'Bund Deutscher Maedel' and fourteen boys of the 'Hitler Jugend' of Hanover. They were accompanied by a leader, Herr Erwin Helms. Some were still at school or university, others were apprentices, typists, or shop-assistants, as was usual in the German Youth organizations. Their fortnight's tour of

English schools was in response to a visit which had been made to Germany by a party of boys from Manchester Grammar School. They arrived in Oundle by motor-coach. Their previous performance at Bedford School had been received with rapture by an admiring audience, judging by an eye-witness's account, full of praise for their appearance, 'brimming with health and vigour'.

They had their meals in the new Tuckshop in Milton Road and were quartered in the boarding-houses and privately. As their performance was not until the Monday evening, the Oundle boys had plenty of opportunity to make friends with their German visitors, and the Tuckshop presented an unusual scene, with groups of boys and girls conversing in a mixture of English and German and playing darts, bagatelle, cards and ping-pong. The Germans were also shown round the Chapel where they attended a practice of the 'Messiah'.

On the Sunday evening some of the Oundle pupils were present at their 'Adventfeier', a traditional ceremony held in many German families on the four Sundays before Christmas. For this a table was laid out with pine wreaths and candles and plates of sweets and biscuits, and with the lights extinguished, candles lit, and all sitting round the fire, a solemn and truly German 'Stimmung' was produced. Songs, music, poetry-reading and a short address by the Leader served to remind the exiles of the Fatherland, the whole providing a foretaste of the Christmas festivities.

The performance on Monday evening lasted an hour and a half, and the enthusiasm with which it was received left no doubt as to the School's appreciation and enjoyment of the excellent singing and playing. The first part of the programme, which the Leader in his introduction describes as 'the serious part', consisted principally of a modern cantata for voices and strings, alternating with a spoken recitative, the whole presenting in rhetorical, somewhat mystical form, the ideals and aspirations of the New Germany. 'It is possible that this item, the playing and singing of which were of a high order, seemed uninspiring to an English audience unable to follow the text and not unreservedly enthusiastic about the New Germany,' recorded an eye-witness. 'But it should be remembered that such ceremonial is dear to the German heart and is not peculiar to the Nazis. In any case it was an interesting experience.' The second, or 'gay' part of the programme was an unqualified success.

The folk songs and dances, accompanied by strings and flageolets, the skill of the accordion player, and the yodelling song by a boy of fourteen from the Harz mountains, were all greeted with whole-hearted applause. The boys' Hitler Youth uniforms were unexpected, but blended well with the peasant costumes of some of the girls. 'It was altogether a delightful and memorable evening.'

In conclusion the Leader extended an invitation to Oundle boys to join a winter-sports party in the Bavarian Alps during the Christmas holidays, and on both sides the hope was extended that the Oundle and Hanoverian 'Kameraden' should meet again.[2]

History master Dudley Heesom gave a less flattering account of the visitors' musical talents during what must have been the same visit by the Hitler Youth party, stressing nonetheless the politeness with which the group was received and the hope among pupils and staff that such friendly visits might make some difference to world affairs.

> After strutting up to the platform of the Great Hall, a little fat boy in shorts who had a Bach trumpet with a Nazi flag on it blew a fanfare. It was appallingly flat. At least five Oundle boys could have blown the fanfare perfectly. But the feeling of responsibility was so high that not a single boy laughed.[3]

A year later, at the 332nd meeting of the School's Debating Society, on 30 October 1937, the motion before the House was 'That in the opinion of this House friendly relations with Germany are essential to the continued existence of the British Empire'. It was clear that the boys appreciated the growing seriousness of the world situation, with France viewing with disfavour the recovery of Germany, and Hitler turning to the Rome-Japan axis. The future author of *Oundle and the English Public School*, Raymond Flower, speaking from the floor, referred to public opinion's support for the view that Germany should be given back its colonies so as to avoid war. After a long and wide-ranging debate the motion was lost by 42 votes to 48.[4]

There were those who believed that Germany's alienation from the rest of Europe was a contributory factor in the oncoming crisis in Europe. At the last meeting of the School's Debating Society in July 1939 before the outbreak of war in September, the motion before the House was that 'This House views with concern any encirclement of Germany'. Michael Mills, who both attended the School as a boy and later taught there, retiring to Oundle to live in Cotterstock Road, was Vice-President of the Society; it was he who had proposed the motion, claiming in his speech that Germany was like 'an old billy-goat, contented when left in the middle of the field, but, if it is driven into a corner, it becomes angry'.

'We have got ourselves to blame for the anti-British feeling in Germany, for she really wants to be friendly with us,' he went on. 'We should give her back her colonies and then she would be satisfied.' But the mood was hardening against Germany. The motion was lost by 20 votes to 67.[5]

Some Oundle people had a clearer insight than most into what was happening in Germany because of their personal experience of the country.

Oundle School's headmaster Dr Kenneth Fisher went on a visit to Jena, where he had taken his PhD. He found the laboratories almost empty of staff as most of the German research scientists had been withdrawn from pure research to work in less pure military projects. On the train a young Nazi struck a posture and said: 'I adore Adolf Hitler.' The conclusions were obvious.

There was even a German, Herr K. Rahmann who taught at Oundle School from 1937-38, and who was believed to be a Nazi agent by many in the town. Michael Mills remembered the flaming row which broke out after a joking remark from the French teacher Monsieur Malan about the German's briefcase, 'Ah! Ze spy papers!' On one occasion during the tense pre-war days of world crisis, when Herr Rahmann was looking particularly haggard in the Common Room, one of the masters said, 'You must have had perfectly ghastly orders from Berlin today.' His reply was, 'It's the complete impossibility of any one man making any difference in this situation.' Later, according to Dudley Heesom, it was to emerge that Herr Rahmann was one of the survivors of the July 1944 plot against Hitler's life.[6]

A Few Tables from the Führer

Benefield Road resident and music teacher Robin Miller remembered well his stay with a German family in Munich before the war, and knew the dangerously attractive nature of the Nazi fever that was sweeping the country.

> My parents were very anti-German — they had been through the Great War and so on — but I had the opportunity when young to be brought up partly bilingual in Germany. My parents

would not have any of it, though. Anyway, when I was a student at the Royal College of Music in 1935 I had an American friend of German extraction, who was going to spend some time in Munich improving his German, living with a German family. At this time Hitler had taken over, and my friend persuaded me to go with him.

The father was a retired Army Major, and the mother kept up appearances — she had a picture of Hitler on the mantelpiece. But she was very two-minded about the whole thing because she had friends who were Jews. She didn't say much about it, however, because it was too dangerous. The daughter was a member of the Hitler Mädchen and was a passionate admirer of Hitler himself.

While we were there, she heard that Hitler was having lunch in a certain café at a certain time in Munich. She asked us if we would like to go and try to see him. I kept a diary:

3: Robin Miller with his diary of pre-war memories, at his home in Benefield Road.

It's all rather thrilling; I should like to be able to say that I have seen him close up.

Sat. Aug 31: Went by bus and train to the Osteria-Bavaria Restaurant in Shellingstrasse. We arrived at about 12.45, and took as long as possible over lunch as Hitler was due at 2.30. At about 2.20, the waitresses began bustling around preparing for him. We began to get excited, and he soon came in followed by eight men, one of whom I now know as Rudolph Hess. Also in the party was Unity Freeman-Mitford, the English girl following him around at that time. He sat down in a corner two tables away from us. All around him sat these big, burly men, I suppose to act as sandbags in case anyone took any potshots at him. It was hard to realise that this little man had revolutionized Germany. He has a simple, sincere face and as he speaks his facial movements accentuate what he is saying. Of course we could not actually hear his voice but we could see his face easily.

Apart from a few old ladies, the only other people in the room were two English gentlemen, one wearing an Old Etonian tie, and a lady. The two men went up to Hitler, 'Heiled' him, and engaged him in conversation. The waitress told us that they were English Fascists come to study German politics, and were telling him how much they admired him. He sat there until about 3.45, and then went out. We followed him out, and saw the most enormous crowd. He had to push his way through them to get to his car. I climbed through the window of the café and found myself saluting him with the rest. And do you know I found myself shouting 'Heil! Heil!' with them. I feel quite ashamed of myself now. Flowers were thrown into the car as he left.

I think that this was the first thing that got me interested in things German, rather reacting against my parents' attitude to them.

Later on, during a return pre-war visit to Germany, Robin Miller was to redeem himself. 'We were on a cycling tour, and of course everywhere we went, children would be raising their arms and calling out "Heil Hitler!" to us. So we always made the point of answering them very politely, "Good afternoon" in English. They always looked very puzzled.'

Witnesses to Persecution

By now, of course, Robin Miller had come into contact with those who were suffering the direct consequences of Nazi persecution, and was disturbed by what he saw.

> In 1937 I travelled to Vienna to stay with a family suggested to me by a Viennese contact in order to improve my German. They were very nice — the father was slightly wounded on the Russian Front, and there was a son two years younger than me and also a daughter. The son and I had a great time together.
>
> In March 1938 was the Anschluss of Austria and I heard from a relative of theirs that they were in trouble. I had not realised, but the father was a Jew and the mother was not, so they were 'out' with the Nazis. In 1938 I found myself in Austria again, singing with a choir. I looked up the family, and landed up at their flat. It was all rather traumatic, as the Nazis were by this time in full occupation and all sorts of dreadful incidents took place. In fact I was there when two SS men arrived and said, 'You are Jews. You have two months to get out.' 'Where shall we go?' they asked. 'In the Danube for all we care,' was the reply.
>
> Anyway, I decided to do something about this. So I went to the Quakers and made arrangements for Heinz (the boy) and his family to come to England. We managed to get the whole family out in the Summer of 1939. When the war started they were in fact interned on the Isle of Man as 'enemy aliens'!
>
> Anyway they got out, and Heinz joined the Army and ended up as a Sergeant, about to go into Normandy. At this time, people like him were allowed to change their name, and Heinz Wolfgang Taussig became Henry William Tyrrell. We have kept in touch ever since — he lives in Kent.
>
> Indeed, he was recently telling me about quite a disturbing experience he had had in Austria during the Nazi occupation. He was in a queue with other Jews for some papers, when some SS men turned up, heavily armed. He decided that he did not like the look of this, and telephoned his mother to ask what he should do. She told him to return home immediately. Nobody in that queue was ever heard of again — a lucky escape indeed for Heinz.

Whatever repugnance he felt for the Nazis, Robin Miller felt a cultural kinship with Germans in general, at least prior to the outbreak of hostilities. 'I did like them, yes. One felt often more in sympathy with the German civilians than the French. I think both sides felt a sort of respect for each other in that way. The Japanese of course were a completely different matter.'

Miriam Rothschild, like many other people in this country, did what she could to help the Jewish victims of the persecution raging in Germany at that time.

> Before the outbreak of war, I adopted and brought out of Germany, under the Baldwin scheme, 49 children, who all came to Ashton. Their ages varied between 9 and 14, and most of them did amazingly well. When one of the boys got to the age of 16, a miracle happened: his mother, who was supposed to have gone into the gas ovens, turned up in America as a refugee working in a laundry, so I was able to send him out to her. At first he worked in a fountain pen factory, but at night studied chemistry and eventually went as a student to the University in Texas. He then joined the American army and rose to be a Colonel in their Secret Service and actually went back to Germany to the town from which he had been rescued. By a strange fate, he had the job of accompanying the German Generals to their prison. On the flight they asked him, 'How did you learn your excellent German?', but he did not tell them. He came to visit me, but time had rolled on and my husband had come back from the war. A year had gone by and my first child was born. I was looking after the baby in a flat in London, a few

days after coming out of hospital, when there was a knock at the door and when I opened it there stood a tall good-looking American colonel. He said, 'Do you recognise me?' I replied, 'My good fellow, I have never seen you before in my life,' and he laughed and said, 'I am Kurt!'

Not all the stories of Miriam Rothschild's adopted children have a happy ending. 'A great many of them were extremely unhappy, having lost their parents and had landed in new and strange surroundings. Two of them killed themselves here, which was a very great tragedy.'

Fears for the Future

Sabre-rattling alternated with the protestations of peaceful intentions during the propaganda war in which both sides engaged as a prelude to the declaration of hostilities. Just before the outbreak of war, on 11 August 1939, Mr F. Stretton, of Milton Road, was surprised to find a letter from Germany addressed to him at the Oundle Golf Club, where he was the green-master. The arrival of the letter, from Herr Goebbels, was notable enough at the time to be mentioned in the *Peterborough Advertiser*, which reported that it expressed 'the German point of view'. Mr Stretton no doubt threw the letter away, as no trace of it remains today. The explanation for its arrival in Oundle was probably that Philip Cotton, owner of the Market Place shoe-shop and President of the Golf Club, had encountered the German Ambassador Herr von Ribbentrop at Gleneagles in Scotland the previous year. Clearly the Nazi propaganda machine recognized that Oundle was an important and influential town in the battle for the hearts and minds of the British people![7]

Naturally there was apprehension at the turn events were taking. 'I was absolutely terrified of Hitler,' recalled Elizabeth Berridge, of Benefield Road, schoolmaster Wilfred Cole's daughter. 'I listened to him on the radio and although I didn't understand German, I could hear all the people in the background shouting "Heil Hitler" and I found it terribly upsetting. Our forces didn't seem to be ready for war — there weren't enough of them.' Her feelings were echoed by Ruth Keens, then a 15-year old living in Stoke Doyle:

> We had been listening to the radio and reading the papers watching with mounting horror how Hitler's troops were taking over, first one country then another. It seemed that no-one had heeded Mr Churchill's repeated warnings about rearmament and we were ill-prepared for what was to follow.

4: Elizabeth Berridge: 'I was absolutely terrified of Hitler.'

Miriam Rothschild was not among those who were surprised by the ease with which Hitler overran Europe in the early stages of the war. Travelling across the continent, on her way home from New York, she found herself in Paris in early November.

A French cousin of mine said, 'Would you like to go up and see the Maginot Line? And what about the Siegfried Line?' I said I would love to see the Siegfried Line, so we drove up into Belgium, which was a neutral country. Then I realised there was nothing in the way of Germans sweeping over Belgium. There were no road blocks and, to my astonishment, the only barriers in the highway were bundles of faggots — it was amazing. We spent quite a lot of time looking for the Siegfried Line through our binoculars.

Fear of enemy action from the air was foremost in the minds of many from the start of hostilities. The night after war was declared, many Oundle people were convinced that a bomb had exploded in the town when the workhouse chapel on Glapthorn Road was struck by lightning in a storm.[8]

Many air-raid shelters had already been built. As early as 1938 each boarding-house in Oundle School had dug trenches which could be occupied in case of bombing, and by April 1939 the School's magazine recorded the completion of the task:

Trench-digging has been the most remarkable event of the term and for the past two weeks most of the School has been busy on this novel form of work. Shifts of an hour have been worked and on the whole we think most of the School have enjoyed the change. However, it is time we in Oundle took these precautionary measures, and 'Something attempted is something done'. Next term we hope to see many of the blemishes we have made on the fields and grounds covered at least partially and made less obvious: we shall then have a complete system of trenches and the satisfaction of having dug them ourselves.
    So another anxious term has passed, and we hope for such an easing of the political situation that we may not have to use our trenches: long may they remain untouched.[9]

The knowledge that science and technology would be used to a far deadlier effect in wartime than they had ever been in the history of mankind was poetically expressed in Sixth Former Ian Grant's *The Might of Man*, published in the School's magazine.

> A giant vessel sails across the seas;
> An engine roars across the country-side;
> A car conveys us whereso'er we please;
> And in the air an aeroplane doth glide,
> And Man controls them all!
>
> A gleaming shaft in perfect rhythm glides;
> And turns in perfect time a giant wheel;
> A flying shuttle through the fibres slides,
> And cotton strands spin fast upon their reel,
> And Man controls them all!
>
> The organ thunders forth a mighty chord
> As wrathful as the fierce Atlantic wave,
> And then it hushes; like a whispered word
> The notes flow forth all sombre, cool, and grave,
> And Man controls them all!
>
> A deafening crash, a fiendish blinding flame,
> A hideous shell goes screaming through the air;
> Machines we have which blacken mankind's name,
> Which neither Man nor any life do spare:
> O God, control us all![10]

ONE ~ BEGINNINGS

Bevil Allen, remembering his part in the preparations for war, was not quite so enthusiastic as his schoolmasters about the building of air-raid shelters.

> I helped dig out the shelter at the top of Blackpot Lane. That was an awful performance; it was very hot weather when we were doing it, and of course when you got below a certain level you had to fill a bucket and haul it up. I can remember losing a lot of sweat over digging that air raid shelter, and of course they weren't really used but I suppose it was necessary to take precautions.

5: One of Oundle School's air-raid shelters, at the top of Blackpot Lane.

These precautions involved a certain disruption to the young Bevil's routine, with schoolboys being led by Laxton School masters down St Osyth's Lane to the underground shelter in the grounds of Bramston House. Peter Higson-Smith, also educated in Oundle and known to local residents today as a Northamptonshire County Councillor, remembers painting the backs of cockroaches while waiting in the cellars of the School's Berrystead House. The different colours served to identify the runners in races that junior pupils organised to pass the time.

There were of course other air raid shelters in the town that have since been filled in, but those at the top of Blackpot Lane outside Oundle School's Chemistry Department, and in the grounds of Bramston House are still visible. Inside the shelters were bunks arranged five deep to accommodate the potential refugees from the Luftwaffe bombardment. Entry to the Bramston shelter was barricaded a few years ago when it was discovered that pupils were using it as a den for various unauthorised activities. They were of course simply following a long-established tradition. Former Oundle School boy John Keene, who left Bramston House in 1945, remembered the air-raid shelters as 'quite good retreats for us smokers. Alas, I looked up one afternoon and to my horror there was Reggie Saunders gazing down at me. I had to report to my housemaster and accept my punishment'.

Less elaborate than the above, and available on a national scale, was the Anderson shelter, based on a simple design involving 14 sheets of corrugated iron buried to a depth of four feet, covered with at least 15 inches of soil and capable of accommodating six people in conditions of discomfort. A distribution scheme was announced a year before the outbreak of war: the shelter was issued free to all earning less than £250 a year, and at a charge of £7 for those earning more than this income. Eventually 2,250,000 were erected in householders' gardens up and down the country. A more solid, concrete version was built in the garden of New Road residents Keith and Margaret Sauntson.

Another example of British ingenuity in dealing with the threat of air-raids, and one unique to Oundle, was soon seen at the School in the shape of the Bungyphone. This was an ingenious device invented by the Science teacher, Herbert Palmer, and so called because of his nickname. In the event of an air attack it could give immediate warning, setting bells ringing in all the boarding-houses simply by breaking the circuit of the electric light. What had not been appreciated was that normal accidents tended to short circuit the lights several times a day, and very soon the boarding-houses had to put out of action the Bungyphone rather than go unnecessarily to the trenches.[11]

Many older Oundle residents suffered from frustration at their inability to contribute to the war effort. Dr Charles Newman, the eminent physician and ex-Dean of Hammersmith Hospital, who lived for a time in the family home at Bramston House on Oundle Market Place, and then in Cotterstock Manor before moving to South Road in Oundle, recalled how everyone who was compulsorily inactive found the war a trial to the nerves. His father Arnold Charles Newman, known as 'The Boss', who was living at the time in Cotterstock, in the depths of the country, had an air-raid shelter dug in the garden, more on account of what he called the 'fidgets of inactivity' than through fear of German bombs.[12]

An Education for War

Confidence in the country's ability to withstand the Nazi threat should have been stronger in Oundle than in many parts of Britain. This was after all the town whose School had provided technologists and leaders for the industrial heartlands of Britain for most of the century, thanks to the ideas of its famous headmaster Frederick Sanderson and the equally famous Workshops. Oundle at this time cultivated the image of a tough, no-nonsense school, wrote a former pupil in his book about Oundle and the English public school tradition. 'Because of its engineering tradition, Oundle tended to attract the sons of parents with family businesses or industrialists; indeed the school lists bristled with household names, from jam to toothbrushes, dreadnoughts to cars.'[13]

Was not a former pupil, Sir Geoffrey Vickers, who had won his Victoria Cross in the First World War, to become Deputy Director-General at the Ministry of Economic Warfare in 1941? Sir George Briggs, who had left Oundle in 1916, was shortly to become Deputy Controller of Iron and Steel Supplies. Was it not Oundle who had provided the education for wartime industrialists like Sir Alfred Owen and Edward Paxman, who had helped to make Britain the workshop of the world? George Nelson, the future Lord Nelson of Stafford,

ONE ~ BEGINNINGS

had been sent by his father, Chairman of the English Electric Company, to the School's Laxton House; he had left in 1934, joining the company in 1939 as superintendent of its Preston works, where over 3,000 Halifax and Hampden bombers would have been produced by the end of the Second World War.[14]

Among the many other companies which contributed to wartime research and production of value to the RAF at this time was Pye Radio Limited, whose chairman Harold Pye, a former Oundle School pupil, had left Dryden House in 1920. The company's wartime products for the RAF included test gear, navigation aids, telescopes, anti-aircraft sights and radar components, while its radios were used in thousands of British tanks.

Oundle School's reputation for science in the 1930s had attracted another unsung hero of wartime technology whose roots were more local. Gerald Touch, from nearby Thrapston, was a leading member of the team whose secret work on developing radar before the Second World War was to help save beleaguered Britain from disaster. Gerald Touch himself, the son of a gentlemen's outfitter, was to end his career as Chief Scientist at Government Communications Headquarters (GCHQ), retiring in 1971.

In a later chapter it will be seen that effective control from the ground was one reason for the RAF's victory. A well-knit defence system with radar stations, operations rooms and high-frequency radio network had been set up in the pre-war years, comprising a coastal chain stretching from Ventnor in the Isle of Wight to the Firth of Tay.[15] The future intelligence expert from Thrapston, educated at Laxton School, studied with Oundle School's Sixth Form before going to Jesus College, Oxford. A brilliant scientist with a double first in Maths and Physics, the young Gerald Touch was finishing his doctoral thesis at Oxford when he was spotted by an aide of the radio pioneer Robert Watson-Watt, then scouring the universities for talent. It was August 1936, and scientists under Professor Watson-Watt at Bawdsey Manor outside Felixstowe were already making encouraging progress towards the goal of condensing radar detection equipment so that it would fit into a military aircraft.

6: Gerald Touch in 1935, hero of the technological war against the Nazis.

The following year, Gerald Touch was one of a party of four which took off in an Anson aircraft to carry out the first trials of airborne radar in the world. From the aircraft the four scientists bounced signals off ships of the Home Fleet in the Channel approaches as part of the development of ASV-2 Bawdsey's code for an air-to-surface vessel Mark-2 system. In 1940 the ex-Laxton School boy moved to the Royal Aircraft Establishment (RAE) at

Farnborough before being sent to Washington as a member of the British Air Commission. His rôle in America, where he was to stay until after the war, was to superintend the fitting of British-designed radar sets to aircraft being dispatched to this country under the Lend Lease programme, and also to advise on the application of British technology to the US air forces.

Not being a member of the Armed Services, Gerald Touch, like other wartime technologists associated with Oundle, is not listed in any of the war archives in the town. Yet his contribution to the war effort deserves to be fully recognised.[16]

7: Gerald Touch, Chief Scientist at GCHQ, celebrating his golden wedding with his wife Phyllis.

It may well have been on Gerald Touch's recommendation that two more wartime scientists of whom Oundle should be proud joined the top-level team working on secret defence research. The first of these was Vivian Bowden, later to be created Lord Bowden under Harold Wilson's government, which considered him as one of the leading technologists in Britain. Vivian Bowden had arrived in Oundle from the Cambridge Cavendish Laboratory to be chief Physics master at the School in 1938. He was one of a pair of outstanding Physics teachers who were whisked away in 1939 to be set to work on projects connected with radar. The other was G. L. Smith, awarded an MBE for his work on night-fighter interception, whose health was to break down as a result.[17]

Yet another ex-Oundle technologist whose skill contributed greatly to the success of the RAF at this time was Hugh Barker, who had left Crosby House in 1923 to follow an engineering career. A future Chairman of Parkinson Cowan, he was seconded to the Ministry of Aircraft Production in 1940 as Deputy Director of Instrument Production. There his chief interest was the development of lenses for reconnaissance photography. He also worked on bomb-sighting equipment.[18]

ONE ~ BEGINNINGS

8: Speech Day tea at Oundle School, 25 June 1938.
(L. to r.) Schoolmasters H. J. Matthews, B. V. Bowden, F. C. Waddams, unknown, C. M. Osman.
Vivian Bowden, later Lord Bowden, was to leave the following year to undertake secret work on radar.
Charles Osman was to die in 1940, from wounds received at Dunkirk.

Whatever fears for the future there might have been, in any case, could not last forever, observed Oundle historian Dudley Heesom. He recalled how the inspired leadership of Churchill made use of despair to turn everything into a joke, and England developed the most surprising mood of confidence and hope. Dudley Heesom's pupils were no exception. One morning during the fall of France a boy, later to become a QC, arrived in school announcing brightly, 'Another couple of countries gone this morning, Sir.' As Dudley Heesom put it, 'the situation had become almost Shakespearean, when boys believed that the fewer we were, the better'.[19] It was perhaps such an attitude prevailing in both young and old which explains Oundle's positive achievements in the war effort.

Notes
1. Dudley Heesom, *The Thirties at Oundle*, in *The Laxtonian*, Michaelmas 1979, p.21.
2. *The Laxtonian*, vol.XIV, no.3, December 1936, pp.171-2. *The Ousel*, vol.XL, no.689, December 16, 1936, New Series, p.173. I am grateful to Mr Richard Miller, Director of Studies at Bedford School, for providing me with information about the Hitler Youth visit to Bedford.
3. Dudley Heesom, *The Thirties at Oundle*, in *The Laxtonian*, Michaelmas 1979, p.21.
4. *The Laxtonian*, vol.XIV, no.6, December 1937, pp.394-6.
5. *The Laxtonian*, vol. XIV, no.11, July, pp.817-9.
6. Dudley Heesom, *The Thirties at Oundle*, in *The Laxtonian*, Michaelmas 1979, p.21.
7. Patrick Duerden, *Aspects of Oundle during WWII*.

8   Patrick Duerden, *Aspects of Oundle during WWII.*
9   *The Laxtonian*, vol.XIV, no.10, April 1939, p.721.
10 *The Laxtonian*, vol.XIV, no.10, April 1939, p.788-9.
11 Dudley Heesom, *Oundle in wartime*, in *The Laxtonian*, Michaelmas 1980, p.17. Vera Lynn, *We'll meet again*, p.11.
12 John Newman Ward (ed), *The Newmans of Barnsley*, pp.8-9.
13 Raymond Flower, *Oundle and the English Public School*, pp.115-6.
14 *The Old Oundelian*, 1975-76, p.30; *The Old Oundelian*, 1982-83, p.67; *The Old Oundelian*, 1994-95, pp.92-3.
15 Guy Hartcup, *The Challenge of War*, p.99.
16 *The Times*, Obituary, 6 December 1994.
17 *The Old Oundelian*, 1963-64, p.47.
18 *The Old Oundelian* 1984-85, p.75.
19 Dudley Heesom, *Oundle in wartime*, in *The Laxtonian*, Michaelmas 1980, p.23.

CHAPTER TWO

Oundle in Wartime

First Changes

Many obvious changes took place early on in Oundle's population as a result of the war. The departure of many of the town's men on active service coincided with the arrival of new faces, and this was noticeable in a small community with at that time a population of about 2,250. Some of the new arrivals were to form permanent links with the town. Ruth Keens remembered the first troops arriving, a battalion of the Leicestershire Regiment, stationed at the Drill Hall on Benefield Road.

9: Oundle's Drill Hall on Benefield Road.

'They were all young lads eighteen to nineteen, probably never left home before. We girls enjoyed meeting them at the local dances and were sad to see them leave — on buses — one of their number playing "Sierra Sue" on the accordion.' Later on, the town became flooded with servicemen, especially from 1942 when the USA's involvement meant the arrival of Americans from the nearby airfields of Polebrook, Deenethorpe, Grafton Underwood, and the fighter base at King's Cliffe. Some well-known faces made their appearance in the area. Marlene Dietrich, Bob Hope and Glenn Miller would entertain

10: 19-year old June Gaunt (left) and Ella Formby in 1943, at the Gaunt family's home in East Road, Oundle.

troops at the local airfields. Joyce Hardick remembered George Formby's sister Ella, who stayed for two months at the Gaunt family home at 50 East Road while working with ENSA.

With Oundle's more compact nature, every house containing extended families or evacuees, people became closer and more friendly, recalled Ruth Keens. One of the local girls who was to marry a soldier from Leicester, Ted Hudson, was Joan Donegani, daughter of the East Road garage owner. Later the couple were to move to Australia.

Those people with houses big enough were obliged to accommodate some of the new arrivals, and Cobthorne, now Oundle School Headmaster's house on West Street, became home for a contingent of the Auxiliary Territorial Service (ATS). Their forward behaviour was evidently a source of surprise for local girls, according to Ruth Keens:

> Some were rather flighty to say the least, and I remember some telling us how they had stayed out with boyfriends after lights out, then been legged over the back wall of Cobthorne, straight into the flock of geese kept in the back garden, which chased them and certainly heralded their late arrival.

Along Barnwell Road where the cement factory now is, was an RAOC depot staffed by members of a REME section. Bevil Allen found himself living with some of them at his parents' house in Benefield Road.

> There was one chap who worked at the RAOC depot who lived with us and he went off, he was in the RAF. We saw an account in the newspaper of five fellows who were shot down in their plane and trekked a terrific distance for days and days in the desert and nearly perished

TWO ~ OUNDLE IN WARTIME

11: Cobthorne, on West Street, a wartime ATS base.

but managed to get back to base. We saw his photograph in the newspaper and then another couple of sorties after that he was shot down and killed, which was very sad.

Outside Oundle, at Polebrook Airfield, constructed in record time as Ruth Keens recalled, the RAF also made a hit with the local population. 'We now had the Brylcreem boys, as they were known; always cheerful, lighthearted and so gay, they were the bravest of the brave.'

The construction of Polebrook Airfield was carried out in a desperate hurry, according to Miriam Rothschild, on whose farmland it was situated.

> The maps provided were pre-1900, and bore little resemblance to the area on which the runways were to be laid, and the buildings erected.

There were some amazing and extraordinary characters among the men who had to carry out this gargantuan task. 'I always remember one chap,' recalled Miriam Rothschild, 'who was responsible for erecting the first huts on the field. He could drink 18 pints of beer without turning a hair, and down at the pub in the village he used to do this for a wager — drink the 18 pints and then end up with a full glass of gin.'

> A team of extremely jolly Irishmen were employed to help lay cables, and every night they got fighting drunk. It was a mystery where they procured their wine or spirits, since they were banned from all the pubs in the area. It eventually transpired that they were bubbling coal gas into milk and drinking that, and this beverage apparently sent them right round the bend.

Lord Rosebery, who was then Regional Commissioner for Civil Defence in Scotland, visited Peterborough at this time and I told him the story. Much to my surprise he knew all about the possibilities of putting gas into milk, which apparently removed the poisonous qualities, but it remained, nevertheless, very stimulating.

It was difficult to get enough slag to put under the runways during their construction. Lorries with their drivers, which came onto the airfield, were paid for their load at the entrance. A number of these then drove out at the other end, returned with the same load of slag and were paid again! One driver boasted that he had made the detour ten times. It was so important to construct the runways as soon as possible that such misdemeanours were ignored. There simply wasn't time to consider such incidents.

Owing to the defective maps, the drainage systems were not understood, and much to Miriam Rothschild's surprise, she found ducks swimming in the newly built WAAF's quarters.

The building of Polebrook Airfield was not without its tragedies. Considerable work had to be carried out to extend the runways, and vast amounts of gravel were extracted in the Oundle area. Charles Foster, living in South Road, who was supervising some of the extraction at the time, remembered the horrifying moment when one of the excavators carrying out work at what is now Oundle Marina slipped, carrying its driver to the bottom of one of the pits. 'We couldn't get him out. There was just nothing we could do at that depth, and in that darkness.'

The influx of new residents had a dramatic effect on the town's social life, remembered Ruth Keens. 'Oundle was much livelier than it is now, with dances and entertainments, most of it provided by the forces. I remember the wonderful sound of the Squadronaires Dance Band. On another occasion the RAF produced a pantomime at the Victoria Hall; it was absolutely hilarious as only service productions can be. Some years after the war, a paint firm representative had made an appointment at the Bursar's Office where I was working. Chatting as he waited, he mentioned that he had been at Polebrook during the war. I looked hard at him and asked, "Were you in the Pantomime?" "Yes," he replied, "I was Dirty Dick."'

Just as dramatic, once flying operations had started, was the noise of the air-traffic over what had been a quiet market town. Oundle was at the centre of an area criss-crossed during World War Two by combat aircraft from more than a dozen airfields. Polebrook, to the east, home to the RAF's 90 Squadron and then the USAAF 351st Bomb Group, and Deenethorpe, to the west, were the two nearest. Former Oundle School boy Patrick Lane remembered the disruption caused to lessons with one of his teachers, W. G. Walker. 'Oundle Church was a landmark for the aircraft at Polebrook Aerodrome and they would fly very low over it. Willie Walker in Room 31 (Great Hall block) would do a sort of Harpo Marx act, mouthing inaudible words, until the racket died down.'

Oundle in fact quickly became a plane-spotter's paradise. Another ex-Oundle School boy, Peter Green, kept an accurate record of the aircraft he saw in the skies above the town during 1942 and 1943. 'It was generally accepted that Air Training Corps (ATC) cadets knew more about new types of aeroplanes than most members of the public — it was a matter of pride to be the first to know.' On 5 May 1943 he noted that there was 'a good deal of flying. I sat and counted 102 different planes in one hour'. Occasionally planes piloted by ex-pupils would land on the school playing-fields. Peter Green recorded a month later that three Austers landed for an overnight stay on 9 June.[1]

12: Oundle's Victoria Hall on West Street, a focus of wartime social life in the town.

Evacuees

Most of the newcomers to Oundle were much younger. Just before war broke out, trains steamed into Oundle station packed with evacuees. A total of three and a half million people are estimated to have moved from high risk to less vulnerable areas in Britain between June 1939 and the first week in September. The county of Northamptonshire, being a low risk area, was designated a 'wholly reception county', and by the start of war had accommodated 45,529 evacuees, a number exceeded only by Somerset.[2]

To start with, the new arrivals in Oundle were mainly women and young children evacuated from London. Arrangements for the accommodation of evacuees were not, it appears, as efficient as they could have been. Many of the women and children returned within a few months, principally because they were forced to live in tents at Barnwell.

Not all the evacuees appreciated the joys of living in the countryside. Princess Alice recalled how two little boys came to stay in the staff quarters of the Manor, now largely habitable after an almost total renovation, and their sister was lodged with the butler and his wife, who had a little house nearby. One morning the boys got up with the intention of walking the 80 miles back to London. They went in the wrong direction and were soon returned to the safety of Barnwell. Asked why they had run away, they said the country was dull and they wanted to see more of the raids and guns.[3]

And Danford Close resident John Hinman, a pupil at Laxton School at the time, recalls a wasted journey which he made in connection with the arrival of the evacuees.

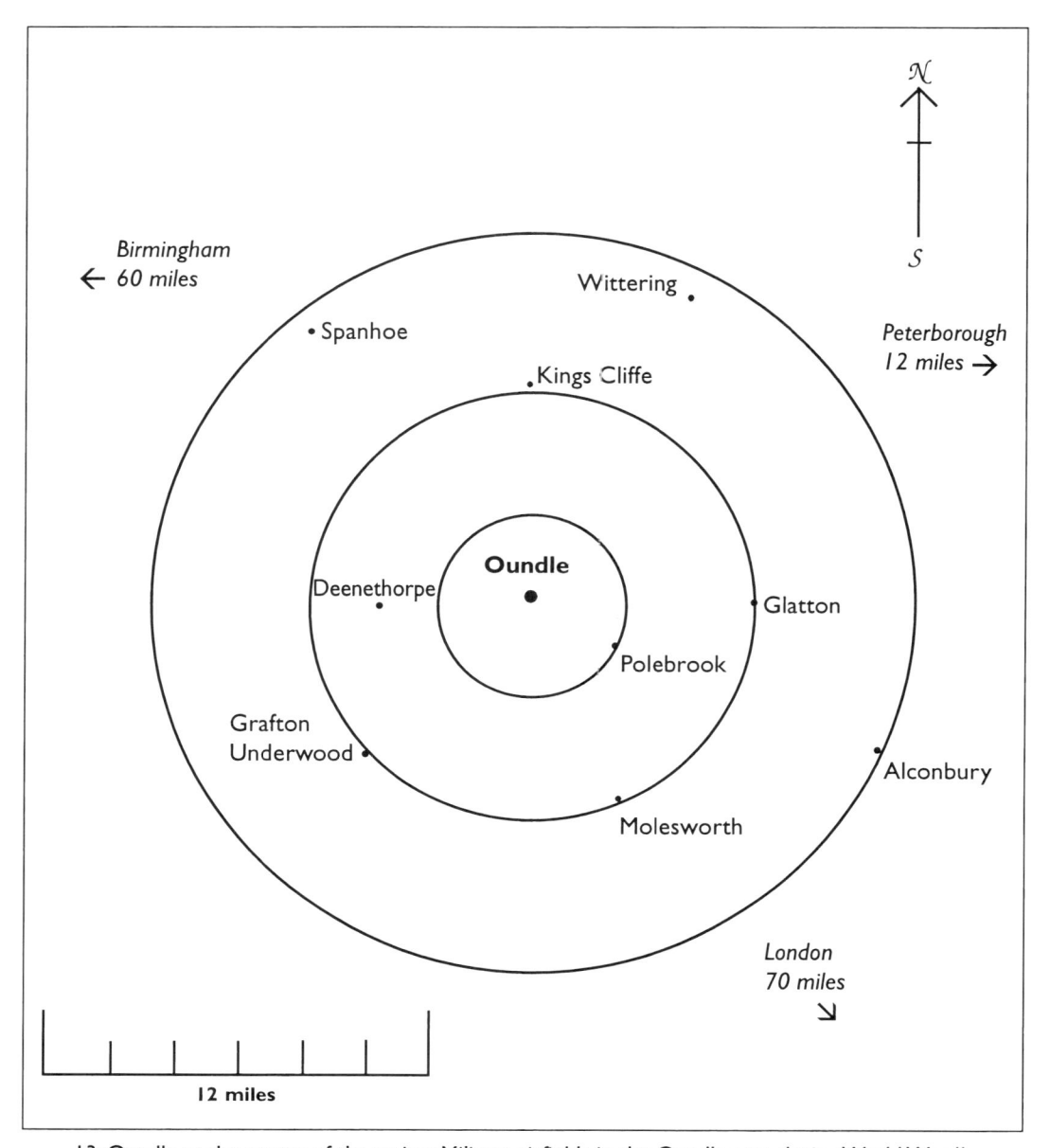

13: Oundle at the centre of the action: Military airfields in the Oundle area during World War II.

There were some girls from a School in Highbury in London. They were supposed to come in by train and then go by bus round to various villages, and some friends and I were given the job of sorting out the routes to the villages on bikes so we could direct the bus drivers to where they were going. But it didn't happen like that, they were just taken out from the station, and so we did all that biking for nothing.

More children arrived in Oundle as enemy bombing of the cities intensified. In July 1940 the Isolation Hospital on Stoke Doyle Road was requisitioned as an emergency hostel for children who might be found on arrival to be 'unsuitable for billeting on private households',

14: A children's Christmas party for evacuees organised by the British Legion in the Victoria Hall, 1939.

and in December of the same year the former hairdresser's shop at 39A West Street was designated as a Welfare Centre under the Government Evacuation Scheme.

At one time there were plans for 2,000 evacuees to live in Oundle, but these did not materialize. Even the small number of evacuee children eventually taken by the town caused problems of accommodation. The headmaster of Milton Road Church of England School recorded the difficulties he was having in the school register on 19 September 1939:

> School reassembled this morning under unusual conditions, after a prolonged holiday due to outbreak of War. Evacuees from London and other districts totalled 69, and with our own numbers of 168, made school for everyone impossible until further arrangements could be made.

By 27 September he recorded that extra accommodation had been arranged at Oundle School's Dryden House in Glapthorn Road thanks to an arrangement with the headmaster Dr Fisher. Local children attended normal classes in the morning before setting off for gleaning at Oundle Lodge Farm in the afternoon, their places at the school being taken by evacuee children.

There was a flicker of excitement in the independent school when green-blazered girls arrived in the town, but the schoolboys were to be disappointed: these particular evacuees soon moved out to Clopton. A rather larger flicker was caused by the arrival at Biggin Hall of girls from an elegant finishing school from Fiesole in Italy. Dudley Heesom rather dismissed their presence because, as he put it, 'boys were busy, and field glasses scarce'.[4]

OUNDLE'S WAR

But School House's Rhidian Graesser and his friends were not as busy as their schoolmasters thought, and certainly found time for the young ladies of Biggin Hall.

> We sometimes saw them in town during our very limited time allowed to the shops, and of course it was strictly forbidden in School rules to chat up any female at any time. So it caused many of us to change our Sunday afternoon habits, when under House rules we had to stay out of the House between 2.30 pm and 3.20 pm, and normally wandered up to and around the School playing-fields or down to the river — instead we walked out past the Golf course on the main road, and the most adventurous went into the Hall grounds, to see what they could see!

The number of evacuees fell as the war went on. By November 1943, there were only 40 in the Oundle Urban District Council area, and the Welfare Centre was opening only at the weekend. However the Isolation Hospital remained officially in use as an evacuee centre until October 1945.

Margaret Gale, of East Road, an Oundle teacher, felt that the town 'did a good job' with its evacuees, and many new friendships were made, with Oundle residents still receiving visits today from their wartime guests. Some, like Rock Road's Ernie Cox, adopted by their Oundle families, are still living in the town.[5]

15: Oundle's Isolation Hospital on Stoke Doyle Road, requisitioned as a hostel for evacuees.

Blackout

Another obvious change at night was the blackout. From Friday 1 September 1939 night-time Britain was plunged into darkness, and Oundle shared in the gloom for most of the war. Only in December 1944 was it noted that 'one by one, as if reluctantly, the street lamps have been springing back to life after five years of darkness'.[6]

The early enthusiasm to maintain a complete blackout had resulted in a stampede for blinds, curtains, brown paper, cardboard and drawing-pins. Oundle School, with its twelve boarding-houses, had a particular problem in observing the new régime. One housemaster's wife remembered that on the first day she had to black out 98 windows.[7]

People's social lives were much affected by the blackout, as Bevil Allen explained.

> You had to have a torch at night. A cycle lamp had to be covered by cardboard with a tiny wee slit in it, and the cars just the same. So it was horrendous going out at night. If you were on a bike you weren't allowed to have any light, and the people in cars could hardly see where they were going. So people didn't go out much at night on vehicles.

Changes also took place in the town's calendar. Many traditional local events were affected during the war years in Oundle. The Football Club abandoned its fixtures, and the Music Festival was cancelled, as were agricultural and horticultural shows, and Speech Days at Oundle and Laxton Schools.

The absence of church bells added to the gloom. 'I used to love to hear the church bells on a Sunday morning, and of course these were silent during the war because they would only ring the bells if the Germans landed — I really missed those church bells,' recalled Elizabeth Berridge. However Nora Blunt remembered the church bells in Barnwell being rung for her wedding-day. It was after all a special day for the village, and by 1944 the Germans were unlikely to invade: there was nonetheless some confusion in people's minds. 'Nobody really knew whether they'd rung the bells because I was getting married or whether there was an invasion.'

Rationing

The restrictions of war also affected people's personal lives. The rationing of items such as food and clothing applied to everyone, as Bevil Allen remembered from his childhood.

> The start of war didn't have any immediate impact at all, but as the weeks went by they started to issue us with gas masks and identity cards, and my mother used to get the groceries delivered. We used to get a big box of groceries once a week, and the first time we were on rations I can remember us all as a family, all five of us, standing in a circle round the table and peering into this little tiny cardboard box and saying, 'But we can't manage on that for a whole week.' A little bit of butter... not much more than you'd put on for three bits of bread.

Oundle's food traders did not find it easy to administer the new regulations. 'Dealing with rations was an absolute nightmare,' recalled Jessie Richmond, the cashier at North's, the West Street butchers now occupied by Johnson's. 'Sometimes people tried to twist your arm, but most people were very good.' What surprised her most was that the population did not suffer from food poisoning. 'The meat was in terrible condition, but no one was ill.'

16: A picture of wartime austerity: Oundle schoolboys gaze at the sign in the shop-window which reads 'NO BISCUITS SWEETS OR CHOCOLATES'.

Even royalty was affected by the restrictions. Two Oundle School pupils interviewing Princess Alice at Barnwell Manor in 1984 heard about the crate of oranges, sent from abroad as a gift to Her Royal Highness, who then had to hand them over to the authorities, thus proving that even princesses were subject to stringent rationing. 'Indeed,' they recalled, as Princess Alice poured out tea, 'we were thankful not to have to produce our own teabags as she had to when visiting friends during the war. Local hedgerows had been ardently searched for rosehips, in order to make syrup for the babies.'[8]

Barnwell, in common with the villages around Oundle, had certain advantages over the towns in having easier access to sources of food. Ruth Keens, brought up in Stoke Doyle, recalled one of them:

> We were fortunate in the village to have a poacher in our midst who provided us with rabbits and pigeons. My mother made tasty stews and I never tired of them, even after eating rabbit every night for a week. Rabbit meat was excellent then, before the days of myxomatosis. We also kept about a dozen hens, so were never without eggs; any surplus could not be given away but had to be collected each Saturday by the Egg Marketing Board; they then became part of the general ration in the shops.

TWO ~ OUNDLE IN WARTIME

Oundle School itself, of course, had the problem of ensuring that its pupils were adequately fed during these difficult times. Rationing at the School was one of the sides of war which was much better handled in the Second World War than in the First, believed schoolmaster Dudley Heesom, who remembered a housemaster announcing in 1917 that roast horse was to be served. 'In 1917 boys at school could not rely even on getting bread. Schools had to provide potato cakes and maize cakes and even cakes made of hay — which were just edible if eaten hot.' At least on one occasion during the Second World War, when supplies of meat were very short, a stew had to be filled out with whale meat.[9]

Rhidian Graesser, who left Oundle in 1942, recorded his memories:

> Food rationing meant that there was some deterioration in the menus, but because it was hardly gourmet in the first place it was not as disastrous as might have been expected. Most of us received parcels from home of extra 'goodies', and I was particularly lucky in having a studymate who was South African and who, surprising as it may sound in wartime, received food parcels from his parents in Western Province. Each boy had his weekly sugar ration, less an unspecified amount deducted by the kitchen staff for use in cooking, in a screw-top glass jar on the dining room table, and there was much bartering with those without a sweet tooth. I remember that the sugar had a rather sickly smell because it was now made from local sugar beet instead of being imported cane produced. We accepted the School grub with the usual criticisms, but everyone was in the same boat. This equality was upset when the Top Table in School House, consisting of any number out of Housemaster, Under-Housemaster, Headmaster's daughter, or Matron, began to be served better food than us at supper — often a cooked meal when we had to make do with cheese or something similar. Great exception was taken, and it resulted in an organised silence at one Sunday lunch at which the Headmaster's wife was always present to carve the joint. The outcome was that fewer staff attended the evening meal with the same menu as ours, and we assumed that they merely had their 'big eats' elsewhere in the House.

Older boys had the opportunity of dealing with shortages in their own way. 'I supplemented the school rations with an air rifle (authorised), and a double barrelled .410 pistol (not authorised!),' admitted Charles Bingham, who spent the war years at the School, leaving Laxton House in 1947.

The School was fortunate in having an efficient and far-sighted Bursar in Griffith Rees. Ruth Keens, tired of the problems of the daily journey to Peterborough, had moved to work at the Bursar's office in April 1941; she credits her employer for his efficiency in keeping the boys fed.

> Food was by then becoming very scarce but we made sure that the boys had enough to eat. The Bursar very wisely registered the various Houses at three different wholesalers; two in Peterborough and one in London, so that if one obtained supplies of something unrationed, it was delivered to the Store or Tuckshop and shared round everyone, scrupulously fairly, and we had to remember a few ounces of this and that for the Sanatorium, Laundry and Laxton School.

Food, of course, was just one of the basic items in short supply during the war years. Bevil Allen's parents ran a shop at what is now Owen & Hartley's in the Market Place selling household goods. He recalled the problems faced by a shopkeeper in obtaining supplies, and the excitement that an unexpected delivery caused at the shop.

My mother used to have Oundle School parents to stay for the weekend. One of these parents, off his own bat, sent my father a great big crate of crockery, and pots and pans, and buckets and things like that to sell in the shop. You couldn't get that sort of stuff, and as soon as we undid this crate of buckets, you got this queue of people down the street, all queuing up to buy a bucket, unbelievable now, a 100 yards queue just to buy a bucket, and they'd just go, just like that. So it did affect the shop in that respect — we couldn't get what we wanted, so it was a case of changing over to something that would sell.

The School itself suffered from an increasing lack of paper, and July 1942 saw its magazine reduced drastically in content. 'We are now compelled to make drastic cuts in paper consumption and we have decided to devote less space to the various games,' the Editor informed his readers. 'So we have only written out a few of the cricket results in full and have contented ourselves with the best scores for all the rest. We are sorry to have to do this, but there is no alternative, especially as the printers are short of staff.'

The petrol shortage was also felt in a variety of ways. Only seven of the School's fourteen grass tennis-courts could be cut during the summer of 1942, and the use of a tractor on these did not improve the surface.[10]

Food Production

But if people found that they could survive without buckets, it was a different matter for food, production of which was given a high priority by the Government. Production rates soared as people found that they were working together for a common purpose.

The predominantly agricultural situation of Oundle gave it a certain importance as far as food production was concerned. The Ministry of Agriculture provided information to each county as to the need for particular crops. This information, part of the programme known as 'War-ag', was passed in turn to landowners and individual farmers.

Northamptonshire saw a considerable increase in the amount of crops grown during the war years. Wheat production almost doubled, soaring from 36,000 acres in 1939 to 100,000 acres by mid-1943. Oats and barley production also increased, though not so dramatically, while potato growing had increased tenfold by the end of the war.[11]

New sources of labour, including women, schoolchildren and prisoners of war were used to maintain food production. Miriam Rothschild returned to Ashton to work on the farm following the Plymouth blitz. As a scientist she had been placed in a reserved occupation and was not allowed to join the forces.

The Women's Land Army

The best known source of labour for food production was the Women's Land Army, which had a hostel at Southwick. The Land Army came into existence in June 1939 following an initiative by Stella, Marchioness of Reading. A register was started of women who would be prepared to give up their ordinary jobs for farm work if war came. By the time that war broke out the Women's Land Army numbered 1,000 volunteers; the figure rose to 20,000 by the summer of 1941 and eventually to 80,000 nationwide.

Some Land Girls like Jean and Margaret Laxton already lived in the area, but many others, some of whom have settled here, came from further afield. Nationally, about a third of the Women's Land Army came from London or other big cities. Frances Pearce, now

17: Cheerful smiles from a Women's Land Army group in November 1940.

living in Southwick, came from Cumbria. Another Land Girl from the North of England was Gladys Ashby, a resident of Cotterstock.

As well as harvesting jobs, the Women's Land Army in the Oundle area dealt with poultry, cows and pigs, although its members were prepared to take on more unusual work. Mrs Peggy Tuffs remembered rat-catching in particular among the jobs she performed as a Land Girl. They also taught boys from Oundle School to drive tractors.

Just as in the First World War, when the useful jobs performed by women to help the war effort had helped the process of female emancipation, the work done by members of the Women's Land Army helped to change men's perception of the role of women in society. Mrs Winifred Smith, a vet in practice with her husband, was struck by the way in which, after the war, local farmers would consult her frankly about problems with their animals which they had never dared to discuss before 1939.[12]

18: Former Land Girl and Cotterstock resident Gladys Ashby in WLA uniform.

19: Gladys Ashby and friends on the stack at the Measures' farm, Hemington, in 1941.

20: Like other wartime associations the WLA is still active today, as seen from this recent picture of a reunion at the Royal Albert Hall in London.

Schoolboy Farmers

Pupils from Oundle School played a useful part in farming work. The pupils contributed to the war effort both outside and within the School. The need to help farmers was clear from the moment war was declared. In Autumn 1939 boys would hurry out of School, race on their bicycles to Barnwell and clear the fields at a speed which amazed the hard-bitten farmer, as described in *The Laxtonian*:

> Members of the School have been helping local farmers this term. We are very glad to have had this opportunity of repaying our friends and neighbours for their kindness in allowing us to roam over their lands and for any damage that we may have done in the past. Throughout the term, parties of boys from each house in turn have been to work; they have been picking and loading potatoes and beet, threshing wheat, and doing other odd jobs. During October, no less than 1,200 hours of work were put in. The wet weather of November and December somewhat curtailed the work, but we have been out whenever the ground was suitable. We hope to continue this useful work so long as the war lasts.[13]

In Oundle itself the schoolboy farmers were just as active, noted schoolmaster Dudley Heesom:

> The School Farm under the ebullient H. P. Hewett produced pigs and sheep; vast hen houses were moved slowly up and down Two Acre to manure the ground and produce for the boys an unexpectedly large number of eggs. Several houses had their own food raising schemes.

21: Oundle School boys at work attaching a pitch-pole cultivator to the school tractor.

Grafton House under A. Cutcliffe had a valuable vegetable garden. Another house bred rabbits on a large scale and a third, ignoring the need for pig-swill, even managed to raise ducks.[14]

It was soon realised that such work was also needed out of term-time, and a regular wartime tradition was established, as the School's magazine records:

> During the whole of the Summer holidays, Oundle and the neighbouring villages were invaded by members of the School who came back to put in some work on the 'good earth'. Besides the boys billeted at Hemington, Lilford Hall, and on Lord Brassey's estate at Apethorpe, there were usually 30 or so staying at Sanderson, Dryden or St Anthony, which were opened in turn during the holidays. Most boys stayed a fortnight or more and were initiated into the mysteries and pains of wheat and barley stooking, threshing and stacking. It was thought at the end of the Summer term that no one would be really needed until the end of August, when harvesting usually begins, but the harvest turned out early this year and full use was made of everyone. Whether the initial motive was the prospect of pay at 6*d* an hour and only a secondary motive the desire to do something in the national effort is unimportant; we are sure the work was well done all the same. There are terrible tales about days when threshing had to be

22: Bramston Digs for Victory: schoolboys hoe between the rows of a fine crop of cabbages, watched by the head gardener. The four acre field behind Bramston House yielded enough vegetables to feed the School.

continued in half a gale, with a stack so dry that it was almost impossible to breathe for dust. We have heard also stories of horse-dragging on cold, wet days with a stubborn mare which simply would not budge! We feel, however, that no one was the worse for their work, and we are only too glad to have been of some service to the farmers.[15]

Former schoolboy Robin Paterson, who left Oundle's Laundimer House in 1943, confirmed the 'official' view that he and his friends enjoyed the holiday work on local farms:

Six of us moved into Churchfield Farm cottage, just outside the town, and spent a fortnight hedging and ditching, haymaking and helping with the harvest. We looked after ourselves with the help of local ladies who prepared some of our meals. There was a general holiday atmosphere away from school restrictions, and although it was a wet summer that year we enjoyed the experience thoroughly. I note that I played my first game of bridge during that farming fortnight, sitting in the cottage after work in the fields, and probably drinking beer and smoking in my best sophisticated manner. We were paid the munificent sum of eighteen shillings a week, of which fourteen were deducted for bed and board!

Ruth Keens remembered seeing the headmaster Dr Fisher supervising the loading of the school lorry on its way to farms in the outlying villages, but the schoolboys travelled to their work in convoys of vehicles of all kinds, as reported by an observer in December 1941:

As far as we can see, the chief new feature in Oundle this term has been the repeated conglomeration of cars, of all shapes, sizes and ages, outside the Science Block at 9 o'clock in the mornings. More remarkable still is the number of boys who have worked themselves into or on each of these cars. For as they moved off the casual passer-by could not have helped hearing the complaining squeaks and groans (of springs and engines) and seeing that the cars were dangerously close to the ground and not quite on an even keel.

Forty-five local farmers had been helped during the summer holidays of 1941. Because of the unavailability of Lilford Hall, alternative accommodation had to be found in cottages and huts at Apethorpe, Benefield, Churchfield, Barnwell and Southwick, as well as under canvas at Achurch. The whole of the organisation for the staffing of these camps was done by the Headmaster's sister Miss Fisher, with help from a colleague Miss Mason, as well as masters, their wives, and many other local people, including Mrs Richardson at Barnwell and Mrs Mycroft at Benefield.[16]

23: One of Oundle School's farm horses being shod by a 16-year old schoolboy in 1941.

A Farm Camp at Achurch

An account of life at the Achurch camp in the summer of 1941 was kept by a Modern Languages schoolmaster, Lawrence 'Tub' Shaw, later to retire to Oundle where he took up residence in New Street:

> A camp was set up in the Lynches by the Scouts to take about 30 boys for farming. The site was excellent, but unfortunately the rain came, and very soon the paths were seas of mud, making camp life most difficult.
> In spite of the rain, most of those who came enjoyed the camp, and all did the work willingly, whether on the farms or in camp. Five farmers were supplied with labour from Achurch. Food was cooked outside on Primus stoves and an open fire, but meals had to be taken in the village hall, for it was too wet outside. This hall was invaluable: here clothes, blankets, &c., were dried; one night a successful sing-song was held, and the camp was pleased to welcome the visitors brought by the untiring ffiske, to whose efficiency all the camps owed a great deal. The Headmaster visited us for a meal, and rejoiced at the sight and taste of Lyle's golden syrup, which he had not seen for months.
> Washing and bathing were done in the river, a raft and a diving-board being built. Insects were troublesome and the eyes of many rats could be seen gleaming by night.

After the first night, all slept well, in spite of the fact that few had camped before; and, in addition to the help given on the farms, a considerable amount of valuable camping experience was gained.[17]

Holiday-work for the war effort continued to be popular. During the summer of 1943 two three-week shifts had been arranged during the summer holidays, from August 9 to 28, and from August 30 to September 18. During the first period nearly 250 boys were involved in camps in Lyveden, Lilford, Churchfield, Apethorpe, and Tansor. The work continued into the term, with over 100 boys being sent out daily and a total of over 100,000 boy-hours being worked.[18]

Following an appeal from the County War Agricultural Committee, congratulating the boys and staff on their efforts in dealing with the harvest but stressing the urgent need for help with the 1945 harvest, it was decided to make the three week Harvest Camp an obligatory activity for all boys aged over 15 years. Free rail travel was provided, and wages were paid at official rates.[19]

Growing Your Own

In 1941, following the Government's decision to promote 'Dig for Victory' as the slogan of the year, Oundle people began to grow more of their own food. Allotments appeared along the main Peterborough road.

In Oundle itself, clubs for those wishing to rear pigs, rabbits and poultry were founded, and pig sties became commonplace. Pigs were fed on boiled up kitchen scraps, turnip tops and official pig food (although this was expensive) throughout the year, and slaughtered in the autumn. It was very sad for 'pig fanciers' to come home and find chops, bacon and hams strung up, and grown men were reduced to tears when the slaughterers came. There were consequently many cases of 'you eat ours, we'll eat yours'. In May 1942 the Oundle WI was invited to a regional lecture at Deene Hall about organising a Pig Club, following the death of many pigs which had been given inadequately prepared food.

Chickens and rabbits were less popular because they produced less meat, and if more than a certain number were reared, as set down by the Ministry of Agriculture, the surplus had to be sold to an approved buyer. This was usually a hospital.

The Oundle Rabbit and Poultry Club was founded in April 1942, and by the following month there were 60 members. They arranged lectures, the sale of young rabbits, bought rabbit food in bulk, and arranged the mating of rabbits owned by members. In January 1944 the Club was awarded a £2 prize for the highest meat production in the Midlands area, the total figure being 6,610 lb. Under strict meat rationing rules this would have amounted to enough food for a meal for 15,000 people.[20]

A new approach to food production meant a different approach to its consumption, and alternative recipes were introduced to cope with the shortages. Not all the innovations met with approval. 'We had dried eggs, foul stuff,' remembered Bevil Allen. 'I think they imported it.'

Yet people adapted to even the most bizarre food-substitutes. Elizabeth Berridge, brought up in Oundle and the daughter of the School's Chaplain remembered: 'The thing I missed most was marmalade, because the marmalade we had was made out of carrots and when we first had it I thought it was disgusting, but after the war I can remember the first jar of 'real' marmalade which I thought was also disgusting, because I had got used to the carrot marmalade.'

Ingenuity

The shortage of clothes was another problem caused by the war which affected the young royal family at Barnwell. Clothes rationing started on 1st June 1941. Princess Alice recalled how parachutes were in great demand, the acreage of silk providing copious underclothes. Such was the scarcity of clothing that old jumpers were unstitched and reknitted as smaller garments.[21]

Adapting to the new conditions imposed by war was essential for survival. People displayed remarkable ingenuity in coping with the shortage of supplies which they had previously taken for granted. Dr Charles Newman, the eminent physician and paediatrician who ran the Home Guard at London's Hammersmith Hospital during the war, but who had been brought up in Oundle, used his gardening skills to grow herbs as well as vegetables, but not just for culinary purposes. Plants such as datura, which contains several alkaloids, were grown in his allotment along with the vegetables to make good the shortage of certain drugs which could no longer be imported because of the war conditions.[22]

Black Market

There was of course the black market. Food and clothes rationing lasted until 1949, but many Oundle people had experience of by-passing the system. The Government was well aware of this as a national trend, and appointed Ex-Superintendent G. Yandell as Board of Trade Chief Investigator of Black Market activities on 25 May 1942. But clearly the authorities who hoped to stamp out illegal trading in rationed goods had a hopeless task: Philip Game, the Commissioner of Police for the Metropolis was reflecting a nationwide picture when he referred in his report for 1944 to the large number of individual transactions in the black market:

> Perhaps we do not realise that if we are prepared to accept without demur a bit more than we are entitled to, we are all to that extent black marketeers.

Almost everyone 'knew a man' who could help them find scarce consumer goods if the need arose, and not surprisingly the 'accident rate' among farm animals saw a dramatic increase during the war. However Oundle's black market was a low-key affair according to Ruth Keens: 'People would remark that they had obtained goods on the black market, but it was not very evident in Oundle, more a case of friends who worked in the shops keeping something "under the counter" if something off ration suddenly appeared, such as oranges.' The School Tuckshop, run by Bill Carter, was another source. 'Quite often Bill would let us have two or three little cakes, a great treat, and from time to time he would have a supply of small bars of chocolate — not available in the shops.'

The black market must have been stronger in Oundle than in many other towns thanks to the proximity of the American airbases, and the generosity of the USAAF personnel who ensured that a constant stream of luxury goods found their way into the hands of willing customers. Elizabeth Berridge was unequivocal about this aspect of the transatlantic impact on the area. 'You could get absolutely anything from the American airbase. My sister and I used to work in the American canteen at Polebrook during the college holidays and that was a very interesting experience.'

Even an ex-German prisoner of war like Charlie Schoenrock, now living in the Oundle area, knew what to do to obtain the necessities for a new life in his adopted country. 'I wanted to buy a suit from Northampton market but I hadn't got enough coupons so then I gave him an extra fiver and he let me have it,' he recalled. Five pounds was in fact the black market value of one clothing book in 1944.

Scrap Metal

Many of Oundle's older residents will feel that the newly opened Recycling Centre off East Road is nothing new. Wartime conditions meant that recycling was essential, and scrap metal was at a premium. 'If you had a saucepan surplus to requirements you'd give it away for munitions,' recalled Bevil Allen.

Collecting began officially on 28 June 1940, although some Oundle residents had already given suitable items for the war effort. Dumps for scrap metal were set up at Nene Cottage in Station Road, and at Jesus Church. The WVS also had a dump for aluminium in West Street, and by 26 July six hundredweight had been collected. The Market Hall was also used as a dump for iron railings and other scrap iron.

An official collection was organised for iron railings in October 1941. Some of those in the town, notably outside Oundle School Cloisters and the Great Hall, were retained because they were considered to be of artistic merit or historical value. Some were also retained for safety reasons.

Silver thimbles were also collected for a fund in London which had already provided a flying ambulance by 12 July 1940.[23]

Comforts for the Troops

Oundle people also proved industrious when it came to supporting those who were away on active service. Comforts for the troops included socks, blankets, gloves and hats, as well as chocolate, tobacco and razor blades, which were sent to the Ministry of Defence in thousands. Indeed there were so many that some were distributed among refugees because the Government did not know what to do with the surplus.

Knitting circles maintained a constant flow of knitted items, and in Oundle this was organised by Mrs Markham, of Lime House in East Road. Her first bundle, consisting of 42 garments, was sent to the troops in France on 15 September 1939.

Mrs Markham's knitting circle began just before the outbreak of war and continued valiantly right until the end, increasing production at an astonishingly high rate. By the end of November 1939, Oundle women had knitted 160 garments to send to the troops. By the beginning of February 1940, nearly 350 garments had been sent from the town, representing about 7,000 working hours in only four months of knitting. Parcels were being sent out every Monday. The end of the same month saw the collection of 3,272 knitted garments at the Red Cross depot at Polebrook Aerodrome, provided by knitters in North Northamptonshire for despatch to troops on active service.

The Oundle WI was also to the forefront in providing useful items for the troops.

24: Knitting for victory: a group of Barnwell residents at work on socks for soldiers at Castle Farm.
Standing: Mrs Dorothy Berridge;
sitting (l. to r.) Miss Ethel Parker, Mrs Robson, Miss Anne Berridge (just visible), Miss Connie Parker, Mrs Short, Mrs Waite, HRH Princess Alice, Miss Dora Robinson.

The first December of the war saw 66 parcels being despatched, mostly to the British Expeditionary Force in France, with 24 parcels following on 10 May in the following year.[24]

Comforts for the troops were also provided by the pupils of Oundle School. An Over-seas League Tobacco Fund was set up, as explained in the School's magazine:

> Each week voluntary collections have been made in the houses for this fund, which provides tobacco and cigarettes for the BEF. The cigarettes are sent free of postage and duty, so that each shilling collected provides fifty cigarettes for a man. Many of the houses have sent their contributions direct to headquarters, so that it is difficult to assess the exact amount forwarded. However it is certainly not less than five pounds each week from the School and Staff.

It is good to learn that cigarettes were not the only gifts whose value would be appreciated by the troops.

> All the houses have been sending packages of books and games to the BEF throughout the term. Mr Cullingford, who is out in France, and has been distributing these gifts to his regiment, has written many letters of appreciation: the men too have sent us letters of thanks. It is worthy of note that the Brigadier in Mr Cullingford's regiment is Guy E. Carne Rasch, CVO,

TWO ~ OUNDLE IN WARTIME

25: HRH The Duchess of Gloucester visits the WI Headquarters on South Road.
Back row (l. to r.): Mrs Win Bamford, Mrs Douglas, Mrs Parnell, Mrs Horn, Mrs Butt.
Seated (l. to r.): Mrs Bamford Snr., Mrs Crawley, Mrs Edwards, HRH The Duchess of Gloucester,
Mrs A. Laxton (President), Mrs Clipston, Mrs Collier, Miss Caborn.

DSO, who was due to become Master of the Grocers' Company soon. He became a Warden of the Company in 1928, but was obliged to retire in 1930 owing to pressure of Army business. He resumed his position in 1938 and has now left it again to serve with the BEF. We have also sent a donation from the Cot Fund with which Mr Cullingford can buy footballs and such other things as may make the soldier's life more pleasant. If members of the School, past or present, have any books or games to spare, will they please be so good as to send them to Mr Hewett, Laundimer House, who has kindly undertaken to have them distributed to the troops overseas.[25]

The Oundle Maids' Club

The School was indirectly involved in another venture which aimed at making servicemen's lives more pleasant. Miss A. M. Wood had arrived in Oundle in 1927, trained as a Librarian, with a Cambridge degree in History, a year's work on the land during the First World War, and ten years' experience in youth clubs and works clubs. Not only did she run the School Library but presided over the Maids' Club in the British School, off West Street, a meeting-place on five days a week, between 3.00 pm and 10.00 pm, for the members of the large staff of maids who looked after the boarding-houses. During the Second World War this became a youth club, open to servicemen who happened to find themselves in Oundle.[26]

26: The British School, off West Street, the wartime base of Oundle's Maids' Club.

The Women's Voluntary Service

Another centre in Oundle which provided social life for servicemen based in the area was in the Crown Assembly Rooms, now Crown Court, staffed by members of the Women's Voluntary Service (WVS). The WVS, like the Women's Land Army had been founded before the war by Lady Reading, and by 1941 had over a million volunteers in its ranks. Among them was Ruth Keens, who helped at the canteen which had been set up for servicemen at the Crown Assembly Rooms.

> My friend from the office and I served one evening a week. We had to cut the bread (no sliced bread then) and make up the sandwiches, etc. My friend was of a flirtatious nature, and as she scraped the butter thinly, made conversation with everyone until there was a queue stretching right to the door, but the men enjoyed a decent cup of tea and the opportunity to chat or play board games away from the depots.

27: Crown Court, facing north. The Assembly Rooms, the WVS base in wartime Oundle, are on the left.

1941 saw the launch of a Pie Scheme in East Anglia, aimed principally at providing good, filling food for agricultural workers gathering in the harvest. However the meat pies provided by the WVS became popular for all country dwellers who found it impossible under wartime conditions to go out for a meal. Orders were taken at the pie-room, the pies being collected from a delivery van on Fridays.[27]

Fund-raising

Along with collecting scrap metal and sending presents to the troops, fund-raising was something which the people of Oundle did in common with the rest of the British Isles. In the latter activity they distinguished themselves at a national level.

The issuing of National Savings Certificates, to be cashed in after the war, was one major way in which money was raised to provide a loan to the government to sustain its war effort. Oundle embraced the idea enthusiastically, buying Savings Certificates on a grand scale. A Savings Association was formed in the town, and £160 16s was lent in just one month, in August 1941.

Competitions were held in many English schools to encourage ideas for a poster design to promote National Savings Certificates. Vic Owen, a pupil at the Junior School, better known today as the Ashton 'Conker King', won a 15 shilling National Savings Certificate and had his poster displayed in the Royal Academy in London after his teacher Miss Gale had submitted it.

28: Ashton's 'Conker King' Vic Owen, with the author's daughter Rosie Downes at the International Conker Festival, 1992.

Throughout the war, 'weeks' were held to raise money throughout Britain. These were something of a misnomer, since they frequently lasted for months. Events during a typical week included military displays, concerts by military bands, sports, whist drives, dances, baby shows, shop window dressing displays and dog jamborees.

The first of these fund-raising exercises was Spitfire Week in 1940, which lasted from 27 September until 6 December. In Oundle the 'week' failed to meet its target of £5,000, raising only £274 18*s* and twopence halfpenny, although it was remarkable for seeing Mrs Fox give her first pension to the fund.

29: War Weapons Week, July 1941: The band leads a march along West Street.

War Weapons Week was held in the following year between 28 June and 5 July, aiming for a target of £35,000. The fund received a boost even before the start of the week, with a donation of £35 from Oundle School. Eventually it raised £124,000, considerably more successful than Spitfire Week.

Early in 1942 Warship Week was organised, with equal success in Oundle since it raised a grand total of £124,250. Of this, £123,859 8*s* 4*d* was lent as National Savings Certificates, with the rest being presented as 'a free gift to the nation.' A telegram was received from Sir Kingsley Wood thanking Oundle for its great efforts.

Later on, Oundle officially adopted a corvette, HMS *Nene*, and connections were maintained throughout the war, with a constant flow of comforts and presents such as a dartboard, dominoes, chess sets and other games being sent.

February 1943 saw a new triumph for Oundle fund-raisers, with Wings for Victory Week aiming to reach a target of £80,000 to provide two bombers. The final total of £135,000 was enough to provide three bombers, with £285 4*s* 10*d* being offered as a gift. Later a letter

TWO ~ OUNDLE IN WARTIME

30: War Weapons Week, July 1941: Nurses at the tail-end of the march, passing what is now the Oxfam shop in West Street.

of thanks was received from the Chancellor of the Exchequer.

The last week to be held was in 1944, from 8-12 July. Salute the Soldier Week had a target of £100,000 to provide two base hospitals. Events organized for this included a fête at Ashton, where a bottle of whisky raised £350 in a raffle. Some 200 people attended the fête, which raised £12,000. Following an extension of the week, and further events such as a talk by a French visitor to the WI, and a dance organised by American airmen from Polebrook, £161,040 was raised.

For its fund-raising efforts Oundle won the county flag, achieving the highest average for savings per head in Northamptonshire.[28]

31: A plaque in Oundle's Council Chamber presented by the Lords Commissioner of the Admiralty to commemorate the adoption of HMS *Nene* during Warship Week, March 1942.

Red Cross Fund-raising

There were of course other fund-raising activities, quite apart from the campaign for Savings Certificates. The Red Cross had many supporters in the Oundle area, and flag days were organised regularly in Oundle. Occasionally there was a conflict between the fund-raising activities. The *Peterborough Advertiser* reported that Red Cross work 'got in the way' of Spitfire Week in Peterborough, necessitating two months for the raising of £5,000 for a Spitfire.

Flag days and the 'penny-a-week' fund were the Red Cross's two principal forms of fund-raising. The organisation collaborated with another group, Mr Churchill's Aid to Russia, which supplied veterinary items for horses among other things.

The 'penny-a-week' collections were made in Oundle by volunteers who went from door to door with tins, organised by Mrs Lottie Mason, Secretary of the local branch of the Red Cross. For the average collection, amounting to £20, Red Cross helpers would have to collect some 4,800 pennies. This was no small physical feat, considering that they called at individual houses and asked for donations in the street.

Fund-raising in Oundle for the Red Cross compared with the rest of the country was again astonishingly successful. The average contribution in the town was a penny half-penny per head per week, double that of the national average. For a town of its size, Oundle raised the third largest amount of money in the country, coming after Sandy, Bedfordshire, and Oakham, Rutland.

Amounts raised by the 'penny-a-week' in Oundle in 1942 and 1944 were as follows:

1942	£	s	d	1944	£	s	d
Jan	18	19	9	Jan	49	19	7
Feb	18	10	8	Feb	41	5	9
March	20	5	8	March	32	14	11
April	22	11	4	April	31	3	4
May	19	14	11	May	38	2	0
June	21	18	8	June	34	3	6
July	17	16	1	July	42	8	4
Aug	-	-	-	Aug	29	4	1
Sept	-	-	-	Sept	28	15	6
Oct	27	0	10	Oct	33	18	1
Nov	17	5	8	Nov	38	1	6
Dec	26	3	6	Dec	46	9	7

Lottie Mason's drive and service to the community were to make her well-known in the post-war years. She became the first woman to chair the Oundle Urban District Council in 1957, and served on the Council for 30 years, becoming Chairman for the second time in 1971 and receiving an MBE for her service to the public interest.

Other fund-raising organisations which were active in Oundle during the war were the Royal National Lifeboat Institution, and the British Sailors' Society.[29]

32: Lottie Mason, MBE, one of Oundle's champion wartime fund-raisers.

33: HRH Princess Alice, escorted by Douglas Whitwell visits the Oundle Ambulance Division unit at Glapthorn Road Hospital in 1942. Molly Wickham in nurse's uniform is behind them.

Defending the Realm

There were of course official groups based in Oundle, and made up of Oundle residents, whose purpose and organisation were more military.

The Civil Defence unit, headed by Douglas Whitwell and equipped with an Ambulance Division, was ready for all emergencies at its base in Glapthorn Road.

Air raids were viewed as a major threat well before the outbreak of war in Britain. As early as 1924, Air Raid Precautions had been set up as a Home Office sub-committee under Sir John Anderson, in reaction to the bombing of civilians, particularly in London, during the First World War. Within 30 minutes of the declaration of hostilities in September 1939, wardens were at the Air Raid Precautions post in Oundle, the building being manned for the duration of the war so that if an air raid was on, information could be passed on to smaller warden's posts in the town, chosen because of their size and because they possessed a telephone.

34: 16-year old Peggy Wade, now Mrs Gidley, in Civil Defence uniform.

The ARP post was at the corner of South Road and East Road. It consisted of a derelict house with two rooms, a working-room, and a resting-room for off-duty wardens. It was conspicuous because it was probably the only building in Oundle flanked by sandbags.

Bevil Allen, whose father was an ARP warden, was somewhat dismissive of Oundle's attempts to protect itself against air-raids.

> We had no siren, so the wardens had to go out into the town with a police whistle and blow short, sharp blasts on this whistle, and I used to go out in the morning blowing on this whistle, and then when you got back to base eventually a message would come through to say it was all clear, and then I had to go out and I would blow the all clear, which was long sustained blasts. My father didn't have time to do this because he had his shop to run, so I did it. And there was another boy in the town who did this for his father, and I can remember cycling down West Street blowing a warning and meeting this other boy cycling the other way blowing the all clear, and we would meet and have an argument, it was quite funny.

The ARP wardens also organised talks about how to deal with incendiary bombs, gas, and other enemy weapons.

The threat of an enemy gas attack was regarded as real, particularly in the early stages of the war. A lecture on Chemical Warfare by schoolmaster Herbert Palmer to Oundle School's Science Society on 29 October 1940 attracted a record audience, and so many

35: The old ARP post: Oundle's defensive nerve centre against Nazi bombs.

juniors had to be turned away that a repeat performance in a modified form was arranged for them a week later. People were told to carry a gas mask with them wherever they went, although as the war went on they tended to less and less.[30]

One of the principal functions of the wardens was to ensure that a total blackout was enforced, and they had the power to prosecute anyone who showed a light at night.

The first person to be prosecuted in Oundle was the housemaster of New House, Mr Burns, who was fined ten shillings after maids in his boarding-house opened some curtains. Mrs Priest, of Glapthorn Road, whose husband taught in Oundle School workshops, and who moved to Oundle just after the outbreak of war, considered that the School, and indeed the town in general, was extremely lax about the use of blackout curtains compared with London, where she had been living previously.[31]

For those who had never been bombed it was easy to see the warden as a self-appointed Peeping Tom peering through the blackout curtains or as yet another strutting arrogant official. But there is no doubt that those wardens like Miriam Rothschild who had direct experience of the bombs in Plymouth, Bristol or London were genuinely annoyed by the lack of any sense of urgency shown by some residents of Oundle and the villages about the danger from above.

> As I was waiting to be directed into a war job, I acted as an Air Raid Warden, and one of the most exasperating jobs I had was going round the villages and various buildings in the area making quite sure that there was not a chink of light showing from the windows. I think an

36: Oundle School staff experiment with a gas mask.

extremely depressing aspect of the war was the blackout. I remember most vividly the lengthening of the days when lighting was no longer necessary in the evenings and it ceased to be such a worry. At Ashton in the war it was possible to recognise the German aeroplanes on their way to bomb Coventry and other important industrial areas. The sound of their engines was very different from that of our own aircraft, so we were always conscious of prospective raids. It was strange that despite this, people were very careless and foolish, and frequently failed to black out their windows properly. I was always afraid that a German plane might unleash a stick of unwanted bombs if they saw a twinkling light.

The only major incident involving an air raid to occur in Oundle was on 30 July 1942, when damage was done to rooftops during a machine gun attack by a German aircraft. The enemy plane, a Heinkel 111 bomber according to former Oundle schoolboy Lindsay Hodgson, was chased by a fighter, which later shot it down. Fortunately the school holidays had started. 'Had it happened during the term, with boys milling around at 11 o'clock, it would have been devastating.'

The incident was recalled by Bevil Allen. 'My father and a friend of his, Mr Williams, both of them Air Raid Wardens, were out walking down Benefield Road and a plane flew over and machine gunned straight down West Street, and there were some stone balls just outside Danfords Yard and they shot one of those off, and they both went white and threw themselves into the gutter, tracer bullets flying about all over the place.' Luckily there were no casualties or real damage, although the attack annoyed Mrs Stokes, an Oundle woman who spent the rest of the war washing in a bucket because she was unable to find a replacement for her wash basin, which was damaged.[32]

TWO ~ OUNDLE IN WARTIME

Another incident remembered clearly by the young Lindsay Hodgson occurred in term-time while he and his friends were walking on a Sunday along Benefield Road. 'A Wellington bomber decided to test his guns, and suddenly empty cartridge cases were pinging on the tarmac.'

Enemy bombs were obviously a much greater cause for concern among Oundle residents. The town itself was very little affected by enemy action during the war. A bomb landed on the golf course, killing a horse. Bevil Allen remembered:

> There was another time that we had a bomb that landed somewhere where these houses are on the left hand side of Benefield Road, there's a brook that runs between the field and the houses and it was in that brook, and it went off with a hell of a bang. On that occasion I was woken up and told, 'Quick! get under the bed', and I suddenly realised there was this terrific high pitched wailing sound going on, it seemed to go on for an eternity, and that was the bomb coming down. They put some whistlers on them so that they would make a noise as they came down and eventually it landed three or four hundred yards from our house.

Over at School House, the young Rhidian Graesser was also disturbed in his sleep.

> I remember waking up that night to hear a series of explosions, each one a little louder than the preceding one as they landed nearer Oundle. We went out next day to survey the field beyond the Golf Course where they landed to find the 10-15' craters containing some evil smelling liquid, possibly a fire accelerant.

As the war went on the fear that Hitler's blitzkrieg would reach as far as Oundle was a real one in many people's minds. Some Oundle residents had had direct experience of the bombing raids on British cities. John Matthews, of Glapthorn Road, who had been teaching at Oundle School for two years when he was called up in 1939, recalled being caught on leave while in Birmingham during an air-raid as his worst wartime experience, particularly as there were no air-raid shelters nearby. Miriam Rothschild had seen all her experiments of seven years of laboratory research destroyed in Plymouth at the beginning of the war. She felt her most appalling experience was the aftermath of the blitz in Bristol.

> The whole city was flat, it was terrifying, like a landscape on the moon. I was not traumatised by the blitz in Plymouth, but after witnessing the Bristol disaster I suffered very much with shattered nerves. I always remember a little kiosk where you could buy a bar of chocolate — very rare in the war — which was the only building standing in the devastated city.

Ruth Keens, who was working in Oundle School offices when the bombing of London Docklands was at its height, recalled how the Bursar, Mr Rees, volunteered to take the place of an Air Raid Warden in Deptford for two weeks, giving someone a much-needed rest in the country. 'The Bursar's standing went up quite a lot as he had no need to do this.'

In this connection it would be wrong not to mention the heroism displayed during the London blitz by a former Oundle pupil, the Rev. Harold Earnshaw-Smith, vicar of All Souls, Langham Place, from 1936. 'None of his people will forget his infectious courage and fortitude at the height of the bombing,' wrote a colleague, on his death in 1950. When his church was hit, Harold Earnshaw-Smith was the first on the spot to rescue those who were trapped in the ruins.[33]

Everyone in the Oundle area knew that they were in the line of the German raids on the cities of the Midlands, and the muffled booms which disturbed the peace of the countryside took on a heightened significance. Jessie Richmond was walking back home to Oundle from Thrapston one evening with her friend Ruth Smart.

> We saw these silver planes going over in droves and droves, and then we heard 'whoomph, whoomph, whoomph...' We could hear the explosions; we didn't know what they were bombing. It's so clear in my memory.

It was the night of 14 November 1940, and Coventry was the target of the Luftwaffe. Jessie Duffin, who grew up near Warmington, remembered staying with friends in Harringworth and being woken up later that night to see the flames of the stricken city lighting up the sky. Ruth Keens in Stoke Doyle remembered the same night:

> I was awoken from a sound sleep by my parents saying we ought to get up; most people were in the street by then. A German bomber was releasing his load and an excited man said: 'That one is going to hit the end house,' which was ours. I went to work as usual and then found it was the night that Coventry was devastated. Later in the morning a train drew into Peterborough North station with the sad-faced people from Coventry who had undergone such a harrowing experience, my employer's son and family among them. 'Our' bomber had disposed of his load on the way home and the incendiaries had fallen, creating small craters in a circle round the village, causing no damage.

Princess Alice's home in Barnwell also had a lucky escape when an enemy plane jettisoned three bombs on its way back to Germany, and it was not an isolated incident. 'The shock waves from the bombs would set the pheasants crowing before we heard the distant "crump" of the explosion,' recalled the Princess. Evidence of the bomb damage can still be seen alongside the main road at Lilford, and at Barnwell water tower some explosive devices still remain because they are too deep down to be dug out. On another occasion at Barnwell, Elizabeth Berridge recalled a German aircraft which actually crashed almost opposite Castle Farm. 'Michael Berridge, who was then farming with his father, was either brave or foolhardy — I suppose he was brave in a way — rushed straight into the flames and pulled the pilot out, and saved his life because shortly afterwards the plane blew up.'

Some believed that the fear felt by humans as the German planes passed overhead could be sensed by animals. The Princess found that the two polo ponies left at Barnwell after all her hunters were commandeered proved susceptible to the vibration of aircraft engines.

> If one of our planes passed overhead, they paid no attention but, when a German plane approached, they began to get fidgety and even to tremble. German engines made a different sound — anumb, anumb, anumb — and the ponies recognised this and associated it with danger. It was the same with the bull mastiff we had. He was terrified of German planes, wriggling under the bed or sofa as soon as he heard them coming.[34]

Records of the total number of air raids in Northamptonshire show that Oundle was lucky to remain so unscathed by enemy action. The county was divided into four Warning Districts during the war. Oundle was in the Peterborough Warning District, where a total of 579 alerts were sounded between 1939 and 1945. The Kettering Warning District came a long way behind, with only 199 alerts. The other two county districts, Northampton and Oxford, registered only 143 and 95 respectively.

Oundle's situation in the path of enemy bombing missions to the Midlands did mean that the danger of air raids had to be taken seriously. Elizabeth Berridge certainly saw the threat to the town from German bombs intended for the strategic targets nearby.

> We were always in great danger in Oundle because of Corby where there were very big steelworks. They used to run their chimneys underground so that the smoke came out somewhere else. The other thing we were told, and I don't know whether this was true, was that the swimming pool at the school, which was open-air in those days, acted as a reflector, and planes could see the reflection of the water and use it as a marker for Corby and I was very fearful that this would be a target.

Approximately 7,800 bombs fell on Northamptonshire during the Second World War. Of these a total of approximately 1,128 high explosive bombs and 6,500 incendiaries fell on the county. 666 incendiary bombs fell in the Oundle and Thrapston Rural District. Approximately 1,943 buildings in the county suffered war damage between 1939 and 1945. 1,629 were damaged as a result of enemy action, while the remainder suffered damage from British or Allied aircraft and bombs.

Oundle's proximity to Allied air bases also made it a potential victim for enemy air raids, and in fact Polebrook was subjected to machine gun attacks on two occasions before the arrival of the Americans, on 2 November 1940 and 11 May 1941. Warmington also was attacked on 3 July 1942.

However Bevil Allen was astonished that the area received so little attention from German bombers in view of its strategic importance.

'Northamptonshire seemed one enormous airfield, with little pockets of land in between that weren't airfields, and the surprising thing was that none of these airfields got bombed.' Towards the end of the war the occasional flying bomb managed to find its way to the county, for 'doodlebug' attacks were by no means confined to the south east of England. One of these fell at Creaton on 22 July 1944, injuring seven people and damaging 94 buildings. Another, carrying propaganda leaflets and booklets, fell at Woodford on 26 December 1944. One of the last hit Irthlingborough at 6.45 am on 13 January 1945.[35]

The Observer Corps

A post of strategic importance which played a part in national defence planning was the Oundle section of the Royal Observer Corps. This had an observation post at the Oundle School farm to the north west of the town, manned by volunteers from both town and school. It was one of a group of four posts, one of the others in the cluster being at Duddington, and the two others in Cambridgeshire. Information was relayed from this cluster to a plotting room at Cambridge, from where it could be relayed to RAF sector operations rooms in stations such as RAF Wittering, and thence to RAF squadrons.

Although the Observer Corps' conditions were initially primitive, its members having no uniforms, they maintained surveillance over Oundle throughout the war, and watched not only for aircraft, but also for bombs, fires and parachutes.

The Observer Corps personnel at their post on the Oundle School farm were no doubt helped by additional information offered by pupils. A Spotters' Club was formed at the School in early 1942, progressing by leaps and bounds until it numbered 125 members by the end of the Lent Term, making it the second largest club in the North Midlands Region.

The Observer Corps post in Oundle has been demolished, only the concrete foundations remaining to indicate what was probably the only position of strategic importance in the town.

The nearest anti-aircraft posts to Oundle which involved offensive action as distinct from observation were situated at Titchmarsh and Alwalton. These never destroyed any enemy aircraft, but they almost certainly surprised them as they headed for or returned from their bombing missions. There was a stage when anti-aircraft guns were taken to Peterborough to defend the cathedral, and many of these passed through Oundle.

There were searchlights at Warmington, and these served to blind enemy aircraft so that they could not see Allied aircraft or aim their bombs accurately.[36]

37: Oundle's Royal Observer Corps post.
Back row (l. to r.): H. Johnson, L. Redhead, V. Leayton, J. Touch, F. Bennett, H. Lewington, C. Vessey, R. Mitchell, J. Richardson, C. Wills;
Front row (l. to r.): A. Laxton, P. Cotton, A. Wright, P. Thompson, F. Stretton, G. Ludlow, H. Mowbray.

Fire-watching

Oundle's fire station was situated in the Market Place, but to deal with the threat posed by enemy bombing missions, and notably the use of incendiary bombs, there were also fire-watching groups. These got underway rather slowly due to lack of interest. Pupils from the

TWO ~ OUNDLE IN WARTIME

38: Oundle Fire Brigade 1938-39:
l. to r. (back row): Bill Carter, Fred Johnson, Ruff Clarke, Jack Hill, Frank Gaunt;
(middle row): Chris Newton, Gordon Clarke, Walter Lee, Ernie Brindsley, Bob Hancock, Bert Dodsworth;
(front row): Percy Spriggs, Fred Carter, Joe Horn, Arthur Riddle, Syd Garrett, Tom Houghton, Mr Blackwell.

School proved themselves of use; one of them, Sixth Former Graham Wilson from New House, was inspired to write in Latin on the subject before leaving Oundle in 1941 to join the Royal Navy:

> *Nos quotiens hostes diffindunt aethera pinnis*
>   *Iacturi piceo fulmina dira polo,*
> *Horrisono totiens vigiles clangore ciemur,*
>   *Haud mora, reicimus gaudia blanda tori.*
> *Induimur tunicam correpta lampade crassam;*
>   *Cingimur ut frustra flammiger ales agat.*
> *Non tonitrus signum sequitur, non ignea flamma,*
>   *Imus et excubiis, laeta caterva, domum.*
> *Sed iaciant hostes fulmen; sumus usque parati:*
>   *Non intacta diu flamma flagrabit humi.*
> *Urceolus siphoque levis rutrumque recurvum —*
>   *Haec habet in promptu iam sibi quaeque domus.*
> *Vae! cuicumque placet nos laedere ab aethere lapso,*
>   *Viribus Undeli fax tua vana cadet.*

A version in modern English has been suggested by one of today's Sixth Form classicists:

> As often as the enemy cleave the skies asunder with wings,
> About to hurl their fearful bombshells down from the black heavens,
> So we, the watchmen, are roused by the dreaded sound of the siren,
> And, without delay, force back the alluring comforts of our beds.
> Snatching up torches, we put on our heavy garments;
> Girding ourselves so that the wingèd explosives have no effect.
> No thunderous noise follows the siren, no fire, no flames,
> So we go home from our watch, a happy band.
> Let the enemy hurl their bombs down; we're ready all the way:
> Not for long will their fires rage untouched on the ground.
> Fire-extinguishers, light-weight pumps, and curved shovels -
> Each House has them now, at the ready, for its own use.
> Woe betide whoever tries to harm us from the sinking skies,
> For the might of Oundle will ensure that your fire rains down to no avail.[37]

By 1943 however, the fire-watching groups were watching from Oundle rooftops and church spires in surrounding areas, as well as delivering a comprehensive series of lectures.

One incident which aroused the attention of Oundle fire-watching posts occurred when a mysterious floating object was seen in the sky. It was reported as a parachute by several observers, finally being identified as an escaped barrage balloon from Peterborough.[38]

The Home Guard

The fear of invasion by Hitler's armies, which had so successfully overrun most of Northern Europe by 1940, was a very real one for Britain. German radio broadcasts could reach Eastern England and on more than one occasion Oundle people found themselves listening to Nazi propaganda in English. Schoolmaster Dudley Heesom remembers going into the kitchen of his boarding-house where he found all the maids and women helpers sitting in frightened misery listening to Lord Haw Haw broadcasting from Germany. The theme was the inevitability of the defeat of Britain and the discomforts which would arise in the course of the inevitable invasion.

39: Members of Oundle School fire-fighting squad at work in 1941. The housemaster carries a bomb shovel up to the roof while prefects put in some stirrup pump practice.

In the earliest days of the war, protection of the water pumps was given high priority, as the contamination of water might have been a quick enemy method of causing distress. Oundle School's Armoury, which contained most of the weapons in the neighbourhood, had to be guarded every night. The earliest plans were to try to contest the crossing of the Nene bridge on the Peterborough road. Coal waggons were to be turned over as late as possible at the railway level crossing, presumably to bar the way to the expected German tanks.[39]

One precaution against invasion which did not please local farmers was the placing of barricades on the many flat large fields around Oundle to prevent enemy gliders landing on them. These were a source of annoyance to farmers, who had to plough and harvest around the obstacles.

A real fear concerning the royal family throughout the war was that German paratroops would kidnap individual members at their country residences. Barnwell's royal residents Prince Henry and Princess Alice were certainly felt to be at risk, but, as the Princess recalls in her autobiography, never at any time were they given instructions what to do in such an event, in spite of being constantly shadowed by a single 'faithful corgi' as she affectionately called her detective, a Welshman who came with his family to live in Barnwell. Indeed she did not seem to have taken the threat too seriously, having decided that she would wait until it happened before deciding what to do. Notwithstanding the array of alarms and floodlights which later surrounded Barnwell Manor, she felt more vulnerable in peacetime than she did during the war, when the enemy could be expected 'from above', as she put it.[40]

The threat of invasion was the principal factor in the formation of the Local Defence Volunteers on 14 May 1940, as the Home Guard was originally known. A broadcast by Anthony Eden, then Secretary of State for War, had appealed for men between the ages of

40: Lt. Col. F. R. Berridge, DSO, MC, JP (facing the camera), Commanding Officer of the 3rd (Oundle) Battalion of the Home Guard, inspects a soup kitchen.

17 and 65 to come forward and offer their services. 'You will not be paid, but you will receive a uniform and will be armed.' It was hoped that the new force would be an effective defence against the use of parachute troops such as those who had just overrun so successfully the Low Countries. Two months later, on July 14, Churchill referred to the new army as 'the Home Guard' and the name stuck. Early in 1942 membership of the Home Guard became compulsory, and the ranks were swelled by 16 and 17-year olds who were provided with valuable training before their call-up.

The Oundle and Thrapston District of the Northamptonshire Home Guard, later to be known as the Third Battalion, was commanded by an ideal leader. This was Lieutenant Colonel F. R. Berridge, DSO, MC, JP who had won distinguished military spurs in the First World War as Intelligence Officer of the Seventh Battalion Northamptonshire Regiment, gaining six decorations for gallantry and becoming known as the Regiment's 'intrepid hero'. Immediately following the LDV call in May 1940, Colonel Berridge contacted those ex-servicemen who he believed would be ready to organise the new force in their villages. A fellow ex-Army officer in the neighbouring village of Polebrook was Brigadier General A. F. H. Ferguson, great-grandfather of the present Duchess of York, although it was his neighbour Lieutenant Herbert Case who ended up running Polebrook's Home Guard. Along with Major R. A. Muntz from Achurch, Captain C. E. Harvey from Thorpe Achurch, Captain E. A. Barnes, Adjutant of the Oundle School JTC, and several others, the group formed a committee and called the first meeting in the Oundle and Thrapston District to undertake weapons training and to secure a suitable leader with a telephone in every village.

The Third (Oundle) Battalion of the Home Guard under Lieutenant Colonel Berridge was finally divided into six companies, with the area reaching from Denford and Addington in the south to Easton on the Hill in the north, and from Lutton in the east to Brigstock and Deene in the west. The companies were as follows: A (Kings Cliffe), B (Bulwick), C (Barnwell), D (Thrapston), E (Oundle School), F (Oundle Town). Two more companies, G and H, were formed later, being off-shoots of the D Company which became rather unwieldy.[41]

The Oundle Home Guard companies were established and ready for action very early during the war, although they never saw any, and only once were members issued with live ammunition. In the early stages of the war there was a shortage of ammunition, maps and instruction, and ingenious efforts were made to remedy the absence of weapons. Rhidian Graesser, as a member of Oundle School's OTC (Officers' Training Corps), was, for some reason that he could never grasp, given the job of 'Explosives Instructor' to lecture LDVs on the various bombs there were for use against German tanks. The 'Sticky bomb' remained for a long time in his memory: 'a 6" diameter sphere with a handle. Inside its outer casing was bird lime, and one was expected to climb onto a tank and whack the bomb on its turret — the bird lime made it stick ready for the explosive contained to go up. If we had ever been issued with the real thing, and used it as required, we could only have ended up as posthumous VC material!'

Molotov cocktails, flame-throwers and 'drainpipe' artillery were all fairly common. 'Imagine my joy at being given a Blacker Bombard to try out,' wrote ex-Oundle School boy David Mycock. 'A six-foot length of four-inch piping on a tripod, which you filled with nails, stones etc. (the etc. was important) and fired with a black powder charge and a large percussion cap.' Rhidian Graesser explained its use in more detail.

It had a crude trigger mechanism consisting of a spring behind a back plate which was compressed into the firing position. Into the muzzle end was put a petrol filled bottle capable of being 'sprung' 100 yards or so. The main drawback was the aiming device — an eye on a threaded shank which fitted into a hole in the drainpipe wall. Unfortunately this hole was drilled right through the wall, and so it was possible to have the end of the eye shank protruding into the bore. In such a case one produced a flame thrower of startling proportions, all right if fired downwind, but not so pleasant if into a wind.

As the war progressed more efficient and official equipment was delivered, including rifles, grenades, and anti-tank weapons.

Major F. Spragg, an Oundle School master, commanded the town-based F Headquarters Company throughout the war and it provided officers and specialists for other Companies. A number of masters from the School had specialist roles in the Third Battalion: Major H. P. Hewett commanded C Company (Barnwell) in the Third Battalion of the Home Guard, combining the male inhabitants of a dozen villages into a unit and receiving the MBE for his leadership; Captain J. M. Branfoot, the Head of Biology, was the Ammunition Officer; Lieutenant D. L. Venning was the Signals Officer; Captain E. A. Barnes, Adjutant of the School JTC was the Weapon Training Officer. Yet another, W. G. Walker, had on his windscreen up to the day he died the initials LDV. Knowing the area as it did, the Oundle Home Guard would have had a considerable advantage over any attacker. Transport was provided by the lorries of Smith's brewery in Oundle, organised by Captain Philip Coombs. Other Oundle-based specialists in the Third Battalion included the Liaison Officer Lieutenant R. K. Yeld, and Captain J. H. Heard, a repatriated prisoner of war from Germany who assisted as one of the three adjutants.

The E Company, the School's own contingent for the Home Guard, was formed under Major P. Priestman, who was at that time commanding the OTC. The second-in-command was Dudley Heesom. That senior boys in the school should take a full part in resistance was accepted by both boys and staff. In the earliest days the NCOs of the OTC were of the greatest value as they were able to give instruction particularly in weapon training to the many members of other Companies who had not handled weapons before. Its disadvantage was that it existed only during term-time, and in due course it came to be seen principally as a mobile unit, to reinforce others if they were short of men during an enemy attack. By the Spring of 1942 the F (Oundle Town) Company was sufficiently competent to be able to give instruction to the boys.

At its largest the School Company included 140 boys. Many boys had four parades a week and asked for more. To the senior School Platoon was given the job of dealing with parachutists if they arrived. One warm June evening in 1940, soon after twilight, one housemaster remembered waking several boys telling them to put on uniform and come down to the study. News had been received that the Germans had landed, and that this was not a practice. He issued live rounds, the first they had seen, and a cigarette each, with the warning that the chief danger of the night was that they would shoot each other or the officers who came round to check their positions. The grim-faced boys were led out to protect the playing fields against a parachute landing. Sections were led out to posts round the field, where they loaded their rifles with live ammunition, and for two hours waited to meet the threat. 'Such is Oundle discipline that none of the officers was shot either accidentally or deliberately,' recorded Grafton House's housemaster Alan Cutcliffe some twenty-five years later. 'Those are days never to be forgotten.'[42]

41: A member of Oundle School's Junior Training Corps gives instruction to members of the local Home Guard.

Both Companies E and F of the Oundle Home Guard were responsible for joint patrols of Polebrook Aerodrome, especially after the arrival of the Americans. Protecting the aerodrome was the aim of one of the wartime exercises undertaken by the Home Guard. A suicide squad of German paratroopers was presumed to have landed with the mission of destroying as many aircraft as possible. An exercise by the E (School) Company on 23 November 1943 was judged by the Battalion Commander as 'an unqualified success'.[43]

Less successful from the USAAF point of view was an exercise in which a former pupil from the School, Tony Jolowicz, remembers taking part: the aim was to destroy as many aircraft as possible with flour 'bombs' launched by an 'enemy' task force. The future Professor of Law at Cambridge University remembered on that occasion the 'incompetence' of the American defenders. A plank resting on the barbed wire surrounding the base had obviously been used as a private exit by GIs, and was accordingly put to good use by the invading force who scored heavy 'losses' against the Yanks.

A major exercise on Sunday 22 March 1942 put the spotlight on the Oundle area of the Home Guard when the Third Battalion organised a test of the town's defence scheme. The attack, made by troops under the command of Captain E. St C. Gainer opened at surprise points around the town. Inside Oundle, the garrison, under the command of Captain H. P. Hewett fought desperately, under orders to fight to the last man. Unfortunately the Drill Hall, Headquarters of the Oundle garrison, had been inadvertently left without a guard, and was taken by an enemy patrol almost before the exercise began! The exercise was made more spectacular by the sight of the RAF dropping messages concerning the movements of the 'enemy' to those besieged in the inner keep of the Drill Hall.

A second major exercise took place in the town later in the year, on 29 November, when the Third Battalion was responsible for the defence of Oundle against Regular troops using light armoured vehicles. Continuous explosions rocked the town's Sunday calm, interspersed with the usual dramatic or comic moments which characterised such exercises. The best example of the latter was recorded by the *Official History of the Northamptonshire Home Guard:*

> At Oundle the comic relief was furnished by the Sub-District Intelligence Officer (Lt. Peter Perry), who penetrated the town in civil attire as a spy, carrying on his person complete plans for the destruction of Oundle.
>
> When challenged, after gaining admittance to the Rectory, he produced a German identity card. A sentry questioned it, but, being assured it was a 'special' pass, let the 'spy' through. He was not caught until he practically forced his own arrest![44]

42: Oundle Rectory: wartime base of the Royal Army Service Corps.

The Rectory, later to become the headquarters of Anglian Water before being bought by Oundle School, was the wartime base for the Royal Army Service Corps, which, in case of invasion was to be one of two 'keeps' in the town. An RASC training unit in the Rectory was to defend itself and at the other end of the town the Home Guard would try to protect the area of the old Police Station on Mill Road. During the rehearsals for this scheme it was discovered that it was possible to walk across the river by using the stones of the ancient Oundle Mill which were still there under the surface.[45]

The availability of real weapons of war as used by the Home Guard in a rural community led occasionally to unorthodox practices especially where livelier and younger members were involved. 'We did all sorts of daft things,' recalled one former resident of a village not all that far from Oundle. After all, what better substitute for fireworks on Guy Fawkes night could there be than a few Home Guard hand grenades, launched by excited teenagers? It was of course 'under strict supervision' assures our source, who prefers to remain anonymous.

Boys from Laxton School had their own ways of amusing themselves with illegally obtained live ammunition. One favourite pastime was to throw live rounds onto the fire before rushing out of the classroom in a mad stampede.

43: A relic of the past: the access from North Street to the Royal Army Service Corps base for 'other ranks'.

The Home Guard had its last parade on 3 December 1944. The end was marked by various events in Oundle and the villages, such as the 'Stand Down' dinner held in the Reading Room at Polebrook on 17 January 1945, where speeches, entertainments and toasts were the order of the evening.

Certainly there were comic and bizarre moments in the operations of 'Dad's Army'. Yet the force whose creation came at such a deadly serious point in the nation's history was an illustration of a mood that many today view with nostalgia. Twenty years after the event, an Oundle observer noted:

> The Home Guard was probably the best example ever of Briton and Briton getting down to the job and forgetting class and background and prejudice; the spirit of 1940 certainly brought out the best in a man; and it brought town and gown in Oundle closer than ever before.[46]

A Comic Opera?

There was of course another less reassuring side which has to be considered. Britain survived, but some might say that this was more through German miscalculation of Churchill's resolve than for any other reason. Hitler, it is said, was counting on the British Government's inevitable agreement to a compromise peace on the favourable terms which he was ready to grant, and the Prime Minister's rejection of any compromise was not at first taken seriously. Besides, at the back of Hitler's mind was his planned invasion of Russia.[47]

Had the German military machine been programmed to deal with Britain as resolutely

TWO ~ OUNDLE IN WARTIME

as it had dealt with the rest of Northern Europe things could have been different. The nightmare of thousands of battle-hardened Nazi paratroopers seizing strategic positions throughout Britain, even indeed appearing in the sleepy shires of the Midlands, could too easily have become a reality.

In Caroline Seebohm's book *The Country House — A Wartime History 1939-1945*, Miriam Rothschild describes her experience on the day that Churchill announced on the wireless that we could expect the invasion at any minute.

> It so happened that men of the Ordnance Corps were billeted in our stables, and the officers were in a house that normally belonged to the estate agent. I was in the habit of inviting these officers to lunch on Sunday. The day that Churchill went on the wireless warning us of the impending invasion, I thought: 'I can't invite these officers to lunch, they'll be standing at the ready.' So I went to find them to ask them for their reactions, but they had all gone away for the weekend. But being rather officious, and a good air-raid warden, I thought: 'I'd better go and see what has happened to the men, since we are expecting an invasion at any minute.' So I drifted off with my gas mask into the stables and there was not a soul there. But all their rifles were on their beds. Well, in the Army you are not supposed to be separated from your rifle, particularly when you are expecting an invasion at any minute. So I collected all the rifles and took them into what was my gun room, where we kept our sporting guns, and carefully stacked them up and locked the door. Then I went home and had my lunch, expecting the invasion at any minute.
>
> There is a famous story about the telegram that went out at that time, saying, EXPECT THE INVASION FROM DUSK TO DAWN. Then a correction went out, FOR DUSK TO DAWN READ DAWN TO DUSK. So at Dawn the next day, the invasion hadn't come and the telephone rang. It was the Captain, who had returned and found his army without arms. He said, 'Have you a-a-a...?' He stammered on the phone, so I said, 'You're looking for your rifles.' And he said 'Yes', so I unlocked their rifles and gave them back to him. I thought at the time, if we win the war it is an absolute miracle.

Caroline Seebohm's book also describes the extraordinary measures which were taken during the period of expected invasion. Every village had to appoint a head man, who was given consignments of food to be stored, so that in case one was cut off and completely isolated, the head man could feed the village. Miriam Rothschild was of course appointed head man of Ashton, and when her food consignment came it was accompanied by an official letter which announced on the front, NOT TO BE OPENED UNTIL THE ENEMY IS WITHIN 10 MILES.

> So I thought, 'Well, I'm not going to wait, I'll open it.' So I opened the letter, and it said, 'When the Germans are within ten miles, you are to round up the cattle and drive them into the church.' I thought I would find out what the next village was going to do about this. The head man of the next village was also a woman, of course, so I went to see her, and asked, 'I'm going to bury the food. Do you know how long tins last underground?' She had no idea, so then I said, 'Did you get a letter too?' 'Oh, yes,' she said. So I said innocently, 'What did it say?' And she said, 'It said "Not to be opened until the Germans are within ten miles," and since I didn't want them to find it, I burned it.' So I never found out whether she, also, had to round up the cattle!

Such experiences were unlikely to inspire confidence in the readiness of Britain's defence.

'In those days I thought there was bound to be an invasion and we would be overrun like other countries of Europe,' admitted Miriam Rothschild.

One should at this point quote the story of what happened at nearby Fotheringhay at one particularly tense moment in 1940. Invasion scares were perhaps heightened in the villages surrounding Oundle because of the sense of isolation. During one of about four alerts, the watch on Fotheringhay church tower thought that the Germans had come at last, picking the village as their invasion point. A power failure in nearby homes was assumed to have been caused by enemy paratroops cutting the supply lines. The panic of imminent attack seized the tower: a cryptic radio message, 'B******s are comin'' was the only information received by HQ that Fotheringhay was about to fall to the enemy, with no details as to its strength or location, and no indication as to the watch's own position.[48]

Spy Mania

Not surprisingly, in view of the proximity of strategically important air bases to Oundle, there were frequent sightings of so-called spies. A real spy had been caught in Northampton-shire on 6 September 1940 after being discovered lying in a ditch in a dazed state. He had been dropped by parachute at 3.00 am, and on landing had hit his head on his wireless set. A search of his person had uncovered £300 in English notes, a compass, maps, food, a forged identity card and a loaded pistol.[49]

Such stories were bound to set the imagination racing, particularly among the young, recalled Bevil Allen.

> There was one boy who was an evacuee and one boy who was a native of the town, and they used to make up spy stories. For instance they'd run an electric wire down a tree into a hole in the ground and there'd be a box buried in the ground, and they'd say 'We've found some equipment that some spy is using.' It was great fun because we used to invent spy stories.

The American authorities' acquaintance with Oundle School members of the Home Guard was unfortunately not enough to prevent the arrest of their headmaster Dr Fisher, apprehended as a spy near Polebrook Airfield on the grounds that he was carrying binoculars near the base. His failure to carry a pass resulted in his detention for some hours in the Guard Room.

The authorities were also involved in investigations of suspected German spies at the School when Scotland Yard sent a man to question the young House Tutor at the Berrystead House on North Street. He had gone behind a hedge to write Greek verses about the head of the Classical Department, and the hedge was close to the war-target of Corby.[50]

Perhaps the authorities had already been alerted by the fact that the Housemaster's wife, a Russian, spoke with a foreign accent. Elizabeth Berridge, living at the Berrystead at the time, remembered the Reverend Cole's paranoia on the subject of his wife's supposed links with the enemy. 'If she ever started to talk to strangers, my father became very agitated because of what they might think.'

Certainly Oundle had its fair share of amusing spy-stories. The naturalist Miriam Rothschild jokingly recalled an incident which arose from her work in various parts of the country with the Agricultural Research Council on the control of wood pigeons, which were considered a great pest to farmers.

> Rather an amusing thing happened in Wales. I was denounced as a spy because I kept carrier pigeons in cages under my bed. Of course they weren't carrier pigeons at all, they were some of the wood pigeons that I had been trapping. My brother was in MI5 and he was very amused to find on his desk a report that someone of my name was sending carrier pigeons to Germany, it was a great joke.

But nearer to home, in the woods at Ashton, she recalled another spy-story, confirmed by her friend Lord Rosebery, the Regional Commissioner for Civil Defence in Scotland, which at the height of the threatened German invasion was no laughing-matter.

> I remember a moment when my heart really sank, when an empty parachute was found here. Somebody had come down in the night. It was so beautifully made of silk, and it had left the factory two years earlier, because it was dated, and I thought, 'They have all those supplies!' Eventually the man was caught. It was Lord Rosebery who told me, which of course he shouldn't have done, as it was deadly secret when a parachutist was captured, particularly as in this case he was almost certainly a spy.

Life at the Manor

The war effort was remarkable in galvanising every section of society into action against the enemy. From country cottages to manor houses, civilians transformed their homes into workshops for manufacturing a vast range of useful items.

Even a royal residence was no exception. At Barnwell Manor, which Prince Henry had bought the year before the outbreak of war, his wife was complaining to her mother-in-law Queen Mary that their horse-box had been appropriated as an ambulance, and that 'numerous workmen still seem to wander in and out of the house finishing various jobs at their leisure. The War is made into an excuse for everything'.[51]

Two Oundle School pupils who visited HRH Princess Alice in 1984 heard how, in the place where they were sitting, there had once been a large table at which village women had made bandages for the hospital supply depot at Southwick.[52]

The male servants and employees at Barnwell Manor were conscripted into the forces, so the royal couple were left with only old people, who, as Princess Alice recalls, dug up the greater part of the garden and turned it over to potatoes. 'It was sad to see the flower-beds that we had cherished destroyed in this way,' she reflects in her autobiography, 'but it was not a very serious sacrifice in the circumstances.' Another sad moment at the beginning of the war came when all the hunters at the Manor's stables were commandeered for service in North Africa.

The Princess was to find that the war extended her duties considerably. By 1940, in addition to being Colonel-in-Chief of two regiments — the King's Own Scottish Borderers and the Northamptonshire Regiment — she was Commandant of the St John's Ambulance Brigade and Air Chief Commandant of the Women's Auxiliary Air Force. There were of course official visits within the county to keep up people's morale, to the Moulton Institute of Agriculture at Northampton, to hospitals, first aid posts, ARP demonstrations and engineering works. But she also saw the grimmer side of the war. Touring Coventry two days after the blitz which had destroyed so much of the city was her worst experience of the bombing, as she recalls in her Memoirs:

> As we visited one factory, an air-raid warning went off and the Lord Lieutenant, who was acting as my guide, asked me if I would prefer to go to an underground shelter or to continue the tour. I said I should much prefer to be bombed than buried, so long as it did not force other people to follow my lead. 'Splendid!' he said. 'It will set a very good example to the workers. They're apt to dash to the shelters at the slightest excuse.' So we continued the tour and luckily no raid materialised.

Such visits were of course a tremendous boost for those who had suffered from the ravages of war. Princess Alice described the visit which she and her husband made to Belfast in April 1941, the day after a devastating air-raid:

> Our visit, as usual, had been planned in secret some time before; but as it coincided, quite by chance, with the day after the raid, we met with an extraordinarily grateful, even hysterical, welcome. The people were so overwhelming in their response that the police decided it was safer to let us walk among the crowds, which they would never have done in normal circumstances. Neither of us had ever witnessed anything like it; nor were we to again.[53]

Other large houses in the area in addition to Barnwell Manor saw changes brought about by the outbreak of war. At Ashton Wold the house was used as a Red Cross convalescent home with 60 beds for wounded military personnel. This was in fact totally illegal according to the Geneva Convention, given the situation only half a mile from a military air base.

Lilford Hall, to the south of the town, the country seat of the fifth Baron Lilford, was used as a base for schoolboy farm workers, and then became a military hospital largely for American forces. Ruth Keens and her mother in Stoke Doyle would often meet the American nurses from the hospital walking or wobbling into Oundle by bike. 'They were wonderfully groomed and the smartest girls I've ever seen — and so pretty! Their very presence must have helped raise the morale of the wounded.'

Barnwell, the nearest station, suddenly gained a grim fame. Such was the length of the ambulance-trains that the platform had to be increased to three times the normal length for the war-wounded to be unloaded. Elizabeth Berridge remembered the scene. 'Watching the train bringing the wounded to Barnwell station was unbelievable, because every carriage was unloaded at the same time. The American ambulances were there on the platform and whisked them straight away. We all thought at the time it was because they were afraid of an air-raid, but looking back on it, I think it was because some of them were in very poor shape and needed urgent treatment.' Her visits to the many ill and convalescing American soldiers in Lilford Hospital made a deep impression on her. 'I remember going there to chat to people and listen to their stories and that was very moving. Some had had terrible experiences and were not much older than I was. They must have aged years as a result of these horrendous happenings. We used to go there at Christmas and sing carols to them.'

When the Americans left in 1945, Lilford Hall was taken over by the British Resettlement Corps to act as a staging-post for some of the thousands of Allied prisoners of war who had spent such grim years in captivity, many of them in the slave camps of the Far East.

Oundle School

One of the most immediate impacts of the World War on the School was that it lost a considerable number of its teaching staff. Former Second Master John Matthews, now living in Glapthorn Road, who had arrived in Oundle some two years before to teach

Mathematics, remembers how the start of war affected some of his colleagues, though he himself was allowed a brief respite.

> I was an officer in the Territorial Army for home service, and I immediately signed up to go anywhere. I arrived in Oundle in July 1939 expecting to go straight off, but I didn't go until 1940. One was quite conscious of the war because, at the time, I was resident tutor in Laxton House and my opposite number in Crosby, a chap called Jack Brittain, was in the regular army reserve of officers and was called up straight away. He went in the expeditionary force across to France and was killed during the retreat to Dunkirk, and one other member of the staff, a linguist called Charles Osman, was very badly wounded in the retreat, and died of wounds in this country.

Another loss to the School was the Adjutant of the Officers' Training Corps (OTC), Lieutenant Colonel Alfred Butcher, who had been awarded the Military Cross in the First World War, and who now rejoined a batallion of the Royal Welch Fusiliers. Alfred Butcher was a former pupil of the School, having left Grafton House in 1913 to fight with distinction in France and Mesopotamia. He was with the Special Forces Executive in 1941 when he died of heart failure as a result of his service.[54]

Some twenty members of the permanent teaching staff of the School served with the Forces during the Second World War.[55]

For the schoolboys, a deep impression was made by the sudden appearance of female teachers in the classroom. 'It did everyone's morale a power of good just to see them about,' commented former pupil Rhidian Graesser. David Mycock remembered the Headmaster's daughter-in-law as 'a Maori with the most stunningly beautiful eyes I have ever seen'. She was in fact the writer Margery Fisher, brought up in New Zealand, but born in Camberwell.

The editorial in the first edition of the School magazine to be published three months after the start of the war, in December 1939, expressed relief that things had turned out to be not so gloomy as had been predicted. In fact the energy which infused the School's war effort had diverted pupils and remaining staff alike, and of course this was the 'Phoney' war:

> The term began under very depressing circumstances. Everyone thought that life would be miserable, that there would be continual air-raid warnings, and that we should suffer from a food shortage. This rather natural depression has been proved unreasonable, and we have all been very glad to give a helping hand to the country, even if only in a small way. We have helped the local farmers and turned the Workshops to national service; the Scouts have collected the waste paper and sent it off to the mills, and gardens are being dug and cultivated by several of the houses. We have had to fend for ourselves considerably more than usual and certainly no one is any the worse for it.[56]

Schoolboy War Workers

The School certainly played a considerable role in the town's war effort. The Oundle area being more agricultural than industrial, the principal factory was the Oundle School workshops, conceived by the headmaster Frederick Sanderson at the beginning of the century, and since 1921 under the direction of the Engineering Teacher, Mr Maurice Lakeman.

The Workshops were doing nothing new in helping the national war effort. From

44: Oundle School boys working at the model lathes in the Metal Workshops, as featured in the *Illustrated* magazine of 21 June 1941.

January 1915 during the First World War they had been kept continuously at work, producing items such as 12,376 brass torpedo gear parts for Brotherhoods in Peterborough, 32,008 tools for Woolwich Arsenal, and 1,393 horseshoes for the Munitions Board.[57]

In this second period of wartime endeavour, many pupils clearly took their duties seriously. A letter written by schoolboy Denis Lake in November 1940 pointed out to Mr Lakeman that the micrometers and other delicate instruments displayed in a glass showcase on the wall of the Metal Shops ought to be removed and used 'to help win the war', and the Engineering Teacher was quick to agree.[58]

However, School House's Rhidian Graesser commented: 'Our one week in the School Workshops during the Summer Term was still looked on as a bit of a bore, although in the Foundry, the Machine Shop and the Woodworking Shop we were making items for the War effort. The same "skylarking" went on, and the reject rate was high.' And judging by a letter written by a Cambridge Old Oundelian to the Editor of *The Laxtonian* in March 1941, there seemed to have been a certain difficulty in maintaining the momentum of production in the workshops after the initial enthusiasm:

> During the war of 1914-18 our fathers saw to it that there should always be an adequate supply of volunteers to produce Munitions of War in the School Workshops. In the summer

holidays, 1940, some 35 boys spent two weeks or more working in the Workshops, in addition to the 200 who worked on the land. Now, when the need is, if anything, even more urgent, it seems likely that for the second holidays in succession the Workshops will be compelled to refuse work of vital importance to the National Effort.

May I through your pages draw the attention of your readers to two points? First, members of public schools, or of universities, now enjoy a holiday which is at least ten times as long as that which their contemporaries in factories receive. Secondly, of this holiday boys are only being asked to give up about one-third. Surely this is not such a very big sacrifice, especially as those who do make it will know that they are doing a job of real importance.

Finally, as one who spent part of August 1940 on this work, I should like to say how thoroughly enjoyable the work was. The hours were not long and the three housemasters concerned in the billeting arrangements, ably supported by their wives, saw to it that we were comfortable (and excellently fed!) If any one is in any doubt as to whether he will have a good time I can only advise him to ask one of last summer's party if he had a good time. For myself it was one of the best holidays I have ever spent and an unforgettable experience.[59]

Perhaps the letter had an effect: four months later, in July 1941, the Editor was announcing that 'we at Oundle are making an even greater effort than last year to keep the workshops in production during the holidays'. In fact a total of 67 boys stayed to help in the workshops, and by December 1941 the number of fittings completed since Easter 1940 had risen to 22,000, and to 30,000 by July 1942.

To maintain production levels throughout the year and accommodate boys who would volunteer to work in the workshops, a system of hostels was set up, using mainly Laundimer House in North Street and Bramston House in the Market Place.

From early in the war a boarding-house was kept open to provide accommodation for boys who had no home to go to and, near the end of the war, when parts of the country became dangerous because of Doodlebugs and V2s, considerable numbers of boys stayed as guests in some of the boarding-houses.

Boxes for hand grenades were made in the Wood Shop — 4,500 had been completed by July 1942 — while the Metal Shops were of particular value as they enjoyed handling small orders for spare parts which munition factories could not stop to supply. The summer holidays of 1942 saw such a good response of volunteers to undertake work that not all the offers were taken up: during this two-month period 1,300 grenade boxes were completed, along with numerous pieces of casting. In July 1943 it was calculated that 600,000 hours of boy-labour had produced a total of 50,000 fittings of various types, including 15,000 metal shop fittings, 13,000 metal castings and 12,000 hand-grenade boxes.[60]

At an early stage in the war the schoolboy factory workers' efforts came to the attention of the authorities in London. Arthur Jackson, Director of the Ministry of Supply for Armaments, while examining the reports from anti-aircraft batteries regarding the requirements for firing-pins, was struck by the fact that alone in the country, the battery in the village of Barnwell in Northamptonshire seemed never to run short. Prompted by curiosity he took the train to Barnwell Station, and over lunch at the Talbot Hotel with the battery's Commanding Officer the mystery was solved for him. 'Well, Sir,' he was told, 'there's a very fine workshop at the School in Oundle. We supply the model to the headmaster Dr Fisher, and the boys make all the firing-pins we need.' The conversation led to an arrangement with the School which resulted in the provision of some 30,000 firing-pins between the autumn of 1940 and the end of the war, including firing-pins for ·303 rifles.[61]

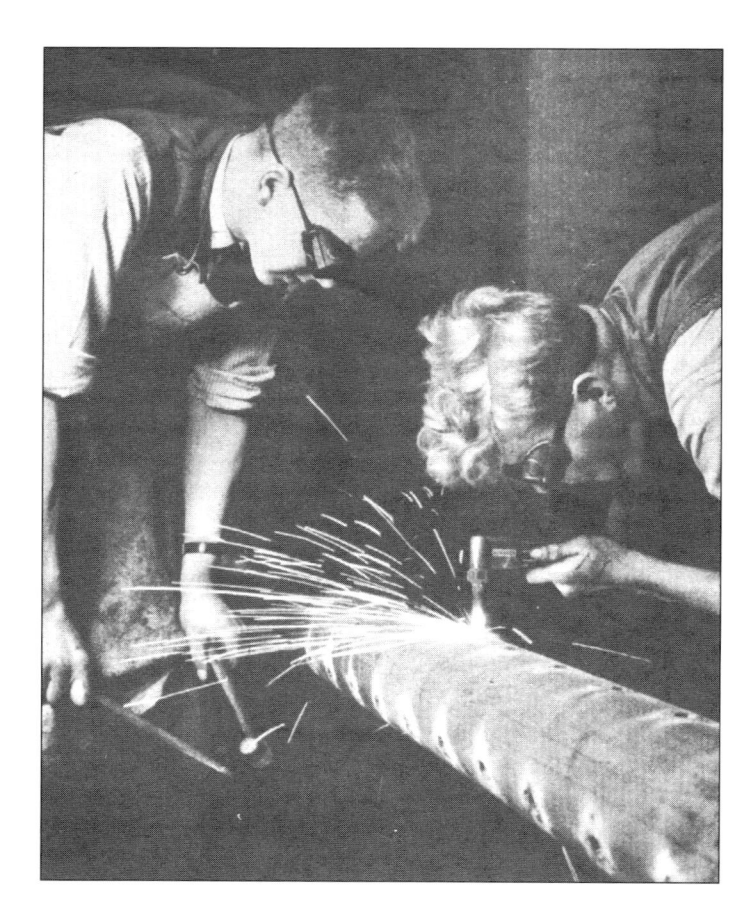

45: Oundle School boys using oxy-acetylene equipment at the Workshops to cut holes in the tube of an artesian well shaft.

Occasionally the Science department was asked to solve problems of some importance. A former pupil was told to find out why large steel hammers making propellers were breaking up. He decided that the man to solve this problem would be Oundle School's Herbert Palmer, and spent a month in Oundle working with senior forms on the project, returning to the RAF with a machine for measuring the wave lengths inside the hammers.[62]

A Schoolmaster's Memories

Oundle School's history master Dudley Heesom evoked a picture of life as it was for the pupils at the School from 1939 to 1945 in an article he wrote for its magazine *The Laxtonian*, published in 1980.

> To most of the boys at school at the time the chief memory will be of darkness and cold. When street lights had been turned off the slightest chink in the black-out appeared as a searchlight and no amount of warning and patrolling could prevent occasional shafts of light which, in the town, caused extreme alarm. The cold of the winters at a time when there was no central heating was a constant problem, for coal was difficult to obtain. Study fires could not be lit until after tea. Heating depended largely on the fact that each boy generates a hundred joules of heat a second. Much ingenuity was shown by boys in acquiring fuel. Indeed even the most gullible housemasters found it difficult to believe that so much coal happened to fall onto the railway lines from the carelessness of the stokers on the engines.

TWO ~ OUNDLE IN WARTIME

Though hard, life was seldom dull, and there were many amusing moments.

> One day at a Masters' Meeting the Headmaster, who had been to see a Marx Brothers film, remarked 'I was bombed near Peterborough this afternoon.' After a time it became clear that the 'I' was geographical rather than personal, and referred to the village of Eye.

The wartime weapons which provided much amusement for the town boys of Laxton School also found their way into the School's boarding houses. 'Blank cartridges on the prep room fire were always good for a minor riot,' recalled Bramston House pupil John Keene. More worrying is Dudley Heesom's recollection of a moment in the same boarding house. 'The Head of the Prep Room came into the study and said, 'I think you ought to know, Sir, that there is a live 3" mortar bomb in one of the lockers, and it is fizzing.' The detail omitted by Dudley Heesom is that he himself supervised the burial of the offensive object on Bramston Paddock. 'Is it still there?' wondered John Keene fifty years later. Eventually, even the boys felt that something had to be done about their illicit arsenal. 'I think it was in the summer of 1945 when various doubtful items of a potentially explosive nature had been assembled by several people in the House. We couldn't hang on to them, and, of course, we didn't want to worry Dudley, so late one evening after 10 pm a trip was organised down to the river behind Bramston where all the items were deposited in the Nene.'

Dudley Heesom believed that many teachers found their subjects became more meaningful for pupils in wartime.

> In spite of the difficulties, the war seemed to add a spur to much of the teaching. Maths and Science clearly had an extra relevance to artillery and flying and many specialist branches. When boys experimented with explosives the Headmaster, who had run an ICI factory in the First War, was angry, not that they should have tried, but that they should have hesitated to ask his help.
>
> Doubtless, privately, boys were disturbed that the escalator of time would remorselessly deliver them into the horrors of battle. But the immediate need to take the steps necessary for survival kept minds concerned mainly with practical jobs. It seemed that morale rose as they became more familiar with war. Before the outbreak the question asked was, 'What would be the safest job?' One boy, who later distinguished himself at Alamein, decided to try for searchlights on the grounds that bombers would, if they could, try to keep away lest they would be hit. By the end of the war, prefects were asking, 'What is now most needed in the war?' and the answer had to be 'Naval Air Pilots', a very dangerous job.
> By great good fortune none of the group was killed.

46: Dudley Heesom, one of Oundle School's wartime teaching staff.

Interest in the war was stimulated by the steady stream of former pupils who came back telling stories about each other.

There was the ex-scout who took part in the midget submarine torpedoing of the *Tirpitz*; there was the gentle ex-pupil from Grafton House in Milton Road, whose serenity Montgomery so much appreciated that he took him from theatre to theatre of war on his staff; there was the ex-School House cox Battle-of-Britain pilot who felt that every minute spent on the ground was wasted, who admitted that as a boy he could have easily imagined that he would shoot down German planes, but could never have imagined that he would be allowed to walk up and down the Housemaster's lawn. There was the Naval Lieutenant who had been landed on the coast of Malaya to make a survey for an Allied landing. The submarine, which was supposed to pick him up, did not arrive, so that he had to spend the rest of the war fighting against the Japs with the Chinese guerrillas. There was the ex-Head of the School who used to fly daily an unarmed Mosquito to measure the weather over Mont Blanc. One evening when he came to supper he was unrecognizable. The plastic surgeons had given him a new face.[63]

Not all the School's former pupils were officers of course. Many, such as Lance Corporal John Warr, ex-Head of Laundimer House, reported by *The Laxtonian* as having been killed in action in France in May 1940, after joining the Seventh Royal Sussex Regiment the day after war began and refusing to take a commission, were proud to serve in the ranks.

Just as for the town, a certain disruption in the calendar was inevitable for the School. The first Speech Day of the war had to be abandoned, causing a certain consternation since such a thing had never happened even in the darkest days of the First World War.

However Dudley Heesom noted the surprise with which it was realised at first how little difference was made to life at school. It was true that in April 1940 the School magazine's Editor was claiming: 'The war has scarcely affected us at all. A little less sugar and a little more margarine will do no one much harm.' And it was true, even by July 1940, that only about twenty Old Boys and masters had been killed or gone missing: 'even this tragic number is not as great as those which filled the Laxtonians of 1915.'[64]

The average junior boy at the School found that the contents of his tuck-box retained an importance which outside events could hardly diminish. 'Apart from rationing and the total absence of things like camera film, bananas, fully-lined jackets, gateaux, chocolate biscuits, branded soft drinks, pleasure motoring etc., the war had little direct effect,' recalled Patrick Lane, who joined The Berrystead on North Street in 1943.

Oundle's War Poets

Indeed it is true in a sense that no event of major importance occurred to bring war physically into Oundle pupils' consciousness. Yet some boys felt as passionately as the young Ben Grantham about the evil which had overtaken Europe, and not in a purely anti-German sense. Oundle School Sixth Former James Alexander was writing *A Denunciation of Nationalism and of Self-Seeking Politicians, the two chief Causes of War*, just as the British Expeditionary Force was preparing itself for the onslaught by Hitler's armies. It did not prevent him from serving as a Lieutenant in the Middlesex Regiment on leaving Oundle the following year.

> Once more the loathsome octopus of War
> Has spread its slimy tentacles around
> The nations of the world, and once again

TWO ~ OUNDLE IN WARTIME

Its horny beaks gape wide, and swallow up
Whole peoples: once again the tortured air
Resounds with bursting bombs, exploding shells;
Once more the rotting corpses deck the earth,
And women mourn for husbands, brothers, sons.
Once more the starving housewives stand in queues
And vainly wait for food; and when at last
With empty hands they wander back in tears,
And little Ivan, Heinrich, Pierre or John
Demands his meal, what does he have to eat?
Not food; foul propaganda, slogans, fill
His empty, aching belly. 'Courage all,'
The rulers say, 'Your country must come first,'
''s ist für das Vaterland,' 'Pour la patrie.'
But, as her children starve before her eyes,
The wretched mother curses in her rage
The politicians and hot-headed youths
Who made the war.
                    Then, when at long, long last
The cannon's roar is hushed, and peace returns,
The well-fed politicians, sleek and smooth —
The men who from the safety of their desks
Sent millions to their deaths — they turn and gaze
In pained surprise upon the rows of graves,
And on the regiments of wounded men,
Who, blind or crippled, must eke out their days
Upon a miserable pension — they
Draw profit from the new-born love of peace,
And, standing on their platforms, they proclaim
'That was the war to end war. Ne'er again
Shall millions die, and millions more remain
Pale shattered wrecks, mere living corpses some.
The Age of War is past; henceforth mankind
Will solve its problems by more peaceful means
And not by force of arms.'
                            So speak they then,
But all is lies, for after twenty years
Another generation rises up
That has not suffered war; that has not seen
War's cruel sights nor heard its dreadful sounds.
This generation in its turn cries out
'Heil Hitler!' 'Britain first!' or 'Vive la France!'
And those same politicians, old and grey,
But still in power, if they can scheme it so,
Stand up once more, but this time they proclaim
Words of another nature; *now* they say
'Our rights must be respected, or we fight.'
They talk of 'Lebensraum' to cheering crowds
Of empty-headed youths, who will not heed
Their parents' counsels, when they sadly say,

> 'You know not war, you only think you do;
> If you had suffered what we underwent,
> You would not wish so much to go to war.'
> Those wily politicians play on them —
> In order that they once again can say
> That they have led the land to victory —
> Rouse patriotic pride, and urge them on,
> Till once again all Europe is at war.
>
> O love of country, curse of all Mankind!
> Virtue once noble turned into a vice,
> Whose name has been besmirched by more foul crimes
> Than any other save religion. Oh
> I would that thou mightst vanish from this earth,
> For then all war and strife would vanish too,
> And then at last would nations realize
> That others are of the same human race,
> And not foul monsters. Then, and only then,
> Would Honour, Peace, and Trust return to earth,
> And Man at last be truly civilized;
> For then would politicians rave in vain
> Of 'self-sufficiency' and 'living-space';
> The crowds would laugh, not cheer, for common sense
> Would rule the world instead of passion. Then
> Would earth become a heavenly Paradise,
> And then at last that epoch would have dawned
> Which every generation of mankind
> Has striven for — 'The Golden Age of Man.' [65]

Here, in 1940, was a worthy expression of humanist anger directed against those who had in large measure been responsible for sowing the seeds of the current world war. Is it possible that the same feelings were responsible for the result of a debate conducted by the School Debating Society just a few months later, at a time when the Battle of Britain was raging? The motion, 'That the dismemberment of Germany is a legitimate war aim of the Allies' was lost by 35 votes to 46.[66]

Certainly there was an intelligent awareness among some of Oundle's young that the humiliation of Germany by vengeful politicians after the First World War had been the gravest of errors. With what sad lucidity such feelings are expressed in the next chapter, by an Old Oundelian who was to die during the Battle for France.

An Interest in the Enemy

The subject of the war continued to provide material for the Debating Society: the motion 'That the British tendency to regard Hitler as a joke rather than as a tyrant has brought us to the present calamity' was lost by 52 to 54 votes on October 11 1941, while the motion 'That the course of the war so far has not discredited the strategy of defence' was debated in a lively fashion on 22 November, and carried by 58 votes to 28. February 1942 saw the defeat, by 35 votes to 14, of the motion 'That this House deplores the declaration of the occupied countries that retribution is a major war aim.'

TWO ~ OUNDLE IN WARTIME

A matter of vital importance to the future stability of Europe was the subject of the Debating Society on 31 March 1945, when it was clear that the defeat of Hitler was only a matter of time. The motion was 'That the willing co-operation of Germany is essential to the peace of Europe.'[67]

Interest in Germany and German culture continued at a high level at the School during the war years. There was no indication of any narrow xenophobia among the boys. The Modern Languages Society held a German evening on 16 November 1939 at which there was excellent fare and a large audience: the programme included a piano quartet, German songs, a paper on Goethe's Faust, recitations of some of Goethe's poems, a sketch, and a well acted short play in German by Hans Sachs. Two years later, on 11 November 1941, Rolf Barber, a languages master at the School known to generations of Oundelians, who was to settle in retirement at Paines Cottage in West Street, gave a fluent and entertaining lecture on student life in Germany. He even prevailed upon the headmaster, Dr Fisher, to give some first-hand stories of the latter's days in Jena, including various instructions for the delivering of blows in duelling. The next term, in February 1942, saw a further German evening: there was a talk on German Baroque Architecture and singing of songs by Schumann and Schubert which, as *The Laxtonian* put it, 'would have done credit to any German wireless programme.' Later in the year, on 17 November, a successful polyglot debate was held, the motion before the House being that 'Reisen ist besser als zu Hause bleiben,' with speeches not only in German and French but also Gaelic, Hungarian, Hebrew, Italian, Yiddish, Zulu and Swedish.[68]

The war provoked extreme feelings of gloom, despair, defiance and elation as appropriate, as seen in the writings of pupils at the School.

Even the Captain of Cricket at Oundle School, Michael Mills, who was to return as a schoolmaster after the war, naming his house in Cotterstock Road after the Cambridge University cricket ground, was inspired to lament the threat to his favourite pastime during that grim summer of 1940, in his *Thoughts of Cricket and War*:

47: Oundle schoolmaster Rolf Barber.

> Swallows are soaring overhead.
> The morning haze is pierced by summer sun,
>   Which, streaming through,
>   Dries up the dew,
> And gives warmth to the earth till day be done.

The mists are gone: see, in their stead,
Flecked with white clouds, the blue vault of the skies.
    On such a day
    'Tis meet to play
The kingliest sport that e'er man can devise.

A stretch of bright green turf, whose edges
Nestle 'neath a belt of oak trees' shade,
    Lies there unfurled
    Far from the world
Of care and trouble: there the scene is laid.

Pavilion, score-board, all are there,
The white screens standing bold against the green.
    Shades of the past!
    These are the last
And sole reminders of what once has been.

I'll see no cricket in this place,
To fight a war must Youth forgo its sports,
    And learn to fly,
    And shoot... and die
For Freedom, Honour, Peace: what mocking thoughts!

Why must this be? When shall we see,
Not guns and bombs, but bats and balls instead?...
    ... My thoughts were these
    As through the trees
I watched the swallows soaring overhead.

Certain events in particular struck a chord in the hearts of Oundle's young people. Here are the defiant *Thoughts of a Frenchman on the Franco-German Armistice, 1940,* another poem contributed to his school magazine in the summer of the same year by James Alexander, studying French in Oundle School's Sixth Form.

'Why look you so depressed and so forlorn
And why so faint at heart?' some say to me;
'Though France is crushed, *we* always shall be free!' —
You fools! prate on, and mock me while I mourn;
It is not your land that is being torn
And ravaged, your towns that are heaps of dust,
Your people that will slake the German lust
For might and riches. God! why was I born
To see my country in so black an hour,
Her honour gone, stripped of her wealth and power,
Her rulers grovelling before the foe;
Her people starved and sweated, while the flower
Of France's manhood has been killed in vain?
No! not for nothing do those bodies lie
Upon Mars' altar. France will rise again

And smash the German yoke. She cannot die;
She is too great: the land of La Fontaine,
Racine, Hugo, Voltaire, Villon, Montaigne
Can never pass away.[69]

While there were no great physical disasters to befall either Oundle or its School there were moments of extreme emotional tension experienced all the more deeply in a small community with so many parents, former pupils and friends engaged in the war effort.

'The war was ever-present, if not directly affecting us,' wrote 14-year old schoolboy Robin Paterson, noting in his diary for 9 February 1941: 'After prayers I listened to Churchill's speech on the wireless — it was superb.' Patrick Lane, newly arrived at the School's Berrystead House for junior boys in 1943 remembered: 'Most of us pinned up the war maps from the papers over our desks, whilst others had charts of the number of days left until end of term.'

Former Bramston House boarder Paul Massey remembered, more than fifty years on, the anguish that he shared with a senior pupil, Richard Watkinson, whose 'fag' he was in June 1939. The latter's father was on board the newly built submarine HMS *Thetis* which had failed to rise after submerging off Liverpool, the target of suspected IRA sabotage. Half-hourly news bulletins on the radio alternately raised and dashed the boys' hopes as frantic attempts were made to attach an airline to the stricken submarine, until it was finally realised that all inside had drowned.

Deep shock was felt at the news received just before the beginning of the summer term 1941 that the Master of the Grocers' Company, G. Maurice Beaufoy, had been killed during an air-raid in London while on ARP duty.

And Paul Massey's memory of the litany of names of former pupils killed in action — by June 1944 there were some 2,050 former pupils serving in HM Forces — jolts us into seeing a new picture of Kenneth 'Bud' Fisher, the very epitome of a headmaster, with his gown and mortarboard, steel-rimmed glasses and piercing look, known to many schoolboys for his strong right hand. 'I remember him blubbing as he read out the names to the whole school. I didn't understand why he was blubbing — I was only 13 at the time.'

Here, in its expression of emotion at the anguish, or, as the war progressed, the elation, was a further way in which the School found a closeness with the Oundle community which it would be difficult to match today.

48: Dr Kenneth Fisher, Oundle's wartime headmaster.

Wartime Morale

An attractively nostalgic image of wartime Oundle can be drawn from the recollections of the vast majority of its residents. A readiness to serve the nation in its hour of need, a sense of duty and the need for a common effort against the forces of evil, aching sympathy for your neighbours in their hour of tragedy, elation at the news of victory — all this was so typical of the traditional wider picture of Britain during World War Two. Glapthorn's Alec Payne expressed such a view:

> During the war, we were all in it together, and I think a lot of social barriers disappeared. I was a gunner for a short time, and I had some South Wales miners next door to me, and the only thing that really mattered was if they were decent, whether they were nice chaps. It didn't matter what their social status was at all, and if you were up against it and the chap next door saves you, or pushes you through or helps you — OK. So social distinction disappeared, and as a result of that there was one goal and everybody shared the same goal. So there was consequently more friendliness than there is now.

In wartime Oundle itself, 'everyone, including schoolchildren worked hard and there was a spirit of "togetherness",' believed Ruth Keens. 'People kept very cheerful in spite of the hardship of rationing, black-out and severe weather during the winters. Of course there were sad times, particularly when the news filtered through of our great battleships being lost and over one thousand brave sailors at a time going down with them.'

What fear there might have been during Britain's darkest hour had vanished as Oundle people like Elizabeth Berridge listened to one of the nation's greatest ever leaders. 'I remember Churchill's speeches. He was the man we would have all died for — he was a wonderful speaker. He certainly got everybody going and we were all absolutely determined then to win. By that time, I was about seventeen and our heroes were the Air Force. Nowadays it is pop stars, then it was fighter pilots. I remember Jack Finnegan, and picking up the paper to read that he had shot down his twenty-first bomber. We had pin-ups of him.'

Awareness of the fragile nature of life in such times undoubtedly led to a keen desire to enjoy it while it lasted. Wartime friendships seemed to have had a unique intensity about them, thought Elizabeth Berridge. 'We did have wonderful parties, but there wasn't the same social life in Oundle as there was before the war, and it has never returned to the way it was.'

Postwar Changes

Just as the start of the war had brought new faces to Oundle in the shape of evacuees, refugees and servicemen both from other parts of the country and from abroad, so its end marked further changes in the town's population. Elizabeth Berridge believed that people's experiences between 1939 and 1945 had a lasting impact in breaking their links with Oundle. 'I think but for the war many would never have moved away but afterwards they saw new horizons and left.'

In the villages the war's impact was even more drastic in bringing about such changes. Nora Blunt in Barnwell noticed how people who had been away in the war seemed older in so many ways.

> A lot of them seemed to be dissatisfied with country life because they'd been fighting away for all this and when they got back country life wasn't much different in a way. In fact to a lot

of them it was worse because there was rationing. They had to find work again. While they had been away the women had been working on the land and that's when they started to look further afield for jobs. We lost the village community then because men didn't work in the village anymore and it got more mechanised and they weren't needed as much.

Notes

1. Peter Green's remarkable plane-spotting diary was the basis of five articles in *FlyPast* magazine, April-August, 1993.
2. *Northamptonshire at War*, p.19.
3. HRH Princess Alice, *Memories of Ninety Years*, p.147.
4. Dudley Heesom, *Oundle in wartime*, in *The Laxtonian*, Michaelmas, 1980, p.17.
5. Patrick Duerden, *Aspects of Oundle in WWII*.
6. *The Laxtonian*, vol.XVI, no.3, December 1944, p.71.
7. Dudley Heesom, *Oundle in wartime*, The Laxtonian, Michaelmas, 1980, p.17.
8. Jonathan Hand & Angus Piper, *The Lady of the Manor, The Laxtonian,* Summer 1984.
9. Dudley Heesom, *Oundle in Wartime*, in *The Laxtonian*, Michaelmas, 1980.
10. *The Laxtonian*, vol.XV, no.8, July 1942, pp.339, 363.
11. Patrick Duerden, *Aspects of Oundle in WWII*. See *Fighting with Figures*, published by the Central Statistical Office, London, 1995.
12. Patrick Duerden, *Aspects of Oundle in WWII*.
13. *The Laxtonian*, vol.XIV, no.12, December 1939, p.913.
14. Dudley Heesom, *Oundle in wartime, The Laxtonian*, Michaelmas, 1980, p.20.
15. *The Laxtonian*, vol.XV, no.3, December 1940, pp.129-30.
16. *The Laxtonian*, vol.XV, no.6, December 1941, pp.267, 274.
17. *The Laxtonian*, vol.XV, no.6, December 1941, pp.274-5.
18. *The Laxtonian*, vol.XV, no.12, December 1943, pp.497-8.
19. *The Laxtonian*, vol.XVI, no.4, April 1945, p.126.
20. Patrick Duerden, *Aspects of Oundle in WWII*.
21. Jonathan Hand & Angus Piper, *The Lady of the Manor, The Laxtonian*, Summer 1984.
22. *The Daily Telegraph,* 2 September,1989, p.13.
23. Patrick Duerden, *Aspects of Oundle in WWII*.
24. Patrick Duerden, *Aspects of Oundle in WWII*.
25. *The Laxtonian*, vol.XIV, no.12, December 1939, pp.913-4.
26. *The Laxtonian*, vol.I (3rd series), no.10, July 1956, p.360.
27. Patrick Duerden, *Aspects of Oundle in WWII*.
28. Patrick Duerden, *Aspects of Oundle in WWII*.
29. Patrick Duerden, *Aspects of Oundle in WWII*.
30. *The Laxtonian,* vol.XV, no.3, December 1940, p.128.
31. Patrick Duerden, *Aspects of Oundle in WWII*.
32. Patrick Duerden, *Aspects of Oundle in WWII*.
33. *The Laxtonian,* vol.XVII, no.8, July, 1950, p.511.
34. HRH Princess Alice, *Memories of Ninety Years*, p.148-9.
35. Patrick Duerden, *Aspects of Oundle in WWII; Northamptonshire at War*, p.47.
36. Patrick Duerden, *Aspects of Oundle in WWII*.
37. *The Laxtonian*, vol.XV, no.5, July 1941, p.264. I am indebted to Tim Robey for his translation.
38. Patrick Duerden, *Aspects of Oundle in WWII*.
39. Dudley Heesom, *Oundle in Wartime, The Laxtonian*, Michaelmas, 1980.
40. HRH Princess Alice, *Memories of Ninety Years*, p.146; *The Laxtonian*, Summer 1984, p.3.
41. B. G. Holloway & H. Banks, *The Northamptonshire Home Guard 1940-1945*, pp.17, 36-7, 75-6.
42. Dudley Heesom, *Oundle in Wartime, The Laxtonian*, Michaelmas, 1980, p.18. A. C. Cutliffe, *Some Memories of the Oundle Corps, The Old Oundelian,* 1965-66, p.9. A full account of the School's participation in the Home Guard is given in *The Laxtonian*, vol.XVI, no.3, December 1944, pp.85-86.
43. *The Laxtonian*, vol.XV, no.12, December 1943, p.501.

44 B. G. Holloway & H. Banks, *The Northamptonshire Home Guard 1940-1945*, pp.182, 223-4.
45 Dudley Heesom, *Oundle in wartime*, The Laxtonian, Michaelmas 1980, pp.18-19.
46 *The Laxtonian*, vol.1(New Series), no.1, July 1961, p.34.
47 See Liddell Hart, *History of the Second World War*, p.87.
48 See Caroline Seebohm, *The Country House — A Wartime History 1939-1945*, pp.120-121; *The Laxtonian*, vol.1,(New Series), no.1, July 1961, p.34.
49 *Northamptonshire at War*, p.44.
50 Dudley Heesom, *Oundle in Wartime*, The Laxtonian, Michaelmas, 1980, p.22.
51 HRH Princess Alice, *Memories of Ninety Years*, p.146.
52 Jonathan Hand & Angus Piper, *The Lady of the Manor*, in *The Laxtonian*, Summer 1984, p.2.
53 HRH Princess Alice, *Memories of Ninety Years*, p.147,148.
54 *The Laxtonian*, vol.XV, no.4, April 1941, p.198.
55 W.G. Walker, *A History of the Oundle Schools*, p.597.
56 *The Laxtonian*, vol.XIV, no.12, December 1939, p.893.
57 I am indebted to my colleague Lindsay Rooms for this information.
58 *The Laxtonian*, vol XV, no.3, December 1940, pp.156-7. Awarded the Distinguished Flying Medal for service with the RAFVR, Denis Lake was killed in action in February, 1945.
59 *The Laxtonian*, vol.XV, no.4, April 1941, pp.211-2.
60 *The Laxtonian*, vol.XV, no.5, July 1941, pp.220, 275-6; no.8, July 1942, p.350; no.11, July 1943, p.462.
61 I am indebted to Mr Richard B. Jackson, son of Arthur Jackson and a former pupil of Oundle School, for this information.
62 Dudley Heesom, *Oundle in Wartime*, in *The Laxtonian*, Michaelmas, 1980, p.21.
63 Dudley Heesom, *Oundle in Wartime*, in *The Laxtonian*, Michaelmas, 1980, p.17. The ex-Scout who took part in the attack on the *Tirpitz* was Robert Aitken, whose account of the operation is given in a later chapter. The Naval Lieutenant in Malaya was Lieutenant A. M. Hood, a former member of Bramston House, who came back to talk to pupils about his experiences in the Lent Term of 1946: see *The Laxtonian*, vol.XVI, no.7, April 1946, p.289.
64 *The Laxtonian*, Michaelmas, 1980, p.17; *The Laxtonian*, vol.XV, no.1, April 1940, p.1; no.2, July 1940, p.60.
65 *The Laxtonian*, vol.XV, no.1, April 1940, p.52-4.
66 *The Laxtonian*, vol.XV, no.2, July 1940, p.66.
67 *The Laxtonian,* vol.XV, no.6, December 1941, p.272; no.7, April 1942, p.312; vol.xvi, no.4, April 1945, p.124; no.5, July 1945, p.159.
68 *The Laxtonian*, vol.XIV, no.12, December 1939, p.909-10; vol.XV, no.6, December 1941, p.273; vol.XV, no.7, April 1942, p.313; vol.XV, no.9, December 1942, p.382.
69 *The Laxtonian*, vol.XV, no.2, July 1940, pp.113-4.

CHAPTER THREE
Active Service

~ 1939 ~

49: Tanks in Oundle Market Place during a recruiting drive.

Call-up

Whatever apprehensions there might have been in that autumn of 1939, Oundle people showed themselves to be more than ready to support the Government in its opposition to Hitler. Fifty-two Oundle men registered for active service on the first day of the war. Laxton School, surrounded by airfields, would have an especially strong link with the RAF, as though its pupils sensed from the preparations at the many bases in the area how important the battle for air supremacy would be. Nine out of the 18 Old Laxtonians who lost their lives were to do so fighting in the air.

Typical were the Monk boys, whose parents ran the Black Horse in Benefield Road. Gordon, the youngest, would see action with the 11th Hussars Tank Regiment in Belgium and Germany following the Normandy landings, being mentioned in despatches after the

50: Flight Lieutenant Bill Monk, (fifth from the left) sporting his Old Laxtonian school colours alongside a Halifax of Coastal Command. The photo was taken in 1944, whilst he was serving with 518 Squadron, on the Isle of Tiree, in the Inner Hebrides.

war, but his elder brothers would both serve with the RAF. Bill Monk flew with Coastal Command, receiving the King's Commendation after the war. John, the eldest, had joined the RAF in 1926 and as Wing Commander would become Commanding Officer of 44 Southern Rhodesia Squadron, based at RAF Upwood near Peterborough, from where he flew Lancasters with Bomber Command.

Of those Britons living abroad not all had managed to return home by the start of hostilities. Robin Miller, who had left England the previous year to make his fortune as an organist in America, was keen to offer his services to King and Country but disappointed by the response of the authorities.

> I was in Philadelphia when war was actually declared. I went to the British Consulate to ask what I should do. I had previously passed my 'Certificate A' in the OTC, similar to the 'Passing out test' in the equivalent in those days of the CCF. They were very off-hand — they basically told me to go home, and that if they needed me they would send for me. Nothing much happened, and they eventually said that I could go back to England as long as I paid my passage. I thought 'To hell with that! If I am going to serve King and Country, you can pay my passage.'

Not until the Americans joined the war in 1941 were his services required.

> They started classifying people according to their 'use'. I was classified 4D, alongside 'Clergymen, Aliens and Persons of unsound mind'. Things began to hot up, and I was

reclassified 1A. I was then 'called up' for a preliminary medical, which I passed. Then I got a letter from the British Ambassador offering me a free passage back if I served the country.

I accepted, and after a while I was inducted into the British Army. We then set out for England on a boat which turned out to be the liner *Queen Elizabeth*, then fitted out as a troop ship — 15,000 American troops and quite a few RAF, and packed in like sardines. Conditions were pretty spartan, with eight of us sharing a single cabin, on double tiered bunks. We were allowed two meals a day. We did not see the sea, as the windows were boarded up, and the journey took us five days. We learnt later that if we had been torpedoed, we would have had no hope at all, as there were not enough life-jackets or boats. The plan was that instead of going in a convoy, we would zig-zag across the Atlantic to try for safety. I then got back to England.

Some Oundle people who were already professional soldiers at the start of the war did not find active service very different from their pre-war existence. Others, like music teacher Robin Miller, who had led a very different kind of life, found their world turned upside down.

To become an 'irk' (the lowest rank in the RAF) was a very considerable change, I can tell you! One was taught that you were absolutely nothing, rather like I imagined prison. It was really quite a salutary experience, and I had nearly a year of that. Actually, I was scrubbing the floor with another chap and it emerged that I had been to University, but he could not believe I had two degrees! He had never met anyone like this before. Another experience: I was in a billet with two other chaps, and one of them was rather interested in culture. The other was a corporal with 15 years' service. I think he had pretty limited horizons. Anyway, we managed to get hold of a radio. The other chap and myself listened to the music we liked, and the corporal just could not understand why we liked it! I applied for a commission to the Intelligence branch. I was sent to carry a message to an officer, whom I suddenly realised had been at public school with me.

'Good God!' he said. 'What are you doing here? You should apply for a commission. How about Intelligence?'

'I am not very intelligent,' I replied.

'That does not matter!'

And so I did. My Sergeant was a bit scathing, but I got it past him, and then found myself at the RAF Officer Cadet School at Cosford, where we jumped over things and marched about and did all sorts of things. Eventually I went to the RAF Intelligence School in London, which was very interesting. We were at last treated as if we had some brains! My first posting after that was in the headquarters of the 'Pathfinder Force' in Huntingdon. These people were the ones who marked the targets in Germany with lights, flares and so on, for the rest of Bomber Command, who were rather an élite sort of group.

The haphazard nature of call-up, and the direction that one might take in active service depending on the whim of others, was for Alec Payne a demonstration of the more absurd aspects of war:

One of the first chaps to be killed was a friend of mine from Neath County School. It was terrible how things worked out. You see, none of us knew very much about soldiering — we didn't know what it was going to be like, and what we would have to do. It happened that this friend of mine was called up just about a week or two before I was, and he was a classical scholar, and classical scholars don't go down too well in war time. So they asked him what he could do: 'Can you fly a plane?' 'No.' 'Can you drive a car?' 'Yes.' 'You're in the tanks!' That was the way it went, you see, and the poor old devil was killed in the desert fairly early on. That was what happened to you — they tried to fit you in, but there were some strange fittings sometimes.

Others were eager to be involved for political reasons. Former Oundle School boy Group Captain Stephen Beaumont, who would receive an OBE for his staff work with the RAF's 84 Group, joined up three years before the outbreak of war. So why, in 1936, aged nearly 26 and engaged to be married, had he joined 609 Squadron Auxiliary Air Force on its formation in February of that year?

Two main reasons are the answer to this question. First, the menace of Hitlerite Germany. In the 1930s Germany was not seen as a threat to Britain. Communist Russia, where the Tsar and his family had been murdered, where the aristocracy and professional class had been destroyed and the proclaimed intention was to establish Communism world-wide, was the major threat. Hitler in his *Mein Kampf* said that his enemy was Communist Russia. A confrontation between Germany and Russia would be no concern of ours. The brutality of the Nazi régime was not at first apparent. Hitler was seen as doing some good things like curing unemployment, giving discipline to the young, building good roads (we did not appreciate that they had a military significance) and making the trains run on time, like Mussolini in Italy. His anti-semitism appeared early, but busy Yorkshiremen did not feel automatic sympathy for German Jews, however regrettable it is to record this now. By 1936 we as a nation were seeing things very differently, and so was I.

The second reason was my admiration for my father who, having no military experience (a thing quite unknown in the Beaumont family), joined as a trooper in the Essex Yeomanry in 1914 and ended the First World War in command of the 2/4th Battalion, King's Own Yorkshire Light Infantry with a Military Cross and bar. In 1914, the country being in obvious danger, my father thought it his duty to play a part in its defence. In 1936, though the danger was not as apparent as in 1914, I felt much the same. I was conscious too that, due to my parents' self-sacrifice, I had been given a very privileged upbringing, so I ought to give something or do something in return. I joined the Auxiliary Air Force, which enabled me to go on with my job and get some training which, in the event of war, might be of use.

Ben Grantham, as we have seen in an earlier chapter, was eager to follow the example of his seniors and fight against Fascism and Nazism in Spain and Germany, but was as yet too young, being only 17. 'The minute war was declared we were prepared to quit and go, and had I been of an age, I'm absolutely certain that that is what I'd have done.'

In his particular case there were added reasons why he was ready to join.

I came from a military family. Before my generation there were six generations of serving soldier. Most of them had reached the rank of Colonel and above, and there was absolutely no question in our minds what one's right and one's duty was. We were not only prepared to fight but we were almost educated, that if the need arose you dropped everything and went.

There were few conscientious objectors in Oundle. Elizabeth Berridge remembered one or two on the staff at the School. 'There were some young masters who stayed on at the School whom we thought were fit enough and young enough to fight and we never knew why they didn't go. People didn't think it was honourable not to fight. However, some were prepared to be ambulance drivers — they were prepared to save lives but not to take lives. One of them joined the London Fire Brigade and had to fight some of the biggest fires in the Docklands area of London. He had a terrible time, but was determined that he would never fire a gun.'

Oundle, it seemed, followed the majority view of pacifists as expressed by ex-Navy man Tom Fiddick. 'Nobody had any time for them at all. When you're in a war you have to fight, it's a fight for survival you see.' However Ben Grantham took a different view.

> Strange though it may seem, although in a funny way one felt that they were wrong, I had enormous sympathy for them. A lot of people thought very badly of them indeed. I personally didn't. I queried their beliefs because of my own, and of course at that age one must be right! But they didn't worry me, and the vast majority of them actually did extremely good service during the war: hospitals, ambulances, all sorts of things they did, and they did it very well and were extremely useful citizens.

The Phoney War

'The Phoney War,' a term coined by the American Press, has become established as a name for the period of the war from the collapse of Poland in September 1939 to the opening of the German offensive in the spring of the following year. It was a period when no great battles were being fought between the Franco-British and German forces, and because of this, as Liddell Hart put it, people 'concluded that Mars had fallen into a slumber'.

In fact, this was a period of ominous activity behind the scenes, involving not only intense strategic planning by both sides, but also a propaganda war. This included the air-dropping of material over enemy territory, and it was an Oundle-educated airman, Flight Lieutenant Caradoc Bowen-Davies, who was in the first 'leaflet raid' over Germany. According to his old school's magazine he had the further distinction at this time of being permanently immortalised as a 'typical British airman' in a work by the painter Henry Lamb, commissioned by the Ministry of Information and exhibited in the National Gallery. Flight Lieutenant Bowen-Davies was later killed in action over England in September 1941.[1]

The propaganda war was also conducted by radio. A former Oundle School pupil, Noel Newsome, was to be given the job of Director of European Broadcasting at the BBC from 1941 to 1944, and would later be seconded to the Supreme Headquarters Allied Expeditionary Force (SHAEF) to take charge of the Allied radio transmissions to occupied Europe. Noel Newsome set the style and called the tune, according to a recently published study of wartime broadcasting, but his was one of the most difficult jobs in the BBC. 'What we have to do in this period of the war when we're on the defensive is to establish our credibility,' he told his colleague Alan Bullock. 'If there's a disaster, we broadcast it before the Germans claim it, if we possibly can. And when the tide turns and the victories are ours, we'll be believed.' Sound advice from this historian who had made himself a reputation as a formidable boxer, thought Bullock.[2]

The War at Sea

The war at sea started early for Britain. Barely twelve hours after the outbreak of war on 3 September 1939, an unarmed British liner, the *Athenia*, on its way to America, was torpedoed without warning 250 miles west of Ireland, contrary to Hitler's specific order that submarine warfare was to be conducted only in accordance with the Hague Conventions. This act by the German Navy marked the beginning of the Battle of the Atlantic, which, had it gone against this country, would have meant starvation and defeat for Britain.

The German Admiral Dönitz's boast in 1940 was that the U-boat alone could win the war. In fact the Battle of the Atlantic had already started by 19 August 1939, when the first ocean-going U-boats sailed from Germany to their war-stations in the Atlantic. By the date of the invasion of Poland 17 U-boats were already in place, while some 14 coastal-type U-boats were out in the North Sea.

Commodore Kenneth Gadd, who was in the Mediterranean in September 1939, described the changes which took immediate effect on the minesweeper on which he was sailing.

> Well, of course you went to what is called 'War Stations'. You had to darken the ship — you could not have any lights, that was the first thing to do so the aircraft coming over could not see you. And then you went into proper war watches. You had the sort of cruising watch and if you suspected the enemy to be nearby you went to close defence stations and when the battle was commencing you went to action stations.

The threat from enemy submarines to Allied shipping from the very first day of the war was something which the future 'Desert Rat' Vic Thorington experienced on 23 October while sailing through the Mediterranean on his way to the East.

> I didn't get back to India because there was a bit of a muck up on the part of the navigators, or one especially. It could only have been half a day out of Malta and to avoid being attacked by submarines the action they took was very like a zigzag. We zagged and this other ship didn't, it kept coming. Unfortunately it didn't go behind us. Oh no, it was almost a head-on collision. Of course there were a few thousand troops down there that didn't know what was going to happen, they thought a torpedo had hit us or something. It so happened that there was an Italian reconnaissance plane up in the sky that we were all looking at until somebody shouted out, 'Look at that wally — he's heading straight for us!' The course was set by the captain and he'd be down having his meal I suppose. When it happened I was hanging on to this rail and I ended up looking right into the water. We couldn't proceed because the front of our bows were split top to bottom, so we were half towed into dry docks in Malta and I stayed there ten days.

Waiting for the Weapons

Vic Thorington's scathing comment about the navigator's expertise was matched by his scorn of the weapons available to British forces at this time. 'For the first half of the war they were useless. When Hitler started this war he was prepared for it, this was why he started it. He was invincible at one stage.'

Other Oundle veterans shared his view of Britain's lack of military preparedness. 'We used the infantry weapons and equipment of the day,' said Charles Tod. 'We thought they were efficient but some were obsolete: for example we soon discovered that the anti-tank weapon we had was just a bad joke.'

The situation at sea was the same, according to Kenneth Gadd's description of his minesweeper's weaponry.

> She had a 4 inch gun and we had a 12-pounder aft and two twin Lewis guns — one on each side of the bridge. That's all the armour we had. We really didn't have any proper anti-aircraft

guns — the 12-pounder was the only one we could use and the 4-inch you couldn't elevate enough. We were very poorly equipped, simply because we hadn't been making enough guns.

A year before the outbreak of world war, former Oundle School boy Robert Butler, serving with the British Army in Palestine, had found himself in a tricky situation when commanding a ten-man reconnaissance patrol. Suddenly faced with 100 or so guerillas in September 1938, he recounts in his autobiography *Nine Lives* how the patrol discovered that its only automatic weapon, a Lewis gun, produced nothing more than a series of clicks. Following their escape, Robert Butler reflected on the incident. 'The Lewis gun was found to have its "Right stop pawl" and its "Left stop pawl" reversed through an assembly error after stripping and cleaning. Disciplinary action was taken; but an error in design which made such a mistake possible should surely have been corrected in a weapon which was used throughout World War I and into World War II.'[3]

Rodney Turner, who had left Oundle School's Sidney House in 1928, joining the 13th Light Anti-Aircraft Regiment, found himself posted as a Troop Officer to 38 Battery at Killinghome, near Grimsby, on the outbreak of war. He recalled the 'very public disaster' which occurred when it was decided to test one of their two Vickers Mk II 40mm guns, sited in the centre of the town square at Blythe, in Northumberland, detached there to defend the Submarine Base.

> The gun jammed every time after one round. The old ex-RN Petty Officer stores man said that when he was in a battleship in WWI this always happened unless the webbing ammo belts were boiled in tallow, and he offered to do the smelly job. The Brigade Staff Captain didn't want to know about it and kept well away, which was sensible as the smell really was appalling! The second test firing went like a dream except that the springs of the railway wagon, on which the gun had been mounted, and the firing rate seemed to be synchronized, so that the gun numbers were bounced higher and higher into the air! The Navy shored up the wagon with old railway sleepers, and we were at war.
>
> (I reported all this to Vivian Hunt, Officer Commanding 38 Battery at Killinghome, and strongly suggested that the belts of all eight Mk IIs there be similarly treated. He told me afterwards that his Brigade didn't take at all kindly to the idea of boiling belts in tallow, and blew their top. Luckily Jerry never visited Killinghome.)

A year later in October 1940, having left Greenock on board the MS *Georgic* bound for the Middle East, he was to witness the sight of the *Georgic's* gun crew unable to defend itself against a Condor flying boat because they had been supplied with the wrong ammunition.

~ 1940 ~

The Overrunning of Norway

Following the German invasion of Poland in September 1939, British forces had moved into Europe to support their allies, with a large concentration guarding the Franco-Belgian frontier. But German attacks were directed further north, with the invasion of Denmark and Norway, and the Allied attempt to counter this aggression was a failure. Brennie Dunkley was one of the British High Command's early victims of its unreadiness. Born in Thorney but now living in Oundle's Rock Road, he had moved to the area in 1935 where he found work on the Barnwell Estate. A member of the Oundle Territorials before the war, he joined the Leicester Regiment and was part of the Allied expeditionary force which set out to save Norway, leaving Scotland on 22 April. Five days later, on 27 April, he was a prisoner, spending the rest of the war in captivity.

Keeping the Sea Routes Clear

Following the sinking of some of its ships early in the war, Britain made haste to arm its merchant vessels, and established a convoy system whereby merchant ships sailed together under the command of a naval officer, with an escort of warships and RAF aircraft. However the U-boat threat continued unabated: in the seven months from June to December 1940 the Germans sank 2,500,000 tons of Allied and neutral shipping. On 27 April 1941 Winston Churchill was to warn the nation that 'in order to survive we have got to win on salt water just as decisively as we had to win the Battle of Britain in the air.' The Prime Minister saw that Britain's survival depended as it had always done on its freedom to trade by traditional means. 'Battles might be won or lost, enterprises might succeed or miscarry, territories might be gained or quitted, but dominating all our power to carry on the war, or even keep ourselves alive, lay our mastery of the ocean routes and the free approach and entry to our ports.'[4] But there was a heavy price to pay: more than 13,500 British-registered merchant ships were destroyed between 1939 and 1945, and more than 30,000 merchant seamen lost their lives.

Willoughby Turnill had left Laxton School in 1913, joining the Merchant Navy the following year, and was one of the many brave men who died in the struggle to keep the sea routes open. A native of Stibbington, he was First Wireless Operator in his ship when it was lost at sea on 21 November 1940.

Enemy submarines were only one threat to Allied shipping at this early stage of the war. On the east coast route mine-laying by air had caused more damage than U-boats in the later months of 1939, and after the German invasion of Denmark and Norway on April 9 the pressure was intensified. Kenneth Gadd came home in that month from the Mediterranean to find himself based in Harwich, from where he undertook the vital work of clearing German mines from British waters, sweeping up the north-east coast.

He explained the technical problems involved in the work.

51: Commodore Kenneth Gadd CBE, DSC, sailing from Southampton in the troopship HMS *Voltaire* in July 1939, on his way to join the Fleet Minesweeper HMS *Ross* in the Mediterranean.

THREE ~ ACTIVE SERVICE

There are various types of mine. The Navy had their own minesweepers, called fleet minesweepers — like small frigates. These were built in 1918. They were called the Hunter class minesweepers and were coal-burning. They could do 16 knots, but they were only equipped to do oropesa (a fish shaped float) sweeping. Now you know how trawlers have their otter boards out, at an angle, well it's the same principle as that: these floats go out and they take the otter boards out at an angle — you can have one or two out, we usually had one — and then each minesweeper is inside the sweep so you have a clear passage doing your sweeping.

Well, in the 1940s the Germans were very clever. They laid magnetic mines and there were some ships which were sunk in the Caymans, which were the first ones sunk. There were big passenger ships sunk in the Thames and they didn't know how they went down. Anyway they managed to recover part of one of these magnetic mines, and these very brave chaps, these bomb disposal chaps — you've got to take your hat off to them here — they gently unscrewed the insides and took the detonator out. Any move had to be very carefully done and they had magnesium screwdrivers and everything because they are not magnetic. Anyway, they got one of these mines, and then we had to degauss the ships — that's when there's a wire that goes right round the outside of the ship and the electric people gave the right amount of current to nullify the magnetic properties of the ship, so there's no magnetism in the ship — and that's done by this coil. All ships had to have it done. And then to sweep the magnetic mines we had what we called a double-L sweep, there were two rolls of enormous cable and it was a question of stretching these cables across and setting up these positive and negative points 200 or 300 hundred yards from the ship and exploding the mines there.

Then, of course, they introduced an acoustic mine, and you used to have a hammer inside the hull and you hammered on that and that sent a sound wave ahead of the ship and that would explode the acoustic mines.

They even went so far as to have a pressure mine and they were very tricky indeed. We didn't carry equipment to deal with them. You had to use specialised barges which were pulled through the water and as the pressure of the water went over the mine, it would explode. But the main ones we had to deal with were the sweep, oropesa, magnetic and acoustic mines.

Kenneth Gadd's duties also consisted of dealing with U-boats.

We also were fitted with ASDICs, that's for 'pinging' submarines. It worked using the Doppler effect. The equipment sent out a 'ping' and when it hit the hull of the submarine it reflected back and appeared on the screen. Then you went hunting the sub and, if it was appropriate, you ran over the top of it and dropped your depth charges which were at the back of the minesweeper. They were set to different depths.

Frequent returns to port were needed for the minesweepers.

When we were in the coal-burners we only used to have enough coal for about four days, so we had to refuel much more frequently than the oil-burners. If we went further afield — we headed out towards the Faroes once — we took a collier, a coal ship with us and we used to anchor and go alongside every so often and fill up with coal again — it was a dirty business I might add, filling up with coal.

Also you had to go into port for maintenance. After so many hours you had your boiler cleaned. We were based on a port. In the Mediterranean we were based on Alexandria, and in home waters we were based on Harwich and eventually on Hull, Grimsby and Gillingham. Up north also, Leith, near Edinburgh, the Firth of Forth and Aberdeen. When we first came home we were sweeping what you call the Ward Channel, up the coast, keeping it clear of mines. The E-boats, the fast German motor boats, used to come over in the middle of the night and lay the mines and we used to have to go out each morning and sweep them to keep the supply lanes clear for the coal coming down from the coal-fields and Northumberland, and the convoys going back and forth.

As might be expected, the work could be dangerous. Along with clearing the British coastal waters of enemy mines, Kenneth Gadd was also involved in laying mines, and one of his worst experiences occurred while doing this.

52: A German 'Oboe' mine exploding a little too close for comfort!

This particular minefield was laid off the north of Ireland, Londonderry, and we laid a big minefield off there, a deep minefield to catch the submarines. You have a particular setting, you drop the mines and they come up so much thanks to their electrical gadgets and so on. These were about 90 feet deep so all surface ships would go over the top of them. Unfortunately one or two of these came up and one or two ships had been sunk. So we had to do what we call a skimming sweep — we set our sweeps at about 60 feet and we got in our formation and swept across our 'lanes'. In the process we cut one or two mines that were too light. In the middle of all this, the ship ahead of us, its sweeper parted. It flipped along the water and it set a mine off and then, spasmodically, mines were going off in a big minefield and we were in the middle of it. You didn't know which way to turn. None of us was hit, one or two of us got a jolt, none of us were sunk but it was quite a frightening experience being in the middle of the minefield not knowing when the next mine would go off. I don't think we really had any casualties, at least not major ones — people were jolted off the deck so there were minor ones there.

THREE ~ ACTIVE SERVICE

53: HMS *Clinton*, one of the new generation of Fleet Minesweepers, built in 1943.

In spite of the dangers, Kenneth Gadd, like so many other servicemen, enjoyed his work for the camaraderie, which he found particularly strong in minesweeping.

> The minesweepers work in flotillas — you have a squadron of battleships and a flotilla of destroyers. The destroyers all go out in a line ahead and the minesweepers the same. We usually had eight minesweepers in the flotilla and you worked together doing your minesweeping exercises. Consequently when you get into harbour you get your 'chummy' ships, and you get to know people and it's quite a friendly life. That's compared with those ships which are completely on their own in some port or other so they don't have those opportunities. So we had that very good opportunity there. The flotilla life, that was very good.

The Battle for France

Not until 10 May did British troops advance eastwards into Belgium in order to repel the attack on the Benelux countries. But the action was too late and too slow. Rotterdam was bombed to ruins, the Dutch surrendered, and in quick succession the Germans took Brussels, Amiens and Antwerp. By May 27 the German push westwards had reached the French Channel ports with the capture of Boulogne and Calais.

Many servicemen with Oundle links performed acts of bravery during the campaign in France. Lieutenant Patrick Hunter-Gordon and Sergeant Denis Evans, both former pupils of the School, were just two who were given awards for their courage. Lieutenant Hunter-Gordon won the Military Cross, while Sergeant Evans won the Military Medal.

Patrick Hunter-Gordon had left Oundle School's Grafton House in 1934, joining the Royal Engineers. Bridges were being destroyed in an attempt to halt the German advance, but the sappers often found that a second demolition charge was needed. On the night of 14 May it was discovered that four of the main girders of one bridge had not been cut through by the explosion, but enemy fire from the opposite bank was so intense that no one could approach the bridge. Towards dawn, as the fire died down, Patrick Hunter-Gordon, 'with great determination and disregard of personal danger' as his citation puts it, led a small party of sappers, running out in full view of the enemy to place further charges and complete the destruction of the bridge.[5]

Denis Evans in particular showed coolness in the face of danger, as testified by the War Office:

54: Major Patrick Hunter-Gordon, MC.

> On May 11th Sergeant Evans was driving a lorry of 3.7" anti-aircraft ammunition during the advance into Belgium. At a halt at Tournai he found his lorry was on fire. Sergeant Evans, assisted by Lance-Bombardier McPherson, off-loaded the 60 boxes of ammunition successfully even though the whole lorry was ablaze, the last few being red-hot at the corners. He then reloaded the ammunition and delivered it intact to the new gun position in Brussels.[6]

Denis Evans was later to be awarded an MBE for his wartime service, reaching the rank of Major.

Among the British servicemen who fell during the Battle for France were two brothers, both educated at Oundle School. Their deaths, both occurring on the same day, 21 May, were a shattering blow for their family. Lieutenant Gordon Potts, was serving with the 8th Royal Warwickshire Regiment when he was killed at Calonne. His younger brother, Captain Michael Potts died in action at Bruyelle.

A letter which Gordon had written on November 10 in the previous year was found among his papers after his death.

> I am writing this in case anything should happen to me. I am not gloomy as to the prospect, but I prefer to be prepared. I want first of all to make it clear that I shall bear no bitterness of any kind to anyone whatever may happen. I hope everyone else will be able to face the future without hate, bitterness, or fear. Inasmuch as we let these passions have a play in 1919, we are, I think, partly to blame for what is now happening. But I feel that our policy for the last three years could not have been otherwise, and I willingly face whatever may come.

THREE ~ ACTIVE SERVICE

There is a tragic echo here of the feelings that some younger Oundelians were expressing so vehemently at their School at this time, as seen in the preceding chapter. There is nothing defeatist about the moving wisdom of Gordon Potts' last message. His blame of the vengeful politicians who had humiliated a defeated enemy after the First World War would surely have been approved by one of England's greatest military leaders. Wellington himself is supposed to have said, two days after Waterloo, that he never wanted to fight another battle because it had been 'too much to see such brave men, so equally matched, cutting each other to pieces'. The future Prime Minister was to be one of the foremost voices in calling for a 'just equilibrium' in Europe after the fall of Napoleon, rather than the punishment of a defeated France.

55: Lieutenant Gordon Potts, killed in action, 21 May 1940.

The double tragedy of the Potts boys was commemorated in the form of a book, entitled simply *Gordon and Michael*, edited by their family. A collection of letters and other material based on their short lives, it was privately printed, with a foreword by Oundle School's headmaster Dr Fisher. Today at Oundle their memory lives on in the Gordon and Michael Potts Reading Prize, awarded annually at the School.[7]

One of two Oundle School masters who died during the Battle for France was Lieutenant John Brittain. A history teacher, he had been called up on the outbreak of war and went to France in October 1939 as Intelligence Officer with the Second Battalion, The Northamptonshire Regiment. He was reported wounded and missing on 28 May. The second was Captain Charles Osman, who had served

56: Captain Michael Potts, killed in action, 21 May 1940.

with the Field Security Corps since January 1940. He was to die in hospital back in England on 24 July from wounds received on the beach at Dunkirk.[8]

The Evacuation from Dunkirk

With the capitulation of the Belgian army on 28 May, it was decided to evacuate as many as possible of the British Expeditionary Force from Dunkirk. A bridge-head some 15 miles long and less than 10 miles deep was established, and the withdrawal to Dunkirk began under the command of General Gort. The naval plan began to function on 29 May, using the celebrated assembly of little ships of all shapes and sizes which had crossed the Channel to help in the evacuation following an appeal by the British Government. By midnight on 31 May some 80,000 of the British troops within the bridge-head had been evacuated, and by 3 June the operation was complete.

The Royal Navy played a crucial role in the evacuation at Dunkirk in 1940. The operation was highly successful in terms of organisation, but for those who took part at the time it must have seemed chaotic. The late Lewis Keens, a well-known resident of Herne Road who spent much of his life in the Royal Navy, was astonished to encounter one of his own brothers whom he had not seen for many years, pulling him aboard his ship, and only later discovered who he was.

Commodore Kenneth Gadd had vivid memories of the evacuation, in which the fleet minesweepers took part to help the destroyers evacuate the troops.

> We were there for about four or five days, going back and forth taking so many troops. The most we could take was about 300 — we were only built to take about 90 people so they were everywhere, even on the deck. The last time out the Germans were really very close to Dunkirk and we were coming out on our last voyage in the morning on the 'Glorious 1st of June', and there were God knows how many Heinkel dive-bombers around. Anyway they almost sunk the destroyer alongside. Another one was hit, we were in the middle and somehow or other we had about four or five of these Heinkels going for us and the bombs were just missing us. The water was being chucked up. The ship was lifted but we actually were never hit which was quite remarkable. We had one person killed by the splinters from the bombs and we had several people wounded by the splinters and bullets — not seriously. But anyway, we got clear of that which was absolutely... how we did it I don't know.

In a humorous vein — and of course there are amusing moments in war — it is worth quoting Arthur Marshall on the British withdrawal from Dunkirk. Oundle's famously funny pupil, who had left the School's Dryden House in 1928 and found himself in the British Expeditionary Force at this time, was grateful for his military training in the OTC. 'During the confused fighting in France and Belgium in 1940, and the rather hasty scamper to the coast, conditions were in some respects not unlike an Oundle Field Day that had, somehow, gone wrong,' he explained in an article written twenty years after the evacuation. 'It was a pinch noisier, and the enemy had taken up positions unknown in Certificate A, but nobody knew where anybody else was and all those assurances that "Blue Force will be protecting your left flank" had turned out to be woefully inaccurate. It seemed impossible not to believe that shortly a whistle would be blown and the Tuck Shop van would come careering round the corner, the trestle tables would be set up and there would be cups of strongish tea and doughnuts for all. This gave strange comfort.'[9]

Arthur Marshall was to end up as a Colonel in Military Intelligence.

Less whimsical in tone was the description of Major General Sir John Winterton, who had left Oundle's Laxton House in 1915. His performance at Dunkirk was to be recorded in his citation.

'During the evacuation from the beaches he exerted himself tirelessly, organizing parties of soldiers and getting them embarked in the small boats which took them out to the larger craft lying offshore. Day after day he spent long periods up to his waist in seawater.'[10]

He was to display similar courage in adversity in the retreat from Burma in March 1942.

57: Oundle's most amusing ex-schoolboy: Lieutenant Colonel Arthur Marshall MBE.

Another former Oundle School pupil who was later to become deputy chief of the Foreign Office's Information Research Department was to claim that during the evacuation from Dunkirk he owed his life to his ex-scoutmaster at Oundle, Eric de Ville, who had taught him so thoroughly to build rafts out of spurs, lashings and petrol cans. Norman Reddaway, of the Reconnaissance Corps, who ended the war as a Lieutenant Colonel at the Allied Kommandatura in Berlin, was one of the last to leave Dunkirk, jumping on board a freighter. Half-way across the Channel an explosion rocked the ship and it began to take in water rapidly: the freighter, laden with troops, had been torpedoed by a German motor torpedo boat. In the ensuing panic only one in ten of the crew and passengers were to survive. Norman Reddaway found himself in the water surrounded by the débris of the stricken freighter, including a few planks which he succeeded in lashing together and clinging to for three hours until he was rescued. In later years the incident was to make him aware of the bizarre and absurd coincidences so frequent in war. 'It does seem quite likely that the German motor torpedo boat was commanded by a close friend of mine,' he believes. The friend was Kurt Theo Gautier, son of a German Air Marshal, with whose family the former Oundle schoolboy had stayed in Kiel in 1934. 'He did not survive the war, so we shall probably never know whether it was his or someone else's motor torpedo boat — but there weren't many of them and MTBs were his line.'[11]

The RAF did its best to keep the Luftwaffe at bay during the evacuation, but its fighters, based at airfields in southern England, were heavily outnumbered and unable to stay for long over the area because of the distance. Among those pilots who lost their lives was Flight Lieutenant George Rex Shepley, who had left Oundle School's Dryden House in 1928 and was based with No.16 (AC) Squadron at Old Sarum. He was killed in action over Dunkirk in May, receiving the posthumous award of the Distinguished Flying Cross for previous action over Calais. His parents were to lose a second son, Douglas, in the Battle of Britain three months later.[12]

On land too there were those who sacrificed their lives or their freedom in order to allow so many thousands of Allied soldiers to escape to safety across the Channel. Lovel Garrett, well-known in the Oundle area for many years as a County Councillor, had also been educated at the School, leaving Sidney House in 1930. A familiar name to countless former pupils, he returned to the town in 1964 to teach history for seven years and later became Hon. Secretary of the OO Club from 1976 to 1981.

In 1939, Lovel Garrett was Housemaster at Cranleigh School. When war broke out he joined the Northumberland Fusiliers, fighting in the disastrous campaign in France against the advancing German forces. Retreating along the coast towards Le Havre, he was trapped with the 51st Highland Division at St Valery-en-Caux and after fierce but hopeless resistance was forced to surrender. The defeat, in which up to a thousand British soldiers died and more than 8,000 were taken prisoner, is one of the most controversial episodes of the war.[13]

58: Flight Lieutenant George Rex Shepley DFC.

Lovel Garrett spent the rest of the war in POW camps in Germany and Poland. His family preserved the letters he wrote home and some of these are now in Oundle School archives. Two letters written during his time as a POW refer back to the battle at St Valery and his capture by General Rommel, later to become the Desert Fox of North African campaigns.

12 June 1941

It is very peaceful here today and I can't help thinking of the very different scene exactly a year ago when we were surrounded on three sides gradually being driven back on to the cliffs; memory is a mixture of noise and horror. I was sent down towards evening to look for the expected ships, the beach was a shambles, littered with corpses, raked by MGs, constantly shelled and periodically dive bombed; it was a miracle to me that anyone was left alive while on my left St Valery seemed one gigantic bonfire. The thing that affected me most was to see the same battered corpses hurled into the air again and again. . .

16 June 1942

The resumption of hostilities on a large scale in North Africa, makes one worry about so many friends I have there. I take particular interest having met General Rommel in France, the meeting on my side was involuntary and as I was on foot armed with an empty revolver and one Mills bomb and accompanied by half a dozen weary troops and as he had a number of tanks, I was somewhat at a disadvantage. However he treated me very well, one of his officers gave me half a bottle of brandy and some cigarettes and they then took me off to a doctor who treated my scratches, that was two years ago almost exactly.

In a third letter Lovel Garrett recollects how lucky he was to survive, as a bullet pierced his gas cape and shrapnel his pack.[14]

Another former Oundle School boy was to join Lovel Garrett in captivity, taken prisoner after a heroic battle to halt the German advance on Dunkirk. This was Elliott Viney, who had left School House in 1932. As a Captain in the Buckinghamshire Battalion of the Oxfordshire & Buckinghamshire Light Infantry, he played a key role in maintaining a defensive ring round Dunkirk during the evacuation. German armour, and lack of ammunition finally brought the defence to an end, and Elliott Viney, with about half his battalion, which he was now commanding due to casualties, was forced to surrender at Hazebrouk. He too was to spend the rest of the war as a prisoner.

Their sacrifice had not been in vain, however. A total of 224,585 British officers and men were evacuated, including 13,053 wounded, and 112,546 Allies, nearly all French and Belgian.

Italy Enters the War: the Defence of Malta

With Italy's entry into the Second World War on 11 June 1940 the Mediterranean island of Malta found itself the object of almost constant bombardment until July 1943.

Lucy Fallace, now a resident of Oundle Market Place, was one of the many civilians trapped along with the military garrison. Her husband, serving in the RAF, had been posted in 1936 to the island, where she had joined him with their four-year old son at Kalafrana, the sea-plane base. She had decided to stay in Malta rather than be evacuated following the dramatic news of the outbreak of war on 3 September 1939, and remembered the first air-raid which ended the uneasy lull of peace that they had enjoyed. They had heard the announcement of Italy's entry into the war while walking to the camp cinema, and had immediately rushed home to pack a suitcase of clothes in case they were evacuated.

> The following morning at about 6.15, I was cooking breakfast on a Valor stove, when I saw my husband come dashing down the stairs, shaving soap on one side of his face, and carrying our son. He had snatched him from his bed; I couldn't understand what the hurry was all about, but he said he had seen a plane fly over the camp and it wasn't one of ours, so I turned off the cooker and followed him to the covered trench not far from the house. Not many people were there because there was no warning siren, but within five minutes there was an earth-shattering thump quite near. We waited for the all-clear before coming out, and then discovered that the first bomb had fallen within yards of our house. The kitchen windows had been blown out, and the frying pan was full of glass and rubble. On looking back, I can't understand why breakfast was so important. However I washed the pan and started frying some more bacon just as the siren went again. This time I put the pan in the oven, then dashed out to the shelter. No bombs this time, and we managed to complete our breakfast just in time to see a covered truck going from house to house picking up women and children to be evacuated, so this was our start to the war.

Preparations had been made to accommodate servicemen's families inland at the Parisio Palace Hotel, which was to be their refuge from the enemy air-raids. The new arrivals were allocated a bunk each. 'Mine was in the ballroom along with my son and 28 other bodies,' recalled Lucy Fallace. 'The mirrors all around the walls were all boarded up, and as the bunks were three tiers high, gazing up at the beautiful painted ceiling from the top one is a novelty at first, but fluffy clouds and cherubs can lose their appeal.'

The cramped conditions were not the only uncomfortable aspect of their time at the Parisio Palace.

> The NAAFI prepared and served all the meals, and the women were expected to keep the bathrooms and wash-places tidy. I was a junior officer's wife at the time and was given the thankless task of allocating jobs. There were so many excuses and grumbles that one Sunday I skipped the church service and cleaned six bathrooms and about thirty wash-basins myself so that nobody used the excuse of 'I did it yesterday!'

The chance of an escape from this tedious routine came soon, bringing Lucy Fallace nearer the front-line of Malta's defence.

> One day someone came who wanted recruits to take a course in First Aid and Nursing. Myself and a friend called Mara were the only volunteers. We were driven to the Governor's Palace in Valleta three times a week to do our training, and after about five weeks sat an exam and became fully qualified VADs (Voluntary Aid Detachment) with sufficient knowledge to work under a doctor's instructions. We were issued with a white overall and head-dress, which was the St John uniform, and so started our duties in a very busy underground medical dressing station where all sorts of wounds and burns were dealt with. I remember thinking, 'I shall no longer be trying to do a perfect bandage on a pretend wound, this is the real thing.' I remember the first morning I was on duty, following the doctor's orders about dressings etc., seemed to run quite smoothly. Then a man came in and when the dressing was removed from the back of his neck I saw a huge hole the size of an orange and the doctor remarked, 'It's nice and clean. Nurse, pack that with a bip dressing.' I looked at it with panic. This was altogether outside my experience, then quickly a young orderly stepped up and said, 'You are a new nurse, aren't you, well I'll do it today and you watch me.' He proceeded to take a jar of this tape-like dressing and with a pair of forceps gently fold yards of this back and forth until the wound was filled. The next day he supervised me doing it, and it was quite a thrill to me to see this wound getting smaller each day.

59: Lucy Fallace (right) with VAD friend Mara Marks in Malta 1940.

Malta was to endure over 3,000 air raids. During the most severe, lasting for a week in October 1942, a total of over 1,400 bombers dropped their bombs into a target area not much bigger than a few square miles.

Further east, near Cairo, where he had arrived at the start of the Western Desert campaign, Oundle's Ralph Leigh was to hear the tragic news of the death of his friend Frank Briggs. Battery Sergeant Major Briggs, a Glapthorn man, had arrived in the Middle East in the autumn of 1940. The two had met quite by chance in Egypt, thousands of miles

THREE ~ ACTIVE SERVICE

from home and after a celebration drink had arranged to see each other again. On 25 October Ralph Leigh was told that his friend had died in a motor-cycle accident.

The War in the Air: the Battle of Britain

With the evacuation from Dunkirk, and the overrunning of most of the continent by Hitler's forces, it remained only for Operation 'Sealion', the invasion of Britain, to allow the Nazis to dominate most of the continent of Europe. Fleets of barges were assembled to transport a great German army across the Channel. But Hitler's generals were apprehensive about the risks that their troops would run in crossing the sea. They were concerned about the British naval threat, and they insisted that air superiority over the crossing area was essential.

Hitler finally accepted that 'Sealion' could not be launched before the middle of September, and allowed Marshal Göring, the Germans' Supreme Commander in the Air, to demonstrate the Luftwaffe's superiority.

Formations of up to 130 aircraft were used to attack British shipping and coastal targets from 3 July. However, German losses proved heavy against the easily manoeuvrable Hurricanes and Spitfires: 364 aircraft were lost between July 3 and August 11.

Göring launched attacks on the fighter aerodromes of south-east England, but British air strength was maintained and the German losses continued to rise. On 15 August alone, 75 German aircraft failed to return and by the 23rd losses had risen to 403. Göring widened the attacks on British airfields from 24 August, still without achieving mastery of the air, and then switched his attack to London. From September 7 to October 5 German bomber squadrons pounded the capital. However by the end of October it was clear that Göring had not achieved his objective. On October 12 Operation 'Sealion' was postponed until the spring of the following year.

Allied losses were high — 915 fighters were destroyed — but the Luftwaffe's was even higher, with 1,733 aircraft shot down from July to the end of October.

Oundle's contribution to the wartime technology which was vital in the struggle for survival on land, sea and in the air has already been mentioned. The School had a strong Air Training Corps, and many of its cadets came from an engineering background strengthened by Oundle's system of Workshops education set up by headmaster Frederick Sanderson at the beginning of the century.

But just as important as the equipment was the bravery and determination of the aircrews, whose defence of Britain in effect caused Hitler to abandon his plans for invasion. 'Never in the field of human conflict was so much owed by so many to so few,' as Churchill said in the House of Commons at the height of the battle. To pick out any one outstanding individual is difficult. Oundle was well represented in the RAF during World War Two.

A previous generation of former pupils who enjoyed illustrious flying careers in the pre-war years had no doubt contributed to the glamorous image of the air ace.

There was Alan Jerrard, the only winner of the Victoria Cross during the prolonged and bloody combat in the skies above Italy during World War I after leaving Oundle School's Sidney House in 1914.

There was the World War I fighter pilot Cecil Lewis, who had left Oundle the following year, and was to win a Military Cross for his flying exploits over the front line of the Somme Battle in 1916. He was later to help found the BBC before picking up an Oscar for the script of *Pygmalion* in Hollywood. George Bernard Shaw had written of his

60: Members of Oundle School Air Training Corps receiving instruction on the working of the School's aeroplane engine as featured in the *Illustrated* magazine, June 1941.

autobiography *Sagittarius Rising*, published in 1936, 'This is a book which everybody should read. It is the autobiography of an ace, and no common ace either... he is a thinker, master of words, and a bit of a poet.'

On the technical side there was the brilliant aircraft designer Amherst Villiers, who left Oundle three years after Cecil Lewis and who had set up his own aeroplane engine company, although his design ideas were applied more in the area of motor-racing, where he worked with leading figures such as Ettore Bugatti, Raymond Mays and Donald Campbell. During the Second World War he did however design a heavy bomber with the ability to fly non-stop around the world. He also became a member of the RAF Transport Auxiliary, delivering Spitfires, Hurricanes and bombers, achieving notoriety on one occasion when he overturned a Hurricane when no one informed him that the runway on which he was landing in fog had been ploughed up for resurfacing.[15] A further link with the past was provided in the person of Air Commodore Ian Brodie, who had left Oundle School's Dryden House in 1916 and now set up the Air Ministry's Central Gunnery School at Warmwell in Dorset, becoming its first commander in August 1940. It was Ian Brodie who had been closely associated with Lawrence of Arabia in that enigmatic figure's subsequent incarnation as Aircraftsman T. E. Shaw. Lawrence, who served as Ian Brodie's clerk at Miramshah Fort on the North-West frontier of India in the late 1920s, was to write from Miramshah that 'we

THREE ~ ACTIVE SERVICE

have had an idyllic two and a half months here under the best and kindest CO of my experience'.[16]

But it was the dashing pilots of the Second World War who were to achieve real star status in the eyes of succeeding generations, and particularly following the victory over the Luftwaffe at this critical stage in the war.

One Battle of Britain pilot who had been educated at the School, and now found himself at Warmwell with fellow-pupil Ian Brodie, was Pilot Officer Douglas Shepley, who had left Dryden House in 1935 and achieved an excellent flying record at Cranwell before joining No.152 Hyderabad Fighter Squadron. In four days of air combat in the Battle of Britain, from August 9 to 12, he accounted for two enemy planes before being shot down over the Channel during his second engagement of the day. His elder brother, Flight Lieutenant George Rex Shepley,

61: Cecil Lewis, wearing his RFC Wings and MC after a visit to Buckingham Palace in 1916.

62: Air Commodore Ian Brodie OBE, a photograph taken in Rome in 1945 when he was an acting Air Vice Marshal.

63: Pilot Officer Douglas Shepley.

flying with No. 16 (AC) Squadron at Old Sarum, had been killed in action over Dunkirk in May 1940, receiving posthumously the Distinguished Flying Cross.[17]

Douglas Shepley, married for only six weeks, was in fact the third member of this North Country family with strong Oundle links to die in the war. The first was Jeanne, who was lost when the SS *Yorkshire* was torpedoed in the early days of the conflict.

Douglas's mother and young wife, in their sadness sought to replace the Spitfire in which he had flown. Within fifteen weeks, £5,700 was collected and a replacement was purchased, called The Shepley Spitfire. This plane gave an excellent account of itself before it too was lost in the Channel. The plane now lives on in the name of a pub, close to the family home, called The Shepley Spitfire, which was opened in 1979 following a conversation between former Oundle School boy Seymour Shepley and the brewery who were seeking a name for their new premises.

Among many other pilots who survived the conflict and went on to achieve illustrious flying records was Squadron Leader Count Manfred Czernin of 17 Squadron, who had left St Anthony House in 1930 and was a nephew of Dr Schuschnigg, Austria's Prime Minister during the First World War. Between 19 May and 24 October, Manfred Czernin destroyed or shared in the downing of 19 enemy aircraft, being awarded the Distinguished Flying Cross. On 17 November, after hitting an Me 110 he had the honour of being shot down by the Luftwaffe's top air ace Adolf Galland, fortunately bailing out in time and surviving the experience. Galland, or 'Dolfi', as he was popularly known, had after all shot down 57

THREE ~ ACTIVE SERVICE

RAF fighters during the Battle of Britain and went on to achieve 104 kills in the war, later becoming a guest at RAF reunions. Manfred Czernin ended his wartime career by winning the Distinguished Service Order and the Military Cross.[18]

Another distinguished airman who survived the war was Air Vice Marshal David Atcherley, a former pupil of Oundle School who had left School House in 1921. On the outbreak of war he commanded No. 85 Squadron in France, and in 1940 was Commanding Officer of RAF Castletown in the Isle of Man. Later he was to lead No. 325 night fighter wing in the 1942-3 North Africa campaign, before returning to Europe where he was appointed senior air staff officer of No. 2 Group, RAF Second Tactical Air Force, going to the Air Ministry at the end of the war. 'David Atcherley will be talked about and idolized as a symbol of what an Air Force officer should be long after the rest of his generation are forgotten,' wrote Air Marshal Sir Basil Embry under whom the former Oundle pupil had served as Chief of Staff, on hearing of his death in 1952.[19]

Equally respected as a pilot was David Atcherley's twin brother, Air Marshal Sir Richard Atcherley, who left Oundle at the same time. He had established his reputation in the pre-war years as a skilful and successful member of the RAF's flying team, renowned for his aerial exploits including the use of 'props' such as hunting pink, saddle, top hat and umbrella at race meetings. In 1929 he won the King's Cup Air Race.

However it was for more practical inventiveness that he made his real name in the RAF. Before the war he had devised a Gannet Moth engine for inverted flight, and was also responsible for developing a flight refuelling system. As Station Commander of the fighter

64: Air Marshal Sir Richard Atcherley KBE, SC, CB, AFC, is briefed for a launch in the 'Grasshopper' during a CCF Inspection visit to his old school in 1958.

base RAF Drem in Scotland he designed an airfield lighting system which gave much help to the pilots while denying to enemy aircraft in the vicinity the same degree of assistance. The Drem lighting system became standard RAF equipment throughout the war and for some years afterwards. In 1942 he was shot down in the Channel; in spite of being wounded in the shoulder by a shell he managed to swim half a mile to reach his dinghy before being rescued. Later he served as Commanding Officer of No. 211 Group in the Middle East Air Force, before returning to Europe in December 1943 for a posting with the Allied Expeditionary Air Forces. 1944 saw him as the first Commandant of the newly formed RAF Central Fighter Establishment, set up to study and develop fighter tactics and techniques, and with war over, Commandant of the newly reopened RAF College, Cranwell, in September 1945.[20]

A Blenheim Pilot Remembers

With the threat of invasion receding in the autumn of 1940 the RAF found itself aiming at new targets on the Atlantic coast of now occupied France. For Richard Muspratt, who had been posted in June to 53 Squadron RAF Detling in Kent, the main objectives were the docks and submarine pens at Lorient and Brest from where the German navy was terrorising Allied shipping. For the first three years of the war he was a pilot and instructor for the Bristol Blenheim twin-engined bomber, an aircraft which had captivated him while he was still at his Advanced Flying Training School. 'I thought, "That is the aircraft I want to fly in this war." It looked purposeful and still does to this day.' The former Oundle School boy, who had left Crosby House in 1935 and was to become a Squadron Leader by the end of the war, receiving the Distinguished Flying Cross for his service, described a typical sortie in December 1940 which he wrote for the Blenheim Society at RAF Duxford:

> We hear at lunchtime it is to be Lorient again tonight, a joint effort by 53 and 59 Squadrons of 12 aircraft, briefing at 5 pm in the crew room. We have two hours of winter daylight to do the essential air test to ensure PZ-S is ready for take-off at 3 am. I do several turns and climb to make sure our directional and horizon gyros are running freely, they are air suction driven by venturi. On a pitch dark night with no horizon if the Gyro horizon topples we are in deep trouble. [If the gyro fails to spin it lies on its side useless, or the direction gyro will spin around madly.] We land and PZ-S is fuelled and bombed up to be ready by the ground crews.
>
> At 3 am we are waiting to move onto the paraffin flare path which extends nearly the full length of the airfield. We are well togged up in Sidcot suits, gloves and flying boots as it is a cold night. We wait with engines ticking over in fine pitch, I set 30 degrees of flap for take-off and check elevator trim settings.
>
> The officer in charge flare path flashes his green Aldis lamp at us. I have our orange cockpit lights turned down to give the best luminosity from the instrument panel. My observer sits beside me; our faces are reflected back from the instruments looking rather anxious. There is no point in looking outside. I close the engine cooling gills and move onto the flare path, lined up. I set zero on the directional gyro and pull out the stop so it is alive, I open the throttles fully and clamp them, release the brakes, then with my right hand reach forward and pull down the +9lbs boost lever.
>
> Our Mercury XV engines instantly respond to their full power of 1700hp. Brilliant flames pour from the exhausts lighting up the cockpit, we are at maximum AUW [all up weight] of 7 tons. Slowly we accelerate down the long flare path and at the last flare but one we unstick at 100 ASI [air speed indicator in mph]. I raise the undercarriage wheels keeping my eyes glued to the gyro horizon; I must not allow a wing to drop only feet above the mud flats.

Our climbing speed increases to optimum 120 ASI; I raise the flaps and reach back with my left hand closing the pitch buttons. The engine revs drop as we change into coarse pitch. I select hydraulic power to the turret. My observer moves forward and prepares a course to steer. At 800 feet I start a wide climbing turn to the left through 180 degrees using the directional gyro. I am still flying blind, the black-out over Portsmouth is complete with no horizon.

We climb to 5,000 feet with a southerly course set on my directional gyro; we relax. We will get a drift fix over the Channel Isles before crossing into France. Away over the Channel there is the glimmer of the horizon. My Mark IV Blenheim PZ-S is an easy aircraft to fly, stable on all three axes and although sluggish at full load, responsive on all controls. I pull the mixture levers up to their lean mixture stops and the throttles back onto them. The engines are now on economic cruise.

I have time to reflect; my total flying hours are 390 (82 at night); I was trained on Tiger Moths, Harts and Oxfords. We have been together as a crew for seven months and after the many operations we carried out over the Channel ports, Low Countries, and sea patrols, I am satisfied we are fairly competent. The only damage we've sustained is a wing tip shot off on a low level attack on St Omer airfield where the searchlights and flak were intense.

The moon is rising and ahead I can see huge cumulus clouds building up along the French coast. I start climbing, at 14,000 feet we cross the coast, flying along valleys and canyons with towering banks of cumulus cloud on either side in brilliant moonlight. It is a truly fantastic sight.

Once into France it is a clear night and shortly we can see in the distance flak and searchlights rising over the target; the 59 Squadron boys have arrived ahead of us and alerted the defences.

I decide to use the bomb sight at 4,000 feet and lay a stick of bombs along the docks and hopefully the submarine pens, and I alert my observer who now has a clear view of the target. We do a long straight run adjusting for drift so that the target moves down the centre of the sight, left, then right, straight ahead, 'bombs gone,' he calls out. I do a climbing turn to the right, we are lucky the searchlights fail to pick us out, probably because there are other aircraft in the area.

We set course for home, changing over our fuel supply from outer to inner wing tanks. We cross the French coast again, flying north. My wireless operator gives me a QDM [radio bearing] course to steer for base. I aim off a few degrees for my own reasons; St Alban's Head and Anvil Point come into view. It is daylight now and I circle down over my parents' home on the seafront at Swanage, but it is too early for anyone to be about.

So, flying low, we set off across Bournemouth Bay, the Solent and Spithead, to turn into the circuit at Thorney. I select fine pitch, and hydraulic pressure for wheels and flaps down for final landing.

I taxi back into flights and we go over for de-briefing and a bacon and egg breakfast. We have been flying for three and a half hours.

It is Christmas Eve and there is to be a party in the mess and some of us will go over to the Sergeants' Mess later to be with our crews.

~ 1941 ~

The Mediterranean: the Malta Convoys

On Italy's entry into the war in June 1940 the numerically strong Italian Air Force and Navy had seemed to present a formidable threat to the British presence in the Mediterranean. The Admiralty's first thought went so far as to contemplate the abandonment of the Eastern

Mediterranean and concentration at Gibraltar. This, as Churchill pointed out, would have meant the doom of Malta. British naval successes against the Italian fleet in the following month helped to persuade the Admiralty that a strong policy was justified. The launching of the naval operation known under the code-name 'Hats', challenging the Italian Navy and Air Force in the Mediterranean, was to lead to the regular convoys of armaments and provisions so badly needed by the defenders of Malta. However the lifeline to the island was maintained only through the immense sacrifice and bravery of the air and naval escorts which faced determined attacks from both Italian and German forces.[21]

By January 1941 Lucy Fallace and her family had decided to leave the protection of Parisio Palace and had rented a flat at Floriana where they could live together again, and not far from the Dressing Station where she worked each morning. She remembered well the grim evidence of the suffering which the convoys had to endure.

> The flat overlooked the Harbour and we could plainly see any ship that managed to get there bringing food and mail, we could see small crowds of Maltese people who gathered to cheer on each occasion. Then one evening when we had taken our coffee to drink up on the flat roof, we were looking into the harbour when in the darkness we saw a big bulky ship slowly coming through the entrance. It was the aircraft carrier HMS *Illustrious* limping in. She had suffered tremendous damage with more than 100 of her crew killed. The rest of the convoy followed her but there was no cheering from the dock side this night.

While the Malta convoys ran the gauntlet of attacks from enemy aircraft and submarines the inhabitants of the island itself faced a blitzkrieg as savage as that which Hitler had launched on British cities.

> The Germans who had joined the Italians in Sicily, just sixty miles away, kept up a continuous barrage of bombs day and night, and we spent many hours in the air raid shelter at night, but sometimes so tired one would sleep through a raid without knowing it. At this time we had a squadron of Hurricanes on the island and they flew continuously trying to ward off the ferocious attacks by the German bombers.
>
> The morning after the arrival of HMS *Illustrious*, as my husband left for work his instructions were to run like hell as soon as an air raid started. This we did, but the big guns were already firing when Tom and I dashed to the nearest shelter. It was packed with Maltese families all frantic and screaming with terror as the guns and bombs made a deafening roar, then a priest started praying and this had a calming effect because they all joined him. An hour later when the all-clear came, we staggered out in the sunshine and the first person I saw was my husband coming along on a motor bike, having watched the raid from the roof of the Mess at Kalafrana. He was so relieved to find us unhurt, but decided it was too dangerous to stay so near the harbour, so we packed our things and found a flat at Sliema a few miles away. We discovered that several of our friends were already living in the same block, and we shared the same air raid shelter in the basement. Food was getting very short especially bread, the grain in storage gradually running out and convoys unable to get through.
>
> I think it was about April of that year that the Germans left Sicily and were involved on the Russian front, so we only had the Italians to deal with. A small convoy of cargo ships carrying much needed food and oil managed to get through, and as there was a brief lull in the air attacks, the powers that be decided to get some families away and back to England.
>
> Everything is kept so secret in wartime so perhaps I should not have been so surprised when my husband came home one teatime to announce that Tom and I would be leaving on a boat the next morning. There was a great rush to empty cupboards and drawers and decide

what to take in one suitcase. Two of our neighbours came in to help, and during this time we had an air raid but didn't bother to take shelter.

The following morning we were driven down to the harbour where five small cargo boats and one oil tanker were waiting for us. I felt very sad at leaving my husband behind because his relief had not arrived. We boarded a boat called SS *Amerika*, manned by a Danish crew who spoke no English. The convoy set off later in the day and we could see the ones in front and behind, but during the night we got separated, so in the morning there was only the oil tanker in front of us. It was a lovely day with a calm sea and blue sky. We sat on the small deck enjoying the sunshine, and we were just passing the small island called Pantelleria when a plane flew over us. I thought perhaps it was an escort, but the second time it came round it dropped a torpedo. It was so near that we lost sight of it round the bow of the ship. We had not been given life-boat drill or even life-jackets, so we went to our cabins and found the jackets on top of the wardrobe. We had only just got them fastened on when we had another torpedo attack which again fortunately missed, then about half an hour later we were just sitting down for lunch when the ship's hooter sounded, we all took shelter underneath the small bridge. This time a bomb was dropped between us and the tanker, our boat was violently shaken with dishes and things crashing all around. The sea rose up like a mountain between us, and we thought the tanker had been hit and they thought that we had, so when everything calmed down again it was such a relief to know that we and our friends were still around. Shortly after this attack three RN destroyers came up alongside, the sailors all waved to us then steamed on ahead, I expect trying to patrol the rest of the convoy. We seemed to have lost sight of the tanker during the next few days but sailed on without further incidents.

I can't remember how long it took us to reach Gibraltar, but this was the first part of our journey; two days later the tanker arrived, she had been hit by a torpedo but managed to get to the harbour.

We all disembarked from our small ships at Gibraltar, and were taken on to a very large French liner called the *Louis Pasteur*. It was being used as a troop ship. We stayed there for about a week, but could go ashore each day. The liner was really luxurious and so was the food which had been taken on board in South Africa. Then without warning early one morning I felt the ship moving and went out on deck. We were being led by the battleship *Renown*, and each side of us protected by three naval destroyers. I thought there must be someone very special in this convoy.

I am not a good sailor and the first day I spent sitting out on deck eating dry biscuits but I felt so ill that the rest of the voyage was spent lying flat in my cabin. Again I can't remember how many days or weeks this took, but one day two friends came to my cabin with a big jug of coffee, which we shared, to inform me we were steaming up the Firth of Clyde. We landed at Greenock, then caught an overnight train to London. There was one other little incident; as we took a taxi to cross London, my son noticed some smoke coming up through a mat on the floor. I tapped on the window to tell the driver, he stopped the taxi and we quickly jumped out just as the mat burst into flames. An hour later we were home safe and sound with my parents at Northolt.

My husband returned to England six months later, but Malta was still being ferociously bombed by the Germans, and the Navy suffered dreadful losses as they tried to get convoys through.

The War at Sea

During the early stages of the war the German Navy placed great hopes in its surface warships as well as its U-boats, and boasted a number of noted battleships, including the ill-fated *Admiral Graf Spee*, forced to scuttle itself outside Montevideo in Uruguay, in the Battle of the River Plate in December 1940. Other pocket-battleships were to prove more

65: Sub-Lieutenant John Heron Rogers.

effective in their attacks on Allied vessels. The *Admiral Scheer* succeeded in sinking five merchant ships along with their armed escort the *Jervis Bay* in the North Atlantic on 5 November 1940. The *Scheer* and the battlecruisers *Scharnhorst* and *Gneisenau* were to cause further Allied losses in March of the following year, sinking or capturing 17 ships.

One of the casualties of the war at sea who has left his name on the Oundle landscape was Sub-Lieutenant John Heron Rogers, a former pupil of Oundle School, who had left Grafton House in 1933. He had joined the Royal Naval Volunteer Reserve in 1936, serving in the Mediterranean and Northern waters in HMS *Coventry*, then transferring to HMS *Borde* for special duty on magnetic minesweeping. He died on active service in HMS *Vernon* in March 1941. Thirty years later his sister Mrs Murray Barber approached the School with the offer of a bequest to commemorate John's death and the sacrifice of all the former Oundle School boys who had died in the Second World War, resulting in the planting of the Heron Rogers Wood on the west side of Oundle.[22]

May 24 1941 saw the sinking of Britain's largest ship, the 42,000 ton battlecruiser HMS *Hood*, with the loss of all but three of its 1,400 crew off the coast of Greenland. Sub-Lieutenant Neville Frodsham and Major Heaton Lumley, both former pupils of Oundle School, were among the dead. The latter's loss was particularly keenly felt in the School's New House, where his son was a boarder.[23]

However, the Royal Navy had its revenge two days later with the sinking of the new German battleship *Bismarck*. The events of May 1941 marked the defeat of Hitler's plans to win the Battle of the Atlantic with surface ships.

War in the Western Desert: the Arrival of Rommel

Veterans of the Desert War have few enjoyable memories. Conditions were hard even during the rare moments when the conflict was not raging. Dust, flies, fleas, a shortage of food, and a lack of drinking water were all part of the North African picture. 'Desert Rats' was an apt name for the Seventh Armoured Division, to which Vic Thorington belonged.

> When you looked at us before we had had a wash, that was just what we looked like. Gerbils, that's all we were! You were as much under ground as above. Tobruk was a whole warren of tunnels. At night time you'd be on patrol above ground.

Following the Italian advance on Egypt from the Libyan Desert in September 1940, the

THREE ~ ACTIVE SERVICE

Allies counter-attacked in an offensive launched by General Wavell in December. By February 1941 the Italians had been swept back: Tobruk, Derna and Benghazi had been taken, and thousands of prisoners had been captured. But the end of March saw a setback for the Allies. German troops reinforced the Italians, and their counter-attack from El Agheila sent Wavell's force racing back to Egypt, leaving an isolated garrison at Tobruk.

Vic Thorington and his 'Desert Rats' had to cope with a new enemy in the person of Rommel, who had arrived in Tripoli on 12 February.

> We'd over-stretched ourselves, I suppose. He was a brainy character, this Rommel and he decided that the moment was right. We woke up one morning to the sound of shell-fire coming from all around us. That was it, you didn't stop to weigh the situation up. When you heard that, you just packed up your gear, got in your vehicle and went.

Churchill's message to Wavell on 7 April had been unequivocal: Tobruk was to be 'a place to be held to the death without thought of retirement'. Former Oundle School boy Rodney Turner, who had arrived in the Middle East in November 1940, found his Regimental Headquarters defending the town and harbour with two Heavy Anti-Aircraft Batteries and one Light Anti-Aircraft Battery.

> From now on, the Fortress was attacked continuously from the air. Dive bombing Stukas by day and high level bombing during the night. We shot down over 200 enemy aircraft. On one occasion when I was attached to 'A' site during a Stuka attack I was blazing away at the diving aircraft with a rifle. As the dust cleared I found I was firing at falling bombs. I can't have done them any harm as they landed with great effect not far away!

Siege conditions contributed their own particular flavour to the stories which Rodney Turner recalled.

> The water supply in the Fortress was very brackish so we fixed up stills using fuel drums as boilers and old ex-Italian lorry radiators as condensers. These were arranged in a line on the beach. The beach rest parties were given the job of firing the boilers with driftwood, swilling the salt out and refilling with sea water. For some inexplicable reason the distilled water made lousy tea unless a little of the brackish water was added!
>
> On one occasion a visiting destroyer brought in an enormous consignment of tinned pilchards as a very special treat. To our amazement the troops wouldn't touch them. As a result the officer's mess served pilchards galore for weeks.

Social life continued amidst the bombardment thanks to other supplies intended to keep up the garrison's good spirits:

> Bill Younger (of the brewery family), Officer Commanding the Light Anti-Aircraft Battery had his Battery Headquarters on the shore of the harbour near the boom. He had put an engine in a lifeboat which he used for visiting gun sites, and also for visiting any Navy ships that came in during the night. As a result he always had a stock of gin. There was open invitation for drinks to anyone visiting between 6 and 7 pm. This was the time that most days 'Bardia

Bill', an Italian 14" Coast Defence gun lobbed shells trying to reach 'A' site just beyond Bill's HQ. On one occasion Mick Gibson and I decided to run the gauntlet. We got there before the shelling started, and as a destroyer had recently come in Bill had plenty of gin. We were so happy on the return journey that we thought the shelling the funniest thing that had ever happened.

Oundle-educated Second Lieutenant Wilfrid Fairclough, who had left Laxton House in 1937, was one of the many British casualties who died in the attempt to hold back Rommel's forces. He had served with the First Battalion, Durham Light Infantry, in Egypt, and taken part in the British advance to and retreat from Benghazi. He was killed on 15 May 1941, while leading his platoon in an attack on an enemy position near Tobruk in what had become known as Operation 'Brevity', the first of two attempts to relieve the garrison. 'I have lost my best platoon commander, in fact the best in the whole Battalion, and also a very great friend,' wrote his Company Commander in Egypt. 'His men worshipped him, for he really got to know them and looked after them.'[24]

Operation 'Battleaxe', the second attempt to drive back Rommel, which started on 15 June, was also a failure, with the British losing 91 tanks while the Germans lost only 12.

Losses in the air among British forces at this time were also heavy. A similar lament by his senior officer was written following the death of Pilot Officer Frank Moss, another former Oundle School boy. He died in action against German fighters and bombers on the Libyan coast on 15 July 1941. 'I can tell you, however, of how much Frank Moss is missed in the squadron. He was one of the best of my younger pilots, and exceptionally popular with all. He had a sense of humour; that means a great deal to a squadron on active service, and his loss is very keenly felt by all ranks.'[25]

Back in England, during convoy manoeuvres which, it was rumoured, had as their destination the Middle East, tragedy also befell the eldest son of a well-known Oundle family at this time. John Burdett, brought up at the White Lion on North Street, had studied at Laxton School, leaving in 1923 to join the Royal Horse Artillery five years later. He had transferred to Coastal Artillery, serving in Malta, and then to Anti-Aircraft, serving in Singapore and Malaya. He left the Forces in 1938 but was recalled a year later to serve with the British Expeditionary Force until the fall of Dunkirk. On 22 July he was in a convoy travelling along the East coast of England when the driver in front made an emergency stop. John Burdett was trapped amidst the crumpled wreckage of his cab,

66: Bombardier Avery John Stooke Burdett, killed on manoeuvres, July 1941.

which had collided with the muzzle of the ack-ack gun in front. One leg was amputated, but doctors failed to save his life.[26]

Operation 'Crusader'

The Allies' failure to sweep Rommel out of Africa in the mid-summer offensives made Churchill even more intent on achieving a desert victory, and more forces were poured into Egypt in the operation code-named 'Crusader'.

The failure of 'Battleaxe' also prompted the Prime Minister to remove the North African Commander, Wavell, replaced by Sir Claude Auchinleck, who had been Commander-in-Chief in India. The enlarged force was renamed as the Eighth Army.

The British advance began by crossing the frontier and moving into Libya on 18 November, hoping to reach Tobruk 90 miles away. A number of engagements took place over the next six weeks between the British on the one hand, and the Germans and Italians under Rommel on the other.

Vic Thorington remembered a clash at Sidi Omar, where Operation 'Crusader' began.

> That was also on the border line between Egypt and Libya. Imagine if you will, that there's barbed wire, great rolls of it... I suppose there would be three miles of that. It came all the way down from the coast following the border. There were bits of it flattened where the tanks had gone through to make these nice convenient gaps. They were twice the width of a vehicle.
>
> On the Libyan side there was this fort — there was very little of it left when I saw it though. We were expecting a little bit of an attack and we were told to patrol that area. We started off 30 or 40 miles further down at Fort Maddelena. We worked our way up, keeping in formation. There would be three cars on patrol, two in the front and one at the back. The two in the front are watching out for any threats of anything. Of course, tail-end Charlie here was on the left hand side, closest to the wire. The first warning we had was the flash from the commander on the right hand side. We stopped, and while we were stopped all hell let loose over the hill. That was an awkward moment for us. Our first casualty Corporal Prior, he was in charge of the vehicle that I was driving. They threw everything at us — mind you, they were far superior, always were from start to finish. Their shells didn't just stop our cars — they went straight through them. You always had a relief driver on the left who had access to various levers that would protect and shield the vehicle, and all I had to do was to hit this bar. The steel shields would come down and leave this little window of glass. We swung the car round and they hit us broadside.

The British plan's aim was to advance its armoured brigades to the village of Gabr Saleh, 40 miles south-east of Sidi Rezegh and then to lure the Axis forces into a tank battle. Rommel recognised the diversion for what it was, concentrating on attacking Tobruk, but was eventually forced to send his panzers to Gabr Saleh. It was here that the first large-scale tank battle of the Desert War took place, with both sides claiming victory.

A combination of factors, including poor communications and ill-luck on both sides, contributed to an inconclusive end to Operation 'Crusader'. The British suffered heavy losses of tanks: under the command of an ex-Oundle School boy, Brigadier John Cockburn, the 22nd Armoured Division, in what Liddell Hart called 'a too gallant assault — carried out in the immortal spirit of the "Charge of the Light Brigade" at Balaclava,' found itself hammered by the Italians' dug-in guns, and lost 40 of its 160 tanks.

John Cockburn, who had left Oundle's Dryden House in 1910, had in fact had a career distinguished by his bravery. Before the 1914-18 war he had taken part in a bullfight at Lima, and in May 1918 had won the Military Cross for rallying troops for a counter-attack at personal risk from snipers and machine-guns. Five months later in the same year, on 8 October, he was to take part in what was probably the last cavalry charge by the British Army, having his horse shot from under him and being taken prisoner.[27]

Operation 'Crusader' resulted in tragedy for a well-known Oundle family. Reginald Black was the youngest son of the late Councillor Harry Black. Educated in the town at the West Street school, he had worked as a cobbler for R. C. Cotton & Sons before being called up in 1941 and joining the 44th Royal Tank Regiment, where he was promoted to Corporal. Christmas Day brought the following letter from his Commanding Officer to his widow Dorothy:

```
Dear Mrs Black,

        I deeply regret to have to inform you, that your husband
Reginald Black was killed in action on the morning of Nov 25th 1941.
Your husband was my Squadron Commander's Gunner. The Squadron Commander
with part of the Squadron were ordered out to deal with some enemy
machine guns in the left flank. They were engaged heavily by anti-tank
guns. Your husband's tank received seven direct hits. When the tanks
came back, we were all sorry to find that your husband, together with
the operator had been killed instantly, and the Squadron Commander
seriously wounded.
   I collected your husband's personal belongings and had them sent to
the Orderly Room Truck. Unfortunately the Truck is now missing,
believed to be in enemy hands. There is a great possibility of our
recapturing it and you can be assured in the eventuality of it
happening the possessions of your husband will be returned to you at
once. Your husband was buried near the scene of the action by a New
Zealand pastor. I, together with Officers and men of the Unit attended
the ceremony. We should all like to convey our deepest sympathies to
you for your great loss and if there is any further information you
would like, I shall be only too willing to supply it.

                Yours sincerely



                        Andrew Williamson
                            (Major)
Sidi Rezegh
```

Along with his wife Dorothy, the Oundle man left a three-month old daughter, Alma.

Fierce fighting by the Eighth Army, supported by the RAF, eventually led to Rommel's withdrawal through eastern Libya. On 10 December, more than seven months after the siege had begun, Allied troops were able to relieve Tobruk. The conclusion of Operation 'Crusader' in January 1942 saw 20,000 German and Italian prisoners being taken, with the Axis forces suffering 33,000 casualties — the Allied figure was only 18,000 — but the operation had ended with a reverse for the British troops at El Haseait on 27 December: a flank of the 22nd Armoured Division lost a further 65 tanks. Three weeks later Rommel was to show that far from being crippled, as had been thought, he was strong enough to sweep the British forces back to the Egyptian frontier, taking Tobruk in June 1942.

The Eastern Mediterranean also saw setbacks for the Allies. John Sharman lived on Oundle's West Street for many years while teaching Modern Languages at the School where he had been educated. Following his call-up into the Army in August 1940 he set sail for the Middle East in March 1941. Two months later he was at the Royal Artillery Depot at Almaza, just outside Cairo, and from there was sent suddenly to report to an officer at the King David Hotel in Jerusalem.

> There I found out that, together with several others who had some pretensions to speaking French, I was to be attached to a unit about to take part in the campaign against the Vichy French in Lebanon. The idea was that we, armed only with a loud-hailer, should advance towards the 'enemy' and tell them what a pity it would be if we had to fight each other. This proved to be a complete failure and the plan was called off, much to my relief, before I had a chance to play my part.

The War in the Air

Though the Battle of Britain had been won, the RAF's war against the Luftwaffe continued, with airfields throughout Southern and Eastern Britain playing a vital role. By now the young Ben Grantham, the future Oundle GP, had started to play a part in the war effort, becoming a Lance Corporal with the Local Defence Volunteers (later to become the Home Guard) at Repton and in his home village, and then transferring to Surrey at the age of 19 as a Second Lieutenant to the Ripley platoon, where he had a section of the Weybridge Aerodrome defences to look after, including a large section of Wisley Woods.

> We had German pilots coming down. We had Canadians. They were supposed to be helping us, but they were an absolutely bloody menace. If a German came down, it behove us to get there first because the Canadians would have cut their throats without turning a hair. They were just anti, and they couldn't see any point in keeping prisoners. If they were bombing England, they were meat to be cut. So one went through the woods like a dose of salts. If you got there after the Canadians you didn't find anything.

Nearer Oundle, from 28 June 1941 until 12 February 1942 the RAF's 90 Squadron was in action at Polebrook, where building work had been completed to equip the airfield with a main runway of 6,000 feet and two smaller runways of 4,200 feet. The RAF had recently bought 20 of the American-built Boeing Fortress Mk I bombers, and Polebrook's concrete runways made the airfield unique in allowing so many different models of the Fortress to operate on high-flying strategic bombing missions over Europe. It was hoped that bombing operations could be carried out in daylight at heights of around 32,000 feet, putting the aircraft beyond the reach of German anti-aircraft and fighter defences.

'A particularly nice group of people, quite outstanding,' was how Miriam Rothschild remembered her RAF neighbours. They had in fact been specially selected for their toughness and stamina: Flying Fortress crews had to survive and function in very thin air, and in extreme cold. The planes were not air conditioned. The medical tests carried out at Farnborough were so stringent that only 40% of the candidates were passed as suitable for the Squadron.

The first high-altitude operation of 90 Squadron's Flying Fortresses Mk I (B-17C) took place in great secrecy on 8 July with a raid on the docks at Wilhelmshaven. The Squadron's existence was made public a fortnight later on 24 July, when three aircraft from Polebrook joined 143 others in attacking the German battle-cruisers *Scharnhorst* and *Gneisenau* in Brest harbour.

Their new Flying Fortresses were a novelty — 'they were the first aircraft to show vapour trails in the sky, a very exciting thing to watch' — and Miriam Rothschild was also inspired at a more practical level. While looking over one of their aircraft at Polebrook in the company of an RAF padre, it suddenly struck her that seatbelts such as those in the aircraft, could, with advantage, be fitted to motor cars. So, after considering the matter, they constructed the first motor car seat belt, made from the saddle girths of a couple of old side saddles, stored in the stables. It was fitted to her Austin 10, but she failed to get a patent for it!

However, in spite of the publicity which 90 Squadron's new aircraft attracted — visitors to Polebrook included Prince Bernhard of the Netherlands, the Duke of Kent and Warner Bros film crews — the early models of the Flying Fortresses experienced numerous problems. Perhaps the padre's pet monkey suspected the difficulties. 'When the aeroplanes went over the monkey used to sit on the branch of a tree and beat its chest in despair,' recalled Miriam Rothschild. Losses among the early Polebrook Flying Fortresses were proof that the aircraft could not escape interception by flying at great altitudes, and operations were therefore run down. The RAF found that the Fortresses were inadequately armed and unable to carry a worthwhile load. However, as has been pointed out, the benefit from the Polebrook experiment was that a spur was given to the development of better models of the Fortress in the USA, and within a year, examples of the improved machines were to make their appearance at the base.[28]

Flying an Inferno

It was during one of the dangerous bombing raids that former Oundle School boy Lucian Ercolani found himself on a mission which was to win him the Distinguished Service Order for his bravery under fire. Flight Lieutenant Ercolani, who had left Oundle's Dryden House in 1934, was the Captain of an aircraft detailed to attack Berlin.

> It was 7 November 1941, I was with 214 Squadron, and it was our twenty-fifth trip as a crew, our third trip to Berlin. It was 10\10 cloud most of the way. We thought we were over target and it was obviously defended, but we couldn't identify it, so we didn't know if we were doing the right thing. We had a load of incendiaries. We dropped them all, and just as we were coming back we were hit with ack-ack. What we didn't know was that one of the racks of incendiaries must have hung up inside the aircraft, and when the ack-ack hit they were set off, and of course they burn for a long time. So we were virtually alight with these things, and they gradually burnt away all of the fabric. The belly of the plane was practically burnt out. The fabric round the mid-part of the fuselage was gone. The fabric on the starboard wing was all burnt away and both wings were badly holed and torn. The plane was nose heavy, although the trimming tabs were wound fully. My pals were marvellous, they put everything they could on the fires; when the extinguishers had run dry, they threw the rest of our coffee over it and peed on it.
>
> There was smoke coming through into the cockpit, and I opened the two lids over my head, which was the worst thing that I could have done, because that sucked all the acrid

smoke past me. I got everybody to put their parachutes on, and we were ready to jump out. I was about to tell them all to jump, but realised we were still flying. Where there's life there's hope, and we kept on flying.

We were burning all the time. We'd lost a lot of power, or rather we had a lot of increased drag, that was really the moment when we could have panicked and done all sorts of silly things. But we kept flying. It was quite difficult to hold the aircraft, all the centre section was badly gone. What made it worse was that it was difficult to find out where we'd actually got to.

We were gradually losing height all the time. As we were approaching the coast I realised that petrol was being used up faster than normal; the question was whether to jump there, or take a chance of getting through. Everybody was very good about it. They were all getting ready to jump out, and I had my parachute handy, but you want to hang on if you can. So we hung on. There was a hell of a wind blowing. We crossed the coast and we still hung on. Our wireless op. had got some sort of message through, but we didn't know where we were.

Then, of course, we were over the water, a couple of hundred feet up. There was a gadget on the Wimpy where you pulled a knob and it put both engines on to both petrol tanks. Normally, one engine ran on one, and the other engine on the other. The two engines didn't always use the same amount of petrol. So when you got right to the end, you pulled this plug and whatever petrol was left in either one, fed both engines. So I did that, and we knew that we didn't have very long to go. We weren't much above the waves. We could see searchlights about the place and were hoping that we'd cross our coast, but we didn't. We had been flying back for three hours and still the plane was ablaze. Then the engines went, and I think I remember saying good luck to everybody.

When you know that you've come to face with the moment of truth there's almost a feeling of relief. I tried to make some sort of landing but the next thing I knew was that there was a terrific crash. Bang we came down nose first and as we went under the water I could hear the sound of things crumpling up and I saw the light of the moon shining down in the water. I felt like a spectator watching it all happen; it didn't seem to be happening to me at all. I tried desperately to get out, but the instrument panel had collapsed back on me, pinning me down. I definitely thought I'd had it then and that I was finished. Then the plane floated up again out of the water; that freed me and I was able to pull myself out through the escape hatch in the top of the pilot's cockpit.

The first thing I saw was the rear turret and the tail of the Wellington twisted right round, facing towards the front. I could see the dinghy and I could hear the rest of the crew calling to each other. I swam for the dinghy but, before we were all in, the aircraft sank.

There was an extraordinary sense of quiet, a sense of relief. We were rather glad to be alive. But at the same time sad. I felt what a pity it was for those waiting at home, particularly my dear wife.

Then, of course, you begin to wonder where you are: do we just sit here, do we try to get back? If we're going to try and get back, what direction do we go in? Everybody was remarkably cheerful. In those days they had rum on the dinghies. We also had water flasks in the dinghy, but unfortunately the yellow stuff they had put in as a marker had got into the water. But the rum did us a bit of good.

The flares didn't work. We could see searchlights, and we thought that we were in the middle of the Channel. We had some funny little paddles, we felt that the right thing would be to aim towards England. We did everything we could to paddle that way. People were in remarkable spirits, we didn't actually have to do anything to keep spirits up. Everybody did it quite naturally. We just paddled and slept, paddled and slept.

We had come down at about three o'clock in the morning. It was very cold. The weather wasn't too bad at first. The next day it got quite rough. The chaps were very good, and we realised we were all in bloody trouble together. We couldn't blame each other for it or anything like that. We had a little miniature compass, an escape compass. We could see searchlights, and we heard two or three aircraft, so again we tried to let our flares off, but none of them worked.

I don't think any of us got to the stage of despair, or thought we weren't going to get out of it. I suppose we weren't there long enough to get to the stage of desperation.

On the third day I saw what I thought was a German submarine periscope, but in fact it must have been a lobster pot marker. It appeared to be moving very fast through the water, but that was just the tide sweeping past it. Then we saw land, and I saw a bit of green, and a football post and thought this is probably England. In fact it was the Isle of Wight. Then we gradually got closer, so we paddled harder with everything we had. We suddenly saw an Air Sea Rescue launch, but to our pride we got ourselves ashore, at Ventnor. By then some people had climbed down to help us in. I stood up to walk ashore, but fell down. My ankle had broken.

I can't tell you what it was like to feel safe again. It was wonderful just to lie back in that ambulance and not have to worry about or think about anything. We were taken to the National Chest Hospital, where we were the only aircrew that they'd had, and they made a tremendous fuss of us. They sent in whisky, everything. In my room there was a wardrobe full of all the booze you could want, including lots of champagne. In the mornings, we sent out for Guinness and played cards drinking black velvet. None of the crew were badly injured. I had my ankle, and they thought that I was badly injured because I had blood all over my face, but in fact it was only a small cut.

It was a remarkable escape. Lucian Ercolani had flown his burning aircraft for three hours after being hit by ack-ack shells, and for most of the time the aircraft had presented a fiery target for the enemy's guns. It was thanks to his encouragement, as his citation recorded, that he had maintained his crew's morale after a 57 hour ordeal at sea.[29]

Further south in Europe the air-battle raged as Britain went on the offensive. Following their success against the Luftwaffe in 1940, British airmen showed their ability to destroy the enemy at sea. While the Battle of the Atlantic was being fought to protect Allied convoys, the Mediterranean saw the British Fleet Air Arm in action. A notable success here in November of the previous year had been the sinking of three Italian battleships lying in a strongly fortified position, by only 21 torpedo bombers. But courage and skill were needed for the dangerous job of facing intense enemy firepower, and losses were heavy. Two years after leaving Laxton School, Sub-Lieutenant Peter Brown, who had been brought up in Lowick, was shot down over Sicily on 28 October 1941 while engaged on such a mission.[30]

Working with the SAS: a Tragedy in the Desert

In the Middle East, Rodney Turner found himself seconded to the RAF, having left Tobruk at the end of August. He recalled a terrifying moment arising from his new job, which involved liaising with the newly formed Special Air Services over paradrop conversion of one of the Middle East transport squadron's Bombay aircraft for a 'stick drop' by the SAS behind enemy lines.

I found the aircraft had already been equipped with an inverted T section rail running from the front bulkhead to a point above the exit door. The door had been removed. On this rail were eight or ten runners, each with four small wheels, below each were attached standard parachute clips. The ring on the end of each para's static line was to be hooked onto one of the clips before making ready to jump. On each man approaching the exit door the runners were pulled along the rail by the static line to a point above the door.

We flew the Bombay down to RAF Kabrit on the Suez Canal, where the SAS detachment were based, and reported to Captain David Stirling, Scots Guards, the Officer Commanding.

It was decided to do a test drop with dummies. Captain Stirling insisted they be overweight to test the strength of the equipment. He and I were in the aircraft during the test drop, which was completely successful. He ordered a live drop with a stick of eight men, and we took off for the dropping zone in the desert north of the Canal. He remained at Kabrit, and left me in charge of the drop. When the pilot switched the signal lights from red to green and the first pair jumped, I saw to my horror that the static lines had become detached from the runners, and the two men fell to their deaths with closed parachutes. The next pair were following close behind. I grabbed them, and after a struggle during which I nearly went out with them, managed to restrain them and reported to the pilot. We returned and landed at Kabrit, where David Stirling was waiting. I explained what had happened, and he remarked 'My God, this will put the training programme back three weeks!'

The crew and I flew back to Heliopolis, and I reported to Air Vice Marshal Graham Dawson, my Chief in Cairo, and explained that the static line rings had somehow twisted off the clips below the trolleys. This problem had not been revealed on the test drop, as the heavier dummies had resulted in a lower angle of attack. He asked me for my suggestions as to what should be done, and I advised that the rails and runners should be thrown away and replaced by a length of steel steam pipe with 'free running' shackles to which the static line could be bolted.

I was told to proceed with maximum urgency. I got the steam pipe supplied and bent to shape at the Nile shipyard of Thomas Cook & Sons, and the shackles made at the workshop of RAF Heliopolis where the assembly was fitted to the Bombay. We flew down to Kabrit the next day, where I thankfully witnessed a satisfactory 'stick drop'.

~ 1942 ~

The Fall of the Far East

Japan had been fighting an undeclared war with China since 1937. Relations between Japan and the Allies had been rapidly declining since July 1941 with the freezing of Japanese assets in the United States and Britain, and it was clear to many that Japan was pursuing a policy of expansion in the Far East similar to that of Germany's in Europe. There was every reason to expect war in the Pacific at any moment, from the last week of July onwards. The attack on Pearl Harbour on 7 December 1941 came however as a surprise to the Americans, and left the Japanese in control of the Pacific in little over an hour. The Japanese naval action was followed immediately by landings of troops in the Malay Peninsula as well as the Philippines and New Guinea.

Hong Kong fell after fierce fighting. The governor had rejected a surrender demand on 13 December, and Allied troops, including a volunteer force recruited from the colony's European community, put up a spirited resistance. John Potter, originally from Kettering, but educated at Oundle's Laxton School as a boarder in the town, was an architect in Hong Kong at the outbreak of war. A Company Sergeant Major in the Hong Kong Volunteer

Defence Corps, he was one of those who fought to the bitter end, dying on Christmas morning. At 3.15 pm the British commander Major General Maltby ordered his forces to lay down their arms.[31]

By the end of January 1942 the whole of the Malay Peninsula was in enemy hands, and on 15 February Singapore surrendered.

A former Oundle School boy, James Bradley, who had left Sidney House in 1929, has given an account of the 'sad and degrading moment' when he and his fellow Britons had to lay down their arms. *Towards the Setting Sun*, written some 38 years after the events, is a sober and objective record of the appalling treatment meted out by his Japanese captors to some of the thousands of Allied servicemen who were forced to work on the infamous Thailand-Burma railway. The young Lieutenant Bradley had set sail from Greenock in Scotland with the 18th Division, Royal Engineers, on 27 August 1941, in the troopship the *Duchess of Athol*. He left behind his wife Lindsay and young son Roger.

Disembarkation at Singapore Naval Base on 13 January was followed by a desperate attempt to hold back the oncoming Japanese forces. James Bradley is scathing about the lack of preparation which hampered him and his fellow-sappers.

> With practically no acclimatization period, we were sent into action on the mainland, not really knowing the difference between the Eastern races; they all looked much alike to us. Never had such a raw and untried group of men gone into action! We had few large-scale maps of the area, and were completely untrained in jungle warfare.

Nonetheless he and his men did their best to blow up bridges and other strategic installations before assuming an infantry role to defend the MacRitchie Reservoir in the central part of the island. Enemy mortar fire was making their position fairly uncomfortable when word arrived of the surrender of Singapore. After only 30 days of action James Bradley was to spend the rest of the war as a victim of the monstrous cruelty of the Japanese.

The defeat at Singapore had caused the Allies the loss of nearly 140,000 Australian, British and Indian troops killed, wounded or captured, compared with 9,824 Japanese casualties. Some of these losses were quite needless, in James Bradley's opinion.

> The other two Brigades of 18th Division, the 54th and 55th, had duly arrived and disembarked at Bombay. However, at a later date they re-embarked and were taken to Singapore very shortly before the surrender, and in my opinion, though I am probably quite wrong, their presence in this theatre of war could have achieved nothing. Singapore was already virtually lost, and I still feel they were sent in as a sacrificial token.[32]

The Fall of Java

On 1 March the Japanese launched an attack on Java; isolated by flanking moves the island fell into their hands within a week.

Aubrey Clarke of Bassett Place, Oundle, captured along with other British troops in Java, related his story in remarkable detail. A native of Upper Benefield, he had volunteered exactly 24 hours before the war started, joining the Royal Artillery's anti-aircraft regiment, whose headquarters were at Stanford-le-Hope in Essex. 'We had Bofors guns, they were for low aircraft really, a bit better than a machine gun and they fired two pounders, two

THREE ~ ACTIVE SERVICE

pound shells.' He found himself serving as a despatch rider because he had a good machine of his own, and the officer in charge had persuaded him to use it for the army. There were a few unpleasant experiences. 'I was despatch riding for about a year, through all the wet winter of 1940. It was a very bad winter, ice and snow, and I fell off about three times with the bike on top of me.'

The destination of his first posting overseas was a secret.

> We left Glasgow, and on our kitbags was the letter N, and nobody knew what that meant. We thought we might be going to the Middle East, where Rommel was, but then we discovered that our destination changed again, and we finished up at Singapore. We got there just as the Nips had taken it, so we were sent on to Java, and from there we went to Sumatra and then back to Java, and that's where we were taken prisoner. You see, we were told if we could get across Java about 250 miles to the coast, we were going to be picked up by the American navy and transport ships, but unfortunately, they got sunk, so there we were, left high and dry, and of course it was an easy walkover for the Nips. We had no guns, we only had about half a dozen rifles between about 500 men which was no good. We relied on our anti-aircraft guns, but you couldn't use them very much for fighting ground troops and that was that, so that's how we were taken.

The situation was hopeless, but before he was captured, Aubrey Clarke had a last-minute service to perform.

> We were instructed by our Commanding Officer that it was no use trying to carry on any longer because we were running short of fuel, food and everything else, so therefore, me being in charge of transport and other things, I had to destroy as many of our vehicles as we could by driving them over the cliff. What I did was to stand on the running board and set the throttle inside, and then jump off at the convenient moment, and I had about fifty to do, and then we had to destroy the guns as well. Me being a gun fitter, I had to go behind the Japanese lines and take the breech blocks out.

Aubrey Clarke was to spend the rest of the war as a prisoner of the Japanese, and had his own story to tell about this aspect of his life, related in a later chapter.

Retreat to India

Simultaneously with the advances on Java and Sumatra, the Japanese 15th Army invaded Burma, pushing all opposition westwards. Major General Sir John Winterton, a former Oundle School boy whose valour had already been demonstrated in the retreat from Dunkirk, was now in the Far East. He played a key role in maintaining the organisation and discipline which ensured the survival of our forces. As General Alexander's staff officer he was sent to restore order to the chaos. A fellow-officer wrote of him:

> Nothing could be done to restore the military situation, but it was greatly to Winterton's credit that so many British soldiers were extricated from the wreck and made their way back to the safety of India. Under the severest stresses he was unflappable and his inspiring presence helped to steady the nerves of others.[33]

On 1 May all British and Imperial forces were withdrawn north of the Irrawaddy river, and a fortnight later had reached Assam.

Life in the Sub-continent

Many British troops who served in India during the Second World War look back on their time in the sub-continent with a certain affection, enjoying a relatively peaceful time compared with the fierce jungle and desert warfare waged by their colleagues in Burma and North Africa. Ben Grantham remembers above all his encounter with the richness of Indian culture, with its caste system and its many languages. Having joined up in Britain he was taken into the Queen's Royal West Surrey Regiment, where he rose to be Lance Corporal before being transferred to India to the Officers' Training School in Bangalore. He never heard a shot fired in anger, and was wounded only when he was hit in the face by a half brick during riots, resulting in a fracture of the upper jaw. His worst experience occurred during the preparations for the partition of India, when he was involved in the mapping out of various routes to get Punjabi Mussulmen into Pakistan. A few miles east of the new border he heard the news of the death of a school friend in the Jat Rifles, who was killed while escorting a refugee train which was ambushed, with everyone on board being slaughtered. Even in those days, massacres of Hindus by Moslems, and Moslems by Hindus were taking place.

'Not a heroic war, but interesting nevertheless,' he commented. After commission from Bangalore he was posted to the Second Punjabs at Meerut. There he was attached to the Chamar Regiment, a newly formed outfit. This was a regiment designed to take in 'the untouchables' of Indian society who were not eligible to serve in the established regiments. He went with them to the Seeonee Hills, and Chindwarra into jungle camp, known to those who have read *The Jungle Book* as the home of Mowgli. It was here that he learned to speak and write Urdu and Hindi, taking his first stage interpreters' exam before transferring to his brother's regiment, the First KGV's (Gurkha Rifles) and going to their centre at Dharmsala, where the Dalai Lama is now based.

There were plenty of opportunities for leisure pursuits. He represented both the Indian Army and the British Army in boxing while in India, and thought that his best experience was being trained by the boxer Freddie Mills to represent the Indian Army against the Americans. 'I am glad to say we won.'

The Battle for Malta

A large British garrison had been stationed on Malta since before the war, and since the first Italian air-raids in June 1940, had been under constant siege. Charles Tod found himself on the island as a Second Lieutenant with the Royal Hampshires, attached to the Malta Docks Control Unit. 'It was a lot of fun as I was given a motorbike to do jobs as a messenger,' he recalled. But the savagery of the battle for Malta left him with painful memories. His worst wartime experiences date from this time, and involved victims from both sides. 'We watched one of our own pilots burn to death knowing there was nothing we could do about it. Another was the time when an Italian parachutist's parachute "Roman Candled": his parachute did not open properly and he landed about twenty feet away from me.'

Also in Malta with his wife Phoebe was Robert Butler, who had left St Anthony House in 1933 to become a professional soldier, and was promoted to Captain after his arrival on Malta in March 1939. He was to spend almost four years on the island, leaving in February 1943.

THREE ~ ACTIVE SERVICE

It was here that the young Robert Butler and his wife were to undergo one of their most harrowing experiences. The beginning of 1942 saw a renewed effort by the Luftwaffe to break the spirit of the defenders of Malta by a savage campaign of bombing. The Germans had realised that too much use was being made of Malta's dockyards for the repair of warships. Robert Butler quotes in his autobiography *Nine Lives* several incidents of which he had direct personal experience at this time.

> We were on a direct line with the length of the Grand Harbour and got all its overs as well as the bombs intended for parked aircraft round the outskirts of Luqa airfield, which, of course, is where my posts were sited. We had every kind of experience. One day an enormous 2,000 pounder landed very near my own private gunpit and failed to explode. Had it been a time-bomb it would have been necessary to evacuate a very large area, because such brutes were designed to make, and did make, the most enormous craters. Acting on impulse I ran forward to it and pressed my ear hard against it to hear if it was ticking. It was silent. Then I began to think. 'If it goes off now,' I reasoned, 'I will feel nothing and there will be nothing of me to feel with, but the moment I leave it and get a few yards away, if I am not killed by blast I could have a complete leg or shoulder blown off or even the lower half of my body.' It was a terrible thought, and for a few moments the brute became my friend and I found great difficulty in leaving it. Common sense prevailed in the end and I tiptoed away for about thirty feet and then sprinted like mad for the safety of my gunpit and telephoned for a bomb disposal party. I have a picture of my entire company sitting in one of these huge craters, photographed on a sunny afternoon when the lunchtime raid was safely over and there would normally be around three hours to the tea-time one.

More shattering was the experience which occurred a week or two later.

> One of our own fighter pilots who had been badly shot up and could not lower his undercarriage, decided to do a belly landing on the grass quite near my command/observation/gun-post, which was situated just above my underground headquarters. I ran forward towards it as it skidded to a halt and was joined by Corporal Greenyer, who commanded the nearby section manning twin Lewis Guns. Before we reached it flames had begun to engulf it and when we finally arrived it was an inferno. The pilot seemed to have his legs trapped and was struggling to get out. We mounted the wings, one each side and managed to get the canopy open, grabbed hold of his shoulders and pulled with all our strength. He never spoke but moved his torso forward and back a few times. We could not free him and were eventually driven back by the heat. I believe that he must have been unconscious from the heat and after a few seconds even dead. The fire truck then arrived with a crew, in asbestos clothing, who sprayed the pilot and plane with foam. When finally extricated by them, the pilot was found dead. Apart from a few singes, Corporal Greenyer and I were unscathed and I will never know how much real burning I would have been able to endure if the trucks had not taken over and we had found ourselves able to move him. I have since wondered if his harness was still fastened, since it would have been until after the crash. Corporal Greenyer and I never forgot those moments when his body was still rocking to and fro even after being covered with foam. We both prayed that if he was alive, that he was at least unconscious.

It was not just the Allied military garrison which suffered from the effects of the Italian and German onslaught on Malta of course. The island's civilian and military inhabitants were brought to the verge of starvation because of the enemy's naval blockade. Robert Butler's wife Phoebe and their 21-month old son Christopher, along with their nurse Polly, were at this time living on Sacred Heart Avenue near Sliema on the north eastern side of the island, as far as possible from the Grand Harbour and Luqa airfield. The house had a concrete air-raid shelter in the basement.

> On Saturday 14 March to 6.00 pm on Sunday 15 March I was taking my 24 hours leave at Sacred Heart Avenue. Christopher heard my motorcycle coming because Phoebe always told him to listen for it. He was ready to run down the steps to greet me and I was early enough to see something of him before he went to bed.
>
> We had a typical siege meal that evening, which Phoebe had cooked as appetisingly as possible, given the ingredients she had available. When I was on leave I thought it prudent not to go down to our shelter, which Phoebe, Polly and Christopher normally did, because I felt that I dare not get the shelter habit. In any case I did not remember any bombing in our area whilst I was at home. Around seven o'clock on Sunday morning the sirens went and distant sounds of bombing could later be heard, but we took no notice until a stick of bombs started coming down very near us and finished beyond us. The glass of the windows blew in and I jokingly shook the sheet and counterpane of my twin bed to project the fragments onto the floor, and said, 'Weren't we lucky, now let's try and get some more sleep.' Phoebe said, 'I think the house has been hit.' I replied, 'Nonsense,' and got out of bed and walked to the door. When I opened it there was no house. We were in the corner room of the first floor and no other part of the house was standing. There was a mound of stone blocks over where the shelter was and I called back, 'Don't worry darling, the shelter was built for that, we'll soon get them out.'
>
> We could not get down until someone produced a long ladder, by which time we had flung on some clothes. Phoebe was taken to Brigadier Ivan De la Bere's house which was only two houses away down Sacred Heart Avenue, and I set to work organising people to lift the heavy square sandstone blocks away from the shelter. Taking two men to lift each block, it was nearly eleven o'clock before we got to the roof of the shelter. For a few moments I was elated and then began to wonder when I saw a huge crack in the roof. When the last stone was pulled clear and I was able to look down through the crack, I saw Polly sitting, crouched protectively forward, on a chair in one corner with Christopher peacefully cradled in her arms. They were both dead, and from their positions appeared to have died instantly from the concussive effect of blast. I walked down to the De la Beres', but did not have to tell Phoebe anything. She just looked at my face and with a choking sob ran into my arms.

With a bitterness which millions of others could understand only too well, Robert Butler questioned his own belief in a divinely ordered universe:

> I could not understand why the Lord should have selected Polly and Christopher, for whose safety I had prayed every night, to the exclusion of ever praying for myself or Phoebe. I did not believe that God had selected Christopher but that such matters were chances run by everyone under the Laws of Nature. The Padre assured me that God had selected Christopher because he loved him so much, but it seemed to me that if he was in such detailed control, why had he allowed him to come to our evil world at all, even for 21 months to be killed by a bomb; it seemed a funny way of loving.

The anger and despair which Robert Butler felt at this low point in his life emerge only too clearly in his autobiography. He went through a phase of needing to seek personal revenge on those who had taken his son's life. He was alone, his pregnant wife having left for Egypt to give birth in more comfortable conditions.

For the first two weeks after the tragedy of Sacred Heart Avenue I regretted that we were not in closer touch with the enemy and wanted to get one in my sights at close range.

On my third day after Phoebe's departure there was an air-raid warning and I climbed into my extremely narrow personal slit-trench and dropped the K gun into its small mounting which I had hammered into the South facing parapet. A low flying ME 109 came in from the West, rather surprisingly, and was engaged by our Bofors and I saw a bit fly off it and opened up myself at about 200 yards range. Drum Major Watts, who had been passing by when the sirens went, had joined me in my trench. At almost the same moment the pilot had bailed out and he started to float down. 'Go on, Sir,' shouted the Drum Major. 'He's already a prisoner,' I replied with a smug feeling of self-righteousness, and realised that my judgement was beginning to return to normal.

Robert Butler's return to sanity was further helped by his interest in a hobby which he had discovered during his schooldays. 'It became my turn to have 24 hours' leave. I had never before had to think where to go and felt completely lost. I remembered that I had a few water colours and a block of water colour paper. I decided to return to painting, which I had kept up intermittently since the Oundle days.'

On 15 April 1942 King George VI awarded the island of Malta the George Cross in recognition of the gallantry of its people.

The following month saw Robert Butler's spirits lifted by his involvement in an action which he describes as a turning point in the Second World War. This was the decisive air battle for Malta, fought on 10 May, the most exciting which the world had ever seen. The former Oundle School boy wrote the only descriptive account of the battle included in the Memorial Book, which was published in 1992, on the 50th anniversary of the lifting of the Siege of Malta:

In April 1942 Malta was in a sorry plight. Several weeks of heavy bombing without a single day's respite had made the garrison weary, dispirited and somewhat 'bomb happy'. Rations had been cut to an extremely low level and the morale of both civilians and those members of the Services who did not have the fortune to be taking an active part in the Island's defence, was low.

Every ship of a convoy which had set out for Malta from Alexandria in March had been sunk, either en route or within twenty four hours of arrival in the Grand Harbour. As a result of this tragedy there was a dearth of every form of material which we of the garrison required to carry out effective and energetic defence. There were very few fighter aircraft and those that remained were worn out and slow. There was very little petrol to keep these few aircraft in the air and they were forbidden to tackle enemy fighters. This was bad for the morale of their pilots, and gave a corresponding fillip to their German opponents who sometimes indulged their Teutonic sense of humour by giving aerobatic displays to anger the helpless garrison. The powerful anti-aircraft defences capable of putting up a barrage which must at that time have been second to none were largely silent. Certain guns only of each site were manned and some sites were forbidden to fire at all unless they themselves were the target of air attack. Those guns which did remain in action were limited to a very small number of rounds per day.

A large number of the civilian population had lived a termite existence in rock caves for months; some children who had been born in these underground shelters had never seen the light of day. Many of the Maltese who only went to ground between air raid warnings and the 'all clears' nevertheless spent periods as long as twenty four hours in their shelters. The Germans arranged these long alerts by sending reconnaissance planes and single nuisance raiders between the big raids thus ensuring that there was a hostile aircraft on the radar screen right round the clock.

It was at this stage that the War Cabinet decided that an adequate force of up to date Spitfires fitted with long range tanks, could be shipped in aircraft carriers from Gibraltar to a point West of Malta from which they could fly to the Island. The part which the soldiers in Malta had to play to ensure the ultimate success of this operation was to construct more dispersal areas and sufficient splinter-proof pens. A vicious circle soon began. The fighters could not arrive until their pens were ready and it was almost impossible to build the pens with constant air interference, which only the arrival of the fighters could curb. We Infantry turned ourselves into Sappers, working in hundreds on every airfield throughout daylight hours at the construction of fighter pens from every conceivable material. When all normal materials were quickly exhausted, we used old petrol tins filled with earth and painted with mud in an optimistic but unsuccessful effort to camouflage them from the prying eyes of the Luftwaffe.

Kesselring, seeming to sense what was afoot, ordered attacks on the empty pens and the cratering of the runways. Work continued however until all airfields were ready. In this final phase of preparations a fine example of Inter-Service co-operation began. Firstly, the RAF trained a large number of Infantry to assist in rearming and refuelling fighters. Next, line communications were established by the Infantry from the control rooms to the proposed squadron dispersal areas on each airfield. These were reinforced by wireless nets and again by military dispatch riders.

In the case of my regiment at Luqa, the CO sat alongside the Controller in the control tower and a company representative was located in each squadron dispersal area. Communication to flights was by motor-cycle dispatch riders and by runners to individual fighters in pens. These pens were manned by our own soldiers who re-armed and refuelled them as they returned from their sorties. We did everything except fly the planes and service the engines but were not oblivious of the fact that we were only the administrative tail of fighting weapons manned by gallant young men. Some of the non-flying wartime RAF officers did not match up to the high quality of their flying brothers and exercised a weak and inefficient control over their ground staff. A substantial number of these took advantage of the lack of roll calls and got shacked up in Maltese villages. When things hotted up at Luqa they tended to fail to make an appearance, and it was for this reason that so many Infantrymen were needed to step in. Lines were also laid to concealed rendezvous about two miles from each airfield where lines of lorries waited, loaded alternately with stones and soldiers. A call for three lorryloads of stones would thus bring six lorries, three of stones and three of soldiers ready to unload them at speed into bomb craters on the runways. Motor rollers, driven by us, stood by on the airfields to level the surface as soon as each crater was filled. All was now ready for 'der Tag'.

The first real trial of strength was a bitter disappointment. The fighters that arrived were hustled into their pens and made ready to take the air once more. It was decided however not to risk more than half in the air at one time. The result was that when the Luftwaffe appeared in great strength the number of Spitfires in the air was insufficient to enable them to hold their own and they therefore received a terrible mauling whilst most of those on the ground were severely damaged. Hopes had run so high that the gloom which descended once more was deeper than ever.

The next operation was now planned to take place on 9 May. This time no mistake was to be made. All the new aircraft had to be prepared to take to the air in defence of the island within ten minutes of landing and experienced pilots who knew the area stood by in some pens to take them over from the ferry pilots. The Senior Controller was now a skilful Battle of Britain Controller. Every aircraft on the island which could get airborne was to be put into the

THREE ~ ACTIVE SERVICE

air — no juicy targets on the ground. Although stocks of AA ammunition were pitifully low every heavy and light anti-aircraft gun was allowed full operational freedom.

A tremendous atmosphere of expectancy pervaded the whole Island and rumours of what was afoot seeped down to the Maltese in even the deepest caves. The planes duly arrived on the morning of 9 May and were quickly made ready for the air by the RAF groundstaff and the newly trained soldiers. Hot drinks were taken round the pens for the incoming pilots and those waiting to take on the Luftwaffe. The enemy duly came to investigate and was appalled by what it saw. Squadrons had taken off from every airfield and were flying purposefully at three different levels. The Luftwaffe withdrew and went back to do some thinking and were punished by our Spitfires on their way home.

May 10 dawned warm and cloudless and I was only one of thousands who flung on their clothes with a feeling of uncanny excitement. A showdown was inevitable and it seemed certain it must come that day. The atmosphere of confident elation which had started on the previous day had taken hold of the entire civilian population. When the air raid warning finally sounded men, women and children instead of going to their shelters solemnly climbed up onto their roofs. Out of holes in the rock came people some of whom had not surfaced for weeks. And quietly they waited. Formations of new Spitfires which had taken off before the sirens went were already high in the sky and lower down at bomber level were the patched-up Spitfires and Hurricanes of earlier days waiting to take their revenge.

The familiar ominous drone began to swell from the direction of Sicily and all eyes turned to meet the oncoming enemy. With a deafening roar the Grand Harbour barrage opened up in full voice. We had almost forgotten what these gunners could do so long had it been since they had last been allowed to fire without restriction. About a minute later the guns of Luqa Aerodrome's defences opened up with the Luqa barrage and the battle was on.

Within a matter of minutes the sky was a mass of whirling aeroplanes. The enemy bombers were jettisoning their bombs anywhere and although it thus became much more dangerous for people away from the target areas than during a normal raid, the Maltese just didn't seem to mind. Parachutes started floating down in all directions. The German fighter cover was being chased all over the sky by planes which really had the legs of them. The war-weary old Hurricanes tore into the bombers and took their long awaited revenge. The gunners put up such a thick barrage over the Grand Harbour that it looked like an enormous eiderdown. I saw one formation of six JU-87s try to dive through it. The first three disintegrated and bits of engine tail and fuselage went spinning down into the water. The last three pulled out and dropped their bombs blindly through the barrage.

The flat rooftops of all the towns were now black with people waving handkerchiefs, shouting, pointing at the descending victims and making that rather rude sign of contempt which is peculiar to the Maltese. Sixty-nine German aircraft were lost in this battle, which exceeds the final proved figures of German losses for any day during the Battle of Britain.

The evening reconnaissance over Sicily that day reported a veritable boat-race going on in the Sicilian Channel as large numbers of defeated aviators whose aircraft had been ditched on the way home rowed northwards like mad in their little rubber dinghies.

From this unforgettable day onwards Malta never again lost her local air supremacy. The constant strain on morale of being the helpless underdog who had insufficient means to hit back and redress the situation was finally over. The battle was a wonderful feat of organisation and Inter-Service cooperation which, in addition to the Royal Artillery and Infantry had also called for substantial use of major units of the Fleet.[34]

For his actions in defence of Luqa Aerodrome during the Battle for Malta, Robert Butler was made an MBE. He was to have a distinguished military career, proud of being the only Oundelian to be twice wounded on three separate occasions, in Malta, Leros and Cyprus.

North Africa

Following Rommel's arrival in North Africa the previous year, the Germans retained their superiority in the Western Desert, taking Tobruk on 20 June 1942 and pushing eastwards. British losses both in the air and on the ground were heavy. Former Laxton School pupil Flying Officer John Kelham lost his life at this time. Brought up in Nassington, he had joined the RAF in 1940, and was posted to 80 Squadron, helping to keep Rommel's forces at bay, but was killed in action over Tobruk on 2 April.[35]

Oundle man Ralph Leigh, familiar to many people in the area as a champion of the Ashton Conker Festival, recalled the events which led to his capture on the day that Tobruk fell to the German forces.

67: An RAF victim of the battle for Tobruk: Flying Officer John Kelham.

> I was Junior Lance Bombardier, joined the army in 1939, had three months' training, and was posted to a regiment already earmarked for embarkation. I fought in the desert for two years. The moment I was captured was an almost unbelievable day. We were put on the outskirts, about ten miles from Tobruk. We were defending Tobruk. We always felt that we were a bait to get the Germans down to Alamein. There were 30,000 men left with little or no armaments, very few tanks. We were on 6" howitzers, the biggest mobile gun in the British Army at that time. They fired 100lb shells. We had to fire from gun-pits, built up from stones or sandbags. The gun itself had a 90 degree arc, and we were told that the gun-pits were to be built, some facing west, some south and some east. We were put in one facing east because the Germans couldn't come any other way. We'd been there only a week, and the CO came round and said, 'Dismantle your guns. The Germans are on the way, the attack's imminent and they're coming from the west.' So we sat there with the guns dismantled. We couldn't fire a shot, and they were giving us all they could give. I was a very lucky man. I don't know how I survived. I was shovelling sand into sandbags to build the gun-pit up, and all of a sudden the blade of the shovel just flew 20 yards away and the shaft had been cut in half. It was an armour-piercing shell. It ricocheted into the gun-pit, cut one man's arm nearly off, smashed against my knee. All I got was a gash across my knuckle. Half an hour later I was standing in the gun-pit and there was a huge explosion. They always used to tell us, 'Never worry about the shell that whistles. If you hear a shell coming it won't hit you. It's the one that you don't hear which gets you,' and I used to think that was a bit of a standing joke. But it wasn't. We never heard a thing until a sound as if the heavens blew up, and the lad standing next to me had the whole of his backside and his back torn off. In the blast we both fell over and he fell on me. I could tell how badly injured he was. I got a doctor there and he said, 'Can you bear with him?' I said, 'I'll have to,' and about an hour later a pick-up truck came to pick us both up and took us into Tobruk hospital. The orderlies came and took him off. I heard afterwards that he'd died that night. I

walked out of the hospital straight into a German tank. And that was the last that I saw of any of my unit for the next 50 years when we had a reunion.

Rommel's forces continued to push eastwards until they were halted at the first battle of El Alamein on 1 July. Fighting continued until the end of the month. Morale on the British side was low, with 13,000 casualties suffered in the latest engagement. But changes were about to take place.

El Alamein and the Turn of the Tide

General Sir Claude Auchinleck was replaced by General Sir Harold Alexander as Commander in Chief Middle East, and the Eighth Army found itself with a new commander, the aggressive Lieutenant General Bernard Montgomery. Within days of taking over, by 6 September, he had beaten Rommel at Alam Halfa. Monty, with a combination of ruthlessness, showmanship and organisation, succeeded in inspiring the Eighth Army with a new-found confidence. The stage was set for the second Battle of El Alamein.

The planning for the North African campaigns was not without its humorous moments. Called up in 1939 after two years of teaching Mathematics at Oundle School, John Matthews became a Second Lieutenant in the Royal Engineers Survey, where his job was to make maps for the army. His most amusing wartime experience was when he found himself in Egypt, helping to plan the battle against Rommel.

> A friend was working on a map that was needed urgently by the High Command in order to formulate their battle plans. This friend of mind had been working extremely hard on this project but he was still being harassed to finish it. Anyway the phone rang and he answered it. However when the bloke at the other end of the line asked him how long it would be until he finished the map, my friend flew off the handle. Then he asked the man just who he thought he was demanding that he hurry up and finish the map. The man just replied that he was a Colonel and my friend's face turned a shade of white.

68: Oundle School's future Second Master, H. J. Matthews, a Major in the Royal Engineers. The photograph was taken in Cairo, 1945.

By 6 October Monty's plan for destroying Rommel was complete. The battle which was to be a turning-point of the Second World War was both an air and a land engagement lasting until the beginning of November. By the end, the Allies had killed or captured 50,000 of the enemy. Monty's victory made him the first British general to beat a German commander in a major World War Two battle. In London, Churchill was jubilant, ordering Britain's church bells to be rung on 15 November, for the first time since 1940.

John Sharman fought at El Alamein with the Seventh Armoured Division. He recorded his memories in diary form:

> Oct 22 — A few days previously my Battery had reverted to being Divisional Troops, and on this evening we were guarding Divisional HQ when three ME 109s appeared and were all shot down, which much impressed the Divisional Commander. We all knew that something big was in the wind, and later that evening my troop and another were sent back to positions that we had previously occupied on the edge of the Ragil Depression. Our orders were to be in position by first light to deny the enemy low level reconnaissance. Apart from ourselves the only troops forward of our minefields in this area were some armoured cars of the Household Cavalry.
>
> Oct 23 — We saw no enemy aircraft all day!
> At last light we moved back to the middle British minefield, and waited to join the rest of the Battery as they came through.
> There was a full moon behind us, and visibility was excellent. At precisely 21.30 every gun in the 8th Army opened up along the whole front — a most impressive display of fire-power, and all kinds of traffic began to pour through the minefield gap: sappers, infantry, tanks, trucks, Scorpions, and then the rest of our Battery with Divisional HQ.
>
> Oct 24-25 — We had a relatively quiet day in our sector, then moved forward again with tanks to cover the gaps that had been made in the enemy minefields. It was soon decided to discontinue attacks in the South, where we were, and the Battery moved back to cover Main Divisional HQ.
>
> Oct 30 — The whole Division moved North to concentrate for the final assault, a very complex manoeuvre that entailed leaving many dummy vehicles behind, and disguising tanks as lorries.
>
> Oct 31 — Another very heavy barrage that night and early next day. We moved slowly forward among marked tracks. Progress was erratic, there was some shelling, but we got through the last enemy minefield at about 18.00. There was much chaos and congestion, and an attack by Stukas. Congestion was such that only one of our guns was able to go into action but we were lucky to have no casualties, and finally halted about 2 am.
>
> Nov 2 — We moved fairly steadily westward all day, and by about 17.00 had reached a point about five or six miles south of Fuka. It then began to rain and poured all night, unusually for that time of year, and fairly unusual at any time in that area.
>
> Nov 3 — The whole army was bogged down — even tanks, and consequently many of the enemy forces, who had the use of the one and only road, were able to escape westwards.
>
> Nov 4 — We reached the landing ground at Fuka, and by next day, the 5th, the chase was on, and apart from brief overnight stops we continued on to Tobruk.

The battle of El Alamein marked the crushing of the German presence in North Africa, but it was a desperate encounter nonetheless. 'It has become a real solid and bloody killing match,' wrote Montgomery at a crucial stage in the battle even while holding the initiative at

THREE ~ ACTIVE SERVICE

that stage.[36] Former Oundle School boy Major William Williamson was one of the many British casualties. He was placed in command of a battery of Rhodesians, and was leading this battery into action in support of the Australian Division in an attack on a Panzer Division near Tell el Eisa when he was killed early in the morning of 31 October. A brother officer wrote: 'His battery put up a most gallant show, destroying several tanks, guns, tractors and vehicles — so much that they were cheered by the Australians.'[37]

Operation 'Torch': the Capture of Casablanca

Planning for a joint Anglo-American assault on the North-West coast of Africa had begun as early as December 1941, and was given added impetus by the reverses which the British had suffered in June with the fall of Tobruk. The project, previously known as 'Gymnast' and 'Super-Gymnast', was re-christened 'Torch', and Churchill agreed that the supreme command of the operation should be given to an American. A three-pronged assault on Casablanca, Oran and Algiers was decided.

Prior to the assault, an attempt was made on the diplomatic front to sound out the possibility of co-operation with the French forces in the area, but this turned out to be a disappointing muddle, described as 'a mixture of a spy story and a "Western", with comic interludes'.

A former Oundle School boy, Lieutenant Norman Jewell, played a key role in the operation. He had had extensive experience of submarine operations in the Mediterranean since the beginning of the war, serving as First Lieutenant on HMS *Otway* and then on HMS *Truant* before taking on his first command appointment in charge of *L27*, a relic of the First World War.

In late 1942 he found himself appointed to command the newly built *P219* (HMS *Seraph*), to which Special Boat Section and Combined Operations Pilotage Parties (COPP), personnel composed of saboteur frogmen and canoeists were attached. One of his operations at this time consisted of putting an SBS team ashore at Genoa in Italy in order to damage the fencing around a POW camp and allow prisoners to escape. The next two patrols consisted of photographing and mapping the beaches in North Africa from Melilla to Algiers. The planning for Operation 'Torch' had begun.

The newly formed COPP, a numerically small group of Royal Navy navigators/hydrographers and Royal Engineers commandos was to play a significant but little known part in the invasions of Sicily, Italy, and Normandy,

69: Captain Norman Jewell, MBE, DSC in 1943.

as well as Operation 'Torch', guiding in assault forces. At least three army officers who had been educated at Oundle, Captain Basil Eckhard, Captain Derrick Freeman and Captain Alec Colson, were members of this élite force involved in top secret operations.[38]

Norman Jewell was entrusted with the task of taking the American General Mark Clark from Gibraltar to a secret landing on the coast of Algeria, en route for a villa 60 miles west of Algiers. The meeting, delayed for 24 hours, allowed General Clark to meet the French commander of troops in the Algiers area, General Mast, for discussions about which French officers might be trusted. It nearly ended in disaster, with the French police making a sudden appearance, and General Clark almost drowning in the heavy surf on the way back to the submarine. Contact was then established with the French officer whom Mast had recommended, General Giraud, who was at that time living at Lyons, and Lieutenant Jewell made a second secret mission in HMS *Seraph* to pick up Giraud from Le Lavandou on the south coast of France and transfer him to Gibraltar. Elements of tragi-comedy persisted in dogging the operation, with General Giraud on this occasion almost drowning during his transfer from the submarine to a flying-boat. On arrival at Gibraltar he was staggered to discover that the 'Torch' landings were to take place on the following morning, 8 November, instead of the following month, as he had been led to believe.[39]

For his part in the daring missions in enemy waters, Lieutenant Jewell was decorated with the MBE and the DSC, and received also the Legion of Merit of the US Navy from the American President himself. Submarine operations were particularly hazardous in the crowded Mediterranean. Norman Jewell remembered frightening moments during a further patrol which he undertook there in 1942.

> On the surface after dark we saw an Italian submarine who must have seen us also, and both submarines dived together. We collided at a depth of 100 feet and resurfaced immediately. After examining the damage to our bows we remained on the surface and about 20 minutes later sighted him again. In our attack we saw one of our torpedoes hit him, but it did not explode. He was later sunk by a destroyer, being unable to dive.

The next year was to see the former Oundle School boy play an equally crucial part in the preparations for the Allied assault on enemy territory.

The Battle of the Atlantic: a Merchant Navy Man's Tales

'Amid the torrent of violent events one anxiety reigned supreme. Battles might be won or lost, enterprises might succeed or miscarry, territories might be gained or quitted, but dominating all our power to carry on the war, or even keep ourselves alive, lay our mastery of the ocean routes and the free approach and entry to our ports.' Thus did Churchill stress the importance of Britain's merchant fleet, so necessary to keep the beleaguered country supplied.[40]

Herne Road resident George Bristow, who moved to Oundle after spending most of his life in the West Country, recalled some of the unexpected wartime experiences that he had during his time with the Merchant Navy. Called up in early 1942 at the age of 18, he served until 1946. A French polisher by trade, he helped in the cabinet making business. Other professional cabinet makers continued until they were 21 before they were called up to help make aeroplanes. Many people joined up under age. This was not due to patriotism,

THREE ~ ACTIVE SERVICE

believed George Bristow, but was because in many cases they came from poor homes and the forces were a better life for them. When called up he went to Pwllheli and boarded HMS *Glendower* for basic training, before embarking at Penzance. His first assignment was to take a load of gravel to Hotwells in Bristol, just 12 miles from where he lived. 'I'll never forget this first trip because we sailed round Land's End in an 800 tonne ship. This was not very big and was very frightening because the ship got tossed about all over the place.'

The merchant ships on which George Bristow served were known as DEMS (Defensively Equipped Merchant Ships). Alongside the regular Merchant Navy seamen there was a gun crew of four naval and four army personnel. The weapons used were a 4" Oerlikon gun, and a magazine of 60 shells which were very sensitive. When using these, it was advisable to take out gunpowder from the first couple of shells, and fire them off, to ensure that any obstructions in the barrel of the

70: Merchant Navy DEMS man George Bristow in 1942.

gun would be cleared. Another weapon used was the Marlins and Hotchkiss ·303 calibre rifle. 'The problem with this was that the instructions for use were in Japanese because they were used by Japan during World War One,' recalled George Bristow. During the early part of the war, the armed forces called for inventions and ideas to assist them because all the Merchant Navy ships had to be armed.

> One invention used was the Horman Projector, literally a stove pipe connected to a steam powered pump. When a plane came over, a live grenade would be placed in the pipe and steam would propel the grenade out to blow the plane up. This was not always reliable, and sometimes, because there was not enough steam in the pipe, the grenade would just drop out of the end, and there would be a mad scramble away to avoid being blown up. Although it was not reliable, the men put it to good use; they used to put any excess food into the pipe and fire it up at the seagulls. There was also something called a Parachute and Cable. This was a metal box situated on the wheelhouse consisting of 600 feet of piano wire connected to a mine and a rocket. When a plane came over, the rocket would be fired up and this would bring the piano wire and mine with it. When the rocket reached a certain height, it would burst and release a drogue which would attract the mine and hopefully blow one of the plane's wings off. The problem with this was that especially in E-Boat Alley, a narrow unmined strip of water between England and France, the convoys went along in two lines, so sometimes if a plane was blown up, it would land and smash on another boat. The final invention used was the Pillar Box. There were two boxes each containing ten rockets, and either ten or twenty rockets could be fired at once.

E-Boat alley was so named because of the threat from the motor torpedo boats which the Germans developed during the war, and which were at their most menacing in Britain's home waters during the first half of 1944. Never more than about three dozen in number, they were nonetheless a danger because they could be switched rapidly from one convoy route to another. 'The most frightening thing in the navy was being on watch on the gun deck in the fog in a convoy,' recalled George Bristow.

> To follow the convoy, the crews devised a machine like an aeroplane which had a metal curve in the water so when it was dragged in the water a plume of water shot into the air. When it was towed, other ships could see which direction to travel by following the jet of water. Sometimes the man on watch could not properly see where to go and so almost rammed the vessel into other ships. The man on watch felt safe in the fog: he knew that the enemy could not see him. It was the most frightening on moonlit nights, you knew that you could be seen and most of the night sinkings were done on moonlit nights. The man on watch spent four hours on duty and four hours off, but in action the men had to spend a couple of days on watch. There was no hot food available because the galley fires had to be put out, and the crew had to live on corned beef sandwiches and slept as close to the guns as possible.

Some of the ships had awful conditions: the DEMS now had an extra crew of eight, and room on the ship had to be found for them. Before the war, ships could carry a maximum of nine without a doctor.

There were of course amusing incidents which George Bristow remembers. 'On one occasion the cook complained that the galley chimney was blocked, so the gun crew poured the contents of a Oerlikon shell down the chimney to see what happened — the powder lifted the top off the galley stove. The poor old cook came out looking like a black man.'

Weather conditions in the Channel could be appalling. The worst storm was when he was in a small ship going past St Ives, and the fuel pumps broke down. The ship was in distress for two days. There was no wireless, only a machine sending out two signals, distress and air attack. A Falmouth trawler and the St Ives coast guard were called out. They had to be towed and this was a very tricky business; having connected the rope the ship had to slip anchor and the tow line had to be slack in the water. If the cable was taut it would snap.

George Bristow's memory of an unexpected encounter with the enemy ranks among the most remarkable wartime stories told by Oundle veterans.

71: George Bristow, in happier times.

On one occasion, we were in a convoy coming down the Bristol Channel and round Land's End, when our ship developed engine trouble. The rest of the convoy sailed on because our ship was only small, and in a short while the engineers got the ship going again. Later on, during the moonlit night, we saw what we thought was a British motor torpedo boat with a loud hailer. It said all the right commands, 'Ahoy there, where are you from?' etc. Our boat gave the correct reply. The voice talking to us was very well educated, and asked, 'Have you seen any E-boats tonight?' We replied, 'No, not at all, sir.' The voice replied, 'Well you bloody saw one now. You have two minutes to get into the boat.' Well, we lowered the boat in double quick time, and the Captain, mate, the two engineers and the two gunners got into the boat. The E-boat took the boat in tow, and set off, with us wondering what was to happen to us. Before going into Falmouth Harbour, you pass a series of buoys, called D1, D2, D3, and D4. Our mate whispered, 'We've just passed D1 buoy.' The E-boat took the ship right into Falmouth Harbour. The German cast us off on the quayside and said, 'I'm sorry to inconvenience you lads.' The Germans then went aboard and flooded the ship so it sank. This meant that I had survivor's leave.

The Submarine War

Some notable figures in the submarine warfare which played so large a part in the Battle of the Atlantic had connections with Oundle. One of these had a legal career almost as distinguished as his years of war service, being Lord Justice of Appeal from 1965 to 1971. Crippled with polio in his youth, the Right Hon. Sir Rodger Winn, PC, CB, OBE, proved himself to be a brilliant student at Oundle School before going to Cambridge and being called to the Bar in 1928. His obituary notice in *The Times* gave Rodger Winn well deserved recognition of his services to the nation, and explained how his work proved so vital in the struggle for control of the seas:

He had an outstanding war-time career in the Admiralty Citadel between the years 1941 and 1945. His work there brought him the unusual distinction for an RNVR officer of four stripes and a CB, OBE and the US Legion of Merit. His skill and authority became legendary.

In the casual way that some of the best intelligence men were recruited into Whitehall, Winn offered himself for the interrogation of prisoners of war. By a mysterious bureaucratic process he was allotted to the submarine tracking room which had been started under Paymaster Commander Thring in 1938. Thring was one of the few survivors of the famous Room 40 which in the First World War had applied the study of decoded German signals to the destruction of U-boats and the diversion of convoys. Thanks to the training and advice of Thring — who had some notable encounters with First Lord Winston Churchill over claims of U-boats sunk — Winn had by 1941 become so adept at the work that he was chosen by the Director of Naval Intelligence, with the approval of the Director of Anti-Submarine Warfare, to succeed Thring when his health made retirement necessary. For a civilian to take on such responsibility, even under supervision by RN officers in the Operational Intelligence Centre, was a notable innovation which proved entirely successful.

Using information from a multiplicity of sources, which varied in volume and accuracy at different times, the tracking room staff under Winn were able to compile the biography of virtually every U-boat that went to sea. This required the most painstaking fitting together of fragments, in which Winn's legal training was invaluable. Still more, it meant the exercise of judgement when it came to routeing important convoys away from known or suspected concentrations of U-boats. In the final stage every decision had to be made by Winn and his colleagues in the Trade Division, and there were errors as well as successes. It is nonetheless true that, until sufficient escort destroyers and aircraft were available in 1943 to capture the initiative from Dönitz's wolf packs, the main obstacle to German success in the Battle of the Atlantic was the work of the section known as 8(s).

The technique of estimating the course and position of U-boats was at first regarded by regular naval officers as sheer guesswork, but in time not only Winn, but also his young assistants, came to be trusted completely. Their advice was always offered and treated as the advice of 'the Room'. More than once, forecasts and diagnoses of U-boat strategy offered by this section affected Admiralty decisions over a wide field. For example, it discouraged in the months leading up to the invasion of Normandy in 1944, too easy optimism about the inability of the Germans to recapture the initiative in the U-boat war.

Winn was a hard taskmaster, who drove his colleagues mercilessly. Their admiration and devotion was none the less for that, and they realised more than once during four years of war — notably in 1942 — that the man was being driven to the limits of his strength by continuous work; 14 hours a day of controversial and deeply disturbing decisions about the destination and fate of precious men, equipment and supplies. He was almost persuaded in late 1942 by his doctor to resign. Fortunately he refused, knowing without any immodesty that his departure at that stage in the U-boat war would have been a national disaster.[41]

Ten years younger than Rodger Winn, but working under him at the Admiralty's Operational Intelligence Centre and coincidentally educated at Oundle School, was another figure of vital importance in the war against the U-boats. This was Lieutenant Commander Patrick Beesly, commissioned in the RNVR in 1939.

Following his retirement after 20 years in the RNVR, Patrick Beesly wrote *Very Special Intelligence*, published in 1977. The book gave a fascinating insight into the Operational Intelligence Centre's work on the cracking of enemy ciphers and codes, much of it based on the Ultra information supplied by Bletchley Park, the Government's Code and Cipher School, soon to be renamed Government Communications Headquarters (GCHQ). Patrick Beesly's work was published in Germany, America and Russia as well as in England. A copy of *Very Special Intelligence* is in Oundle School Library, presented by Patrick Beesly with an inscription to his former history master Dudley Heesom.[42]

The third Oundle-educated figure of note in the Battle of the Atlantic was a man who made British submarines as feared by the enemy as any U-boat was by Allied shipping. Rear Admiral Ben Bryant, who died at the age of 89, was described in his obituary in *The Daily Telegraph* as 'one of the most aggressive and successful submarine captains of the Second World War'.

After leaving Oundle in 1919 Ben Bryant was a cadet at Osborne and Dartmouth, joining the submarine service in 1927. His first wartime appointment was to the submarine *Sealion*, which he commanded for three years in the Mediterranean, off Norway and in home waters. Off Norway in 1940 the clear water, almost continuous daylight and constant air surveillance made submarine operations extremely difficult and hazardous. Off Stavanger in July 1940 he had what he described as his 'worst patrol', during which *Sealion* was depth-charged several times and attacked by aircraft whenever she surfaced to try and recharge her main batteries.

Awarded the Distinguished Service Cross in May 1940, he was mentioned in despatches for clandestine missions off the coast of Brittany. Between May 1942 and July 1943, Ben Bryant, commanding *P211*, later renamed *Safari*, sank some 30,000 tonnes of enemy shipping in the Mediterranean, winning a DSO and two bars. Boldly using *Safari* as

THREE ~ ACTIVE SERVICE

a submersible gunboat to disrupt coastal traffic, he even shelled coastal railway lines and rolling stock on several occasions. He never lost the attacking spirit, often saying that he 'loved to hunt and chase the enemy and beat him up on his own doorstep'. Tracking and sinking the enemy was, he claimed, 'the finest sport in the world'.

By the time he left *Safari* Ben Bryant was a full Commander and one of the most experienced submarine COs in the Navy. But he never allowed himself to become over-confident, and there were grim moments of depression and stress. Once, after *Sealion* was forced to remain submerged for nearly 24 hours, her air quality was so poor that when she finally surfaced, the diesel engines would not start until the boat had been ventilated.

It was one of the few times when Bryant was downcast. The war was going badly, and two submarines commanded by friends of his had just been lost. But when he went up into the fore ends, where the sailors lived, his mood changed. 'Suddenly,' he recalled, 'the atmosphere of unworried serenity passed from them to me. I realised that they would go into action on the morrow without backward thoughts, that with a crew such as I was privileged to command we could not be beaten; the depression left me.'

72: A wartime picture of Rear Admiral Ben Bryant, DSO, DSC.

In his tenth and last patrol, described by the Commander-in-Chief Mediterranean as 'one which will rank among the classic exploits of the submarine service,' *Safari* sank an armed liner, a tanker, a tramp steamer, a minesweeper, an anti-submarine brigantine and a trading schooner.

Promoted Captain in June 1944, Bryant was appointed to command the depot ship *Cyclops* and the Seventh Submarine Flotilla at Rothesay, and then the depot ship *Forth* and the Second Flotilla in Holy Loch.

Unusually for an ex-Oundle man Ben Bryant never took any exercise, having noticed that men who did so on their return from patrol often fell sick. He stayed fit throughout the war. Even when most of *Sealion's* officers and men were prostrated by flu, their Captain remained immune, dispensing medicines to the sick crew until the epidemic was over.

Ben Bryant looked the part. Edward Young, one of *Sealion's* officers, who later became a submarine Commanding Officer himself, wrote of him:

> With his erect height, his sea-dog beard and arrogant eye, he was a typical submarine captain of the public imagination. He had a fine command of the English language, which he used to

good effect in recounting yarns in the wardroom, inventing ballads or expressing his opinion of some ineptitude on the part of one of his officers or men. He had the rare gift of being able to switch without loss of dignity from CO to entertaining messmate.[43]

Ben Bryant spent only three years at Oundle, but evidently remembered his days at The Berrystead with affection as he sent his son Jeremy to the School in 1956.

Not all submariners were as fortunate as Ben Bryant. In the Mediterranean in 1942 submarine losses were high; at one time a boat's chances of survival were no better than 50-50. Another former pupil of the School, Sub-Lieutenant William Hardwick, was one of the many who perished in the dark and tense battles of submarine warfare, killed in action in the bay of Taranto on 8 December 1942. William Hardwick, who had left Sidney House in 1939, had spent the early part of the war on destroyer patrol in the North Sea. From the vantage-point of the bridge, he had been able to indulge one of the passions which he had enjoyed at Oundle, the birdwatching on which he wrote an article published in *The Field* in 1941.[44]

On the subject of submarines it is worth noting that the Royal Navy owed a considerable debt to the Oundle School workshops. The former pupil, Edward Paxman, who had left Grafton House in 1920 to join the Colchester-based family firm of Davey, Paxman & Company made it one of the foremost producers of diesel engines in the world. His brilliant engineering ability was seen in the high-speed lightweight diesel engine which he designed, and which was fitted to more than half the Royal Navy's submarines during the last war.[45]

The War on the Surface

German warships continued to pose a formidable threat to the Allies, and a former Oundle School boy, Sub-Lieutenant Robert Parkinson, was one of many servicemen who lost their lives in the attempt to destroy the enemy at sea. An ex-Head of Bramston House, which he had left in 1938, he joined the Fleet Air Arm and met his death while piloting a Swordfish in an attack on the *Scharnhorst, Gneisenau* and the *Prinz Eugen* in February 1942. A total of six Swordfish torpedo planes, 20 bombers and 16 fighters were lost in the attack. Enemy fighter losses came to 16. For this gallant attempt to destroy the German ships despite a terrific barrage of anti-aircraft fire and the persistent attacks of enemy fighters he was posthumously mentioned in despatches. His courage and that of his comrades was described in the *London Gazette* in the following words:

> The last that was seen of this gallant band who were astern of the leading flight, is that they were flying steadily towards the battle-cruisers, led by Lt. Thomson. Their aircraft shattered, undeterred by an inferno of fire, they carried out their orders, which were to attack the target. Not one came back. Theirs was the courage which is beyond praise.[46]

Also involved in an attack on the *Scharnhorst* and the *Gneisenau* was another Oundle School boy, Charles Ordish, who had left Laxton House in 1936. Decorated posthumously with the Distinguished Flying Cross for his part in the attack, he was to lose his life later in the year on 31 December 1942.[47]

THREE ~ ACTIVE SERVICE

The War in the Air

The Luftwaffe's bombing of Rotterdam on 14 May 1940, and the accidental bombing of London on 24 August, were among the factors which helped to change the climate of opinion about the acceptability of indiscriminate bombing of enemy territory. The day after the destruction of Rotterdam saw Churchill's authorisation of attacks east of the Rhine by Bomber Command, and this is generally taken as the start of the strategic air offensive against Germany. Operational difficulties meant that strategic targets were not always hit, and as German air defences improved, the toll of Allied aircrews became disturbingly heavy. For the first two years of the war the results of the bombing campaign proved disappointing.

February 1942 saw a renewal of the campaign as Bomber Command was issued with the instructions to destroy the morale of the enemy civil population, and in particular of the industrial workers. Decisions on targets were now being taken by Air Marshal A. T. 'Bomber' Harris, who had taken over as Commander-in-Chief, Bomber Command, on 22 February.

Soon the pattern of '1,000 bomber' raids had been established, with the USAAF attacking by day and the RAF by night. At least two ex-Oundle School boys found themselves in key positions on the first of these raids, when 1,046 bombers were sent to destroy Cologne on the night of 30 May. Wing Commander Donald Simmons, who had left School House in 1932 and had been personal assistant to the Chief of Air Staff, Air Marshal Sir Charles Portal, was in command of 142 Bomber Squadron on this occasion. His death in a flying accident in March 1945 prompted Lord Portal to write:

> He was a young man with all the fine qualities — loyalty, good humour, conscientiousness, courage and cheerfulness — that have made the Air Force what it is, and I could never have had a more devoted worker in the capacity in which he served me personally. Equally fine and very courageous was his work in Bomber Command, and he also showed much ability in Staff work. It is heartrending to lose such a valuable and brilliant young officer at this late stage of the war.[48]

The second ex-Oundle School boy involved in the Cologne raid was Lucian Ercolani, who had been awarded the Distinguished Service Order the previous year. Having completed his tour of operations on Wellingtons with 214 Squadron he was posted to take over the flight of 1483 Gunnery Training School with Wellingtons and Lysanders. He remembered flying out of the race course at Newmarket. 'This was very good luck for us as that year, 1942, they held the Derby at Newmarket, cancelled all flying, and gave us tickets for the Stewards' Enclosure!'

The effectiveness of these raids has been questioned: German air defences increased dramatically in 1942 with day-fighter strength rising from 292 to 453, and night-fighter strength from 162 to 349. In the same year the loss of British bombers had risen to 1,404. Yet a report commissioned by Hitler's Armaments Minister Albert Speer in January 1945 on the results of Allied bombing during the previous year speaks for itself: 35% fewer tanks than planned, 31% fewer aircraft and 42% fewer aircraft. Certainly, Lucian Ercolani was in no doubt about the results of his missions, and was proud to have taken part in the first five of the raids.

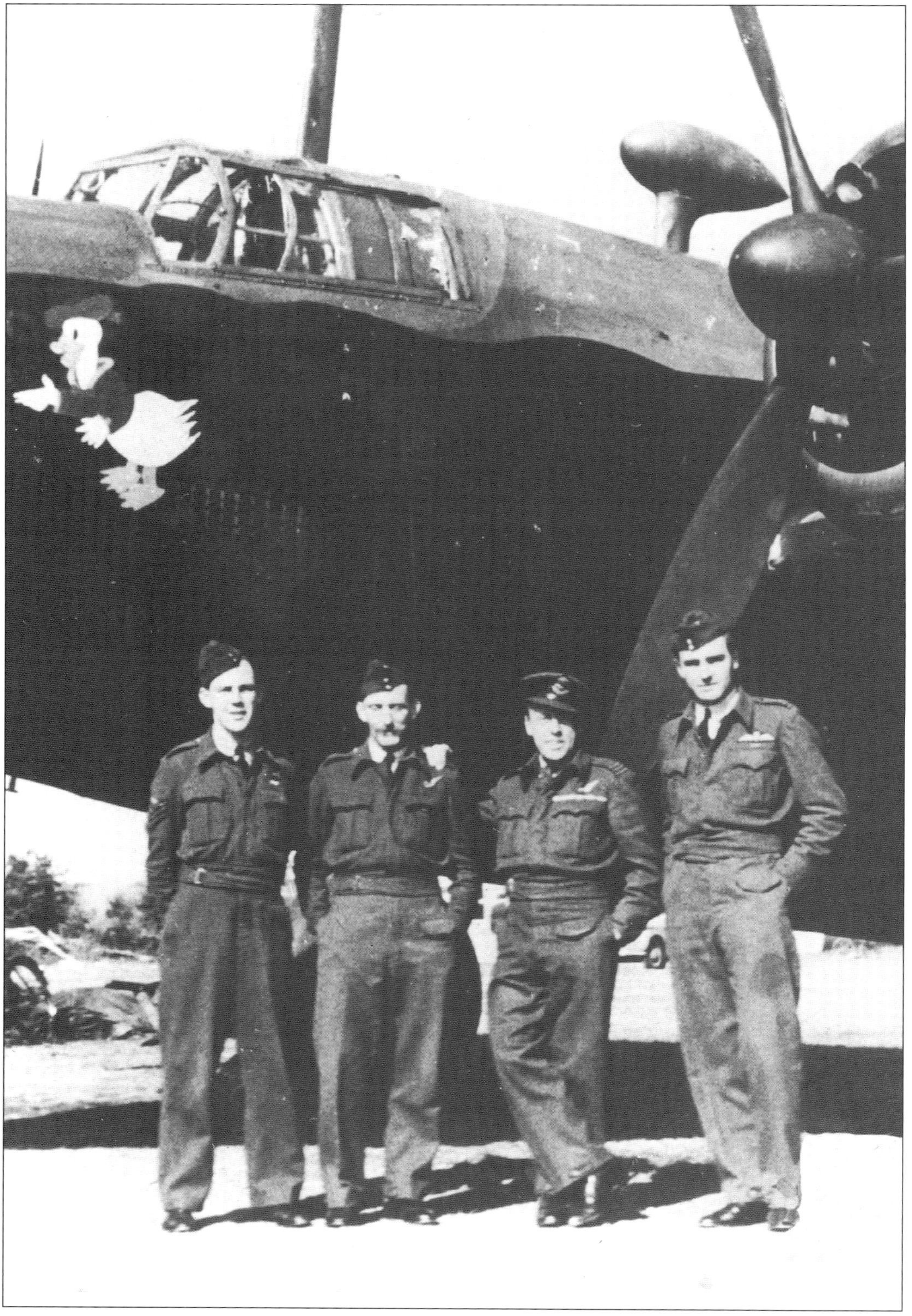

73 *(left)*:
Wing Commander Lucian Ercolani, DSO, DFC (on the right) with fellow aircrew of Bomber Command who took part in the first 1,000 Bomber Raid on Cologne in May 1942.

74 *(right)*:
Sergeant Pilot Alfred Taney.

Two Oundle airmen, Sergeant Pilot Alfred Taney and Flight Engineer Sergeant Peter Richardson, died tragically within a few days of each other at this time. Alfred Taney, whose family lived in North Street, had left Laxton School in 1933, joining the RAF in 1941, and was killed when his aircraft crashed in this country on his return from night operations on 7 November. Peter Richardson, brought up on Benefield Road, had left Laxton School in 1935, joining the RAF in the same year and was posted to Bomber Command. He was on his 22nd mission over enemy territory when he was killed on 10 November 1942.[49]

The Allied Counter-offensive in the Far East

Japan's hold over the islands of the Pacific had extended itself so far by late 1942 that Australia began to prepare itself for an invasion. Towns in the north of the country had been raided by enemy bombers, and it was clear that the Japanese were aiming to secure Port Moresby in Papua so as to establish an airbase from which to attack Queensland. Australian reinforcements were rushed to the Papuan peninsula, and a series of fierce battles took place to push back the enemy.

Colonel Ralph Hodgson, who had left Oundle School's Dryden House in 1922, found himself in Australia at the outbreak of war, an officer in the British Territorial Army, and on War Office instructions joined the Australian Army, becoming Commanding Officer of the 2nd/6th Armoured Regiment. As part of the First Armoured Division, Ralph Hodgson's regiment was selected to take part in the attack on Japanese positions launched at Cape Endaiare in New Guinea in December 1942. The Australian *Official History of the War* goes into some detail about an incident in the attack. The former Oundle School boy, described as 'tall, spare, aloof, a cool and confident leader and hard taskmaster, greatly respected by his men,' was instructed to take an enemy position that was tremendously strong, desperately defended by a fanatical foe, in conditions that were appallingly difficult for tanks. Shortly after the attack went in, one of Ralph Hodgson's Squadron Leaders was blinded in one eye by a Japanese firing through his observation slit. 'The bleeding officer was scarcely clear of his tank before his colonel took his place,' continues the Australian *Official History*. 'As he plunged into the fight, Hodgson, true to his own teaching, was looking out of the open turret of his tank to get a full view of what lay ahead. An inevitable fate overtook him when a machine-gun burst spattered his vehicle. He slumped back into the turret badly wounded.'[50] In spite of his injury Ralph Hodgson went on to become Commandant of the newly-formed Australian Armoured Corps Training Centre in 1943, and was awarded the DSO for his part in commanding the Second Beach Group in the Borneo landing of May 1945, which is described later in this chapter.

~ 1943 ~

The Far East: the Arakan Offensive

The Australian counter-offensive against the Japanese in New Guinea was matched by similar moves planned by General Wavell against the enemy in the Arakan coastal region of Burma. The 14th Indian Division started to advance in December 1942, but progress was slow, and the sending of Japanese reinforcements resulted in a check.

The whole operation had seemed over-ambitious from the start, and the Japanese were not the only enemy. Many British soldiers succumbed to diseases which were endemic in India and the Far East. Gunner James Roughton, an Oundle man with the Second Survey, Royal Artillery, was one of the thousands of such victims. He died of dysentery in India on 21 October 1943, aged 20. For every Allied soldier wounded in the struggle for Burma in 1943, more than a hundred fell sick. Malaria was the chief problem: the annual rate of those struck down by the disease in this year was a staggering 84% of total manpower. Conditions in jungle warfare were grim. Torrential rain, marching in oozing black mud, the fearsome red ants, leeches, spiders, and the prickly bamboo which cut both flesh and clothes to ribbons,

75: Gunner James Roughton.
He died in India on 21 October 1943.

THREE ~ ACTIVE SERVICE

were all hazards faced by troops in what sometimes became known as the Forgotten Army.

Terence Tinsley, who left Oundle School's St Anthony House in 1940, had been born in India where his father was a civil engineer in the Indian Canals Service, and it was no surprise to his family when he joined the Bengal Sappers and Miners in 1942. In a book entitled *Stick and String*, published in 1992, he recalls his part in the Arakan campaign for which he was mentioned in despatches; the work consisted of building, in extremely difficult terrain, adequate roads, bridges and jetties to provide supplies for the front-line troops. The choice of title for his book epitomises the improvisation constantly needed to overcome shortages of equipment or materials, a skill that, like Norman Reddaway at Dunkirk in 1940, he claimed to have learnt in the Scout troop at Oundle.[51]

The appointment of General William Slim as commander of the newly created 14th Army marked a turn in the tide for the Allied forces in Burma. The supply of ammunition and stores to the Assam front was improved by the building of all-weather roads, and a new offensive against the Japanese was launched. But the end of 1943 was to see a second tragedy befall an Oundle family. Captain Christopher King, educated at Oundle School where he had been Head of Grafton House, was the son of Henry King, a former housemaster of New House who had moved to live in Cotterstock. Leaving in 1935 to read Mechanical Science at Cambridge, he had joined the Royal Army Ordnance Corps in 1942, and had been killed in an air-raid on the Isle of Wight in April of that year. Now came the news of the death of his elder brother, Lieutenant John King. He too had been Head of Grafton House, leaving in 1932, and joining the Royal Artillery at the outbreak of war. He had taken part in the Madagascar landing, later serving in India. His death in Assam, in December, was another cruel blow for Henry King and his wife Olive.

Clearing Up in North Africa

After Montgomery's victory at El Alamein in October 1942, the Eighth Army pushed Rommel's forces westward, taking only 80 days to cover 1,400 miles. The fortified Mareth Line, a formidable barrier of tank traps, pillboxes and concrete bunkers some 80 miles west of the frontier between Libya and Tunisia held up the British advance, but on the night of 20 March 1943 a frontal assault was made. Heavy rain had turned the Wadi Zigzaou, which ran in front of the Mareth Line, into a moat. Casualties were heavy as Rommel's troops fought a desperate rearguard action. A former Oundle School pupil, Captain Charles Rob was the first doctor to make a parachute descent on active service at this time; he flew 350 miles to Biza in Tunisia, landed by parachute and performed 140 operations during the battle, receiving the Military Cross and being mentioned in despatches.[52]

A spirited counter-attack by Rommel's 15th Panzers halted Allied progress until the afternoon of 26 March, when the RAF were called in to the attack. Many prisoners had been taken among the British infantry, unable to defend themselves with anti-tank guns against the Panzers. Ian English, who had left Oundle School's Laxton House in 1938, was one of these: he described the Battle of Mareth as one of the most bitter which the Durham Light Infantry Brigade with which he was serving had fought during the entire war.

Among the casualties on the British side in the attempt to break through the Mareth Line was Captain Benjamin Guy Measures, of the Northamptonshire Regiment, the eldest son of local landowners Mr and Mrs Benjamin Measures, of Hemington Manor. Guy Measures had been educated at Oundle School, leaving School House in 1931 to take up

76: Captain Guy Measures, killed in action in North Africa, March 1943.

farming. He was attached to the Second Battalion, The Hampshire Regiment, when he was killed during a reconnaissance operation.[53]

British troops finally cut their way through into Tunisia and joined up with an Anglo-American force there, already in position since the success of Operation 'Torch' in November 1942. Tunis fell to the Allies on 7 May, and by the 13th all the Axis commanders and their troops had submitted: the vast number of German prisoners taken was significant in depriving Hitler of the battle-tested troops which he would need to face the Allies in the first of their invasions of Europe, through Sicily.

John Sharman, who had fought at the Battle of Alamein with the Seventh Armoured Division, remembered the moment of triumph as he found himself among the first troops to enter Tunis. 'The local population gave us a great welcome and we had people riding on the guns as we went through the city to take up positions round the harbour.' It was in North Africa at this time, while on leave in Tripoli, that he contracted polio and was later invalided out of the Army as 'permanently unfit', beginning his long career as a teacher in September 1944 at the school where he had been educated. He looked back on the experience without bitterness. 'I had a fairly easy war really, when you think of what some folk had to put up with.'

The battle for Tunis was marked by the fall of many brave soldiers on both sides. Lieutenant Colonel Alexander Birkbeck, another former pupil of Oundle School which he had left in 1924 to become a professional soldier, was one of the many who lost their lives at this time. His sacrifice was not in vain, as described by his Brigadier:

> He was killed instantly while most bravely leading an attack which led to the restoring of a position we had lost. It was most gallant leadership and typical of him. He knew his job better than most of us and he gave the Battalion every ounce of his knowledge, enthusiasm, fairness and cheerfulness.[54]

Another Oundelian whose bravery was equally remarkable, and who was to die tragically during the advance on Tunis was Lieutenant Donald Foster-Anderson. He had already distinguished himself while still at the School, using his ingenuity in many original ways and experimenting with all sorts of machinery, and when he left Dryden House in 1938 it was naturally enough to read Civil Engineering at Cambridge University. He had volunteered for the Army after Dunkirk, and gained his commission in the Royal Engineers in 1941. In

THREE ~ ACTIVE SERVICE

April 1943, while serving with the First Army near Medjez el Bab, his skill and daring attracted the attention of the national Press. In order to save an important bridge from demolition by the enemy he crawled forward under fire in full daylight to remove ten 200 lb charges, some of which were connected to booby traps. He cut the wires connecting the four charges under the bridge, and then, in spite of concentrated fire from snipers, wormed his way to the top of the bridge, cut the remaining wires, and returned in safety to the British lines.

A short time later, while lifting mines for the advance on Tunis on 29 April, he was killed in action.

By mid-May 1943 all resistance to the Allies had ceased in North Africa.[55]

The Battle of the Atlantic: Closing the Gap

The most critical period in the Battle of the Atlantic was during the second half of 1942 and the first half of 1943, when new U-boats were going into service at the rate of 14 a month. However RAF Coastal Command were becoming more active and more expert in anti-submarine warfare. A new advantage in the Battle was gained when escort aircraft carriers, converted from merchant vessels and able to carry 30 submarine-hunting aircraft, were sent to accompany the convoys. By July 1943, the mid-Atlantic gap, in which Allied shipping had had to travel unprotected because of the limited range of shore-based aircraft, had been closed. Merchant Navy losses, however, were considerable: a total of 2,426 ships with a gross tonnage of over 11 million were lost in the Second World War through enemy action.

Kenneth Gadd had direct experience of escorting Atlantic convoys at this time, and remembers one posting in connection with his duties which turned out to be the most enjoyable of the war. He was sent across the Atlantic to Canada in April 1943 to collect a ship which was being built in Toronto, and found that his visit was an agreeable escape from a severely rationed Britain.

> I spent about four months there with no food rationing! It made your mouth water. Everything... butter, eggs... So we fed very, very well while we were there and, of course there were no alerts or bombing, no air-raids, and lights were on in the town and all that sort of thing. It was a nice relaxing period except that one had to watch the ship being built and eventually, I think it was about October 1943, we completed that and we came back. We acted as an escort to an Atlantic convoy going back to the United Kingdom and back to war again. That was a good experience.

The Attack on the *Tirpitz*

A boost for British morale later in 1943 was the attack on the German battleship *Tirpitz* in a Norwegian fiord by midget submarines which managed to penetrate German defences in what was known as Operation 'Source'. The submarines, known as X-craft, were of no more than 35 tons and just over 50 feet in length; they carried two detachable explosive charges on the outside of the pressure hull which each contained two tons of explosive that could be set to explode by clockwork timers from inside the boat.

Sub-Lieutenant Robert Aitken, a former Oundle School boy who had left Sidney House in 1940, was one of the officers involved in the operation. 'Reading about compensation now being paid by the Ministry of Defence, I am considering making a claim for loss of memory due to oxygen starvation,' he joked. He was able nonetheless to give an impressively detailed account of events more than fifty years later:

> After a medical on the morning of my first day in the Navy, I was told I had defective colour vision. This turned out to be the first step towards joining the 12th Submarine flotilla about 18 months later. I completed a preliminary training course as an Ordinary Seaman before being sent to an old 1914/18 destroyer escorting convoys in the North Atlantic. I then got posted to HMS *King Alfred* for a Non-executive Officers Training Course for those who had some physical handicap, often poor eyesight, and were not able to undertake watchkeeping duties. Not having had my 20th birthday on completion of the course I became a Midshipman RNVR (Special), an unusual rank of which the Admiralty had little experience.
>
> Not knowing what to do with me I was left kicking my heels at *King Alfred*. After some months I was asked if I would be interested in special duties, for which colour vision was not thought to be important. I could obtain details by attending a meeting at HMS *Dolphin*, which I learnt on arrival was the Navy's principal Submarine Base.

77: Robert Aitken DSO, photographed in 1941, wearing an Ordinary Seaman's uniform during preliminary training, one year after leaving Oundle School.

> During the first briefing about two dozen officers and ratings were told we had volunteered as human torpedo men. My first experience of hearing a pin drop! Having been told we could drop out at any time I think nearly all of us decided to 'give it a go' if only to find out more about this new weapon with which the Italians had been very successful, when first used in the Mediterranean.
>
> Training started at *Dolphin* wearing DSEA (Davies Submarine Escape Apparatus) in a tank about 36 feet deep used for training submariners to escape from sunken submarines. We then moved to a canal where we struggled into light, so-called dry diving suits. After strapping on a couple of oxygen bottles we tried to get used to walking around on the bottom, in relatively shallow water. Later in heavy deep-sea diving suits with large brass helmets and breathing compressed air we were lowered to the bottom of the harbour, about 100 feet down, to see if our ear drums could take the strain. This was to prepare us for a similar dive wearing the light suit and breathing pure oxygen to let us experience the early symptoms of oxygen poisoning: a hazard which offset the advantages of diving on oxygen. No bubbles on the surface to arouse suspicions, but the tolerance of individuals varied. On oxygen divers could work at 30 feet for extended periods but tolerance decreased as the depth increased, and at 100 feet or more most divers could only work for a few minutes.
>
> The next move was to HMS *Titania*, an old coal-burning submarine depot ship, moored in a small, and more importantly shallow, loch in the west of Scotland known as HHX. Here we were introduced to Chariots, the name given to small battery powered submersibles which two divers could sit astride and use rather like an underwater motorbike. Tanks could be

THREE ~ ACTIVE SERVICE

flooded to submerge. To surface, compressed air was used to blow the water out and also operated a net cutter. An explosive war-head could be attached to the hull of a ship with magnets. An officer sat in front and operated the Chariot with a rating behind. His job was to cut the A/S (anti-submarine) nets and attach the warhead.

Our days were roughly divided into three periods. During one we learnt to handle the Chariots, manhandle them through holes we cut in the nets, attach dummy war-heads and find our way back to *Titania*. In another period we tried to keep fit, mainly hill walking but there were opportunities to sail, fish and once or twice try and learn some Highland dances in a village hall on the other side of the loch. In the third period we slept.

After a few months *Titania* moved to HHZ, a larger and deeper loch on the West Coast in the far North of Scotland. Here the routine was much the same but there was more night work, the exercises were longer and the dives often deeper, usually by accident. It was not necessary to go very deep to avoid being seen by lookouts. One day we were asked if we would transfer to X Craft, three-man midget submarines. We knew little about them although they were also members of the 12th Flotilla. We were reluctant to transfer, but the Captain of the Flotilla, who had made a special journey from his base in the Clyde, persuaded us to join the X Craft for their first operation, saying we could then return to Chariots without losing our position in the operation ladder.

X Craft were about fifty feet long with a displacement of some thirty tons, scaled down versions of larger submarines. A diesel engine, similar to those used in London buses, powered the boat on the surface and charged the batteries which underwater drove the boat. The Commanding Officer was the navigator, the First Lieutenant the electrician and when we dived kept the trim (maintained the correct buoyancy) by operating pumps. He also kept depth with the hydroplanes. An Engine Room Artificer (ERA) was responsible for the engine, all mechanical equipment and was at the helm when underway. However, each member of the crew had to be able to do some of the work of the others to provide an understudy for each job. In addition the First Lieutenant and the ERA had to be trained as divers.

A special feature of X Craft was the W & D (wet and dry) compartment. This small section between the control room and the battery compartment in the bow, also used as a bunk, had a hatch giving access to the casing (deck). It had watertight doors on either side to isolate it from the rest of the boat. If an X Craft ran into an A/S net a fully dressed diver could, with difficulty, enter the W & D, close the watertight doors and operate a pump to flood the W & D by pumping water from one of the ballast tanks into the W & D without disturbing the trim. To enable the hatch to be opened when the W & D was full, a small valve in the hatch had to be opened to equalise the pressure

78: Robert Aitken DSO, photographed in 1942 wearing RNVR Midshipman's uniform, a year before taking part in the midget submarine attack on the German battleship *Tirpitz*.

in the W & D with that outside. The diver climbed out, collected a compressed air cutter stowed in the casing and cut a hole in the net.

The Captain of the Flotilla, explaining the reason for his sudden request, said during training two divers had been drowned, and a last minute decision was taken to increase the crew to four by including a specialist diver. Charioteers in the same Flotilla were a natural choice and six were seconded to X Craft, much to the annoyance of their Commanders, who didn't want an extra body on board. Space was extremely limited and more importantly they had, understandably, no intention of sending a diver out if that could possibly be avoided. There were risks of the diver losing contact with his X Craft, by being on the wrong side of the net if a wire unexpectedly parted and let the X Craft surge through the hole he hadn't finished cutting, getting carried away by the current, getting his breathing bag cut by the jagged end of a wire he had just cut, or losing consciousness due to over exertion in deep water. A diver might allow some of his oxygen to escape and bubbles on the surface could attract the attention of enemy lookouts. There were many other hazards and there was a real risk a diver might draw attention to his X Craft or worse still compromise the entire operation.

The X Crafts' first target was that for which they had been specifically developed, to attack the German fleet in its protected anchorages in fiords on the Norwegian coast. In September 1943 major units of the German fleet were anchored in Kaa Fiord in the north of Norway, beyond the range of X Craft which had to be towed across the North Sea by large submarines. For security reasons it was decided the operation should sail from HHZ where, at different times, both Chariots and X Craft had trained. In mid August a Charioteer diver was allocated to each of the six X Craft. They began to familiarise themselves with the craft, the crew and practise cutting the X Craft through A/S nets. The mesh of A/T (anti-torpedo) nets was too small and the wire gauge too large to be cut by an X Craft's cutter.

At the beginning of September, two T and four S Class submarines fitted with special towing equipment arrived at HHZ. Towing trials and trials of changing over passage and operational crews at sea began. I was the diver of X7, commanded by Lieutenant B. C. G. Place, DSC, RN. Towed by HMS *Stubborn* we were the last but one to leave HHZ on the evening of 11 September. During the tow the X Craft remained submerged, apart from 15 minutes on the surface every six hours to ventilate. On the afternoon of the 15th, the tow parted and I was floated down in *Stubborn's* inflatable dinghy to pass the auxiliary tow to X7, a manoeuvre I hadn't rehearsed, but floating down was no problem. The return proved more difficult until I found a rope on the inflatable had attached itself to X7 and I was trying to pull both the inflatable and X7 back to *Stubborn.* Climbing aboard I found a very anxious CO because both boats had been on the surface in daylight for more than an hour and at risk of being spotted from the air.

Shortly before towing recommenced X6 appeared! Her tow had parted from HMS *Seanymph*, and with X7 in tow and X8 in company *Stubborn* started to look for *Seanymph*. The Admiralty was informed and passed the information to *Seanymph* who proceeded to intercept. However, before contact was made *Stubborn* had lost X8 and had to leave *Seanymph* to look for her errant charge whom in due course she found.

On the evening of the 18th, *Stubborn* transferred the four operational crew to X7 and took the three passage crew on board. On getting underway again the auxiliary tow parted and with some difficulty a two and a half inch wire rope was passed. On the 20th a floating mine caught in *Stubborn's* tow, slid down the wire rope and lodged on X7 bow. The CO got on the casing and kicked it clear! Shortly afterwards the tow was slipped and X7 set course on the surface to cross the declared minefield to the west of Soroy Sound during the night. After crossing the minefield another X Craft was sighted, almost certainly X5 which was later lost with all hands, and shouts of good luck were exchanged. Early in the morning of the 21st, X7 dived and proceeded up Stjernsund. Apart from having to dodge several vessels our passage was uneventful and the CO and the ERA took the opportunity to stretch out in the battery compartment. While the First Lieutenant kept the trim and depth I steered, which wasn't difficult. However when he wanted to check our position I had to do his job and come up to periscope depth. There had been little opportunity for me to practise this in HHZ, and as we proceeded up the fiord fresh water mixed with the sea water and pockets of different densities made it difficult to keep a stable trim.

At a depth of about nine feet in these conditions there is little room for error and on one occasion I had to shout to the First Lieutenant, 'Flood Q!', the emergency tank which could be rapidly flooded for a quick dive. To my surprise the CO, who I thought was asleep, heard my shout and was none too pleased at the thought we might have broken surface. On the evening of the 21st we sighted the Brattholm group of islands in Alten Fiord where we had planned to spend the night ventilating the boat, charging batteries and making good defects. One of these was the leaking exhaust pipe, but the flange of the spare one had been incorrectly drilled and the original had to be refitted and sealed with a mix of chewing gum, canvas and tape in roughly that order. Our night was somewhat disturbed by various small boats and minor war vessels. One came close enough to cause the CO, keeping watch on the casing, to call 'Dive, Dive, Dive', down the hatch. I was seated in the steering position where the valves which vented the tanks were located. This was the first time I had done this in pitch darkness and had difficulty in locating the right valves, another example of lack of training. The CO, at the best of times somewhat impatient, didn't like a crash dive being delayed in enemy waters.

Early on the 22nd, we left the shelter of the Brattholm Islands and headed for Kaa Fiord where *Tirpitz*, our target, German's largest and most powerful battleship was moored. The gate of the A/S net had been opened for a small trawler and we were able to follow through in her wake. Our luck and my relief at not having to cut our way through the nets was short lived. An outward bound boat forced us below periscope depth and whilst blinded X7 became entangled in a bunch of A/T nets, previously used to protect the German battleship *Lutzow,* which was then exercising at sea. Constant wriggling, hard ahead, hard astern, light trim, heavy trim did not extract us. We were concerned that our somewhat violent movements were disturbing the buoys holding up the nets and someone might investigate. The CO decided to stop wriggling and send me out to see what the problem was. I got into my diving suit but, as I was about to climb into the W & D, the CO realised we were free. An hour had been lost and the violent action had put the trim pump and gyro compass out of action.

We headed for the *Tirpitz*. Intending to go under the A/T nets, the CO ordered 75 feet but again we got caught. Little time was now left before the start of the first 'firing period', during which any of the three X Craft attacking *Tirpitz* could set their charges to explode. It was essential to get out as quickly as possible. Blowing to full buoyancy and going full astern extracted X7 but we broke surface alongside the buoys supporting the nets.

The CO was not sure exactly what happened during the next fifteen minutes or so. We got stuck in the nets again, this time at about 95 feet. Wriggling and blowing got us out but the compass had gone wild. To check our position the motor was stopped and X7 brought gently up for the CO to get a sighting. Much to his surprise he saw we were inside the A/T nets with the *Tirpitz* only about thirty yards away. He did not know whether we had passed under the nets, found a gap, perhaps where two sections overlapped, or by luck passed through the boat gate. X7 struck *Tirpitz* at twenty feet and slid under her keel where the starboard charge was released under B turret. After going astern the port charge was released, when the CO estimated we were under X turret.

Hoping to get out by going under the nets the CO ordered 100 feet but at 60 feet we were again caught. During the next 45 minutes X7 was in and out of several nets, had little compressed air left, was increasingly difficult to control and broke surface on more than one

OUNDLE'S WAR

occasion. Fortunately, we were too close for any of *Tirpitz* guns, but we heard bullets, probably machine gun, rattling on the casing but none penetrated the pressure hull. A few minutes before 0800, X7 settled on the bottom and the compressor was run to boost the last air bottle. We were very conscious that our charges were set to go off in less than an hour and any laid by either of the other two X Craft attacking *Tirpitz* might explode any time after 0800 am.

Indeed, Lieutenant Donald Cameron on X6, despite a flooded periscope and compasses out of action, had succeeded in breaking through the anti-torpedo nets and getting alongside *Tirpitz* before releasing both charges, scuttling his craft and then surrendering to the Germans. It was 7.25 am. Robert Aitken continued his story:

> Coming up to periscope depth to set the direction indicator and put as much distance as possible between X7 and the forthcoming explosion we ran into yet another net.
> Shortly after 0800 there was a tremendous explosion. It shook the net off X7 but on coming to the surface the CO saw *Tirpitz* was still afloat and wondered if the explosion had been a depth charge and took X7 to the bottom to survey the damage. Little structural damage could be seen but diving gauges and compasses were out of action and the boat proved impossible to control. It was decided to abandon X7 on the surface rather than escape using DSEA because of depth charge activity. Each time X7 broke surface bullets were heard on

79: Robert Aitken DSO, standing alongside the remains of the bow of X7 at Duxford. The craft was salvaged by an enthusiastic group of aqualung divers in 1975.
IWM DUX.91/2/3.

the casing, so the CO grabbed a rather dirty sweater, the whitest thing he could lay his hands on, and waving furiously, shouting 'Here goes the last of the Places,' clambered onto the casing through the W & D hatch. He saw X7 was about to ram a moored practice target and knowing X7 had very little buoyancy tried to close the hatch whilst I, following behind him, tried to push it open. An inrush of water both closed the hatch and sent X7 down to the bottom again at about, we thought, 120 feet.

On the bottom, the options of a DSEA escape or getting out on the surface, if we could get X7 there, were discussed. To do the latter the compressor and pumps would have to run and it was thought their noise would bring the depth charges closer. It was decided to flood the whole boat. The First Lieutenant would escape from the after hatch, the ERA through the W & D hatch and I, who was at that time next to the W & D, would follow the first one out. We waited until there had been no depth charging for some time, then strapped on the DSEA sets. We were unable to open some of the valves and flooding was very slow. In time the water reached the electrics, something fused, the boat filled with fumes and we had to go on oxygen. We then discovered that with our DSEA sets on it was impossible to change places, but the ERA signalled he was all right where he was. When I thought the boat was nearly flooded I entered the W & D to try the hatch. It would not open. On my return to the control room I found the ERA slumped on the deck. Checking his breathing bag I found it flat and the two small emergency cylinders empty. Without oxygen he had drowned. I returned to the W & D and tried the hatch again. It wouldn't open. Then my oxygen bottle ran out. I broke open my two emergency cylinders but at that depth they only seemed to give me an extra couple of breaths, but enough to try the hatch again. It opened and I climbed out by standing on the WC housed in the W & D. As I rose the pressures reduced, the oxygen in my lungs expanded and I could breathe. My breathing bag inflated and provided the buoyancy required to shoot me to the surface. As I rose the pressure continued to reduce and it was essential to breathe out to avoid bursting a lung. I unrolled the apron under the breathing bag and held it out at arm's length to act as a brake to slow up the ascent. I remember thinking how pleased my instructor would have been to see the correct drill being carried out!

My delight on reaching the surface was short lived. *Tirpitz* was still afloat and there was no sign of the First Lieutenant. A motor boat picked me up and I was taken aboard *Tirpitz*, stripped, given a blanket and taken below for a preliminary interrogation. Five other X Craftsmen had already been questioned and the main line was, 'You must give us sufficient information so that we can convince the Gestapo you are a British Naval Officer and not a saboteur. If you don't we will have to hand you over to them.'

Then we were put on a train and taken to the Naval Interrogation Camp. After six more weeks in solitary we were transferred to Marlag O, the POW camp for Naval Officers, except X5's ERA who was sent to the ratings camp nearby.

In view of the damage that had been inflicted on their battleship — the pride of Hitler's navy after the loss of *Bismarck* in May 1941 — one might have expected the Germans to react even more menacingly. Relationships with his captors on board *Tirpitz* depended on when you arrived, explained Robert Aitken. 'Only the crew of X6 were on board before the charges exploded. Understandably the German officers were nervous and excited and inclined to emphasise their threats by sticking revolvers into ribs. By the time I arrived everyone had calmed down and relationships were formal.' He was then locked in a cage used to store hammocks, all the cells having been taken by his CO and the crew of X6. The following day they were all put aboard a trawler, kept in solitary confinement and taken to Tromso from where another trawler took them to Tronheim. 'The only contact with German naval ratings was on the trawlers taking us down the Norwegian coast. They were friendly and surreptitiously gave us cigarettes. I sensed the comradeship of seafarers to whom the sea is the common and most powerful enemy.' On the train, in a carriage modified for prisoners and manned by POW camp staff, relationships were cool or cold depending on the duty guard.

'With hindsight I think the conception and execution of the operation was too hasty or not provided with enough resources,' believes Robert Aitken. But in spite of all the unexpected difficulties, and the sad loss of crew from the X craft, Operation 'Source' had been a success. The *Tirpitz* log makes clear that complete surprise was achieved. The order to close watertight doors and man the AA guns was not given until 15 minutes after the first sighting of an X craft.

Although not sunk, the *Tirpitz* suffered considerable damage to her hull, machinery and armaments, including fuel tanks, all three engines, two gun turrets, her two aircraft, and her lighting and electrical equipment.

Temporary repairs were started in Kaa Fiord, but it was then decided that *Tirpitz* would have to be repaired in a northern port. In April, more than six months after the attack, *Tirpitz* was moved out of Kaa Fiord. There she had been immune from air attacks by being moored under the high and steep sides of the fiord. On her way south to be repaired *Tirpitz* came within bombing range and was attacked by Lancasters of 617 (Dambusters) Squadron. An RAF attack caused further damage before the battleship was finally destroyed by one of their blockbuster bombs on 12 November 1944.

80: A survivor of Operation 'Source':
Robert Aitken DSO, in 1995 during a visit to Oundle.

THREE ~ ACTIVE SERVICE

Robert Aitken spent the rest of the war as a prisoner, but was awarded the Distinguished Service Order for his part in Operation 'Source'. The attack on the *Tirpitz* eliminated the threat to Atlantic convoys which the German battleship, the largest built in Europe up to that time, had presented for the previous two years.[56]

Godfrey Place, Commanding Officer of X7, received the Victoria Cross and remained in the Navy after the war, becoming Admiral Commanding Reserves and Director-General of Naval Recruiting. He must have been impressed by the young Oundelian who had served under him. He was to send his son Charles to be educated at Oundle in 1963, and visited the School for the General CCF Inspection in 1968.

81: Rear Admiral Godfrey Place, VC, CB, CVO, DSC, at Oundle School's General CCF Inspection in 1968.

A victory which Churchill described as 'a naval episode of high honour and importance,' and of which an ex-Oundle School boy could be proud, was the sinking of the *Scharnhorst* on Boxing Day 1943 in the Battle of North Cape off the coast of Norway. Lieutenant Denis Swithinbank, awarded the Distinguished Service Cross for escaping from a German prisoner-of-war camp in Greece two years before, was mentioned in despatches for his part in the sinking of the German battlecruiser. It would be natural to feel that he had, without knowing it, done something to avenge fellow-pupil Robert Parkinson, a near contemporary of his at the School, who had died heroically in the attack on the *Scharnhorst*, *Gneisenau* and *Prinz Eugen* in February 1942. But Denis Swithinbank makes it clear that the notion of vengeance never entered his thoughts: 'I find the term inappropriate in the context of the War at Sea, which was always of necessity an impersonal one.'

Nonetheless the Royal Navy's success was one of the turning-points in the Battle of the Atlantic. 'The sinking of the *Scharnhorst* not only removed the worst menace to our Arctic convoys, but gave new freedom to our Home Fleet,' wrote the Prime Minister. 'We no longer had to be prepared at our average moment against German heavy ships breaking out into the Atlantic at their selected moment. This was an important relief.'[57]

The Invasion of Italy: Delivering 'Major Martin'

In April 1943 Lieutenant Norman Jewell was summoned to Submarine Headquarters where he was given the following top-secret document.

OPERATION MINCEMEAT

1. *Object*

To cause a briefcase containing documents to drift ashore as near as possible to HUELVA in Spain in such circumstances that it will be thought to have been washed ashore from an aircraft which crashed at sea when the case was being taken by an officer from the UK to Allied Forces HQ in North Africa.

2. *Method*

A dead body dressed in the battle-dress uniform of a Major, Royal Marines, and wearing a 'Mae West,' will be taken out in a submarine, together with the briefcase and a rubber dinghy.

The body will be packed fully clothed and ready (and wrapped in a blanket to prevent friction) in a tubular air-tight container (which will be labelled as 'Optical Instruments').

The container is just under 6 feet 6 inches long and just under 2 feet in diameter and has no excrescences of any kind on the sides. The end which opens has a flush-fitting lid which is held tightly in position by a number of nuts and has fitted on its exterior in clips a box-spanner with a permanent tommy-bar which is chained to the lid.

Both ends are fitted with handles which fold down flat. It will be possible to lift the container by using both handles or even by using the handle in the lid alone, but it would be better not to take the whole weight on the handle at the other end, as the steel of which the container is made is of light gauge to keep the weight as low as possible. The approximate total weight when the container is full will be 400 lb.

When the container is closed the body will be packed round with a certain amount of dry ice. The container should therefore be opened on deck, as the dry ice will give off carbon dioxide.

3. *Position*

The body should be put into the water as close inshore as prudently possible and as near to HUELVA as possible, preferably to the north-west of the river mouth.

According to the Hydrographic Department, the tides in that area run mainly up and down the coast, and every effort should therefore be made to choose a period with an onshore wind. South-westerly winds are in fact the prevailing winds in that area at this time of the year.

The latest information about the tidal streams in that area, as obtained from the Superintendent of Tides, is attached.

4. *Delivery of the Package*

The package will be brought up to the port of departure by road on whatever day is desired, preferably as close to the sailing day as possible. The briefcase will be handed over at the same time to the Captain of the submarine. The rubber dinghy will also be a separate parcel.

5. *Disposal of the Body*

When the body is removed from the container all that will be necessary will be to fasten the chain attached to the briefcase through the belt of the trench-coat, which will be the outer garment on the body. The chain is of the type worn under the coat, round the chest and out through the sleeve. At the end is a 'dog-lead' type of clip for attaching to the handle of the briefcase and a similar clip for forming the loop round the chest. It is this loop that should be made through the belt of the trench-coat as if the officer has slipped the chain off for comfort in the aircraft, but has nevertheless kept it attached to him so that the bag should not either be forgotten or slide away from him in the aircraft.

The body should then be deposited in the water, as should also be the rubber dinghy. As this should drift at a different speed from the body, the exact position at which it is released is unimportant, but it should be near the body, but not too near if that is possible.

6. *Those in the Know at Gibraltar*

Steps have been taken to inform F.O.I.C. [Flag Officer in Charge] Gibraltar and his S.O.(I). [Staff Officer, Intelligence]. No one else there will be in the picture.

7. *Signals*

If the operation is successfully carried out, a signal should be made 'MINCEMEAT completed'. If that is made from Gibraltar the S.O.(I) should be asked to send it addressed to D.N.I. [Director of Naval Intelligence] (PERSONAL). If it can be made earlier it should be in accordance with orders from F.O.S. [Flag Officer, Submarines (Admiral Barry)].

8. *Cancellation*

If the operation has to be cancelled a signal will be made 'Cancel MINCEMEAT'. In that case the body and container should be sunk in deep water; as the container may have positive buoyancy, it may either have to be weighted or water may have to be allowed to enter. In the latter case care must be taken that the body does not escape. The briefcase should be handed to the S.O.(I) at Gibraltar, with instructions to burn the contents unopened, if there is no possibility of taking that course earlier. The rubber dinghy should be handed to the S.O.(I) for disposal.

9. *Abandonment*

If the operation has to be abandoned, a signal should be made 'MINCEMEAT abandoned' as soon as possible (see Para. 7 above).

10. *Cover*

This is a matter for consideration. Until the operation actually takes place, it is thought that the labelling of the container 'Optical Instruments' will provide sufficient cover. It is suggested that the cover after the operation has been completed should be that it is hoped to trap a very active German agent in this neighbourhood, and it is hoped that sufficient evidence can be obtained by this means to get the Spaniards to eject him. The importance of dealing with this man should be impressed on the crew, together with the fact that any leakage that may *ever* take place about this will compromise our power to get the Spaniards to act in such cases; also that they will never learn whether we were successful in this objective, as the whole matter will have to be conducted in secrecy with the Spaniards or we won't be able to get them to act.

It is in fact most important that the Germans and Spaniards should accept these papers in accordance with Para. 1. If they should suspect that the papers are a 'plant', it might have far-reaching consequences of great magnitude.

(Signed) E.E.S. MONTAGU,
Lt.-Cdr., R.N.V.R.
31.3.43

The former Oundle School boy to whom this document had been entrusted was indeed to play a key role in a mission of the greatest importance. Operation 'Mincemeat' was to be a key which would open one of the doors of Hitler's 'Fortress Europe' to the Allies approaching on its southern flank. The meticulous attention to detail in Lieutenant Commander Ewen Montagu's letter had all the hallmarks of a top-secret military intelligence operation.

Norman Jewell, still Commanding Officer of the submarine HMS *Seraph* at the age of only 29, had been chosen following his part in the preparations for Operation 'Torch' in November of the previous year.

On 19 April Norman Jewell and the crew of HMS *Seraph* left Holy Loch with their unusual passenger, nicknamed 'Major Martin'. Lieutenant Commander Montagu's book *The Man Who Never Was*, the basis of a film of the same title about Operation 'Mincemeat', used the following eye-witness account of the voyage:

> As the *Seraph* slid from the shadow of her depot ship and down the Clyde, the commander — he was only twenty-nine — saluted from the conning tower, then went below.
>
> Of the five officers and fifty ratings on board, only he knew the secret of his odd piece of cargo.

~ ✧✧✧ ~

The cylindrical metal canister now rested in a forward chamber of the submarine.

Because of its weight and shape, the six ratings who manoeuvred it into place joked about 'John Brown's body'. And there was many a wisecrack about 'our new shipmate, Charlie'.

Today, ten years later, those fifty ex-members of the *Seraph's* crew will be shaken to learn how close to the truth they were.

They had been told in the briefing for the trip that the metal canister contained a secret weather-reporting device to be floated experimentally off the coast of Spain. It was actually marked 'Handle with Care — Optical Instruments — for special F.O.S. shipment.'

For ten days the *Seraph* sailed and her crew saw nothing of the sun. Surfacing only at night, she was off Huelva, on the south-west coast of Spain, undetected and according to schedule, on April 30.

The spot selected for floating 'Major Martin' ashore was 1,600 yards off the mouth of the Huelva river.

In the afternoon the Seraph ventured an inshore reconnaissance. The periscope revealed a fishing fleet of about fifty vessels. But the prevailing mist and a mile detour helped the submarine to escape detection. Then she went back to the sea bed for the rest of the day.

~ ✧✧✧ ~

Zero hour was 4.30 in the morning. When the *Seraph* surfaced again it was dark as pitch. The new moon had set and the ebb tide was just on the turn.

Through the conning tower went the five officers, and the submarine was trimmed down until an inch of the calm sea lapped over the casing. The mysterious canister was hauled aloft.

Only then, with all ratings below, did Lieutenant Jewell let his officers into the secret. Lieutenant Jewell told them that the canister at their feet contained a corpse. The operation, he said, was part of an Allied plan to deceive the enemy into drawing his defensive forces away from the spot selected for the main thrust of the Mediterranean invasion.

Phoney invasion plans were to be 'planted' on the enemy through the medium of the body of this man purporting to be 'Major Martin', victim of an air crash at sea.

THREE ~ ACTIVE SERVICE

Huelva had been chosen for the 'plant' because it was known that the German agent there was being well fed with military intelligence by local collaborators.

What a story to be sprung on you suddenly in the middle of the night with the Atlantic lapping round your boots. But if the junior officers were shaken by their commander's dramatic and gruesome revelation, they did not betray it.

Only reaction was the comment from one of them: 'Isn't it pretty unlucky carrying dead bodies around?'

~ ✧✧✧ ~

Then quickly and quietly the five set about their task. While three kept watch, the other helped Lieutenant Jewell to unlock the bolts of the canister with the spanner attached to the case. Ten minutes they worked before the lid came away.

Then the blanketed body was slid gently from its vacuum coffin. For a moment the tension was relieved as the officers stiffened with silent respect in the presence of death.

On his knees again, Lieutenant Jewell plucked at knotted tapes and the blanket fell away.

There followed the final check. Were the Major's uniform and badges intact? Was his hand gripping the handle of the all-important despatch case? Was the case securely strapped to his belt?

Everything in order, Jewell bent low to inflate the Major's 'Mae West'.

Only one thing remained — though it was not in the routine instructions. Four young officers bent bare heads in simple tribute as their commander murmured what prayers he could remember from the Burial Service.

For them, sworn to secrecy, these words from Psalm 39 held a special significance:

'I will keep my mouth as it were with a bridle: while the ungodly is in my sight. I held my tongue and spake nothing: I kept silent, yea, even from good words; but it was pain and grief to me.'

A gentle push and the unknown warrior was drifting inshore with the tide on his last, momentous journey. 'Major Martin' had gone to the war.

The former Oundle School boy's role in the operation was crucial, and his daring was acknowledged by its originator. 'The risk that Lieutenant Jewell had taken in going so close to the shore had given us every possible chance of success,' said Lieutenant Commander Montagu. It was not long before evidence of this success reached London. 'Major Martin' had been carrying a letter revealing details of the Allies' totally fictitious plans for the invasion of Greece, and an examination of the briefcase and its contents, when it was

82: Captain Norman Jewell, MBE, DSC, on a visit to Oundle in 1995.

finally returned to England by the Spanish authorities, showed that the letter had been examined and its envelope re-sealed. German agents in Madrid had passed on the vital information to Berlin, and Hitler's Commander-in-Chief of Naval Staff, Admiral Dönitz himself, had seen a translation of the letter and been convinced of its veracity. 'Major Martin' had done his job perfectly. 'Mincemeat swallowed whole', was the coded message sent to Churchill by his Chiefs of Staff.

The aim of 'Mincemeat' had been to divert the Germans' attention from Sicily, the intended landing point of the Allies for the coming invasion of Europe from North Africa. 'The operation succeeded beyond our wildest dreams,' wrote Churchill's Chief of Staff Lord Ismay. 'To have spread-eagled the German defensive effort right across Europe, even to the extent of sending German vessels away from Sicily itself, was a remarkable achievement. Those who landed in Sicily, as well as their families, have cause to be especially grateful.' So convinced were the German Intelligence Service and the High Command by the contents of 'Major Martin's briefcase that on 23 July, nearly a fortnight after the Allied landing in Sicily, Hitler still believed that the main operation was going to be an invasion of Greece, sending Rommel there two days later to command the German forces that were being assembled.[58]

The Assault on Italy

Sicily, invaded on 10 July, was in Allied hands by 17 August, allowing British and Canadian forces to land in Italy on 3 September. A fierce battle with the German defending forces under Kesselring took place following the Allied landings at Salerno on 8 September, but the enemy was forced to withdraw northwards.

During the invasion of Italy many Oundle people were saddened to hear in September 1943 news of the death of a young man whom they knew as a resident of the town as well as the eldest son of the School Chaplain, the Reverend M. Brown. Lieutenant Commander Anthony Brown had attended the School as a boarder, leaving School House in 1921 after being its Head of House, and joining the Royal Naval Volunteer Reserve in 1939 and transferring to the Royal Navy in the following year. Mentioned in despatches for 'skill and bravery in mine-laying operations in the Mediterranean early in 1943,' he lost his life while on HMS *Abdiel*, where he was Chief Engineer.[59]

Major Russell Elliott had left Oundle School's Laxton House in 1930, joining the Honourable Artillery Corps on the outbreak of war, and later obtaining a commission in an infantry regiment. He had been among the first to enter Tunis, and took part in the landing at Salerno. His conduct under fire drew from his Company Sergeant-Major the following words of praise:

> I have been with the one and only Capt. Elliott as company commander. I would go into action any day with him, as he is a fine leader of men when shells are dropping around and we are in a tight corner. I was with him when he was wounded at Alamein; he carried on then until the battle was over.

Sadly, Russell Elliott was to die in action in Normandy on D-Day the following year.[60]

A Hero of the SAS

Another distinguished former Oundle School boy who played an important but top secret part in the Italian campaign, and whose bravery was praised by the Germans, was Captain

THREE ~ ACTIVE SERVICE

Patrick Dudgeon. Having been Head of St Anthony House, which he left in 1938, he had joined the Royal Corps of Signals, and won the Military Cross for 'gallant and distinguished service in the field'. Later he was engaged on various secret and dangerous missions by submarine and air in North Africa while serving with the Special Air Service Regiment.

Operation 'Speedwell' was Patrick Dudgeon's last mission. The plan was to reduce the rate of German reinforcements to the south of Italy by attacking rail communications between Genoa and Spezia, Bologna and Pistoia, Bologna and Prato, and Florence and Arezzo. Had the operation been properly supported in terms of aircraft and supplies, it has been argued, the strategic advantage gained would have been immense.

As the sun set over Kairouan in Tunisia on 7 September, two aircraft took off from North Africa carrying two groups of SAS men. By midnight they had landed successfully in the mountains north of Spezia, some hundreds of miles behind the German lines. Patrick Dudgeon set off with his six men to attack the Genoa-Spezia railway, the other group under Captain Pinckney being dropped south of Bologna.

Patrick Dudgeon divided his group into three, each to deal with a separate objective before meeting at a rendezvous. Two members of his group succeeded in blowing up two trains on the Spezia-Bologna line, and finally made their way back to British lines. The success of his group's important mission earned a letter of thanks sent to Patrick Dudgeon's unit by General Alexander. But two others in the group were never seen again, and were presumed killed. Patrick Dudgeon, with Trooper Brunt, then ambushed a German amphibian and succeeded in killing a number of the enemy before being captured near Parma. It was clear to the Germans from the explosives he was carrying that the former Oundle School boy had been hoping to reach a further objective, but nothing could make him give any information about the target. In the presence of his staff the German General responsible for the interrogation expressed admiration for the British officer's courage, but gave the order for him and his companion to be shot the next morning on Hitler's orders.

News of Patrick Dudgeon's capture and death came after the war in the form of a letter to his father from the German army Captain who had acted as interpreter at his interrogation, and who wanted to fulfil his pledge to the person he described as 'the bravest English officer I have ever met'. One can only imagine the grim circumstances which had prompted a German to salute such courage.

A fund was set up at the School in 1949 in Patrick Dudgeon's memory, to encourage individual initiative and the spirit of adventure.[61]

83: Captain Patrick Laurence Dudgeon MC.

The Aegean Campaign

With the anti-war coup d'état against Mussolini on 25 July and the capitulation of Italy on 3 September, the Joint Allied Command felt that an advantage might be seized by occupying the large number of Aegean islands which were garrisoned by Italian troops, including Samos, Leros and Kos. Rhodes, however, was still in German hands.

Robert Butler, serving with the Queen's Own Royal West Kent Regiment, was part of the British force which embarked in Haifa on 19th September, arriving on Samos two days later with the aim of making contact with the Italian garrison. Within a short time, first-class German troops from the Greek mainland combined with German naval forces had engaged the Allied troops. The only airfield available for the latter's protection, situated on the island of Kos, was lost on 3 October. Following a severe bombing, Leros was invaded on 12 November and Robert Butler, as Company Commander, was given the task of landing on the island and repulsing the enemy. He gives a dramatic account of the battle for Leros in his book *Nine Lives*:

At 0830 we moved forward in complete silence and I began to think that the enemy had abandoned the highest bump on Rachi Ridge, which was our objective, during the night. Not until Hewett's platoon was within fifty yards of the crest did all hell let loose from the German position. I saw Hewett's leading right section almost on top of them when his men started going down and Hewett (Second Lieutenant Hewett, one of his platoon commanders) was killed. I decided to run forward so that there would be an officer on the objective, and as Company Commander, I would be well placed to marshal my second wave in. I paused in my tracks to look over my shoulder to see how my second wave was faring and saw that they had passed through the start line and were beginning to come down the little saddle which separated the start line from the Germans. At that moment, the enemy machine guns switched their fire onto this second wave and I saw my old friend CSM Spooner and several of those with him fall. He was in fact killed instantly. Those in the second wave who had not breasted the rise took cover. Once the

84: Lt Col Robert Butler MBE, MC, hero of the Battle for Leros.

Germans had their heads up and were not fired on they had complete fire superiority over the saddle and anything that moved on the forward slope of our start line Point 103 was mercilessly machine gunned. I turned my attention to Hewett's other sections and saw the left hand one go round the left of the German position and vanish. His middle section were crawling about right under the noses of the Germans and I joined them. I told them to worm their way round via the left and attack from there whilst I remained fairly central to marshal the others in when they arrived. They never did. I was beginning to feel isolated as the only live person on the

THREE ~ ACTIVE SERVICE

front apron of the German position. My nearest neighbour was a dead subaltern of the Royal Irish Fusiliers who must have been lying there since their attack the previous morning. A silence fell on the immediate area. Since the left side of the objective seemed the only entry point I crawled round to the left feeling extremely lonely. I gingerly stood up and moved forward in a crouched position until I was suddenly confronted by a German light machine gunner lying completely in the open but just over the crest. The military term is 'a reverse slope position'. We both saw each other simultaneously and I thanked my stars that I had played scrum-half for my Regiment for a whole season. I flung myself to the ground, shooting my feet rearwards at the same time so that I fell full length. His stream of bullets crackled a good two feet above me and I wormed backwards as fast as I could. He never fired a second burst and his job had obviously been to protect his right flank and not to expose himself by crawling forward. I then wormed my way across the front of the German position until I was in front of their forward strong-point, a stone sangar. They seemed to have no idea that I was there and no-one fired at me. I was to be on my own there for nearly three hours. I still had my Luger which I had acquired in Tamra in Palestine and had managed to get a supply of 9 mm ammunition for it whilst in Samos. It was then much used by Axis troops, but rarely in our Army. I wriggled into a natural hollow a few inches deep, alongside one of the outcrops of rock which dot all those hillside fields. It was about eight inches high and had a base around three feet by two.

The next time their machine gun was poked through the slit they had made in the rough stone sangar I was already in the aim position and let fly. A long burst was later directed by them across the valley to where my second wave was still lurking. The sun was out and I repeatedly tried to flash a reflected beam at them by using the base of my wrist-watch. I also hoped that if they got their act together and continued the assault that any covering fire that they planned would take my unwilling presence into account! In between times I kept the dark slit in the stonework, which was no more than thirty feet from me, covered with my Luger. I got in three shots altogether and they all went through the slit, or they would have ricocheted all over the place. Always the face vanished and a machine gun would be poked out to fire blindly across the valley. I suppose a 9 mm pistol shot close-to would sound not unlike a sniper's rifle from one of our people across the saddle.

Meanwhile communication between me and the rest of the world was nil, and the first thing to prove it was a series of soft crumps behind my old start line followed by the whistling down of our own mortar bombs all round me. I nestled into my hollow, dug my face into the earth and eased my tin hat back to protect the back of my neck. The mortar team which had come to support us after we had left our start line was from our friends the Royal Irish Fusiliers. They took their time, and the attack seemed to last till all eternity. They were aiming at the stone machine gun-post, and I was literally part of the target. When the last of the bombs landed and I had counted up to twenty I gingerly raised my head and looked around. The nearest bomb had landed just the other side of the little outcrop, about four feet from my head. Our 3" mortar bombs were designed to explode when the elongated nose hit the ground, thus showering metal pieces outwards with a flat trajectory. The tail-fin of the bomb lands in the centre of the shallow crater and there it was.

I felt that I would be in an extremely uncomfortable position if Ben Tarleton (the battalion commander) mounted a battalion attack to compensate for 'A' Company's inadequacy and wormed my way round to the right to see if there was any chance of shooting up the men manning the post from that side. I had already seen no entrance to the left. I thought I might apply Major Grant-Taylor's principle of surprising them from the rear and shooting them in the order in which they moved. I hastily dismissed the thought that they might all move at once! I soon found that I was out of luck, as that flank was also guarded by a single light machine gunner lying in the open slightly back in a reverse slope position. I somehow managed to repeat the gymnastics I had rehearsed earlier on the left, missed his stream of bullets and wormed my way back. For the first time, the men in the post spotted me. I fired two shots at faces which appeared, then a plastic grenade was lobbed over the top and rolled towards me.

I remembered an old Charlie Chaplin film as I leaped out of its way and lay down to my right. I knew that another would come down there and that I would have to go and lie down in the wispy cloud of dust which the first had created. After this had happened and I ran back to the right again, I knew that next time there would be two simultaneously, one each side, and there were. I ran back about fifteen yards and took cover behind a pile of small rocks just before they took courage and popped their heads up and managed to be down before a long burst of machine gun fire began to tear into my little mound of rocks. These are made by the local farmers who walk round every month or so and pick up any stones and small rocks which have worked their way to the surface.

The whanging and pinging that followed was most disquieting, as bits of stone and bent bullets sailed over my head and my cover began to erode. I decided that it was time to make a move. I rubbed all the chinagraph markings of the battle plans off my map, and took a large swig from an Eno's bottle of Italian brandy which someone had pressed into my hand when I disembarked at Portalago, and began to run like a madman down the Eastern side of the ridge towards our own positions. In the course of the morning I had worked my way across from the Western side.

It was downhill and I went like the wind, weaving left and right, and every German who saw me had a go. Eventually I just had to have a breather and flung myself down as if I had been hit whilst my heart raced and I puffed and panted. The firing stopped and I sighed with relief. Then some vicious opponent fired a single shot and a bullet hit between the underside of my wrist and the ground on which it lay and flung my whole arm up in the air, as if in a sort of gesture of surrender. 'Damn,' I thought, 'now the beggars will know that I'm alive after all,' and off I set once more, aiming more down-hill and out of their line of sight.

I eventually made my way round to the rear of my held-up second wave and climbed up to them to everyone's surprise. On my way up I encountered an officer of the regiment who had felt unable to spare us any grenades. He was shouting, 'The Jerries are coming, the Jerries are coming.' I pointed my Luger at his midriff and told him to go back to his men, or else. He said, 'Don't be a fool, I'm carrying an urgent message.' I reflected that his presence in the front line would probably do more harm than good and allowed him to proceed. All the racket he had heard was the Jerries firing at one frightened Butler.

The machine-gunning had alerted both sides as I crawled forward for the last fifty yards, and when I reached Bill Grimshaw (my second-in-command) he looked a bit shifty, but I simply told him where I had been all the morning, asked why there had been no look-out who would have seen me and my signals, and then took stock of what we had left. The answer was one platoon and Company Headquarters, less their dead and wounded, some of whom were still unrecovered on the slope that faced the enemy.

I got on to the only wireless set that worked, the set to Battalion Headquarters, and managed to raise the Adjutant, Donald Cropper and then Ben Tarleton. I told him that I could divide my remnants into two weak platoons but that with all my subalterns and my CSM killed or wounded, I and my second-in-command Grimshaw would have to command them. I said that I was sure that a left hook would take the position, and that I would support them in with my own Brens which I would deploy to the right so that they could keep up fire to the last moment. I asked for smoke and for continued use of the Royal Irish Fusiliers' mortar detachment, which had so nearly written me off that morning; all good chaps who said, 'Sorry Sorr,' when I recounted my experience of their morning's firing. There was only one 25 pounder gun left in action and I was given its support to fire smoke. I said that we could attack

THREE ~ ACTIVE SERVICE

at 1430 hours, and we did. The two wounded subalterns were Johns, who was temporarily blinded by the flash of a near miss from a bomb, and Groom who had a flesh wound in the calf. It was bandaged with a field dressing and he seemed to be walking alright, but said he couldn't face the walk. I put him in charge of the Bren Guns. My instructions were that the guns would fire in turn, never together and that the one firing would rake the ridge in front of us, its whole length, to be taken up by the next etc, until we took the position. The moment we were seen on the position I wanted them up there at the double. At 2.30, the mortar, the 25 pounder and the first Bren opened up, and off we went at a fast trot with bayonets fixed. I took them all well down the Western side of the saddle and then we turned in and rolled the position up from left to right. Unfortunately I was shot in the thigh, right through the sciatic nerve, and bowled over; and Grimshaw had a nasty wound in the wrist which hit bone. We did however clear the entire position, and seeing no signs of movement from my Bren gunners, I sent a runner back with orders for them to join me at the double to defeat the inevitable counter-attack. The runner returned to report that the CO of the regiment through which I had attacked had refused to allow my men and their Brens to leave his Battalion area. I was absolutely shattered. I had been obliged to leave my Brens to provide my covering fire because the men of the regiment supposed to support me had been fighting more or less continuously for three days without sleep and seemed reluctant to put their heads up; and now their CO was keeping my men and their Brens to protect his own positions.

I crawled forward on my elbows to look to the North and, taking a peep over a low wall, whilst one of my chaps put a field-dressing on my leg, I found that I could see to the far end of Leros. The appearance of my head produced streams of German bullets from every direction which clattered against the two foot thick wall. I was down to about twelve men with only rifles and bayonets, both Grimshaw and I were wounded, and in my case I could only proceed on hands, bottom and one leg.

My Regimental History states, 'Major Butler, who had himself been badly wounded in the knee in the final assault, realised that he had insufficient men to hold the position and as his requests for reinforcements were unanswered, he ordered a withdrawal to Point 103.' The truth is that I never asked for any reinforcements, but for my own men and my own Bren guns to join me on the objective which we had captured with such heavy loss of life, and could have held with my eleven Brens and the 22 men who manned them against anything the Germans threw at us. With no automatic weapon, however, and the Luftwaffe's air supremacy, it was only a matter of minutes before we would be bombed out of existence, and my survivors would have had short shrift from the Brandenburgers, who would not have appreciated being thrown off Point 100.

I took my remnants almost straight down the Western slopes of Pt. 100 before turning South towards our own positions. I had been so preoccupied by the prickles which were assaulting my bottom that I was quite taken by surprise to find us being machine-gunned from the air. Now that I was no longer effectively controlling a military unit I was able to take these things in. One of my men said, 'They've been at it all day Sir, haven't you noticed?' I honestly hadn't, and even to this day my memories are crisp and clear about the ground and the ground battle and only hazily do I remember the odd aeroplane. Our tin hats screened us from the sky unless we made the mistake of looking up, which we were trained to avoid.

As we got further down the slope, I spotted a couple of jeeps on the mountain road which led back towards the valley in which Battalion Headquarters had been sited. Both jeeps carried stretchers but only one was used, for me, as I was the only walking wounded who couldn't walk. The worst injured of the others climbed into the spare seats of the jeeps and the others walked on down to Battalion Headquarters. My jeep turned off at a cross-roads called 'The Anchor' and went on down to Portalago. As I made myself comfortable on my stretcher which was laid across the back of the jeep, over where the rear seat is situated, I thought my dangers for the day were now over, but my feet stuck out on one side and my head on the other and on that narrow road, bounded by uneven stone walls, I missed decapitation by inches at least twice and had to plead with the driver, when in doubt, to keep to the left and let the walls hit my feet.

Down at Portalago the quayside was littered with stretchers each bearing a wounded soldier awaiting evacuation. This could not take place until at best an hour after darkness, as the naval vessels to evacuate us could not leave their hiding places in the surrounding islands until darkness had fallen. A Medical Officer appeared and insisted on giving me a shot of morphine. I was in no pain whatsoever as my leg was completely numb and remained so for nearly three weeks. He then said, 'We can't have senior officers lying around out here, I'll get you moved to the hospital.' He indicated a buff coloured building which had already been bombed and its nearest door was hanging drunkenly by one hinge. I said, 'Please leave me here with the others, I don't want to go in there and probably be buried with rubble in the next air attack.' By now two nights of little sleep, followed by one night of no sleep, followed by more nerve-shattering experiences than one would expect in a decade, plus the effect of the morphia beginning to tell, weakened my resistance and I found myself being carried through the drunken door. My last memory was of saying, 'I know what's going to happen, the boat will come in and everyone will be loaded on except me because I'll be forgotten.' I was assured that I would not be forgotten and closed my eyes. The next I remember was my shoulder being shaken and a voice saying, 'I'm very sorry Major, but we did forget you and the minesweeper is nearly full, they're now taking walking wounded only.' I peered into the darkness which now prevailed.

I felt that I had had enough of Leros, flung off the brown Army blanket which covered me, leaped up onto my good leg and said, 'I'm walking wounded', and began to hop towards the quay on my left leg. Two of my soldiers who had seen me taken into the dark and unlit hospital appeared out of the darkness. Both had their arms in slings, luckily different arms, so they fell in on either side of me and helped me to the gangplank. I believe we were the last three on board as the gangplank was already being manned. A Naval Officer shouted, 'Find yourselves somewhere to lie down on the open deck, there's no more space below.' I settled down on the already crowded after-deck, grateful to be on board at all and hoping we would make a safe passage to Turkish waters. In next to no time an officer appeared and cast an eye over his charges. I thought he looked familiar and then he saw me. 'Into my cabin Sir,' he said, with a broad smile of welcome. He looked relaxed and confident and had obviously overcome the stunned shock that his lapse the previous day had done to him. He came in to see me for a minute or two after we had cleared Leros waters and been at sea for about twenty minutes. He had already heard that I had been wounded, and asked me how we had got on. It was only then that I realised that I had only been on Leros for twenty-seven hours. It seemed like two lifetimes. We had left around 2 am and Leros fell in the early afternoon.

When we returned in 1977 I was amazed to see that the door of the hospital was still hanging on one hinge and the interior was still full of rubble. The slit trenches between the trees and the hospital were still as I remembered them and had not been filled in; presumably left as a memorial. I took Phoebe (my wife) up to Rachi Ridge and found the outcrop of rock which had saved my life from the mortar bomb. I stirred up the earth where the bomb had landed, and out came a bomb fragment over an inch long. It now lives in a glass case amongst other souvenirs and treasures.[62]

Robert Butler was awarded the Military Cross for his brave leadership in the attack on Rachi Ridge.

THREE ~ ACTIVE SERVICE

The War in the Air: Bomber Command at Work
At the Casablanca Conference of January 1943 the purpose of strategic bombing by the Allied Air Forces was defined as 'the progressive destruction and dislocation of the German military, industrial and economic system, and the undermining of the morale of the German people to a point where their capacity for armed resistance is fatally weakened'.

The application of this principle was seen in operations such as the Battle of the Ruhr, a series of 43 major air-raids between March and July 1943, ranging from Stuttgart to Aachen. Incendiaries were used, but also explosive bombs as heavy as 8,000lb. The RAF continued to bomb by night, while the Americans bombed by day. This was followed by the Battle of Hamburg, involving a series of 33 major attacks between July and November. 17,000 bomber sorties were made, opening with a raid on July 24 by 791 bombers. Three days later the city was hit by 787 bombers, and on the 29th by 777. A fourth attack, on 2 August, was less effective, but horrendous damage had been inflicted on the city. The German capital was a more difficult target in view of the distance involved, but was the object of 20,000 sorties between November 1943 and March 1944, known as the Battle of Berlin. Losses on some of these raids were extremely heavy: the attack on Nuremberg on 30 March 1944 resulted in the loss of 94 bombers and damage to 71 out of a total of 795 employed.

Among numerous Allied aircrew casualties Flying Officer William Birdsall, Sergeant Navigator Alan Cooper, Flight Lieutenant Gerald Hyne, Flying Officer Andrew Illius, Flying Officer Charles St Leger, and Flying Officer David White, all educated at Oundle School, lost their lives during these hazardous raids on German cities.

Clearly, 1943 saw an intensification of the bombing campaign against Germany. A total of 200,000 tons of bombs were dropped, nearly five times as many as in 1942. However the campaign did not succeed in its aim of crippling Germany's war productivity, and civilian morale remained high. It did however allow the Russians to advance in the East by drawing off a large proportion of Luftwaffe resources and anti-aircraft force.

In Southern Europe too, the RAF continued to harrass German shipping, preventing supplies from reaching Rommel's forces in North Africa. Over the Aegean Sea on 3 January, Elton man Flight Sergeant Edward Meadwell lost his life in the battle for control of the Mediterranean. A former pupil of Laxton School, which he left in 1928, joining the RAF in 1940, he was shot down while attacking enemy shipping with torpedo.[63]

An Oundle Airman
To read through the documents received by the families of those who were killed in action, recording moment by moment their increasingly probable fate, is a salutary experience. Those thin and yellowing telegrams, official letters and messages of condolence, fifty years on, can give us only an inkling of the feelings that they aroused. The following pages commemorate in such documents the sacrifice of just one of so many.

Sergeant John Marlow, an air-gunner with No 75 (New Zealand) Squadron, based at RAF Newmarket, had completed six bombing missions over Germany when a telegram addressed to his mother arrived at his home in East Road on 17 April 1943. The message was terse:

> Deeply regret to inform you that your son 1353768 Sgt Marlow JL failed to return from operations on night 16/17 April letter follows.

85: Air-gunner Sergeant John Marlow,
killed in action on 16 April 1943.

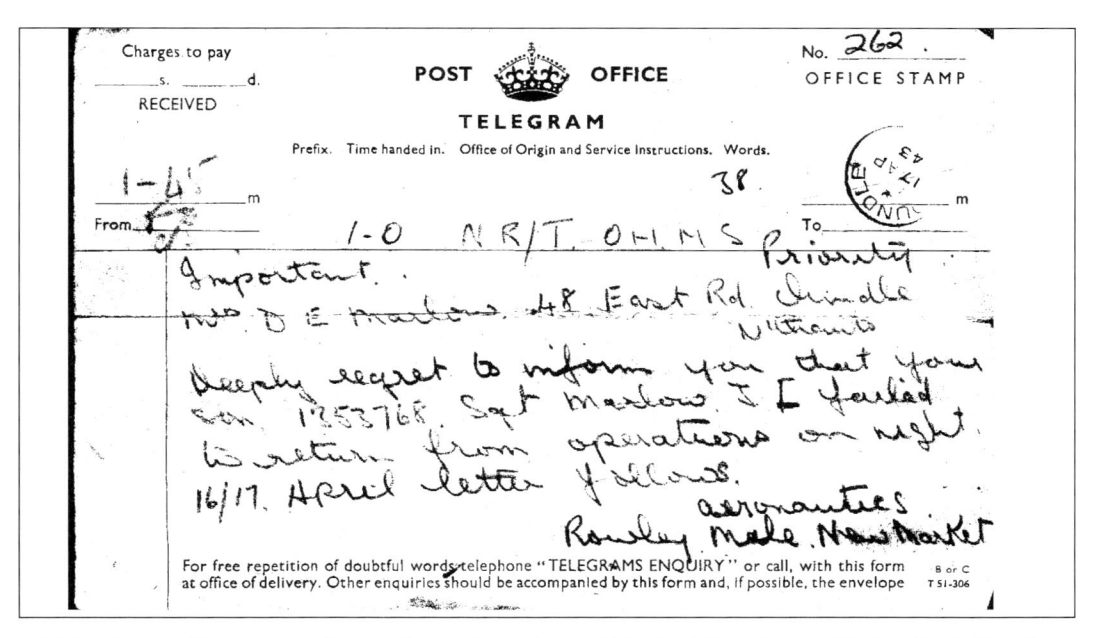

86: A telegram like so many thousands of others, dated 17 April 1943 arrives at 48, East Road, Oundle.

THREE ~ ACTIVE SERVICE

The following letter from his Commanding Officer duly arrived almost a week later.

```
                                     No. 75 (NZ) Squadron,
                                     R.A.F. Station,
                                     Newmarket, Suffolk.
Ref: - 75NZ/1053/CAS

                                     April 21st 1943


Dear Mrs Marlow,

   I find it a sad and difficult task for me to write a letter of this
description. During your son's all too short stay with my Squadron, he
had quickly and happily settled down and become extremely popular
amongst all ranks for his cheerful and willing disposition. He was an
excellent air-gunner, at all times displaying great skill and was
ever keen to strike a blow against the enemy. His loss, a temporary
one I pray, is a heavy blow to the Squadron, to the Service and to the
great cause for which he so nobly fought.

   On this fateful operation, his tenth with my Squadron, the crew of
which he was a member were detailed to attack once again a strongly
defended target in Germany. He had already completed six successful
operational trips over German territory. No further message was received
from the aircraft after it had left base, thus we have no clue as to
the cause of their non-return. Knowing however, the skill and efficiency
of this crew, and the prudence and determination of their captain, who
would do all that was humanly possible to preserve the safety of his
men, I feel we may learn during the course of the next few weeks that
they are all safe and well, although in enemy hands.

   In the meantime, all your son's personal effects have been carefully
listed, packed and despatched to the Central Committee of Adjustment,
Colnbrook, Slough. They will be forwarded to you from there after
certain formalities have been completed.

   The whole of my Squadron joins with me in expression of deepest
sympathy during the sad and difficult time through which you are
passing. We pray with you for his safety and well being.

                       Yours sincerely,
                         S.A. Lane,

                       WING COMMANDER, COMMANDING
                       No. 75(NZ) Squadron, R.A.F.

Mrs. D. E. Marlow,
48 East Road,
Oundle. Northants.
```

WAR ORGANISATION
OF THE
BRITISH RED CROSS SOCIETY and ORDER OF ST. JOHN OF JERUSALEM

President:
HER MAJESTY THE QUEEN.

Grand Prior:
H.R.H. THE DUKE OF GLOUCESTER, K.G.

WOUNDED, MISSING AND RELATIVES DEPARTMENT

Chairman:
THE DOWAGER LADY AMPTHILL, C.I., G.B.E.

TELEPHONE NO.: SLOANE 9696
TELEGRAPHIC ADDRESS: WOMIREL, KNIGHTS, LONDON

In replying please quote reference: OA/AT RAF/C 6791

7 BELGRAVE SQUARE,
LONDON, S.W.1

14th May, 1943.

Dear Miss Green,

    Your letter of May 6th in which you make an enquiry for your nephew Sergeant J.L.Marlow No.1353768.has been passed to us by our Prisoners of War Department at St.James' Palace as they do not deal with correspondence until it has been definitely established that a man is a prisoner of war.

    We are so sorry to have to say that no news has yet reached us about him since he was reported missing from operations on 16/17th April. All possible enquiries are being made ,and we can well understand your sister's anxiety for her only son, particularly as you tell us that her husband died from the effects of the last war.

    We should be grateful if you would pass on to her the contents of this letter together with our assurance that should any news become available she will be notified immediately.

    We will also write to you, and we should like to express our sympathy both to yourself and your sister in your anxiety.

Miss A.Green.
Glencairn Cottage.
Waterloo. Larne.
Co.Antrim. N.Ireland.

Yours sincerely,

Margaret Ampthill.

Chairman.

87: A mother's anguish about her son's disappearance continues:
'No news has yet reached us about him.'

THREE ~ ACTIVE SERVICE

The next day brought a letter from The Royal Air Force Record Office at Gloucester, dated 22 April, confirming officially that John Marlow was missing. It seemed to be the worst possible news that a mother could receive. But there was still hope that he might be alive as a prisoner of war. His aunt, writing from her home in Northern Ireland, undertook to make the necessary enquiries on behalf of her distraught sister. Three weeks later came grim confirmation in a letter from the Wounded, Missing and Relatives Department of the British Red Cross Society and Order of St John of Jerusalem's War Organisation: John Marlow had not been recorded as a prisoner.

Another letter, this time from the Air Ministry's Casualty Branch in London, arrived at the end of August. It announced to Mrs Marlow, with deep regret, that all efforts to trace her son had proved unavailing, but that enquiries would continue.

Not until the end of the year was Mrs Marlow given news that her son was officially presumed dead, in the following letter from the Air Ministry:

```
                                        73-77, Oxford St.,
                                        London, W.1.
                                        4th December, 1943
P.403076/6/43/P.4.(b)

Madam,

    I am commanded by the Air Council to state that in view of the lapse
of time and the absence of any further news regarding your son,
1353768 Sergeant J. L. Marlow, since the date on which he was
reported missing, they must regretfully conclude that he has lost
his life, and his death has now been presumed, for official purposes,
to have occurred on the 16th April, 1943.

    The Council desires me to express again their sympathy with you in
the anxiety which you have suffered, and in your bereavement.

                          I am, Madam,
                          Your obedient Servant,

                          Charles Evans

Mrs D. E. Marlow,
48, East Road,
Oundle,
Northants.
```

Among two more documents received by the Marlow family was a letter of condolence from the King, and a commemorative scroll sent to the relatives of all those who died in the conflict.

Finally, on 5 January 1954, the Marlow family received notification from the Imperial War Graves Commission that a memorial had been erected at Rheinberg War Cemetery in Germany.

GVI RI

This scroll commemorates

Sergeant J. L. Marlow
Royal Air Force

held in honour as one who served King and Country in the world war of 1939-1945 and gave his life to save mankind from tyranny. May his sacrifice help to bring the peace and freedom for which he died.

88: John Marlow's commemorative scroll of honour.

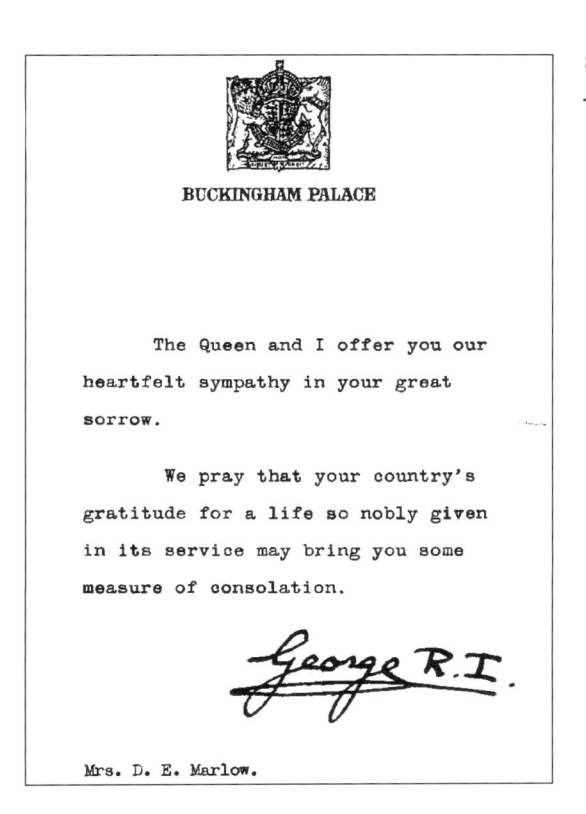

89: A message from the King to John Marlow's family.

> BUCKINGHAM PALACE
>
> The Queen and I offer you our heartfelt sympathy in your great sorrow.
>
> We pray that your country's gratitude for a life so nobly given in its service may bring you some measure of consolation.
>
> George R.I.
>
> Mrs. D. E. Marlow.

Busting the Dams

One of the spectacular successes of the bombing-raids in Northern Europe from a morale-boosting point of view was the precision targeting and destruction of the Möhne and Eder dams in the Ruhr on the night of 16 May 1943 by the specially trained 617 Squadron known as the 'Dambusters', led by Wing Commander Guy Gibson. It was a former Oundle School boy, Air Commodore John Whitworth, who as Station Commander of RAF Scampton where the 'Dambusters' were trained and from where they took off, was directly responsible for the preparations leading up to the historic raid. Later in 1943 John Whitworth became Deputy Director of Bomber Operations at the Air Ministry.

A Hero's Death in the Pyrenees

Vital work was carried out not only by the bomber and fighter crews of the RAF but also by reconnaissance flight teams working with RAF Coastal Command, and usually flying in hostile and remote situations. Wing Commander Donald Walker, also educated at the School, had left School House for Sandhurst in 1933, being seconded five years later to the RAF. It was known that he had been killed in action in a mountainous region of Spain on 11 November 1943, but not until 1967 was the location of his grave discovered, thanks to a villager who wrote to the Ministry of Defence in London. The discovery and an interview with his 85-year old mother were the subject of a story which appeared in *The Sunday Express* on 28 January 1967. Apparently Donald Walker had ordered his navigator to bale out of his photo-reconnaissance Mosquito, which had then crashed amidst the jagged peaks of the Pyrenees. Villagers from nearby San Guesa buried him in a tiny graveyard, and each year since have gone up the mountainside to tidy the grave, plant flowers and hold a service.[64]

~ 1944 ~

The War in the Far East
The end of 1942 had seen the Japanese in control of most of the Pacific, from the Aleutian Islands in the north to the Solomon Islands and New Guinea. However the following year was marked by Allied counter-offensives. Australian troops held back the Japanese in Papua, and American forces re-took many of the Pacific islands inflicting heavy losses on the enemy. By early 1944 the communications of the Japanese troops in the Pacific were growing more and more overstretched.

Burma: the Arakan and Kohima
With the Allied advance into Burma, many decorations for gallantry were won by servicemen with Oundle links. Former Oundle School boy Arthur Marment, who had left Dryden House in 1935, spent most of the war in India and Burma. After eight weeks at Bangalore Officers' Training School he was posted to the Indian Army's Fourth Battalion, 15th Punjab Regiment and served in the Datta Khel campaign of 1942, near the Afghan border. The beginning of 1944 found him involved in the famous battle of Admin Box. The Box, in which Major General Frank Messervy had set up his headquarters, was an area of half a square mile near Sinzweya. The British force, preparing for an attack towards Buthidaung, were surprised by a ferocious Japanese offensive on 4 February. There were heavy losses on both sides; the British garrison was finally relieved on 24 February. Air support from the RAF's newly arrived Spitfires played a crucial part in the battle.

A contemporary of Arthur Marment at the School was Denis Eadie, an ex-New House boy serving with the Royal Engineers. Both were to be decorated following the battle for Kohima, one of the most savage engagements of the Burma campaign.

The Japanese crossed the Chindwin River in mid-March. Under the command of Lieutenant General Renya Mutaguchi the 15th Army attacked the British, Indian and African forces in the area of Kohima and Imphal, near the Burmese border. Kohima was held by only 440 men of the 4th Battalion Queen's Own Royal West Kent Regiment along with some Punjabis and Rajputs, and both sides knew that it was the key to India, commanding the only all-weather road on the Indian-Burmese frontier. There was fierce fighting around the town of Kohima until April 20, when two relieving brigades broke through to the exhausted garrison and went on to drive the Japanese off the surrounding heights. General Slim's 14th Army was then able to raise the 80-day siege of Imphal further south. The battle for Kohima continued with savage determination on both sides, but on 8 July General Mutaguchi gave the order to fall back to the Chindwin.

One of the most vicious episodes of the Kohima campaign was the battle which took place around the British Deputy Commissioner's bungalow and its tennis court, overrun by the Japanese during the night of 9 April. The enemy proved impossible to dislodge, being well dug in. Denis Eadie succeeded in mounting an operation to manhandle a six-pounder anti-tank gun and was decorated with the Military Cross for his bravery. His citation praised him for defying accurate enemy fire and accompanying the gun up the hill, later carrying back the dead and wounded. The Japanese were finally overcome, he remembers, when with the use of a small bulldozer, a Lee-Grant tank was winched up to the crest by the Royal Engineers. 'It virtually finished the Japanese foothold in the town.' It was one of his

90: Burma veteran Major Denis Eadie, MC, with his two sons, also educated at Oundle School.

officers, Jamie Ferris, who designed the memorial to those men of the Second Division who died at Kohima. The inscription reads: 'When you go home, tell them of us, and say: For your tomorrow, we gave our today.'

Denis Eadie's fellow-Oundelian Arthur Marment was also awarded the Military Cross for his part in the battle for Kohima.

The siege of Kohima, it has been said, deserves to rank beside Rorke's Drift and Arnhem in the annals of British military valour. Lieutenant Antony Orchard, of the Royal Engineers, a former pupil of Oundle School which he had left only three years before, was among those who were killed in the battle. The letter to his mother from his Commanding Officer Lieutenant Colonel K. F. Daniell praised him in the following words:

> He was beloved by his men, and rightly so, as all his thoughts were of them and their welfare. In consequence I could always rely on them to do a first-class job of work, and they never looked like letting me down... I am proud to have had such a gallant officer under my command, and to have had him as a friend too.[65]

Further south in Burma, another former Oundle School boy displayed bravery in a unique role which was to gain him both the Distinguished Flying Cross and the Military Cross as well as two mentions in despatches and a Certificate of Gallantry signed by Mountbatten. Captain Edward Maslen-Jones, who had left the School's Laundimer House in 1939, was one of the small group of Royal Artillery officers belonging to an Air Observation Squadron. Within a Squadron there were three Flights, each Flight having four Sections. Each Section was completely mobile, equipped with an Auster aircraft, a three-ton truck, a jeep, and a combination of two Army and two RAF personnel under the command of a Royal Artillery captain, whose job was to spot enemy targets from the air. 'We could actually take the wings off the aircraft and put it in the back of the three-tonner, and we had everything we needed to go into action. It was a support role of course.'

Although the role of an air observer had appealed to him, he admitted to having some early anxieties.

> When it came to the pinch I was really quite frightened of the idea of flying, and I think in the early days I hadn't got much moral fibre about it actually, but it did me a power of good. My flying instructor was a Canadian called Ted Schofield — he was a Canadian mounted policeman, and he was absolutely super because he knew I was terrified, but he still got me going solo in about five to five and a half hours I think. He threatened me with a return to unit, so that did it, and after that the flying bit was terrific, absolutely marvellous.

The job gave him some unusual privileges.

> I was carrying in those days, in my wallet, a piece of paper that allowed me to land anywhere; it had an authority on it, and also allowed me to low fly anywhere in the country. That was fantastic because, quite apart from being on exercise, one could perhaps nip home for a weekend, which actually did happen once.

He also remembered a visit to his old school in about 1942.

> I had been on an exercise in Northumberland, with my section. On the way back we arranged a rendezvous at Oundle, and I landed behind the Pavilion. The ground crew joined me, and I visited Laundimer in my jeep, When driving back past School House, 'Bud' Fisher (the Headmaster) appeared on top of the steps. He recognised me immediately, calling me by name and bidding me to stop and talk. Before leaving — it was OTC day — the cadets inspected the aircraft, and I buzzed the parade as I flew away.

Edward Maslen-Jones was well aware of the dangers of flying in such proximity to the Japanese lines. Enemy fire was a constant hazard, 'but you didn't actually know too much about it because of the noise of the aircraft and also the fact that you were listening to the radio most of the time, but you sort of sensed it. I came down with some holes on one occasion. Obviously one got fired at but one didn't really know too much about that. There was a job to be done, I suppose, and one was concentrating on that....'

From 26 March to 11 May 1944, Edward Maslen-Jones flew as an air observer in support of the 25 Indian Division Artillery. His patrols covered the

91: Captain Edward Maslen-Jones, MC, DFC.
A former Oundle School boy, Captain Maslen-Jones was a Royal Artillery officer in the Air Observation Squadron.

open country south of Maungdaw in the Arakan coastal region of Burma. 'During this period he has ever been the first to suggest some cunning ruse to outwit the Jap, and has ever been eager to go into the air to carry these schemes into effect,' reads his citation for the DFC. 'Day after day this officer flew long hours to accomplish his task. In addition he was used to search for Jap guns and observe in the hill country. Frequently shot at, his courage was unfailing. He was ever ready to take extra risks in low flying to report some minute detail of a target or observe the results of fire.'

Another airman with Oundle links who recorded his memories of flying in the Far East was Lucian Ercolani, who had moved from bombing raids over Germany to missions directed at the Japanese presence in Burma.

92: The Certificate of Gallantry signed by Earl Mountbatten and given to Captain Maslen-Jones, was awarded in November 1944, following work with 15 Corps and 11th East African Division in the Arakan region of Burma.

There was an entirely different atmosphere flying in the Far East compared to the European show. The risk from enemy action was considerably less in the Far East, but, really, the anxiety and fear was probably worse. However badly one thought of the Germans, at least there was an element of European civilisation, as against our real fear of the Japanese and of coming down amongst them.

I had a three-year spell out there and, apart from a six-month stint at Group Headquarters, I was fortunate to be on squadrons all the time. Our bases were always in the Eastern part of India, in Bengal, fifty-sixty miles from Calcutta. This meant that there was a lot of flying before we actually got to the business end, across the Bay of Bengal and, more often than not, flying over the Burmese mountains. To start with, mostly at night.

Returning back in the mornings, though, could be a joy: the sun rising behind you, a glorious gold, lighting up the tops of the mountains, the valleys shrouded in mist, still in the dark. Although you had the worry of getting over them, they were very beautiful. The aircraft with less fuel and no bomb-load now, light to the touch, quite free and relaxed. It was quite an emotional feeling. I often thought I could hear the 'Ave Maria' being sung.

I joined 99 Squadron as a Flight Commander and, within a few days of arriving, was off over the other side. They still had the dear old Wimpys, but conditions were quite rustic. If you needed to change an engine, you had to push the aircraft under a tree and use a block and tackle from a branch.

At that time, the Japanese were pushing right up through Burma and we were involved in bombing aerodromes and communications — anything that could help the Army. They actually got as far as Imphal and it was only the leadership and strong personality of General Slim which tipped the scales against their breaking into India.

After some months, we heard that our Air Force was being built up with Liberators, that is, the American B-24, a four-engine job. They seemed very big to us in those days. They could carry probably four times as much as the dear old Wimpy and could be pushed to flights of nearly 3,000 miles. To start with they were intended to be crewed by twelve people, but we soon skimmed that down to six.

I was posted as Flight Commander to 355 Squadron and was, for some time, Senior Officer to form up the squadron. When I arrived, there were only huts on the aerodrome, quite bare of equipment. Then people started arriving. We didn't even have enough knives and forks. We went round begging, borrowing or stealing equipment. Then the great day when, one by one, the Liberators came in. We did a quick conversion course and before long, to our great excitement, we were flying them.

After a few trips over the other side, I was posted to Group Headquarters in Calcutta. I didn't think I was ever really cut out to be a Staff Officer, and was only there for six months, but I learnt a lot. Then I was offered the great pride of the service, the command of a squadron, and went back to my friends with 99 Squadron, where my experience with the Liberators was immensely valuable, as our first job was to convert 99 to the wonderful new Liberators.

The scene over Burma had now begun to change. Although the Army was having a very rough time indeed in the Burma jungles, they first held and then began to push the Japanese back. We changed our role and switched mainly to daylight operations and learnt the art of flying these big aircraft in formation. It was a wonderful sight to be with your own squadron with twelve or sixteen aircraft all round you. Very small compared to Europe, but exciting for us. For some time, our targets were closely linked to a form of Army cooperation, clearing areas ahead of landings. We cleared the ground for the invasion of Ramree Island, off the Burmese coast, we attacked aerodromes, supply depots and generally made life uncomfortable for the Japanese troops.

It was then that we began to get involved with the infamous railway line linking Singapore right up through to Burma, built over the bodies of thousands and thousands of prisoners of war. It was a real 'hate' operation.

Bridges and the trains themselves were the bomb targets. The Liberators were, of course, designed for medium- and high-level bombing, but as they were the only aircraft available which could do the considerable distances involved, we had to evolve new low-level techniques. We could hardly claim ever converting a Liberator into a fighter-bomber, but we must have come fairly close!

Having flown 1,000 miles plus, to find our objective on the railway line, we would have to come right down on to the deck to try and knock out the engines. The terrible worry in our minds was that these trains, and the lines, were crowded with our own people. It was a very deep emotional experience to see your own people on the ground, right down there in those terrible places, waving to us and encouraging us on. I cannot believe that some accidents did not happen, as many were very close to the engines, but their welcome was always the same. We felt awful when we had finished and pulled up to go home again, leaving them all behind.

I was next offered the opportunity to move from 99 to 159 Squadron and to re-form the squadron into what might loosely be called the Pathfinder role. I was allowed the privilege of selecting the most experienced crews from those just being posted in and from the other squadrons. It could have caused a lot of bad feeling, but everyone was very generous and it seemed to work well.

Our squadron was made up roughly in equal proportions of British, Australians, New Zealanders and Canadians. There was probably a higher proportion of the latter. This was far better than having British, Australian etc. squadrons. By mixing us all up together, you certainly had plenty of rivalries, but healthy ones to make things go even better. We all made many

THREE ~ ACTIVE SERVICE

lifelong friends. Fine pilots amongst many other fine pilots.

Strangely, whilst with Bomber Command, one used to do very little practice bombing, but bearing in mind our new role, we decided to work at it. Quite often we got down to 25 yards, but we used to post up the results in the Mess overnight and anybody who was outside 50 yards had to buy the drinks.

This stood us in good stead when a large Japanese submarine depot ship ventured up the Gulf of Siam. We found her just south of Bangkok, scored several direct hits, sinking her under a great cloud of smoke. As we hadn't used up our bomb load, we left her sinking and went after the escort vessels; but we missed them all, as they bobbed around like little 'water boatmen' beetles on a pond. Perhaps that taught us not to get too cocky!

For this particular operation Lucian Ercolani was awarded the Distinguished Flying Cross.
Destroying the enemy's lines of communication now became a priority.

We evolved a new method for low-level bombing to knock the bridges down. Bridges are, in fact, quite difficult to hit. Amongst many other successes, our squadron led the flight that knocked down the famous bridge over the River Kwai. Great annoyance was caused later amongst the crews by the film when it was said that the bridge was too far away for the Air Force to reach!

The technique we worked out was to go as low as possible and fly slightly diagonally across the bridge, and on each run to only use three bombs. Flying diagonally gave one just a little latitude fore and aft and also sideways. We used delayed-action bombs, certainly to avoid blowing ourselves up, but particularly so that they could really settle down before exploding, trying to get them as close as we could to the bridge supports themselves.

The monsoon season used to be the season when everything stopped. Obviously we couldn't, so we had to find a way of getting through these frightening clouds. If you went in high, the up-currents had been known to break the wings off. We treated them with great respect. If we had to cross them in the middle of the Bay of Bengal, and very often they were at their worst there, we found that our best way through was to go right down on to the deck, then try to work our way along the side of the cloud. At that level, beneath these enormous cumulus clouds and flying along their edges, it was rather like flying under the overhang of a railway station. I don't know quite how wide that overhang would be, but when we flew under the edges of these clouds, about 200 feet below would be the sea, a very strange feeling. We were very frightened of them.

Out there we were rather a small Air Force, and as a result knew almost everybody. We were allowed incredible independence; once given our detailed objectives, it was left to us how we set about it.

93: Lucian Ercolani DSO, DFC, on a return visit to Oundle in 1995.

Our squadrons were still units complete in themselves; they had not been 'rationalised' as in the UK with the squadron being flying crews only, with joint, combined, maintenance. We had the advantage of being a total unit along with all the chaps who kept our aircraft flying. There was a tremendous pride of squadron, with everybody feeling that 'together' there was hardly anything that we couldn't accomplish.

To have command of a squadron under these circumstances, with all those exciting opportunities at twenty-seven years of age, with probably 1,000 people to be responsible for, was a very great privilege.

We had this freedom, had been wonderfully well taught how to fly, but had had virtually no service training. We were presented with our job and got on with it. Where the lack of service training showed up was when we had the VE Day celebrations and had to hold a parade. Although I was supposed to be the Commanding Officer, I hardly knew my left from my right. Fortunately for me, there were one or two people who did know what to do, so I just walked on and walked off.[66]

Lucian Ercolani's younger brother Barry, educated like him at Oundle, was also in Burma with 159 Squadron at this time. An outstanding rear gunner, he later became chief gunnery instructor for the RAF in India.

Oundelian Chindits

In Burma one of the most celebrated groups of forces in the fight against the Japanese was the Chindits, led by Major General Orde Wingate. The group took its name from the mythological beast, half-eagle, half-lion, which we know as the griffin, and was composed of British troops, Burma Rifles, Gurkhas, units from the Royal Corps of Signals, Indian troops, RAF officers to act as liaison with aircraft, and a few Commandos. Wingate's imagination had been caught by the way in which the mythological chindit symbolised the close ground-and-air cooperation needed by such a force in its operations. The Chindits' first excursion into enemy-occupied Burma took place on 14 February 1943. It caused a certain amount of disruption, but the Chindits were forced to retire in mid-April, leaving behind most of their equipment and a third of their strength.

The group was increased from two brigades to six after August 1943, and Wingate himself was promoted to Major General, having inspired Churchill with his ideas and arguments for fighting the Japanese. A larger airborne force was dropped behind enemy lines on 5 March 1944, having learnt many lessons from the original group, and taking the Japanese by surprise. By 13 March some 9,000 men had been landed to the rear of the enemy lines.

Among some notable Chindits with Oundle connections was Captain John David Butler, who died in the final successful battle for Mogaung in June, three months after the airborne landing. He was killed after the company he commanded had captured the railway bridge to the east of the town. His former Commanding Officer wrote to express his sadness:

> I must write and tell you what a very great regard I had for David. He was a real tough little man, independent, and loyal to a high degree. He had a very strong sense of duty, which, with his kind and lovable nature, endeared him to us all. His loss has left a great blank in the Battalion.[67]

THREE ~ ACTIVE SERVICE

Apart from the above qualities it was also true that John Butler had literary gifts and a splendid sense of humour, as well as boxing and linguistic skills — he had gained an Exhibition in Modern Languages at Cambridge in 1940. The British Press, eager to seize on heroes of the Burma campaign, had written what the Chindits no doubt considered was a lot of patriotic nonsense about their exploits. The following verses entitled *The Airborne Chindits* were discovered among Captain Butler's papers after his death:

Characters: The Poet — News Correspondent, Special Force
The Muse — His Editor

Poet: My song is of that gallant motley band
Who, far in Burma's forest-covered land,
Challenged the hordes of Nippon's armoured might,
Smote them and put them shamefully to flight.
Be near me, muse; inspire my noble lays
That all the world may hear and shout with praise.

Muse: You mean the Airborne Chindits? Yes, I will
Be glad to hear the story. O.K., — spill.

Poet: In wingèd monsters borne by night, these men
Flew right into the heart of Burma, then
Disgorging from the monster's gaping belly
Amidst the reeking swamps and tangled trees,
Living on lizards, roots, snakes and tinnèd peas,
They hacked and slashed and crashed their toiling way,
Yet marching forty, fifty miles a day.
For raging torrents, towering mountains they
Cared not a whit, and left them by the way.
At last from RIPUM'S summit, looking down
They saw the fertile vale of MAWLU Town.
Then spoke their gallant leader, 'Look here, chaps,
That place down there is simply full of Japs.
So, come on now, let's have a damn good show.'
He spoke, and with a flourish, plunged below.

Muse: This is terrific. Front-page, Headline stuff.
I'll feature it: 'Our Jungle boys are tough.'
It's what the British Public's waiting for.
Come on. Don't stint yourself. Let's have some more.

Poet: The warriors, with sword and naked knife,
Leapt after him, all eager for the strife,
Each vying for the honourable place
Beside their Leader, foremost in the race.
So, sweeping down the mountain-side they came
With bursting bomb and muzzles belching flame.
How can my halting pen, O Muse, portray
The fearful battle scene, the bitter fray,
The crash of musketry, across the plain,
The rivulets of blood, the piles of slain?
I can no more. I faint. My spirits droop.

Muse: Come on, don't slacken off. Gee, what a scoop!

	Let's have a bit of dope about the Japs.
	Just give the outlines, I'll fill in the gaps.
Poet:	The Japs, that day, in mortal terror flying,
	Left on the field a thousand dead and dying.
	And then the Heroes, flushed with victory,
	Brewed and imbibed the life-restoring tea.
Muse:	Good God, he's going potty. O.K. son,
	You've earned a rest after the job you've done —
	Pack up at once and take a spot of leave.
Poet:	To Bombay will I go, and there will weave
	A pretty step upon the dancing floors.
	There will I knock in turn upon the doors
	Of every Night-club, every evil dive,
	Nor will I once retire to bed till five.
	To Bacchus will I dedicate my pay.
	So, to the Golden City; Come, away.
	Moral: The moral of this super-fatted story
	Is, — never mind the truth, let's have the glory.[68]

Notwithstanding John Butler's modesty, the Chindits, by all accounts, were a group which included many extraordinary characters. One of these must surely have been Frank Baines, an ex-Oundle School boy described in his obituary as 'writer, traveller, soldier, and navvy'. His life as a Chindit so exhausted him that after the war he became a monk in a Hindu monastery in the Himalayas, where he spent the next three years recovering. His wartime experiences were later to be distilled into a book, *Officer Boy*, published in 1971 during three months spent in Brixton Prison for refusing to pay his National Insurance contributions: none of this was to prevent him from travelling to India by bicycle at the age of 65.[69]

The conditions of jungle warfare were indeed tough, and some of the Chindits found themselves patients of another former Oundle School pupil, Major Kenneth Blythe. It was Kenneth Blythe who, after volunteering for service with the Army Medical Corps in 1942 was responsible for establishing the first Malaria Forward Treatment Unit at Lucknow in India, moving it to the front in Burma where he dealt with casualties from the battles of Imphal and Kohima.[70]

Another Oundle-educated doctor who was serving in Burma at this time was Lieutenant Colonel John Armstrong, of the Royal Army Medical Corps. He was killed at Sahmaw in Burma on 6 December. The only son of an Oundle bank manager, he had spent one term at Laxton School in 1925 before going to Bedford School.[71]

The Liberation of France: D-Day

> I peered through the porthole wheelhouse trying to recognise the place where we had to land. Then I suddenly spotted this German gun emplacement about 30 yards to the right, and two gun barrels poking out towards us. I thought to myself, 'This is it!'

Royal Navy coxswain Rex Milborne, a familiar face to customers at Owen & Hartley's electrical goods shop on Oundle's North Street, was steering his landing craft loaded with six tanks weighing 30 tons each. The target was Gold Beach, just east of Asnelles. It was 6 June 1944. The landing-craft was hit twice, but no serious damage was done.

I suddenly found that the terror I had inside me vanished. All hell was let loose but there was so much to concentrate on I forgot my fear. The next instant we hit the beach at full speed and our ramp crashed down. The noise was overwhelming... the noise of six tank engines, the guns opening up at us at point blank range... I was fighting with the wheel and at the same time listening to the voice pipe from the bridge. How long we were getting six tanks off, plus dealing with a folding boat full of ammo that collapsed on the ramp, I don't know. It seemed like hours, but it could only have been 20 or 30 minutes.

We finally dragged ourselves off the beach to let the second wave in. It was then that I thought to myself, 'How the hell did we get away with that?'[72]

Planning 'Overlord'

Courage and determination were of course only part of the answer to Rex Milborne's question. Operation 'Overlord', as the invasion of Europe was known, was also a triumph of planning and organisation. Ever since Hitler had launched his attack on the Soviet Union on 22 June 1941, Britain had been under pressure from Stalin to open a 'second front' in Europe. The entry of the United States increased the pressure. General George C. Marshall, the US Army Chief of Staff had begun a massive build-up of American troops in Britain from 1942 in an operation codenamed 'Bolero', aimed at invasion. Churchill, aware of the difficulties involved in mounting such an operation, was more cautious. Nonetheless the Casablanca conference of January 1943 saw Allied agreement on the plan, while accepting that it should not be implemented before 1 May 1944.

The choice of a landing area was crucial for the Allies. RAF high-altitude reconnaissance photos, pre-war holiday snaps from British tourists, and intelligence reports from the French Resistance were among the many sources of information which were used in the long run-up to D-Day. Special forces were also sent secretly across the Channel to assess the strength of the German defences. Miriam Rothschild's husband was in one of these groups of brave, specially trained commandos. She remembered the unusual treatment which they enjoyed while billeted at Littlehampton in Sussex.

> My husband was in a specially dangerous job. He was in a Commando group which was trained to be dropped in Germany during the war, and one of the curious things was that people who were in No 3 Troop of No 10 Commandos had to be trained as individuals and so they were never billeted in camps, but in lodgings, and were allowed to take their wives with them to the places where they were training.
>
> We were stationed right on the south coast of England, so we had a raid every night. Altogether we lived a very peculiar life. We would be in bed at night and there'd be a knock on the door. 'Sir, there's a raid on,' and George would get up and dress in his battle dress, and left, and we never knew if we would see each other again. It was very hectic — I was expecting our first child, I don't know how I survived it.

Finally, during an intelligence-gathering mission across the Channel to examine coastal defences Captain George Lane was captured and spent the rest of the war as a prisoner, being awarded the Military Cross for his bravery.

> What the Commandos were looking for was some sort of special bomb or floating mine, which had appeared on photographs taken by the Air Force. The orders that my husband and his men received, were to go and fetch these bombs or mines and bring them back in their boat. It was very important to examine the defences along the French coast before D-Day,

and these bombs or floating mines seemed to be of a sort which required investigation. George was successful, in that he found the mines, brought them back and loaded them on to the boat. He himself was captured because he returned to measure a second obstacle on the beach and a German troop came down the coast and got between him and the boat. There was an arrangement that at 4.00 am the boat was to return to England, and by the time he got back it had gone. He had to throw his equipment into the sea, the various detecting gadgets he had with him, and then give himself up.

It was six weeks before Miriam Rothschild discovered that her husband was a prisoner, but alive.

The planning of the D-Day landings involved a mammoth exercise in co-operation between all the services as well as between the Allies. Music teacher Robin Miller of Benefield Road, serving in RAF Intelligence, counted his part in the operation as his most exciting wartime experience.

I happened to be 'duty dog' in the 24 hours up to and including the D-Day landings in Normandy. On this particular day we received quite different instructions over the telephone. I was told to go and get 'Bomber Command Operational Order No 1' from the safe upstairs. It was an enormous sealed envelope which I had to open in front of the Air Vice Marshal. Laid out were all our operations for the D-Day landings. None of us really said very much, but there were murmurs to the effect of 'If you want any help, come to me', and so on. We all knew that this was the thing that we had been planning for years. So I worked on that through the night, and then a very senior officer waltzed into the office at 4.00 in the morning, singing, 'Happy D-Day to you!' I suppose then we thought, 'My God, this really is it.' So we went back to the Mess at about 9.00 to listen to General Eisenhower on the radio telling us that our troops had landed in Normandy that morning. That was probably my most exciting experience.

Keeping the supply lines open was a vital part of the successful planning of Operation 'Overlord'. George Bristow found himself involved in the crucial supply line during D-Day. 14,000 tonnes of drinking water were sent to France for the troops. 'We had been carrying oil and diesel used by other troops,' he recalled, 'so after emptying the tanks we went back to Britain, cleaned out the tanks and filled them with water.'

Medical supplies were also vital. One former Oundle School boy who performed a vital service in maintaining the morale of British troops abroad was a member of the Royal Army Medical Corps, Lieutenant Colonel Francis Hellier, who was to establish a reputation for himself as one of the leading dermatologists of his day. In 1940 he was appointed dermatologist to Western Command. Throughout the war, scabies was a scourge of troops in the field, and Francis Hellier did a great deal, through his centre at Ragley Hall, to cure soldiers who otherwise might well have had to be demobilized.

Along with the many other medical teams he went to Normandy and remained with 21st Army Group until the end of the war, playing a considerable part in keeping units in combat condition. This was no easy task. Penicillin was scarce. Supplies were earmarked for serious casualties and none could be spared for the ravages of skin diseases which were damaging morale.

A colleague remembered how he commandeered a batch of out-of-date penicillin which was about to be destroyed, and created a preparation which could be used externally to treat the impetigo and sycosis which were taking their toll. This initiative produced dramatic results, and men who would have had to be sent home were able to get back into battle within two or three days.[73]

Back in England, former Desert Rat Vic Thorington also played a part in preparing medical supplies for the invasion, having volunteered for an unusual job which he continued doing up to the end of the war.

> I was in Doncaster then. I'd volunteered for this. I ended up with horses again. At one time we were not supposed to speak about what we were doing there. I was billeted first of all on the grandstand at the race course at Doncaster. But there was another section that was offered to me that would bring in a couple more coppers. So I said, 'Yeah all right, I'll have a go at that.' Once you had said yes, you did not tell anybody what you were doing there. It's very possible that if the public had known, there would have been a big outcry.
>
> They were getting a lot of horses that were past their best. There were huge stables there and we were based at the old hospital. We used to start in the morning, you may have ended up doing four or five horses. Some people, when they found out what they had to do, automatically transferred. I used to like to drink, and to get that you had to have money. And this is how I joined the Veterinary Corps. We were bleeding horses! Taking gallons of blood from horses as a build up to the Second Front in Normandy. They could only store this blood for a limited number of weeks or months, and it had to be replaced. Like human blood you could only keep it in the blood bank for so long, frozen. That was what I was doing when peace was supposedly called in!

A key role in the Allied invasion of Europe was played by the Royal Army Service Corps, responsible largely for maintaining supplies, communications and transport of troops. For his part in the invasion campaign of north-west Europe, former Oundle School boy Lieutenant Colonel Duncan Riddell was appointed MBE. The official citation records that 'in all respects he has been outstanding in his devotion to the affairs of the RASC regardless of any limits of duty'. He had already been awarded the Military Cross for his service with the Seventh Armoured Division, the 'Desert Rats,' in North Africa in June 1942, before taking part in the Normandy landings.[74]

The Battle for the Beaches

In spite of the tremendous feat of organisation of D-Day, casualties were inevitable.

One of the earliest was the husband of Molly Melton. Now living in Mason Close, and Chairman of Oundle's branch of the British Legion, Women's Section, she recalled the moment when she heard the news that she had been dreading. Her 27-year old husband Bert, attached to an intelligence gathering advance party, was badly wounded during the first assault. He was evacuated back to England within hours, but died in Southampton on 8 June 1944.

'We couldn't understand why they got him and the other wounded men in his group back to England so quickly,' she recalled. Molly Melton's son David eventually discovered the answer. His father had been carrying vital maps which might have revealed Allied strategy to the Germans had they fallen into the wrong hands.

Barnwell resident Donald Akroyd, a member of the Fourth Survey Regiment, was just metres away from landing on D-Day when he was told to stop due to bad weather and the craters which repeated shelling on the beaches had created. His landing-craft stood only 200 yards offshore, but the danger of vehicles being lost in these shell-holes caused his particular landing to be postponed until 5.00 am the next day.

Many British servicemen with Oundle links were to lose their lives in the assault on the Normandy beaches. Major Russell Elliott, who has already been mentioned for his bravery during the landing at Salerno in Italy in September 1943, was killed instantaneously by a shell during the Normandy landings.

A week after the D-Day landings the Normandy bridgehead was 50 miles long and 12 miles deep. Losses had proved, in Montgomery's words, 'much lower than had seemed possible'. Among the casualties during the subsequent push into France was Gunner Arthur Francis, of the Royal Artillery. Brought up in Polebrook, he had left Laxton School in 1934 hoping to become a glider pilot but eyesight problems had prevented this, and he had ended up in the Royal Artillery. He was killed in action on 8 July.[75]

News of the D-Day landings was a tremendous boost to morale in Oundle as it was throughout the country. Ruth Moisey, later to become Ruth Keens, was in Peterborough when she heard about the Allied assault on Europe:

> My call-up had been deferred owing to several illnesses, but eventually I received orders to report to the Employment Exchange at Peterborough for instructions. I was puzzled to find everyone running to and fro, making tea, listening to radios and no-one took the slightest notice of me. I stopped a woman in full flight to ask if something had happened in the country, as then the V bombs were causing havoc in London. 'Haven't you heard?' she replied. 'The invasion has started; it will all be over in a couple of weeks, you may as well go back to your own useful job.' It was 6 June 1944 — it took a little longer than that.

The Battle of Normandy

Six days after D-Day Michael Lewis landed in Normandy without incident. The future Oundle doctor had sailed from Newhaven as an officer in the Royal Army Medical Corps. He remembered being puzzled by some of the equipment that he saw transported across the Channel as the Allies consolidated their hold on Fortress Europe. 'There were bits of the pontoons for the Mulberry harbour being towed across but we only looked at them and wondered what on earth they could be, we had no idea that they were to build this harbour. One or two battleships were standing off the coast of Normandy, firing inland.'

94: Former Oundle GP Dr Michael Lewis, an officer in the RAMC in 1944.

THREE ~ ACTIVE SERVICE

By now the beachheads had been well secured.

> We had an almost dry landing. I just got my feet wet. The tide was pretty low and for these landings for the infantry, they had ramps down the side. You could just walk into the water. So we just marched into the sea and out, and up the beach. There was really no resistance on the beach. There was a little bit of shelling, but it didn't come near us. An occasional German plane came over, but they were mostly chased off by the RAF. We marched about five or six miles inland to a reception area where we were joined up the following day by all our transport, because that had been sent across separately.

But two miles further on the Germans were resisting fiercely, using the hedgerows and sunken lanes of the Normandy countryside to good effect.

> That was where the fighting really started. We were fighting continuously along that side of the bridgehead to try and advance slowly to the east, and to hold back the German counter-attacks, which were very heavy, particularly the tank attacks. The Germans had very cleverly dug in their tanks in the bocage countryside, high hedges and ditches, and very easy to hide a tank. They were very difficult to take because they were hidden from view and they had a good field of fire, and that was really why the advance was so slow. We never experienced a major breakthrough by the tanks — the armoured divisions were the ones that had terrific casualties. The Regiment was badly affected. We lost a lot of people, officers and men killed and many wounded, so by the end of the Normandy bridgehead, about three months, we were relatively small. A battalion which went in 800 or 900 strong was probably down to 200.

Working conditions for the young medical officer were makeshift and hazardous.

> If you are a Regimental Medical Officer you are right up in the Front, and all you can have is a first aid post of some sort. It had to be sited in the right place so that it wasn't in a position that was very likely to be shelled, visible and so on, and usually consisted of a hole in the ground, or a slit trench. Very occasionally we got into a building, but there weren't many buildings that were suitable and anyway the Germans were bombing the buildings; it was much safer to sit in the middle of a field in a big hole in which you were standing, or lying when necessary. So they were very primitive conditions in which we worked, and in fact all one did was to do essential first aid and get the wounded back from the battle area as fast as you could. There was an ambulance attached to each regimental aid post so you had this, and it would be replaced as soon as it went off with another from the Field Ambulance. We used our

95: Happier times for Normandy veteran Dr Michael Lewis, in his garden on East Road.

jeeps to collect casualties from the battlefield. We were able to modify the jeeps so that we could take two stretchers on top and two below, so you could get four casualties away to the regimental aid post. There they would be attended to by me and my aides, and then taken to the Field Ambulance where they could do emergency surgery and transfusions, and from there back to the Casualty Clearing Stations, where the major surgery was done.

German resistance, while strong in places, was patchy. It seems that morale among some was at a low level, judging by a strange meeting between a former Oundle School boy and an unexpected past acquaintance. Lord Davies had been a brilliant chess-player and Classics scholar, as well as Head of St Anthony House, which he had left in 1928. A Major in the Royal Welch Fusiliers, he was among the first British troops to be put behind the German lines. While helping wounded French civilians he was captured in the neighbourhood of Falaise. The enemy unit which took him prisoner amazingly numbered a certain Herr W. Lassen, who had taught German at Oundle School during the last year before the war. Four days later, during a German retreat, his unit was surprised to see Lord Davies reappear along with a number of his former captors, whom he had in his turn taken prisoner, including Herr Lassen. One can only imagine the moment at which both men discovered the Oundle connection. The interrogation which Lord Davies conducted at his battalion headquarters is supposed to have concluded with Herr Lassen's question, 'Anyway, who won the Uppingham match this year?' Sadly, Lord Davies was to be killed in action in Holland, in September 1944.[76]

Montgomery had hoped for the capture of Caen on the first day of the D-Day landings. However, not until 19 August was he able to say that the Battle of Normandy had been won.

The television scriptwriter and producer Christopher Bond came to know the Oundle area well following his education at the School, later living in the nearby village of Glapthorn for many years. The future creator of award-winning comedy shows such as *To the Manor Born* and *Keeping up Appearances* gave this graphic account of his experiences as a young Captain in the Eighth Battalion The Rifle Brigade:

> We didn't know at the time, of course, but the events of 17-20 July might have shortened the war in Europe.
>
> On 17 July we were forming up for what was officially known as Operation Goodwood. Later and unofficially it became known as the Charge of the Light Brigade, with General Roberts (commanding 11th Armoured Division) in the role of Lord Cardigan. On the same day, Rommel was wounded. But he left behind a plan based on fortified villages and hamlets, strongpoints of stone farmhouses 15 km in depth in three lines of defence.
>
> At dawn on 18 July my regiment had reached the start line. We were the Motor Battalion of 29th Armoured Brigade, close support infantry to the armoured cavalry regiments, some of whose forebears had charged at Balaclava. We found ourselves amid the abandoned gliders which had landed on D-Day bringing 6th Airborne to take Pegasus Bridge. The wind whistled eerily through the broken frames of these flimsy craft, but failed to blow away the ferocious mosquitoes. I sometimes think the bites I received that night inoculated me for life.
>
> The grand plan was for the 750 tanks of VIII Corps under Lieutenant General O'Connor to thrust into the open country south-east of Caen, and break through to Falaise. 11th Armoured were to lead, followed by 7th Armoured and Guards Armoured. But 11th Armoured was ordered to separate its Armoured brigade from its Infantry brigade (not to be confused with the Rifle Brigade) and fight parallel actions with different objectives.

THREE ~ ACTIVE SERVICE

Like Cardigan ninety years earlier, General Roberts demurred. He argued that combined armour/infantry tactics were required to take out Rommel's fortified villages. And like Cardigan before him he was told to obey orders. So the stage was set for a repeat performance.

At 0545 RAF Lancasters and Halifaxes arrived, almost lolloping over in single file at what seemed tree top height. They dropped their bombs, banked, and made for Blighty. They were followed by some 400 Mitchell Marauders and Havocs, assisted by naval salvoes from the battleships anchored off Juno beach. The rolling barrage we had been promised had started.

We began to move forward. At first it seemed easy, as we drove in our lightly armoured half-tracks behind our tanks. Now our artillery joined in, laying a barrage 2,000 yards wide moving at five miles an hour. Germans were surrendering, dazed and defeated. We looked up into the bright blue sky to see incredibly high above us formation after formation of Flying Fortresses. A very different approach to that of the RAF. We hoped the American bomb sights were as good at that height as they were said to be.

As the day wore on things began to change. Our leading tanks were meeting determined opposition, not only ahead but also from the flanks. The rolling barrage began to move faster than the tanks could. We learnt later that a German 88 Flak battery was ordered to use their guns in an anti-tank role. With a crew of only eight men they destroyed the reserve squadron of one of our cavalry regiments. The tall corn through which we moved provided excellent cover for German snipers and panzerfaust. Camouflaged Tiger tanks opened fire, destroying twenty of our tanks in minutes. Then from the opposite flank German Panther tanks appeared. Sherman after Sherman went up in flames. 'Cannon to right of them, cannon to left of them, cannon in front of them volley'd and thunder'd.'

It was now all too apparent that our massive bombardment had not had the desired effect. Nor had it reached the Bourguebus Ridge, our main objective.

The battlefield was now littered with burning tanks, flames belching from their turrets. Tank crews scrambled out, some on fire trying to douse the flames by rolling on the ground. But we were in corn, and the corn caught fire, adding to the pall of smoke.

Shells exploded, ours and the enemy's. The sickly smell of gunpowder and death.

As darkness fell we held a line overlooking our objective, but not in possession of it. Fifty per cent of 11th Armoured Division's tanks were out of action. We suffered 336 killed or wounded.

A word here about weaponry. The German tanks were superior in fire power and thickness of armour. The British used American Sherman tanks, which could be knocked out by any German tank at 1,000-2,000 yards. Not for nothing was it known as the 'Tommy-Cooker'. It could also be knocked out at 2,500 yards by the German 88 mm, an incredible all purpose gun. (In the course of writing this I came across an allegation that the 88 was offered both to the British and the Americans in the thirties. Both turned it down. True or not I don't know. But certainly believable.)

In contrast, the Sherman with its 76 mm gun had to get very close to the German tanks, something like 500 yards in the case of Tigers and Panthers. Some British Shermans were fitted with a 17 pounder gun which evened things up a bit. Even these could not penetrate a Tiger head on at over 1,000 yards. In any case, as usual, there were not enough of them. The Germans also had the 'Moaning Minnie', a really nasty multi-barrelled rocket projectile which caused a horrifying number of infantry casualties in Normandy.

On the British side we had 6 pounder anti-tank guns, Vickers machine guns, Bren guns and the faithful Lee Enfield rifle. Only our 3 inch mortars and our brilliantly directed 25 pounder field guns were superior to anything the Germans had. Why was it that a country which could create the Spitfire, invent Radar, and crack Ultra, was never able to produce a tank the equal of the German, let alone better it? Fortunately we were blessed with almost total air superiority, particularly the 'Tiffies' who could be called in for close support work.

The sight of these RAF Typhoons zooming into attack never failed to raise the spirits.

The morning of 19 July was bright and sunny. We had spent an uncomfortable night. Digging proved impossible. Under the top layer of turf we struck solid chalk. The best we could do was scrape out a shallow depression and hope for the best. Some units were bombed by the Luftwaffe during the night. Miraculously reserve crews came up with some fresh tanks, stragglers arrived, all units concentrated on re-organising their men and vehicles.

As well as the German bombers we were attacked again by mosquitoes. My face had now swollen up like a balloon. I decided to visit the RAP half-track to see if the MO had anything to help. I felt distinctly vulnerable away from my vehicle and what passed for my slit trench. There was no sign of anybody. I was about to turn back when the Germans said good morning with a ferocious stonking, hitting us with everything they'd got. I dived head first into the RAP half-track, lying on the floor between the stacked medical equipment, pretending it was thick enough to absorb armour piercing shot. Certainly the Germans were not interested in the Red Crosses painted on the sides and roof. The half-track reared and bucked, the noise was terrifying. It seemed to go on for hours. At last things quietened down. I crawled out surprised to find myself still in one piece.

On my way back I passed a tank. Under it was one of the crew, and beside him one of his legs. Tank crews hated digging, and would far rather take cover inside their tanks, or if caught in the open, underneath. This frequently proved the worst place to be. I helped him fix a tourniquet, hoping he wouldn't lose any more blood. He was remarkably stoical, probably still in shock. I went off to find stretcher bearers.

I returned to my own half-track thinking how little damage there appeared to be. All our vehicles were well spread out, and most seemed to have survived. But when I reached my own I found my driver looking disconsolately into the bonnet. 'Engine's kaput, sir,' he said. Shrapnel had sliced through the armour plating and created havoc in the engine compartment. My crew had to be distributed among the rest of the company, and I transferred to my Company Commander's half-track.

The CO held an 'O' Group at which we learned that because of the previous day's heavy tank losses any idea of reaching Falaise had been abandoned. Instead, 11th Armoured would attack and hold the objectives which ought to have fallen the day before. Once again the tanks moved forward — and once again they ran into heavy fire from enemy tanks and 88s. As we discovered later, the Germans had reinforced the Bourguebus Ridge during the night.

Guards Armoured Division was level with us, attacking on the left. 7th Armoured was still trying to reach us through the heavy rear echelon traffic. Now General Roberts decided to put into action the plan he had always preferred — a combined tank and infantry attack. This was meticulously planned, involving all the fighting units, the Divisional 25 pounders, and the VIII Corps medium artillery. The first salvo from these 5.5 guns fell 500 yards short, and was distinctly unpleasant. Nowadays this is called 'friendly fire'. Who was the bright spark who thought of that contradiction in terms, I wonder? Nobody who'd ever been up the sharp end, that's for sure.

By evening, we had attained our objectives, though at heavy cost. The Germans had been quick to see the danger, and reacted by reinforcing their front with four Panzer Divisions plus an Infantry Division, together with the forces already on the ground which had re-grouped, something the Germans were very good at.

Once our objectives were achieved we were ordered to withdraw, handing over our positions to 7th Armoured Division. Thankfully we turned our vehicles and headed back through the battlefield littered with burnt-out tanks and support vehicles. But we had one more gauntlet to run. It was necessary to cross some open ground before reaching safety, and we were still in German range. They let fly with a barrage of Moaning Minnies. I was standing

THREE ~ ACTIVE SERVICE

up with my Company Commander in the front of our half track, and got hit, the force knocking me back into the body of the vehicle.

I had been wounded in the left arm. Our Signals Corporal very efficiently slit the sleeve of my battle dress jacket, I got my first Field Dressing out of the special pocket provided in battle dress trousers, and the wound was covered.

My war was over until I was able to rejoin my regiment in Holland in September. Operation 'Goodwood' was over too. 11th Armoured Division's butcher's bill came to 191 tanks and 735 killed or wounded. 'Into the valley of death rode the six hundred.' The descendants of the men who charged at Balaclava acquitted themselves with equal bravery in Normandy. I am proud to have been of their number, though even today still saddened at the loss of so many comrades in arms.

The journey back to England was a demonstration of medical efficiency. From the Regimental Aid Post wounded were sent back to an Advanced Dressing Station, still on what had been the battlefield. Here two labels were tied on to every casualty. One was white, containing a record of sulphonamide drug administered. The other was yellow, and recorded the penicillin injections. Next stop was the Casualty Clearing Station, where casualties were graded according to the severity of their wounds. I was 'walking wounded' and took my turn after the stretcher cases. From the CCS we were sent back to Base Hospital, a huge collection of marquees at the beach head.

Once again we were sorted into 'emergency' and 'Blighty ones'. Those of us lucky enough to be 'carried back to dear old Blighty' were loaded on to an empty TLC (tank landing craft). The entire tank deck was filled with stretcher cases, head to toe. I was reminded of that scene in *Gone with the Wind* where the wounded are laid out in the square at Atlanta.

The next day we reached England and were once again sorted and despatched to various hospitals. This was 20 July — the day of von Stauffenberg's bomb attempt on Hitler's life. If only it had succeeded.

By way of postscript, I recall one day standing in the hospital lavatory. Next to me was a regimental Medical Officer with a leg wound. I remarked on the degree of difficulty we were having, he balancing on one leg, me with an immobile arm. 'True,' he said, 'but do you realise how lucky we are?' He told me that in the last war we would probably have died from gas gangrene. At best we would certainly be amputees, since that was the only certain way of preventing the spread of infection. The timely invention of penicillin had saved our limbs, and probably our lives as well.[77]

There were many other soldiers with Oundle connections who were not so lucky. One of the early casualties in the Battle of Caen was Captain George Milliken, who had left Oundle School in 1936, and having landed in France on D-Day was killed in the heavy fighting around the city on 19 June.[78]

Two young officers who died in the Battle were former fellow-pupils of George Milliken who both received the Commander-in-Chief's Commendations for gallantry from Montgomery himself. One was Lieutenant Peter Howitt who was killed in an attack on the enemy at La Bijude, near Caen, on 28 June, and was awarded his honour posthumously. The second was Lieutenant Geoffrey Cooke, who had left the School's Laundimer House in 1938, enlisting in The Canadian Black Watch in 1942. He had already been honoured for his gallantry, and was killed in action on 30 July. Yet another casualty for the School at this time was Second Lieutenant Michael St John Booth, who had left Sidney House in 1941, and was killed while commanding a night patrol near Caen on 25 July, not long after his 21st birthday.[79]

The city of Caen itself was the scene of stubborn resistance by the Germans. The delay in the Allied advance provoked Montgomery into calling for one of the heaviest air attacks of the Normandy campaign as a prelude to a full-frontal assault, Operation 'Charnwood', scheduled for 8 July. On the evening of 7 July, 467 Lancasters and Halifaxes dropped 2,560 tons of high explosive on the city's northern outskirts. Michael Lewis was not impressed by the bombardment.

> All it did was kill a lot of innocent civilians and reduce a beautiful town to a pile of rubble — it was quite pointless. There weren't enough Germans there, and they wouldn't be sitting in barracks anyway: there wasn't a concentration of German troops or equipment in Caen. We saw it, a colossal cloud of smoke and explosions going on, three or four miles in front of us. It slowed up any advance because even the fields around Caen were filled with massive potholes.

A precarious situation had developed for the Allied attacking force, as testified by the letter written by an officer to the mother of a former Oundle School pupil who died in the fighting. This was Major Thomas Lovibond, who was with the 144th Regiment, Royal Armoured Corps, having left Laxton House in 1928:

> Early last August, in the attack on Caen, the position was very uncertain and part of the regiment had become lost. I reached the head of the leading squadron and managed to reorganise. On starting off again the troops ran immediately into a hell of fire. The leading officers were killed, and chaos redeveloped. When a left-flank movement was attempted in the stickiest conditions, there looked like being a total collapse when Tom took over, calling on people to follow him, and his example won the day. Steady progress was made. At one stage he was hit and shell-shocked, but later recovered sufficiently to carry on. That night he saved the regiment and was killed just as he succeeded.[80]

Also educated in Oundle and a victim of the battle for Caen was Corporal Frederick Bull, who had been a pupil at Laxton School from 1927 to 1930. Brought up in Ringstead, he had joined the Forces in 1940 and was killed in action on 8 August whilst carrying out his duties as a wireless operator.[81]

Slowly, however, the Allies were pushing through into Normandy and overcoming enemy resistance. One ex-Oundle School boy who won praise for his bravery during Operation 'Overlord' at this time was Colonel Sir Alastair Graesser, serving with the 53rd Welsh Division

96: Colonel Sir Alastair Graesser DSO, MC.

Reconnaissance Patrol. Towards evening on 15 August his squadron was advancing ahead of the infantry down the Leffard-Falaise road when its progress was halted by heavy enemy machine-gun and mortar fire. Cut off from headquarters by radio-jamming, 'Buster', as Alastair Graesser was known, moved up to the front, reorganised his troops, restarted the advance, inflicted heavy casualties and took 70 prisoners. He received an immediate Military Cross for his coolness, and calm, clear thinking under fire. Later he was to win the Distinguished Service Order.[82]

The Secret War

The planning for the invasion of Europe had also involved cooperation with those who were already fighting the Nazis on the Continent. The Allied forces' penetration of occupied France was considerably helped in the aftermath of the Normandy landings by the work of the French Resistance. The two dominant forces in the Resistance, Communist and Gaullist, formed a tacit and temporary alliance against the Germans from 1942. After the liberation of Corsica in September 1943 the Corsican term 'maquis' was given to the armed groups of resisters who took refuge in the wooded and mountainous regions of France to fight against the Nazi occupiers.

Help from Britain was given to the Resistance movement with the formation of groups such as the Special Airborne Service. Major Peter Goddard, educated at Oundle, was one of their number who lost his life helping the Maquis behind the enemy lines. In September 1944 he was in Northern France on patrol with a party when he met a German convoy. He immediately gave the order to attack and drove his jeep straight at the leading vehicle, firing all that he had until he put it out of action. He went on fighting until he ran out of ammunition, when he was killed, his body being recovered by the Maquis and buried at Tannay (Nivernais). He was Mentioned in Despatches and awarded the Croix de Guerre for his bravery.[83]

Also decorated for bravery in the war behind enemy lines was the former Oundle School boy and Battle of Britain air ace Manfred Czernin. After being shot down by Adolf Galland in November 1940, Manfred Czernin took command in a variety of RAF postings, both in Britain and in India. In September 1943 he was officially transferred to an Air Ministry Unit, but in fact went to the Special Operations Executive where he trained for the next eight months in warfare behind the lines. On 13 June 1944 he was parachuted into enemy-occupied Northern Italy, close to the Austrian frontier. For his secret operations here he was awarded the Military Cross in December. The following year in March saw him dropped just south of the Swiss frontier, where his operations culminated in the surrender of the German forces at Bergamo.

In fact it was another former pupil of Oundle School, Brigadier James Alms, described by a colleague as 'one of the outstanding staff officers of the 1939-45 war' who, as a member of SHAEF (Supreme Headquarters, Allied Expeditionary Force) was responsible for co-ordinating all the Western European resistance organisations placed under Eisenhower's control, being mentioned in despatches for control of Maquis operations. He was also responsible for the operational 'vetting' of the Psychological Warfare Division's devious attempts to sap the German will to resist. In 1943 he had been appointed GSO 1 (Strategic Plans) to the Chief of Staff to the Supreme Allied Commander, Lieutenant General F. E. (later Sir Frederick) Morgan, involved in much of the spadework on Operation

'Overlord', the outline plan for the invasion of France. He was decorated for his services, being awarded the OBE, and later the American Legion of Merit, and the Polish Gold Cross of Merit; he was also honoured as Chevalier Légion d'Honneur, as well as being awarded the Croix de Guerre avec Palmes.[84]

Alec Payne, a resident of Glapthorn for most of his life since the war, having retired from teaching Modern Languages at Oundle School, gained a special insight into the workings of covert organisations such as the Special Operations Executive (SOE) set up by Churchill for the purpose of sabotage in occupied Europe. A friend of his in Military Intelligence had in fact been involved in Operation 'Mincemeat' which had been so effective in putting the Germans off the scent of Sicily as a landing-point for the Allies in 1943.

Uncertain as to what he could do on being called up he had volunteered for service with the Field Security Police, after seeing an advertisement in the Press which called for language skills. After a period of training with the 29th Anti-Aircraft Regiment in Swansea, he was introduced to the serious business of spying:

> Somewhere about November 1940, I was called up to the Field Security Police's HQ in Winchester, which had gone up-market and decided to call itself the Intelligence Corps. So I went there for training, and towards the end of the training, they decided to send down from London, to find people who could talk Spanish, because Churchill had decided to have a thing called the Special Operations Executive, and the object of that was to send saboteurs behind the lines in Europe. So I went to this Special Operations Executive, and there they had 200 Spaniards, who had fought in the Spanish Civil War, and had got over the Pyrenees and into France when the war was over. And then they had been given the opportunity of either being interned, or joining the Foreign Legion. They joined the Foreign Legion, and were sent abroad. On their way back, France had fallen, and they refused to go back to France so they were landed here. The SOE was going to use them as saboteurs in case Spain came into the war. I spent a year or so with them training; jumping off things and blowing things up (well, they did that — they knew more about it than the instructors!). I was supposed to be the interpreter, fooling around and jumping in with them, and doing odd things. The actual training was done up in Scotland, which was SOE's home — it had a lot of safe houses up there, and of course we raided each other, and blew each other up.

Following this spell of hyper-activity Alec Payne acted as interpreter for MI5 officers who were interrogating suspected spies. He recalled one episode which involved a long journey to Kirkwall in the Orkney Islands where the Navy had seized a suspected German spy-ship masquerading as a Spanish vessel.

> After about a month doing that, I was sent back to SOE HQ, and I received instructions that I was to report to the War Office, which meant that I had joined Room 055, or MI5 as it is now known. I was then sent down to be an interrogator at a place that in peace-time was called the Royal Victorian Patriotic School. This was turned into a reception centre for all people coming into this country during the war who had to be detained. They all had to be detained and questioned. There were a lot of people coming into this country, as you can imagine. There were people coming over the North Sea from Norway and escaping that way, and there were also people escaping from France. But I was concerned with the interrogation of Spanish-speaking people from the Iberian Peninsula and from South America. We had all the relevant languages covered — there were about twenty officers there, and they then promoted me from being an acting Lance-Corporal, so I ended up with a very impressive title

THREE ~ ACTIVE SERVICE

as Captain in the Intelligence Corps attached to the War Office with Special Duties. Sounded terrific didn't it? So I masqueraded as that until the end of the war, and spent the rest of the war just interrogating people.

Alec Payne's fluency in Spanish was particularly useful to MI5 at this time because of the number of refugees from Spain who had been engaged by the German Abwehr Intelligence Service to spy in Britain.

> The object of the exercise was to get them into this country so that they could pass back information about what we were making and so on, and I had to find out if they were spies. To start with, the refugees all had to be detained and if in fact we thought that they were going to be spies, they had to go before a court, and were detained at a place called Ham Common, which was the centre for these people being investigated, who were probably going to be spies anyway. They were investigated by a chap called Colonel Scotland, and then one or two were turned round and used as double agents if they were intelligent, or they were disposed of. Often they were interned on the Isle of Man.

In spite of the fearsome reputation which Alec Payne gained among some of his pupils at the School, he was insistent that he and his colleagues in MI5 used nothing more than guile and piecemeal intelligence-gathering:

> In interrogation, you had to learn by experience and talking it over with the other chaps, because the only fellows in the department who had had any training were the barristers, who often gave you the tricks of the trade. You had to develop your own way, and as far as we were concerned, you had to get it out by what a Spaniard described to me as the 'fuerze de la lengua'. Now I remember this vividly because he himself was in the Spanish Secret Service, and during our conversation, he said something to the effect: 'This is a good job you've got here — getting the truth from people by the strength of the tongue.' Very often if they think you are believing them you will get more truth than if they don't. Every now and again you've got to be tough with them, but as far as we were concerned, there was never any bullying, tormenting or anything like that. There was nothing physical at all; you simply did it by the information that you got. You see, we were very lucky in the sense that there were all sorts of information available, and we ourselves built up information. For instance, in my particular case, I was interrogating a Spaniard who was recruited by the Germans in France, and had been sent back to do a job here. Now it happened in fact that he came to a place in the north of Spain which was a prison not very far from San Sebastian, and he told me this story of having walked there and having been put in this prison and how he had got all his documentation. I knew in fact that the place was a centre for the Gestapo where they had trained people to come to spy. So it was a cake-walk, and that information was on my desk. We built up that information ourselves, and we had information from MI6. MI6 were the people who did foreign espionage. MI5 were counter espionage and we looked after what happened in this country. We had information from the Enigma code breaking as well.

Out in the field it was a different matter. Alec Payne gave an insight into the tactics employed by the Navy on suspected spy-ships:

> After the Spanish Civil War, the Germans established a secret service in Spain, and employed Spanish fishing boats with transmitters to check up on our shipping in the Atlantic. They would use their transmitters to send information back to the secret service stations in Spain.

One of the things the Navy would do when they found these boats was to sail up very close to them and just to give the trawlers a nudge which would turn them over and keep them out of the way.

Pushing Into Europe

Although the Allied High Command had counted on a speedy capture of the French ports on the Western coast following the Normandy landings, the Germans held out in parts of Brittany until the end of the war. Brest was not taken until 19 September, but one incident during its capture was marked by boldness on the part of a former Oundle School pupil which won him the Distinguished Service Cross. Lieutenant Commander Tony Hugill, who had left Grafton House in 1934, landed in Normandy on the second day of the invasion and later recounted his adventures in a book *The Hazard Mesh* which he wrote in 1947 to buy his fiancée an engagement ring. With only eight marines under his command, he succeeded in persuading 280 German troops under their Luftwaffe officer to surrender at a radio station in St Paby, near Brest, telling the enemy that they were surrounded and threatening an aerial bombardment and tank attack which he was in no position to order.[85]

While Allied troops during their advance into 'Fortress Europe' found some Germans demoralised and ready to surrender, there was also fierce enemy resistance. Tony Hayward, a Birmingham man who settled in Oundle's Millfields, and well-known as the churchwarden of St Peter's, had volunteered for active service in October 1942, joining the First Battalion The Rifle Brigade. August 1944 saw him landing in Normandy at Sword Beach with the Seventh Armoured Division, the 'Desert Rats'. Close combat with the enemy at this time taught him respect for the average German soldier, but also an awareness of the fierce loyalty to the Nazi cause being shown by certain units.

> The ordinary German army were ordinary soldiers just like us. They had a job to do and they did it. The SS weren't so pleasant and the Hitler Youth were a damned sight less pleasant than they were. They were absolute fanatics. They were the most dangerous of the fighting troops who we came across. There seems to be the theory that the SS never surrendered, but our unit took quite a few hundred, along with their officers. Yes, the SS did surrender.

German snipers continued to be a threat to Allied forces during the advance into Europe. John Robinson, of Benefield Road, a British Army sergeant who had landed in France on 27 June, recalled an incident in Holland. His platoon was being pestered by a sniper, and he was given the instruction to root out the German. With the aid of some eight soldiers and another sergeant he ventured towards a barn from where the shots seemed to be coming. Deploying his men at various points around the barn, John Robinson waited until he heard a burst of gunfire, but made the decision for him and his men to 'sit it out' to avoid the risk of being picked off by renewed shots. Eventually, a German corporal came out and was taken back to the Allied headquarters. As he put it, John Robinson resisted the temptation of achieving synthetic glory from capturing the sniper while risking the lives of his men; in his words, 'A medal comes when you grasp an opportunity without trying to make one.'

The Disaster of Arnhem

Operation 'Market Garden', which centred on Arnhem in Holland, took place three months after D-Day and was an attempt to capture the bridge over the Rhine. The town lay deep in enemy lines, so troops from the Parachute Regiment were to be flown in and dropped near the bridge, the plan being that they would hold Arnhem until the Allies broke through the German lines and relieved them. This was the theory, but sadly the events of that September must rate as one of the great military disasters of the Second World War. Out of a strength of some 11,000 the British and Polish parachute and glider-borne troops suffered more than 7,000 casualties.

Former Oundle GP Michael Lewis had now moved from Normandy to Holland and was part of the army which was supposed to link up with the airborne drop on Arnhem. 'We didn't get there on time to link up with them or to be any use to them at all. Partly because it was difficult terrain to move fast across, and also because German tanks got into some of the convoys of troops and damaged a lot of vehicles and did a lot of harm as they crossed Holland.' He was bitter in his condemnation of those responsible for the failure of Operation 'Market Garden'.

> I suppose the worst mistake was the Arnhem adventure. It wasn't properly timed, it wasn't properly thought out, it was a terrible and totally unnecessary waste of life, and of first rate, very well trained soldiers. That was a terrible mistake, there was a lack of co-ordination somehow, there should have been some sort of much better co-ordination so that the advancing infantry and armoured vehicles coming through Holland linked up at the right time.

Retired gamekeeper Albert Spring, brought up in Winwick, was one of those who took part in the operation, but never arrived at his destination. The nine Paratroops of 697 Platoon whom he commanded were part of the second wave to be launched to Arnhem on 18 September.

Take-off was from Spanhoe Airfield in gliders piloted by American crew. The rallying point for some 1,000 aircraft and gliders was above Boston Stump in Lincolnshire. 'Our first offensive action was to bomb the civilian population below with green oil paper vomit bags filled with urine,' he recalled with a grin.

The task force then assembled headed off to the Hook of Holland. En route he saw at least two gliders plunging into the sea.

> As our plane flew into occupied territory a red light was illuminated, and almost immediately small arms fire began to burst around us. Within minutes heavy anti-aircraft fire began to pummel our plane. Directly in front of us a glider received an impact to the tail, blasting it off. It was a pathetic sight, it fell like a leaf with men falling out of the back. These gliders had no parachutes.

97: Veteran of the ill-fated Arnhem operation and Winwick ex-gamekeeper, Albert Spring.

They were approaching their destination and had 'hooked up' ready to jump. They were, as Albert Spring described, 'tremendously loaded, looking like Christmas trees, with rifles, kit bags, hand grenades, 303 ammunition and Sten guns'. Suddenly an explosion virtually destroyed the aircraft. It began to plunge from 1,000 feet to 200 feet, with its cockpit on fire. The co-pilot managed to pull the aircraft out of its death dive, but machine guns were tearing into the plane. 'I instructed my men to bail out. The plane flew on about 200 yards, struck a pylon tearing off a wing, and burst into flames. I began to collect my men together. Private Penwell was barely conscious when I found him. "What have I done?" he said. I gave him morphine but he died shortly afterwards. Corporal Hollis was also dead. Both men's parachutes had failed to open.'

The paratroops then noticed three men approaching, waving Union Jacks and singing 'God Save the King'.

> These brave Dutchmen doused the injured with water from the dyke and pulled the co-pilot out of the burning wreckage of the plane. He had received terrible injuries, his clothes were burnt to him, both his arms and legs were broken and his face was wounded with shrapnel. We owed the fact that we were alive to him. The Dutchmen introduced themselves as Harri, Hans and Fay, and later Johan van Zanten, who was in charge of the local Resistance at Kesteren arrived.

Already German units were closing in on the area, but not in force. Sporadic fire could be heard in the distance. The impact had taken place at 2.08 and they were still 25 miles from the dropping zone.

> The Dutch Resistance did a thorough reconnaissance of the area, hid the plane and escorted us to a farmhouse outside Kesteren. We turned the house into a state of siege, removing tiles from the roof for a lookout, and the local doctor placed a fever sign on the door. The Germans were billeted 250 yards away. Johan van Zanten was employed by the Germans and was in the Dutch artillery, as all personnel in occupied countries had either to enlist in the German armed forces or be sent to labour camps.

On the following day, the funerals for the American corporal and Private Penwell were to take place. Albert Spring thought it only right that he should attend, and went, dressed as a Dutchman, having been warned to remain silent by his Dutch friends in the event of their meeting a German patrol. They did meet a patrol but were allowed to pass: it was a tense moment. 'I kept a cocked pistol and grenades in my pocket.' But they had been advised to avoid confrontations with the Germans in such a situation.

> If the Germans suspected the Dutch were helping the Allied soldiers, they would surround the village, herd people together and force them to confess, otherwise they would shoot every 25th person. If they still would not confess, every tenth person would be shot. For the same reason, we were discouraged from any act of sabotage.

After the funerals, Albert Spring was taken to visit their brave co-pilot. He was being kept for safety in the doctor's coal cellar, and was so heavily bandaged that only his mouth and eyes were visible.

THREE ~ ACTIVE SERVICE

When it was decided that they should try and head for the British lines, they were provided with papers to say that they were Dutch bakers, and they started the long walk towards Nijmegen. At one point they saw a German patrol coming towards them, but a suitably placed ditch saved them. 'Our next problem was the River Waal. It was 600 metres wide with a very strong current, and we only had one rowing boat.' However by 2.00 am all the men were across. They waited in another safe farmhouse, and just before daybreak a Guards Regiment picked them up.

On his return to Allied lines Albert Spring completed the following detailed report to vouch for the bravery of the American crew:

```
REPORT ON PLANE CHALK NO. 697

   The plane, a Dakota, was piloted by 1st Lt SPURRIER, Co-Pilot was
2/Lt FULMER, Radio Op was Cpl William T. HOLLIS, Crew Chief was Cpl
Russell M. SMITH they were all in the American Air Force.

   On the 18-9-44 I was stick commander in plane 697 it carried 17
paratroops. At 1410 hours while flying over Holland we were hit by
flak the plane lost some height and the Crew Chief who was in the rear
end of the plane said that the Pilot had been hit but the Co-Pilot had
it under control. At this time we received another hit by flak and the
Radio Op opened the door which parts the cabin from the main compartment
and we could all see the flames in the cabin. The Crew Chief ordered
us to jump which we did. I must say that throughout the whole of this
rather critical period the behaviour of the Crew Chief Cpl R. M. SMITH
was superb. He stayed in the plane until the last paratroop had left
and then jumped himself, injuring his right foot. Also the courage of
the co-pilot was of the highest and coolest type. He stuck to the
plane right to the ground although he was wounded twice by shrapnel,
and the aircraft was blazing fiercely.

   Whatever award any of them receive it will be very richly deserved.

                  (Sgd) /s/ 4805452 Sgt A. SPRING
                        /t/ Sgt A.Spring.

THIS IS A TRUE COPY:



WILLIAM L. BRINSON
Major, Air Corps
```

Albert Spring was demobbed in 1946, but kept in touch with the friends in Holland whom he had met through the fortunes of war. He returned to Holland in 1987 and met again some of those who had helped them — Hans by then had become a Professor of Medicine. He never forgot the bravery of the Dutch Resistance and the selfless help they gave to him and his comrades. Their leader Johan van Zanten was shot by the Germans shortly after he had

98: Repaying a debt: Albert Spring (left) with two former wartime comrades at the ceremony in Kesteren, Holland, marking the events of September 1944.

enabled the Allied servicemen to escape. In May 1995 Albert Spring attended a ceremony at Kesteren at which a commemorative plaque was unveiled in honour of Johan van Zanten and the brave Dutchmen who had helped him to escape. By doing so the former paratrooper felt that he was doing something to repay a debt: for many years, rightly or wrongly, he had felt in some way responsible for the Resistance leader's death.[86]

The launch of 'Operation Market Garden' on 17 September also involved the seizure of towns to the south. It was during the battle for Nijmegen that Private Philip Colbourne was seriously wounded, dying in Brussels Hospital on 5 October. Brought up in Kettering, he had lived in Oundle as a boarder while he attended Laxton School from 1918 to 1925. He had joined the Royal Army Ordnance Corps as a private soldier and was later attached to mobile workshops of the Royal Electrical and Mechanical Engineers.[87]

The Fatherland Under Threat

In spite of the reverse of Arnhem, seven Allied armies pressed on towards Germany in appalling weather conditions. Autumn 1944 was one of the wettest and most miserable on record in North West Europe. Tony Hayward and his fellow-soldiers remembered a succession of surprising experiences at this time.

> We reached a canal, and a small party got across a bridge which had been demolished but was still able to get people across on foot before it eventually collapsed, and we held that bridgehead overnight, about 12 of us, and we were the only troops from our side on that side of the canal. The following morning the Royal Engineers got the rest over with a scissors bridge, and we got ourselves out of difficulty. But I have to say that that was quite a hairy experience. When

99: Turnhout, Belgium 1944: Oundle churchwarden Tony Hayward with the remnants at that time of 5 Section 2 Platoon A Company 1st Bn Rifle Brigade.
(L. to r.) Tony Hayward, Bob Healey (standing); George Winser, Blondie Pike (sitting).
All except Tony Hayward were later killed in action.

we got back across the bridge and had joined our own half tracks, we discovered that one of the other platoon's half tracks was out of service — the hose to the radiator had burst. Anyway, our half track had to tow this one and try to keep up. We didn't keep up, it was hopeless, and we got completely lost. We were missing for about a week after that, just sculling around the country trying to find our unit. On one occasion when we had been driving all morning, it got to lunch time, and there was a German wagon pulled up out of action on the side of the road, and we realised that we could get the required hose for our own radiator off this vehicle. While we were doing this, a unit of the Fourth Royal Army Infantry Brigade arrived and more or less arrested us, because apparently we had driven straight through the German lines, and they thought that we were a German crowd dressed up as British infantry. It took quite a lot of convincing but eventually we got away. On the same trip, our vehicle then broke down. It had water in the petrol, and the one we had been towing finished up towing us. We got to a town

> in Northern France called Carvin which had a big square with a main road going along beside it, and we stopped in this square overnight. We were sleeping on the cobblestones overnight — we were quite used to that sort of thing — when a large German armoured division came through on the road. We lay there just watching these Germans go through, we couldn't do anything about it. We were hopelessly outnumbered, and they didn't spot us, which was a bit of luck.

Some of his luck was eventually to run out.

> I was wounded in January 1945 when I received a wound in the head. An 88mm shell burst about five yards away from me, and that put me completely out of action. I was very lucky to escape like that. The chap just around the corner of the building got absolutely peppered from the same shot.

New Enemies

With Rommel's forces defeated at El Alamein in October 1942 and the British Eighth Army's push into Tunisia in the following year, it was clear that the battle of the Western Desert had been won. German and Italian resistance in North Africa had ceased by mid-May 1943. British forces in the Middle East no longer had to fear the threat from the Axis.

But victory for the Allies in many parts of the world as World War II drew to a close revealed new enemies for British soldiers.

In India it was clear that the old imperial order was over. The stirrings of nationalism had been felt in the sub-continent under Gandhi's leadership: as early as 1942 General Sir Archibald Wavell, Commander-in-Chief India, had been forced to use some 57 British and Indian battalions to quell demonstrations in the eastern provinces. The Japanese had taken advantage of anti-British feeling, notably by supporting and training guerillas who were part of what was known as the Indian National Army.

Palestine

Palestine too had seen insurrections against British rule in the 1930s and freedom fighters such as the Stern Gang and Irgum Svai Liumi were forces to be reckoned with no less than the Germans in terms of acts of terrorism and outrage.

Robert Butler found himself in the summer of 1944 appointed Military Assistant to the Commander-in-Chief of Middle East Land Forces, General Sir Bernard Paget, in Cairo, before moving to Jerusalem as a General Staff Officer at HQ Palestine. The headquarters were in fact on an upper floor of the King David Hotel, with access by the lift and staircase well guarded against the threat of terrorism. No one imagined that the headquarters would eventually be blown up by the simple expedient of leaving a bomb in the room underneath, which is what happened after Robert Butler's return to England later in the year.

A training in counter-terrorism, with instruction in bomb disposal work from the skilled and celebrated Inspector 'Grip' Elson, was followed by Robert Butler's being given security at the King David Hotel as his special responsibility. A dramatic account of one episode of his work is given in his book *Nine Lives*:

> In Jerusalem a big event took place during this period. Grip Elson telephoned me early one afternoon to say that the Police had information that a suspected explosive cache of mammoth proportions had been reported in the modern area of Jerusalem, not far from the King David

Hotel itself, and that he would appreciate my help. The other three instructors were too far away for immediate availability, so I grabbed my little box of tricks and joined him at his headquarters. We proceeded to a quarter which was slightly squalid and found a small single storied building already cordoned off by Police.

Grip was the first to enter the front door, which had been left ajar, with me rather foolishly too close to his heels. He peered through the crack in the door with a torch, to see that it was not wired or booby trapped with some movable object and gently pushed it open. We both entered the dark room, whose windows were all shuttered, and shone our torches round. There was an enormous pile of what looked like builders' sand rising to about four feet in height, and the walls were lined with what, in the dim light, appeared to be bricks stacked against them. About two feet from the threshold lay a khaki haversack. Elson made no attempt to pick it up or to undo the flap. He very gently slid his hand under the flap and slowly moved his fingers left and right, feeling for any suspicious wires. He duly found them.

'It's a booby-trap all right,' he said, 'if you shine your torch in through the gap in the flap, I'll cut the wires one by one if they're single.' (If wires are double, then pliers join them electrically and act as a switch.) When we had eventually made the booby trap safe, we discovered that it was set so that the floor itself pressed up a wooden rod which projected down through a hole in the base of the haversack. This rod was surmounted by a piece of flat metal, thus forming a 'T' which was poised above the positive and negative terminals except when the haversack was on the ground and the rod and plate forced up and away from them. To lift the haversack without first disconnecting or cutting the live wires meant curtains for the lifter; and in our case countless lives and many buildings. We removed the charge and detonator and passed them gently to the nearest policeman who was, very sensibly, not too near the door!

We then opened the doors wide and took a good look around. The actual pile was not sand but ammonal, a grey and highly explosive powder. The things which had looked like bricks, stacked against the walls, were prepared hand bombs, each consisting of four sticks of gelignite, bound together with sticky-tape, with a detonator thrust into their centres already fitted with a short length of safety fuse. The floor was littered with tubular brass detonators, showing that a very hasty exit had been made. If, in the dark, one of us had trodden on one of them, it would not have been a case of losing a few toes, though we would have done, but a very large number of houses would have gone up with them. We would have been non-existent.

The explosion of just one detonator would have set off the bottom of the pile of ammonal which was spread over a wide area, and the first flash or spark to touch just one of the safety fuses would have set off its four sticks of gelignite, which would have set the whole lot off.

100: Lieutenant Colonel Robert Butler MBE, MC, on a return visit to Oundle in 1995.

Moving slowly and methodically, we gradually cleared the floor of all detonators and then began passing the prepared gelignite bombs out to the police helpers, who were now becoming braver and more inquisitive. We decided that it would be prudent to defuse all the gelignite bombs by hand at an area far enough away from the cache to be relatively safe.

The job of defusing them was not highly skilled. It was simply necessary to use no force, to draw the detonators slowly from the bunch of four sticks, then remove the safety fuses from the detonators, and finally place the gelignite sticks on one pile, the safety fuses on another, and the detonators, each separately, on laid-out pieces of soft cloth. I think there were three of us on the job in the end, and that we did around twenty bombs each. I did not know before that if one handles enough gelignite, one gets the most appalling headache. Next day I added a pair of rubber gloves to the contents of my little suitcase. Grip Elson, who was a brilliant and fearless bomb disposal expert seemed to lead a charmed life, and I was humbly proud to have been instrumental in passing on his knowledge and experience to others who made good use of it.

He was one of the people to whom I paid a warm and meaningful farewell when I eventually left Jerusalem two months later. After nine years, when I again met John Fforde, who by then had become the Commissioner of Police in Lusaka, Rhodesia, I asked for news of Grip Elson and learned that he had been killed 'on the job', mercifully almost instantaneously, not long after I left Jerusalem. A sad loss for the Police and all his many friends in Palestine. Since writing the above I have learned that his reputation was of international proportion.[88]

The Crisis in Greece

In Europe the uneasy alliance between Communist elements in the Resistance movements and British forces came under increasing strain in the vacuum caused by Germany's withdrawal.

A crisis came in Greece in late 1944. For ex-Oundle School boy Cecil Lewis, commanding a staging post at Tatoi airfield some miles north of Athens the situation was intolerable, not just because of the threat posed to the men under his command by Greek communist Resistance fighters but because Greece, the birthplace of democracy, was under threat from a new tyranny. 'I, for one, have not given ten years of my life defending the democratic principle to be content to see the first "liberated" country in Europe fall victim to an opportunist communistic minority, trying to shoot its way to power with a few Tommy guns,' he wrote to his wife on 30 December. 'This is exactly the sort of terrorism by which Hitler gained power.'

The author of *Sagittarius Rising*, having rejoined the RAF reserve of officers in 1939, had spent the early part of the war in Britain, first as a controller responsible for briefing and debriefing Anson crews during their flying patrols, and later at the Air Ministry where he joined the RAF publicity staff, concerned with the daily communiqués put out from Whitehall during and after the Battle of Britain. Then in early 1941 the course of the war was changed for Cecil Lewis, when the First World War air ace found himself in demand as an instructor, training hundreds of young men to fly. One of them was a certain Ivor Lewis, whom he was proud to get solo in seven hours and twenty-five minutes, the only instance in the RAF, he believes, of father teaching son to fly.

His wartime career was changed yet again in December 1942 when he was posted overseas to command an air terminal in the recently formed Transport Command under Air Commodore Witney Straight, whose famous 212 Group operated over the length of the

THREE ~ ACTIVE SERVICE

Mediterranean from Casablanca to Bahrain. The air terminals of Transport Command, known as staging posts, were responsible for looking after the miscellaneous aircraft of all kinds flying between the UK and various battle-fronts.

After his nine month successful first posting at Catania in Sicily, Cecil Lewis was moved northwards to form a new staging post at Bari in Italy, ready to move into Athens when the Allies reoccupied Greece. In hindsight it was clear from the information supplied by intelligence officers working with the Greek Resistance that trouble was brewing. The two main resistance organisations had for some time been stockpiling for their own ends Allied money and supplies provided to fight the Germans. One of them, the Communist-affiliated ELAS, seemed to have heavily armed members everywhere, and many more who were undercover agents assessing the British strength in Greece. It was obvious in retrospect that ELAS would never accept the British High Command's plans for a return to the pre-war set-up with a welcome back for the King of Greece, still in exile in Claridges. And the Allied forces sent in to reoccupy Greece were not fighting men but were concerned with the country's rehabilitation: these were units intended to rebuild roads and railways and to reopen postal and telephone services.

However all such concerns were forgotten as Cecil Lewis shared in the elation of arriving in the country where he was eventually to settle.

> It is 14 October and we have liberated Greece! Night has fallen and I am sitting in a hotel bedroom in the heart of Athens. The window is open and through it, high above, I can see the light that crowns the tiny shrine of Mount Lycabettus. From below comes a mutter of joy. It wells up from the brightly lit streets — for the Hun seems to have left the power stations intact — where processions pass carrying banners and singing. The whole city is a flutter of flags. One wonders where did they manage to hide them. They hang from the housefronts, literally in hundreds. It is like a Carnival. The whole of Greece seems to be in the streets, singing and cheering and applauding as we pass, throwing flowers at our lorries and surrounding every stationary group of men. I suppose they remember the tragic days in 1941 when we came to their help only to beat a hasty retreat ourselves! They have longed for our return. Well, here we are!

Later he recorded: 'I have just been out for a stroll. The whole city is in the streets. Crowds throng everywhere, the buildings are floodlit, processions pass, singing, and we are cheered wherever we go. People come up and wring your hand and talk away quite oblivious that you can't understand a word! Loudspeakers are relaying political speeches, the whole place is one big smile. This is the moment of joy, freedom, liberation. Impossible to describe — but impossible to forget.'

Amidst all the joyful celebrations an Allied-backed government was formed. But beneath the surface in every sense there were still dangers. Commodore Kenneth Gadd, still on minesweeping duties to prepare for the return of the Greek President, had an unpleasant experience at sea.

> We were sweeping out there, sweeping ahead of the President of Greece. The trouble with minesweeping in the Mediterranean is that there are no tides — the tide there doesn't move up and down like it does here. Consequently when you lay the mines there's no tide and they never bend over like they do here. If you wait until the tide is running well, then the mines lean over on their moorings and you can go over the top of them. Out there you can't do it. So

we had to be very, very careful indeed. We sent a couple of very small motor minesweepers, but something went wrong and they didn't get there as quickly as they should have. The senior officer's ship, which was ahead of us, struck a mine and keeled right over. There were many casualties. I was right behind and I hit a mine, but, fortunately, all I did was go down by the bow. The bulkheads held and we managed to turn around and we came back to a nice little island called Poros which I believe is now a very popular holiday resort — just south of Athens. We waited in Piraeus and had a patch put on the hole in the bows. Again we got away with it. One or two people were injured to a certain extent, but it was very minor and despite the explosions we had no real casualties.

With the fading of the glorious days of the Greek autumn and the arrival of the chill mountain winds came the political realities. A Victory Parade several miles long staged by EAM, one of the resistance organisations, was a tacit though obvious demonstration of power by thousands of young men and girls with guns, bandoliers and banners. The General Officer Commanding Greece, General Scobie, together with Sir Rex Leeper the British Ambassador to Greece, and Harold Macmillan the future British Prime Minister, were desperately negotiating with the partisans for a return to peacetime conditions involving the surrendering of all weapons. But this was highly unlikely, as Cecil Lewis wrote to his wife.

> These girls and boys of seventeen and eighteen were no more than children when the Hun came in. They lost all chance of education, all home influence, they fled to the mountains to escape the forced labour gangs, they lived like animals. War was a licence for lust, theft and murder. It was easy to destroy — and fun. They were brought up to it. Most of them have never dreamed of living a peaceful life or studying to work or make a living; all they can do is use a gun. They have been well paid for it too. But now the pay has stopped and, what is more, we are asking them to return the gun! The only tool they can use, their only capital asset![89]

Inevitably General Scobie's ultimatum was followed by refusal. A general strike, during which ELAS seized the power station in Athens, was followed by orders to evacuate the Tatoi staging post, bringing its 200 men, 42 vehicles and 60 tons of equipment to the relative safety of the Athens suburb of Kifissia, and Scobie's ordering a full offensive against ELAS.

But this was no simple war against an obvious enemy, as Cecil Lewis discovered.

> To defend a residential suburb like Kifissia would have taken several thousand men. Besides, to defend it against whom? No enemy appeared. In the villas were many Greeks, people who were friendly to us. We could not turn them out. Only our Greek servants, pointing to some faceless man in a mackintosh strolling by, would say, 'That man is a member of the ELAS. I know him well.' It gave us a creepy feeling.
>
> The men were unhappy and mystified. Only a few days ago everything had been perfectly friendly and now suddenly they felt cut off, besieged by people against whom they had no animosity whatever. It was our first experience of guerrilla warfare. There was no front, no back, no sides. Attack might come from anywhere. The feeling of being constantly under observation, and yet unable to locate it, was very odd. Morale fell quickly. None of us had anything to do and idleness is a subtle enemy in situations like this. We had no means of defending ourselves, no arms or ammunition and nothing to do but wait.

Cecil Lewis, alarmed by the increasingly gloomy news of ELAS aggression, persuaded his Commanding Officer, Air Commodore Geoffrey Tuttle, to allow his unit to make a further withdrawal to the main airport at Hassani. Two convoys were successfully evacuated under only sporadic fire before the partisans blocked the road. This time they meant business. Charges of dynamite blew holes in the walls of the hotels where the remaining British troops were trapped in Kifissia and 600 men and officers were rounded up by the partisans. Many of them would have white hair when they were released in the New Year.

Only after General Alexander had come to see for himself what was happening was order restored, following his immediate instruction to send in a division.

The triumph of organisation in which Cecil Lewis was involved to ensure the success of the airlift was something which he long remembered.

> The arrival of that airborne division was, I think, the most exciting and inspiring episode in my RAF career. Top-secret signals began to pour in: 'Forty Liberators arriving!' 'Twenty Wellingtons arriving!' 'Fifty Dakotas arriving!' For the first three days these aircraft all turned up at precisely 11 am. I have never seen anything like it. The sky was thick with aircraft.
>
> All normal landing procedures were scrapped. The boys played it by ear. Stacked up one behind the other, wheels and flaps down, it was nothing to see six on finals at the same time. A bewildered aircraftsman at the head of the runway fired volleys of red lights to space them out, of which the pilots took absolutely no notice whatever. One burst tyre or one faulty landing and there would have been a monumental pile-up. But it was a magnificent display of airmanship. Coming in hard on each other's tails, so that before one aircraft was off the runway the next had touched down, they rolled in perfectly, and followed the jeep with its chequered flag to their parking position. An army lorry slid alongside from the rank of 100 we had organised, the load was transferred and the pilot moved on to the prepared park for take-off.
>
> At this pitch of over 100 aircraft arriving simultaneously, the airlift lasted for three days. Then they got it organized. Arrival times were spaced out and the heat was off. But even so they were terrific days; organizing scratch meals for 400 aircrew was a strain on our resources. The night when the weather clamped in Italy and 100 aircraft crews could not get back was the climax. They thought they might all be shot up before morning. This amused us greatly, for we were used to the conditions and couldn't believe we were in much danger — which was far from the truth.[90]

The organized sweep of regular seasoned troops against ELAS strongholds swiftly resolved the situation, and peace was finally reached after Churchill himself flew to Athens on Christmas Day to state publicly British government policy on the future of Greece.

But the episode, coming as it did in a country which he already loved for its beauty, was to sicken Cecil Lewis.

> I revisited our billets at Tatoi. I have never seen anything like it. Not a stick left. Everything had been looted, furniture, doors, window frames, even floors, ripped out, destroyed, smashed for firewood. At the airfield I couldn't believe my eyes. Absolutely useless things had gone, huge scrapped aero engines, weighing hundreds of pounds, technical gear of which they can't even have known the use, a huge amount of stuff which must have needed hundreds of carts or lorries to move — all, bar our domestic stuff, quite, quite useless.
>
> Somehow this was more terrible than the inhuman destruction of bombing. It was the barbarism of men gone mad with greed and nihilism and it left a very ugly taste in my mouth — as if one had suddenly been allowed to see into the black depths of men's souls. How terribly thin is the veneer of our so-called civilisation. How much evil still seems to grow in the world. How men seem to have a genius to turn good to bad. How much easier it is to destroy than create.[91]

The War in the Air: the Bombing Intensifies

Preparations for the invasion of Normandy from early 1944 resulted in a change of target after the bombing campaign directed at the German heartland, and under Sir Arthur Tedder, who had taken over as Deputy Supreme Commander to General Eisenhower, the German, and notably the French transport systems bore the brunt of the bomber offensive. Improvement in precision bombing meant that such raids were considerably more effective than the earlier blanket bombing of German cities, particularly when it became clear that the ability of the enemy to reinforce itself with supplies against the invading Allies had been severely crippled. Oil installations also became an increasing target for Allied air attacks: by July 1944 every major oil plant in Germany had been hit. Opposition from the Luftwaffe had diminished to such an extent by June that Bomber Command was making its first raids by daylight, first to targets in France, and then in the German Ruhr. In the last three months of 1944 Bomber Command dropped more bombs than during the whole of 1943. The price in terms of lives and aircraft was high. Some 55,573 aircrew died during the 307,000 night sorties and 80,150 daylight sorties between 1939 and 1945.[92]

Many members of the aircrews on these raids had links with Oundle. One was Flight Sergeant Edward Brown, a Nassington man known to his friends as 'Cricketer' Brown, who had left Laxton School in 1937 and had joined the RAF in 1942. By the beginning of 1944 he had completed the required 27 missions with 166 Squadron, No. 1 Bomber Command, but due to a shortage of aircrew had volunteered to do three more. It was during the next, on 14 January, that the Lancaster which he was navigating was hit by enemy fire over Berlin. The aircraft burst into flames. Only the co-pilot survived, recording his testimony

101: Flight Sergeant Edward Brown, killed in action over Germany on his 28th mission. A former pupil of Laxton School, he was known in his native Nassington as 'Cricketer' Brown.

THREE ~ ACTIVE SERVICE

102: The Memorial Window in Lincoln Cathedral, dedicated to the men of Edward Brown's Bomber Command group who lost their lives.

of Edward Brown's devotion to duty in a letter to the dead man's father. 'Your son was a splendid navigator, thoroughly reliable, meticulously precise and infinitely painstaking. We were always on time and the Squadron Navigation Leader had the highest opinion of the charts of our journeys which he presented for analysis... I actually had the papers before me to recommend him for a commission a day or so previous to our last flight.'[93]

Michael Maw, who had left the School in 1931, had joined the Reserve of Air Force Officers (RAFO) soon after going up to Cambridge in the same year. Like his distant relative Roger, he reached the rank of Wing Commander. While the latter had been shot down over North Africa in August 1942, and was to find fame as the originator of the 'Wooden Horse' used in the escape from Stalag Luft III, Michael Maw was piloting Halifax bombers. After spending the first part of the war instructing at Cranwell, the Central Flying School and Calgary, in Canada, he was posted to 10 Squadron, and in 1944 took command of 640 Squadron. He was to die in action over Germany during a raid near Frankfurt on 13 August 1944, one month after being awarded the Distinguished Flying Cross.

103: Wing Commander Michael Trentham Maw, DFC, a portrait painted by his aunt, Dorothy Kenrick.

David Maw, a prisoner of war in Germany at the time and also educated at Oundle, had often thought anxiously about his two brothers Michael and Denys, both of them bomber pilots. Allied aircraft often crashed in the area of the camp during raids on nearby targets. He recalled one night in June 1944:

> I had a most terrible nightmare, a very vivid dream from which I awoke in a cold sweat, and never slept another wink the whole of that night. Quite simply, I saw Mike at the controls in the cockpit of a bomber, the whole thing enveloped in flames, going down at an angle of 45 degrees, and I saw exactly where the plane fell, in a mass of flames, in a clearing of a forest where two tracks crossed one another. I saw no other person in the plane, only Mike, rigged out in his flying kit, just as I used to see him sometimes before the war. But my overriding memory of that dream, which seemed to transcend absolutely everything else — it seemed strange at the time, but now I take it as a very great comfort — was Mike's utter composure and confidence. I would almost say happiness, in that moment of disaster. Quite the reverse of what one might expect, and certainly the complete opposite to my own sweating panic. Naturally I tried to rationalize the whole affair as just a consequence of my shattered nerves, and how could a mere dream bear any relation to reality? Surely my subconscious was just portraying what I feared so much. And so I tried my best to dismiss that terrifying night entirely from my thoughts, and I am sure that I never mentioned a word to any of my closest friends.

In the early autumn of that year came a letter from his mother, bearing the news that he had been dreading: Michael had failed to return from a mission.

After the end of the war, while stationed in Germany, David Maw set out on an

THREE ~ ACTIVE SERVICE

expedition, determined to discover the crash-site and his brother Michael's grave. In what must have been a remarkable moment, given his premonition, he succeeded in identifying the exact spot where the aircraft had come down, using information about the raid and matching it to the details of his dream. A German priest in the village helped him to confirm that an unmarked grave was indeed that of his brother.

Later, David Maw met one of the survivors of the bombing mission, who had succeeded in bailing out before the plane crashed in flames. It was clear from the account of the last moments of the doomed aircraft that Michael Maw had died as a hero, doing what he could to save his crew, four of whom had escaped.[94]

Lieutenant Albert Sikkenga of the USAAF was one of the few American former pupils of Oundle School. Having left St Anthony House in July 1938 he returned to the USA to study medicine, and when the Americans entered the war became a bomber pilot, completing 45 missions over Germany as the pilot of a Flying Fortress before he was shot down and killed at Magdeburg on 28 September, 1944. He was awarded the Distinguished Flying Cross as well as the Air Medal with four oak-leaf clusters.[95]

Another tragic loss was that of Flight Lieutenant Noel Tatam, who had left Oundle School's Bramston House in July 1935 and who was killed in action on 18 December 1944 while returning from a raid on Duisburg. He had joined the Peterborough firm of Baker Perkins Ltd in 1938, and had continued to pursue his studies in engineering, one of his chief interests, during the war years, graduating at the Institution of Mechanical Engineers in November 1943. Mr N. I. Baker, writing from Peterborough, expressed the firm's sense of loss in the following words:

> I had a profound admiration for his determination, strength of purpose and courage. The way he studied for and took the examination of the Mechanical Engineers at a time when he was engaged in frequent dangerous operations was quite remarkable and very greatly to his credit. I had looked forward very greatly to his taking an important position in our works organisation, and his death is a sad loss to Baker Perkins. Noel was certainly a son of whom to be very proud.

Noel Tatam's loss was felt particularly deeply in Oundle, where his father was Director of Music at the School.[96]

Two other Oundle airmen died in action in 1944. Pilot Officer John Mason, whose family lived on Benefield Road, had left Laxton School in 1938, joining the RAF three years later. Following his posting to Bomber Command he took part in 40 operational flights, including three as a Pathfinder pilot, and was awarded the Distinguished Flying Cross. He was killed when his aircraft was shot down over Lille on 11 May. A keen cricketer, his loss was felt in Oundle sporting circles as well as by his family.

Flight Sergeant John Horsford, the only son of an Oundle farming family living at Oundle Lodge on Stoke Road, had left Laxton School in 1941. He joined the RAFVR in January of the following year and was later attached to 272 Squadron. He was mentioned in despatches in July 1944 for the bombing of enemy supplies in Italy, but on 6 September the Beaufighter which he was piloting during operations against enemy shipping was shot down over the Gulf of Genoa in Italy. He was posthumously awarded the Distinguished Flying Medal. The citation read: 'Flt/Sgt. Horsford has consistently displayed courage and devotion to duty of the highest order.'[97]

104: Pilot Officer John Mason, pictured with his DFC and service medals.

THREE ~ ACTIVE SERVICE

105: Flight Sergeant John Horsford, DFM.

106: The grave of
Flight Sergeant John Horsford, DFM,
in Genoa, Italy.

The Doodlebug Menace

Just a week after D-Day, Britain was struck by the first of Hitler's secret weapons, the V-1 pilotless flying bomb. Carrying 850 kilos of high explosive, the destruction wrought by the device recalled the worst days of the Blitz. The Germans had planned to launch up to 500 V-1s a day to terrorize the civilian population, but intelligence reports from Resistance agents allowed the RAF to bomb the launch sites in Northern France. Nonetheless 6,725 of the new weapons — 'doodlebugs' or 'buzz bombs' as they were known — fell on England, killing 6,000 people and badly injuring nearly 18,000. Alec Payne, the retired schoolmaster living in Glapthorn, recalled seeing one of the 2,420 V-1s which fell in the London area during his time there. He was sitting in a bus at the time. 'It sort of went over the top, and we didn't know it was coming. I was going along the Upper Richmond Road and it was coming down another road. We reached the crossroads, the bus stopped, and the flying bomb went by in front of us.'

The V-1 was followed by the V-2, which made its appearance on 8 September 1944. More terrifying, since it arrived without warning, the explosions which it caused were put down at first to gas explosions by the bewildered civilian population. Only in November did Churchill reveal the truth.

While there was little that could be done to stop the V-2s once they had been launched, anti-aircraft gunners and fighter pilots found that the slower 'doodlebug' could be dealt with successfully. An impressive 1,859 of them were shot down by anti-aircraft guns between June 1944 and March 1945. A total of 1,771 were also downed by the RAF. Oundle-educated Charles Steele was to play a key part in the battle of the V-1s. The former Oundle School boy had left Crosby House in 1915, joining the Royal Flying Corps the following year and winning the Distinguished Flying Cross. 1940 saw him mentioned in despatches for his part in the Battle for France. Four years later, as the victorious Allies pushed towards Hitler's fortress, he was commanding the base group of the RAF's Second Tactical Air Force responsible for the night defence of bases in France and Belgium. During this time the Group's aircraft shot down 835 of the V-1 flying bombs, while Mosquito night-fighters operating under his command destroyed over 190 enemy aircraft. He was to end his career as Air Marshal Sir Charles Steele, KCB, CB, DFC.

~ 1945 ~

The Final Advance

December 1944 had seen the Germans making a last stand with a counter-attack penetrating 40 miles through the Ardennes, but this was repulsed by the advancing American and British troops. By March 10 the Allies had reached the Rhine, and the bridge at Remagen, near Bonn, was seized. A major crossing of the Rhine was made some 130 miles downstream at Wesel on 23 March, and the build-up of Allied forces ensured steady progress eastwards.

There were still pockets of German resistance. Lieutenant David Berridge, of the Barnwell farming family, showed a bravery worthy of his father 'the intrepid hero of the Northamptonshire Regiment', winning an immediate Military Cross for his actions on 1 March. The middle son of Colonel F. R. Berridge, educated at King's School, Peterborough, he was posted to the First Battalion, The Herefordshire Regiment after being commissioned

THREE ~ ACTIVE SERVICE

to the Northamptonshire Regiment. His citation recorded what happened to David Berridge and his platoon during the advance on German positions.

> The forward section became pinned down in open ground by heavy and accurate Spandau fire from their front and right flank, and were suffering heavily, all except one man became casualties.
>
> Lieut Berridge went forward to see the position for himself, and tried without success to signal to his supporting tanks. He then crawled 100 yards under intense fire to the nearest tank, and successfully directed its fire on to the enemy position that was holding up the advance of his platoon.
>
> In the meantime enemy shelling had commenced in the immediate neighbourhood of this platoon. Nothing daunted, Lt Berridge collected the remainder of his platoon and cleared the area of enemy, capturing 20 prisoners and the MGs which had held him up.
>
> Lt Berridge's prompt action and complete disregard for his own safety undoubtedly ensured the complete success of the attack. Throughout the operations on this day this officer's gallantry and leadership were an inspiration to his Platoon.

Colonel Sir Alastair Graesser, whose bravery in Normandy had won him a Military Cross the previous year, was awarded the Distinguished Service Order in April 1945 for fighting off a counter-attack and opening up a vital road. Earlier he had launched an attack at Ochtrup which resulted in a nine-mile advance and the taking of 200 prisoners. The citation for his DSO stressed his coolness in action, complete disregard for his own safety, and magnificent example to all ranks. 'I cannot imagine a better leader of a Squadron,' wrote his Commanding Officer. 'Since landing in Normandy, this Squadron, under his command, has shown a consistently offensive spirit and this has been the direct result of Major Graesser's leadership. His determination to overcome the opposition and to reach his objective has been reflected throughout his entire Squadron.'[98]

A loss which was deeply felt in the local community was the death of Lieutenant Richard Berridge. A former Oundle School boy, he was the third son of Colonel Berridge. Leaving Laundimer House only two years before, he had joined the Army in 1943 and on arrival in Germany had been in much severe fighting with the Second Battalion, The Scots Guards. He died on 9 April, of wounds received in an engagement with enemy paratroops during a reconnaissance patrol.[99]

107: Lieutenant Richard Berridge, killed in action on 9 April 1945.

The Bombing Goes On

The Allies continued to punish Germany from the air, with the RAF taking an increasingly offensive role.

The relentless bombing of the enemy's cities, including the devastating raid on Dresden in mid-February, would make a deep impression on an Oundle man who witnessed the event on the ground. The firestorm, as described in a later chapter by Ralph Leigh from his prison camp outside the city, would fill him with anger at the horror of war.

The wisdom of targeting areas of high civilian populations in an attempt to shorten the war has been rejected by many. Former RAF Intelligence officer Robin Miller recognized the issue as 'tricky':

> The object was to area bomb the big German cities. We knew perfectly well that we were not just fighting troops, but also destroying civilians' homes as well. But you did not think about that. However, with hindsight, one wonders whether that was the right thing to do. There are rumours that Harris went beyond his brief and destroyed a great deal more than he was supposed to. Before the Normandy landings that was the only thing we were really doing. I think probably that the (bombing) campaigns were a great mistake.

108: Planning a low level attack at No. 2 Group HQ, Second Tactical Air Force: Former Oundle School boy David Atcherley, DSO, DFC, an Air Commodore and Senior Air Staff Officer in 1945 (left) with l. to r. Air Vice Marshal B. E. Embry, CB, DSO, AFC, Air Officer Commanding No. 2 Group, 2nd Tactical Air Force, Group Captain P. G. Wykeham-Barnes, DSO, DFC, and Wing Commander H. P. Shallard, Group Intelligence Officer.
IWM CL.2738.

THREE ~ ACTIVE SERVICE

Flight Sergeant Thomas Pollard was a casualty of the war in the air at this time. A King's Cliffe man, he had left Laxton School in 1941, joining the RAF two years later and being posted to Bomber Command. He was shot down during an operational flight over Mönchen Gladbach on 24 February.[100]

Another former Laxton School pupil was Warrant Officer Donald Barber, who lost his life when his aircraft crashed in this country on 6 February. Tragically for this Oundle family living on West Street, his elder brother Leslie, a private with the Cheshire Regiment, was to die in a motor accident in Algiers exactly a year later on 6 February 1946.[101]

Discovering the Death Camps

As early as July 1944 the evil of the Third Reich had been discovered in eastern Europe by Russian troops who had come across camps such as Majdanek, and later, in January 1945, the better-known Auschwitz. With the sweep towards Germany from the west, the full extent of Hitler's monstrous programme of genocide came to be known. Reports of the discoveries had been dismissed by many as Russian propaganda, and for British soldiers the reality of Belsen, near Hanover, was a shock which they will always remember. Barnwell's David Berridge, serving with the 11th Armoured Division under General 'Pip' Roberts, recorded the moment:

> I was the first officer, together with my chaps, to come across this concentration camp. It was a great surprise, hidden as it was in the silver birch woods, and we had *not* been forewarned, although, looking back, we should have expected something. A day, or maybe more before, we had been given DDT and instructed to put it in the seams of our battledress as there was typhus in the region which we were attacking. In fact we had observed a German party under cover of white flags visit our HQ. We thought the war was over — how wrong.

The Germans were indeed worried that typhus, which had broken out in Belsen, would spread to the entire region, and during their visit to the British forward positions on 12 April, had declared that they wanted the area around the concentration camp to be declared neutral. David Berridge continued his account.

> As we moved, riding on the backs of our tanks, we came across, on the outskirts of the woods, bunches of two or three POWs who said they had escaped their prison. We gave them water, biscuits and cigarettes as we moved forward. They were in very poor shape — dirty, ragged, thin, with deep hollow cheeks. After about a quarter of a mile we came upon the camp itself with its high wire fence upon which a hundred or so living corpses were clinging and faintly waving at us as we moved along the perimeter. It was not until we got to the wide open gates that we saw bodies littered all over the place. The smell, better described as stench, was horrible.
>   Reporting all this on my radio to my C.O., I received stern instructions NOT to stop, ignore everything, and press on. 'Don't even give water and rations.' Frankly I was relieved by this command. I subsequently learnt that our Padre, who wrote a book on Belsen, and our Doctor, stayed behind.

Victory in Europe

Three weeks later, on 30 April, Hitler committed suicide along with his wife Eva Braun amidst the ruins of the Chancellery in Berlin. The surrender of German forces was quick to follow, with the war in Europe coming officially to an end on 8 May.

It seems appropriate that an Oundle man should have found himself at the scene of the tyrant's death just as an Oundle man should have observed Hitler at a moment of triumph in Munich in the pre-war years. The late Roy McComish, a retired headmaster who moved to Oundle eight years ago, was among the first British troops in Berlin in May 1945, and brought back a souvenir of his visit.

> I went right into the badly damaged Reich Chancellery where Hitler had been in residence right up to one or two days before. The Russians had reached Berlin first, and the large room which had been Hitler's study was now in complete disorder. A wooden chest, standing under one of a dozen windows along one wall, had been ripped open but was still half-full of documents, all of them signed by Hitler.

Roy McComish was unable to resist the temptation of pocketing one of the documents signed by Hitler as a memento of his visit.

> I proceeded on through a doorway until Hitler's tiny bedroom with bathroom en suite. The Russians had pulled off the lavatory seat and nailed it to the wall over a portrait of Hitler. Outside was the bunker where Hitler and his mistress, Eva Braun, had ended their lives, an evil-smelling mass of débris.

The Collapse of Japan: the Capture of Burma and Borneo

Although the Japanese offensives at Kohima and Imphal on the Indian-Burmese border had been halted in the Spring of 1944, the enemy still controlled Burma. The second half of 1944 had been devoted to improvement in supply lines to General Slim's Fourteenth Army, as well as reorganisation of the command structure. With the end of the monsoon rains in mid-October, Slim began the push southwards with the ultimate aim of the capture of Rangoon.

The town of Monywa, situated near the rivers Chindwin and Irrawaddy, was one of the many which became a focus of fierce Japanese resistance. By January 1945 General Montagu Stopford's 33rd Corps had reached the town. Captain Edward Maslen-Jones, the former Oundle School boy who had gained his Distinguished Flying Cross for the brave missions he had undertaken on aerial reconnaissance, was again to prove himself invaluable. This time his work was with the 20 Indian Division, and gained him the Military Cross for 'outstanding service and continuous gallantry in action'. The honour was presented 'in the field' by Brigadier Stevens, Commander Royal Artillery 33 Corps. The citation reads as follows:

> The enemy was well dug in, in perfectly camouflaged positions which proved most difficult and expensive in casualties for infantry ground patrols to locate. Capt Maslen-Jones, in addition to his normal duties, and at great personal and continuous risk from enemy small arms fire, made many tree top reconnaissances over enemy positions in compiling sketches on which were based the final plans for artillery and air strikes for the assault on Monywa.
> It was only after the capture of Monywa that the full value of the daring work done by this officer and of the risks he must have taken in doing it could be appreciated after examination of the enemy positions.
> It is no exaggeration to say that the success of the assault on Monywa and the comparatively small casualties incurred by our infantry are due in no small measure to the

THREE ~ ACTIVE SERVICE

initiative, personal continuous gallantry and devotion to duty with which this intrepid young officer carried out his reconnaissances.'

The increasing damage inflicted on Japanese shipping by Allied forces in the final stages of the war was one of the most powerful factors in destroying her military capability. April 1945 saw the Americans landing on Okinawa in Operation 'Iceberg,' with Japanese losses estimated at 110,000.

The following month saw the disabling of enemy forces in Burma, and the neutralising and surrender of enemy garrisons on New Guinea and the neighbouring islands. Rangoon was captured on 3 May. Denis Eadie, who had won a Military Cross at Kohima, was to discover on returning home that one of his neighbours had been in the group of impatient POWs in Rangoon jail who had written in huge letters on the roof: 'JAPS GONE   BRITISH HERE   EXTRACT DIGIT.'

Borneo's recapture was considered of supreme importance because of its oil and rubber supplies, and operations to secure a foothold were started on 1 May by two divisions of the Australian First Corps under Lieutenant General Sir Leslie Morshead, with the protective aid of the US Seventh Fleet.

Colonel Ralph Hodgson, a former Oundle School boy who had left School House in 1922, took part in the landings on Borneo at Tarakan and Balikpapen, and gave an eye-witness account of the assault, one of the last important amphibious operations of the war. A major difficulty in the attack was the presence of minefields, both Japanese and Allied, which had to be destroyed.

> The Japs had built up really strong defensive positions and the country was ideally suited for defence. However U.S., British and Australian cruisers and destroyers put up an exceptionally heavy preparation which was thickened up by RAF and USAAF Liberators and Mitchells. We finished up with rockets and got ashore with very few casualties — mostly caused by guns hidden in the hills well away from the beachhead.
>
> The most impressive part in the assault were the oil fires from the big storage tanks near the refineries. The flames were estimated up to 600/1,000 ft. and the smoke certainly 5/6,000 ft. in rolling black clouds — typical of all oil fires.
>
> The Japs put up considerable resistance further inland but by that time we had our mortars and artillery ashore and could give very heavy support when we ran into trouble.
>
> I actually landed about 35 minutes after H hour and by that time we decided the beach was safer than sitting in a craft out at sea and being shelled!
>
> The Japs were clever jungle fighters but all our troops (the 7th-9th Australian Divisions) have a lot of experience and they dealt successfully with the usual Jap tricks. They set many booby traps and at nights would creep in through the jungle and throw earth to try and draw fire — if they succeeded a grenade followed — or they would roll 75-pr. shells down a hill with a delay fuse attached. More disturbing than dangerous but one lost a lot of sleep. There were tunnels in all the hills — hundreds of them, and often coming out the other side. We sealed them at each end whenever possible but some were always missed and we had a Jap come out of one of them with a grenade within 200 yards of the beach six days after the landing.
>
> The unforgettable memory of the Japs is the smell! They live in the greatest filth and more like animals than humans. They were very clever at getting their wounded away at night but would leave their dead and after two days in the tropics one can only burn such bodies — you can't move them.

> The natives were a pitiful sight — the women and children not in too bad a condition but the men who had been forced to labour for the Japs were just skin and bone and nearly all with malaria and beri-beri. Some had gaping wounds on their backs where Japs had slashed them with swords.
> We also managed to liberate a number of Indian POWs who had been captured at Singapore, whose discipline and morale after three years' imprisonment was an amazing reminder of their training and loyalty.
> It was a great experience to help in the recapture of some of the great rubber and oil centres and a type of fighting quite unique in military history.

Ralph Hodgson went on to consider the problems that he and his force would face after the recapture of Borneo, chief of which would be the disarming of the thousands of Japanese still on all the neighbouring islands and the desire for revenge on the part of the ill-treated natives of Borneo: 'It will be a tremendous work and when it is done I'm afraid one of the difficulties will be to persuade the Dyaks in Borneo that the open season for heads is over.'[102]

Back in Burma, Arthur Marment had been given a Bar to his Military Cross for the action at Myingyan, at the junction of the Irrawaddy and Chindwin rivers. He was then involved in one of the final engagements against the enemy during the war in the Far East. Lieutenant General Hyotaro Kimura, the new commander of Japanese forces in Burma, was determined to make a stand east of the Sittang river, near the Burmese-Thai border. His forces fought bravely, but the result was a crushing defeat for the Japanese. By 4 August the British Fourteenth Army had killed and captured 11,500 of the enemy, for the loss of only 96 Allied lives.

The Arrival of the Atom Bomb

The news of the dropping of the atomic bombs on Hiroshima and Nagasaki on 6 and 9 August took almost all Allied troops by surprise. Mill Road resident Tom Fiddick, serving as a seaman in the Royal Navy, had strong views about the justified use of what many considered as a barbaric weapon.

> We felt that we were going to have a very hard and long battle against the Japanese — none of us were particularly worried about it. But I think the general idea was that it would be at least another year before the war would be over and a lot of hard fighting. We were in Ceylon to invade Malaya, the Americans were coming round the other side and the plans were all ready for the invasion of Malaya under Mountbatten and in Trincomalee they had hospital beds for 7,000. But, of course, as soon as the bomb was dropped that was called off.

He recalled the elation with which he and his companions greeted the news of the bombing.

> I remember that I was in Columbo and everybody went wild with joy, excitement that it was over and, I can't remember the exact timing, but the Gall Face Hotel, for instance, which was closed, was immediately thrown open and hundreds of people poured in, drinking and dancing and shouting. It was remarkable.

Following the dropping of the two atomic bombs Japan signed the 'instrument of surrender' on 2 September 1945. Edward Maslen-Jones, on leave in Calcutta, had a double reason for remembering the occasion. His brother Bob, also educated at Oundle before being seconded to the Indian Army, had served in Burma where he was wounded at Pegu; the two had not seen each other since Edward's twentieth birthday in October 1940.

> On VJ night I checked in to the Grand Hotel, and as I made my way from Reception to the lift, a hand clapped me on the shoulder. It was Bob!!
> What an incredible time for us to meet up again. Needless to say, it was quite a night, which we shall never forget!

However, many Allied servicemen knew that even though the Second World War had come to an end they would have to continue to be on their guard, particularly in outlying areas. Old Oundelian Lieutenant Colonel Robert Butler, for example, describes in his *Nine Lives* how, while stationed in Burma at the end of the war, he had spent a pleasant two days' leave at a marvellous hotel up in the hills at Maymyo, east of Mandalay, which had been turned into an officers' leave camp. The return journey was made by boat, sailing 130 miles up the River Chindwin. Escorted by only a two-man Burmese crew, Robert Butler was well aware of the dangers.

> We were going unescorted through jungles which had been occupied by the Japanese until the previous month and I knew, from experience, that many Japanese had been cut off and were making their way south-eastwards, and that some of these were even unaware that their higher command had agreed to a cease-fire. I also knew that some of the Northern tribesmen of Burma had sympathised with the Japanese and might be hostile.

It was therefore with a certain trepidation that he found himself in some of the more isolated villages. Having been bitten on the ankle by a possibly rabid dog, with no chance of obtaining any anti-rabies serum for at least five days, he was not in the best of spirits. He did not know how soon the serum had to be injected and hoped that he would not start barking before they reached civilisation.

> On the third evening and on all successive ones I was very careful to keep an eye on my heels as we went through the villages. I had partaken of a few shots of Haywards Gin to cheer me up and we found the villagers sitting round a camp fire and having a rather tuneless sing-song. They responded very favourably to my mellow condition and the skipper and I were invited to sit cross-legged and join them. After a while I decided to chip in with a tuneful and extremely rude after-rugby song, which I sang at the top of my voice. There was complete silence as I sang, and when I finished I wondered if perhaps I would be for the pot. Not a bit of it, the applause was deafening, laughter uproarious — although they could not understand a single word I was saying — and I continued my one man concert for a short time. At Oundle we had one of the best Bach choirs in the United Kingdom and used to broadcast every Christmas and usually cut a record; so I tried to sing one or two tuneful numbers with a good melody. They simply loved it and had never experienced anything quite like it before — nor had I.[103]

Strangely enough there were those who had found their niche in wartime service, and who were almost enjoying their work. Admittedly the vast majority of such people were not involved in combat operations. Robin Miller, for example, had begun to specialise in his own brand of RAF Intelligence work.

When the war was about to end, we were shipped out to India to continue the war against the Japanese. I had by that time become interested in Escape and Evasion — teaching aircrew what to do if they came down over enemy territory and so on, and also ensuring that if they went to a prison camp that they should make a bloody nuisance of themselves, not just settle down. I thus volunteered for a similar post in the Far East and found myself doing that. In fact, one was almost disappointed when one heard of the Hiroshima bomb and that it was all over. We then kicked about in India for a few months more before being allowed home.

One of the jobs which the future Head of Music at Oundle School enjoyed during his time in Bangalore, India, was staging entertainments for the troops with the help of what was known as The Southern Army Orchestra.

109: L. to r. Ex-Head of Music at Oundle School Flight Lieutenant Robin Miller working on the score of *Crescendo, a musical fantasia*, with producer Captain Richard Gordon and fellow-musician Captain Teddy Shurrock.

THREE ~ ACTIVE SERVICE

Later, Robin Miller was to find himself posted to the Cocos Islands, a staging post between Singapore and India, where he enjoyed meeting a wide selection of VIPs. One was Gracie Fields, who with her husband Monty Banks, had come to sing to the troops. Among his VIPs were individuals whose past had caught up with them now that the Allies had won. One was the Sultan of Selangor.

> He was under arrest for collaborating too willingly with the Japs, and heading for internment. I never heard what happened to him eventually. As a Moslem, when taken off for internment he was given the option of taking a couple of his wives with him. He apparently couldn't decide which ones to choose, so he took with him a couple of young boys!

Notes
1939
1. *The Laxtonian*, vol.XV, no.6, December 1941, pp.292-3.
2. Tom Hickman, *What did you do in the War, Auntie? The BBC at War* 1939-45, p.106; *The Old Oundelian*, 1977-78, p.31.
3. Robert Butler, *Nine Lives*, pp.41-2.

1940
4. Winston Churchill, *The Second World War*, vol.III, p.98.
5. *The Laxtonian*, vol.XV, no.2, July 1940, p.107. Patrick Hunter-Gordon's brave exploit was the subject of an article which appeared in *Everybody's Weekly* the following year, on 21 June, 1941, p.14.
6. *The Laxtonian*, vol.XV, no.2, July 1940, p.107.
7. *The Laxtonian,* vol.XV, no.2, July 1940, p.102. See Longford, *Wellington — Pillar of State,* London, 1972, p.5; *Wellington — The Years of the Sword,* London, 1969, pp.385-6.
8. *Oundle Memorials of the Second World War.*
9. *Private Marshall remembers*, in *The Old Oundelian*, 1960, pp.14-15.
10. *The Old Oundelian*, 1987-88, p.79.
11. *The Old Oundelian*, 1982-83, p.68.
12. *The Laxtonian*, vol.XV, no.2, July 1940, p.100 ; vol. XV, no. 3, December 1940, p.150.
13. See J. B. Salmond, *The History of the 51st Highland Division*, and Saul David, *Churchill's Sacrifice of the Highland Division.*
14. *The Old Oundelian*, 1993-94, p.29.
15. *The Old Oundelian*, 1991-92, pp.89-90.
16. *The Old Oundelian*, 1993-4, p.87.
17. *The Laxtonian*, vol.XV, no. 3, December 1940, p.150.
18. *The Old Oundelian*, 1962, p.54; Norman Franks, *Battle of Britain,* pp.18, 32, 59.
19. *The Laxtonian*, vol.XVIII, no.2, July 1952, pp.80-82.
20. *The Old Oundelian,* 1970-71, pp.65-66; *The Laxtonian*, vol.XV, no.8, July 1942, p.371; *The Laxtonian*, vol. XX, no. 9 (3rd series, vol. II), March 1960, p.356.

1941
21. Churchill, *The Second World War*, vol.II: *Their Finest Hour*, pp.388-395.
22. *The Laxtonian*, vol.XV, no.5, July 1941, p.255.
23. *The Laxtonian*, vol.XV, no.5, July 1941, pp.256-7.
24. *The Laxtonian*, vol.XV, no.5, July 1941, p.256.
25. *The Laxtonian*, vol.XV, no.7, April 1942, p.325.
26. *Oundle Memorials of the Second World War.*
27. *The Old Oundelian*, 1979-80, pp.75-6.
28. Michael L. Gibson, *Aviation in Northamptonshire,* pp.96-100.
29. *The Laxtonian,* vol.XV, no.7, April 1942, p.331. I am grateful to Mr Max Arthur for permission to reproduce Lucian Ercolani's account from his book *There shall be Wings.*
30. *Oundle Memorials of the Second World War; The Laxtonian*, vol.XV, no. 9, December 1942, p.399.

1942

31 *Oundle Memorials of the Second World War*.
32 James Bradley, *Towards the Setting Sun*, pp.12-17, 9.
33 *The Old Oundelian*, 1987-88, p.79.
34 Robert Butler, *Nine Lives*, pp.76-7, 80-81, 85, 88-91.
35 *The Laxtonian*, vol.XV, no.9, December 1942, p.400.
36 Nigel Hamilton, *Monty: The Making of a General, 1887-1942,* p.837.
37 *The Laxtonian,* vol.XV, no.10, April 1943, p.437.
38 Alec Colson has been working with co-author Ian Trenowden on a book to appear in 1995 entitled *Stealthily by Night — Clandestine Beach Reconnaissance and Operations in World War II*, published by Crecy Books.
39 B. H. Liddell Hart, *History of the Second World War*, pp.318, 320.
40 Winston Churchill, *The Second World War*, vol.III, p.98.
41 *The Times,* 5 June 1972.
42 *The Daily Telegraph*, 22 August 1986.
43 *The Daily Telegraph*, 25 November 1994.
44 *The Laxtonian*, vol.XV, no.10, April 1943, p.439.
45 *The Laxtonian*, vol.XVII, no.5, July 1949, pp.283-4.
46 *The Laxtonian*, vol.XV, no.7, April 1942, p.327.
47 *Oundle Memorials of the Second World War.*
48 *The Laxtonian*, vol.XVI, no.6, December 1945, p.236.
49 *Oundle Memorials of the Second World War*; *The Laxtonian*, vol.XV, no.9, December 1942, p.406.
50 *The Old Oundelian*, 1988-89, p.84.

1943

51 Terence Tinsley, *Stick and String,* Buckland Publications Ltd., London, 1992; *The Old Oundelian*, 1993-94, p.82.
52 *The Laxtonian*, vol.XV, no.10, April 1943, p.445.
53 *Oundle Memorials of the Second World War*.
54 *The Laxtonian*, vol.XV, no.11, July 1943, p.481.
55 *The Laxtonian*, vol.XV, no.11, July 1943, p.482-3.
56 I am greatly indebted to Robert Aitken for his full and detailed account of Operation 'Source'.
57 Churchill, *The Second World War*, vol.V, pp.146, 245.
58 Ewen Montagu's book *The Man Who Never Was,* provided me with most of the information relating to Operation 'Mincemeat'.
59 *The Laxtonian*, vol.XV, no.12, December 1943, pp.512-3.
60 *The Laxtonian*, vol.XVI, no.1, March 1944, p.62.
61 *The Laxtonian*,vol.XVI, no.5, July 1945, pp.186-7); John Strawson, *A History of the SAS*, pp.90-92, London, Secker & Warburg.
62 Robert Butler, *Nine Lives*, pp.121-28.
63 *Oundle Memorials of the Second World War.*
64 *Oundle Memorials of the Second World War.*

1944

65 *The Laxtonian*, vol.XVI, no.2, July 1944, pp.61-2.
66 Max Arthur, *There shall be Wings*, pp. 279-282.
67 *The Laxtonian*, vol.XVI, no.3, December 1944, p.97.
68 *The Laxtonian*, vol.XVI, no.5, July 1945, pp.198-99.
69 *The Old Oundelian*, 1987-88, p.74.
70 *The Old Oundelian*,1992-93, p.85.
71 *Oundle Memorials of the Second World War.*
72 *Peterborough Evening Telegraph*, Wednesday 1 June, 1994, p.xiii.
73 *The Old Oundelian*, 1986-87, p.79-80.
74 *The Old Oundelian*, 1993-94, p.93.
75 *The Laxtonian*, vol.XVI, no.5, July 1945, p.189.

76 *The Laxtonian*, vol.XVI, no.3, December 1944, p.101.
77 I am indebted to Christopher Bond for so kindly taking the trouble to give this graphic account of his experiences.
78 *The Laxtonian*, vol.XVI, no.2, July 1944, p.63.
79 *The Laxtonian*, vol.XVI, no.2, July 1944, p.98.
80 *The Laxtonian*, vol.XVI, no.3, December 1944, pp.134-5.
81 *Oundle Memorials of the Second World War.*
82 *The Old Oundelian*, 1992-93, p.86.
83 *The Laxtonian*, vol.XVI, no.3, December 1944, pp.101-2.
84 *The Laxtonian*, vol.XVI, no.11, December 1947, p.489.
85 *The Old Oundelian*, 1986-87, pp.80-81.
86 Albert Spring's story was the basis of an article by Christopher Emmott in the *Oundle Chronicle*, Summer 1994, p.5.
87 *Oundle Memorials of the Second World War.*
88 Robert Butler, *Nine Lives*, pp.156-58.
89 Cecil Lewis, *Sagittarius Surviving*, pp.139, 92-3, 109-10.
90 Cecil Lewis, *All my Yesterdays*, pp 128-9, pp. 130-1.
91 Cecil Lewis, *Sagittarius Surviving*, pp.140-1.
92 Max Arthur, *There shall be Wings*, p.198.
93 *The Laxtonian*, vol.XVI, no.8, July 1946, p.330.
94 *The Laxtonian*, vol.XVI, no.3, December 1944, p.99.
95 *The Laxtonian*, vol.XVI, no.6, December 1945, p.232.
96 *The Laxtonian*, vol.XVI, no.4, April 1945, pp.135-6.
97 *The Laxtonian*, vol.XVI, no.4, April 1945, p.135; *The Laxtonian*, vol.XVI, no.5, July 1945, p.187.

1945
98 *The Old Oundelian*, 1992-93, p.86.
99 *The Laxtonian*, vol.XVI, no.5, July 1945, p.190.
100 *The Laxtonian*, vol.XVI, no.6, December 1945, p.240.
101 *Oundle Memorials of the Second World War.*
102 *The Laxtonian*, vol.XVI, no.6, December 1945, p.252-3.
103 Robert Butler, *Nine Lives*, pp.177-78.

CHAPTER FOUR

Friends and Allies

The Yanks

The Second World War brought Oundle into unexpected contact with the outside world. The arrival of evacuees from London and other big cities was just one of a series of waves of new faces, accents and habits which were to make their impact on this quiet Northamptonshire town.

As the war progressed, with Europe thrown into turmoil, foreign refugees forced out of their homeland would make their appearance in the area, in addition to the German and Italian prisoners of war. Some of these new arrivals were to settle here.

The most dramatic foreign influence was of transatlantic origin. Following the Japanese attack on Pearl Harbour in December 1941 and the consequent involvement of the United States in military operations against the Axis powers, Oundle was invaded by American servicemen. Many of them were to find homes and families with whom they have kept up enduring links for more than fifty years. Phil Coombs, who was responsible for organising transport for Oundle's Home Guard, was one of the many local people who allowed their homes to be used as a haven for off-duty Americans. At Cotterstock Hall, Lady Ethel Wickham kept open house to all American servicemen, whatever their rank; Irish coffee was served at 11.00 am.

During the Second World War, two groups of American airmen were based at Polebrook Airfield. In June 1942, Polebrook became the headquarters of the 97th Bomb Group which was the first US Heavy Bomber organisation to arrive in the UK, stationing two of its B17E squadrons at Polebrook and two at Grafton Underwood.

Operations began from Polebrook in the summer of 1942, when on 17 August the 97th Bomb Group flew the first Eighth Air Force mission of the war, an attack on the Rouen-Sotteville marshalling yards in France. The leading aircraft was piloted by the Group Commander, Colonel Frank Armstrong. His co-pilot was Major Paul W. Tibbets, who later flew 'Enola Gay' to Hiroshima with the first atom bomb. Lorna Sloan, the daughter of Phil and Sybil

110: Phil Coombs, one of the many friends that USAAF personnel made in Oundle.

Coombs, remembered the party held at her family home in Cotterstock Road on the very evening of 17 August, when some of the guests arrived late, having just come back from this first bombing mission. Their excuse was that they had run into 'a flock of birds'. They did not mention the mission, but Mrs Sloan remembered that they were, as she put it, 'hyped-up'. In October 1942 the 97th was removed from operations and transferred to the Mediterranean theatre. Polebrook air base remained unoccupied until January 1943.

On 15 January 1943, the 304th Service Group arrived at Polebrook and began preparing the airfield for the arrival of the 351st Bomb Group. They were assisted by the 320th Service Squadron, 1052nd Ordnance Squadron and 166th Quartermaster Squadron. An advance party of the 351st arrived on 15 April 1943, when a B17 landed with Major Milton, Group Deputy CO, Major Bowles, Group Executive Officer, Captain Scott, Group Intelligence Officer and other key personnel. The main force aircrews arrived the following day.

Prior to the start of the 351st's operational missions, Colonel Hatcher, the Group Commander, and other senior staff flew their first combat missions as observers with the 303rd Bomb Group from Molesworth.

The first successful mission for the 351st was on 14 May 1943, against Courtrai Airfield in Belgium. The final mission was on 20 April 1945, when they bombed the Brandenburg marshalling yards in Berlin. Between these two dates the 351st Bomb Group flew 311 credited missions comprising a total of 9,075 aircraft. These aircraft dropped 20,778 tons of bombs and fired 2,776,028 rounds of ammunition. Of the aircraft despatched, 98 B17s were missing in action over occupied Europe, 13 ditched in the English Channel, 11 landed in neutral countries with battle damage and 33 crashed in the UK as a result of battle damage or mechanical failure.[1]

First Impressions

It was small wonder that many of the Americans came across as larger than life figures. Their arrival, whether from small towns in the mid-West of the USA or great cities like New York and Chicago, was a complete culture-shock to a wartime Britain which must have seemed to them quaint but impoverished. 'The Americans certainly opened the eyes of people in Oundle. They were nothing like anything we had seen before — from the other side of the world,' recalled Elizabeth Berridge.

Certain individuals made a remarkable impression. For Miriam Rothschild, who entertained many of the Americans at her home in Ashton, the Commanding Officer in particular stood out because of his incredible courage and coolness: he was 'an absolute star'. A Colonel at the age of 26, Eugene Romig, who commanded Polebrook from 3 January to 12 October 1944, was to figure in the tragic story of the crash involving the B17 known as 'Ten Horsepower'.

Hollywood in Polebrook

One of the notable Americans based at Polebrook and still remembered by many Oundle residents was the film star Clark Gable, celebrated for his role in the film *Gone with the Wind*. His posting at Polebrook gave that particular base a glamour all of its own.

After the death of his wife Carole Lombard on 16 January 1943, Clark Gable was described as 'inconsolable' and 'unapproachable'. She died in a plane crash on Potosi

111: Clark Gable as a B17 air-gunner, photographed during an interview on 6 June 1943.

Mountain a few minutes out of Las Vegas, Nevada whilst on a War Bonds campaign. Rumours spread around Hollywood that he was contemplating quitting the movies and enlisting. This prompted an approach from H. H. Arnold, Lieutenant General Chief of the Army Air Forces.

On 12 August 1942, film star Clark Gable enlisted at the Los Angeles recruiting office and was sworn into the Air Corps as a private. Private Gable 19125741 applied for admission to Officers' Candidate School and became Corporal Gable, assigned to Miami Beach.

On 15 August, Clark Gable and an MGM cameraman Andrew McIntyre were inducted. Then followed a 13-week course of gruelling 18-hour days, seven days a week. He tackled the job with great dedication and enthusiasm, and on 27 October Corporal Gable was discharged to accept his commission. Second Lieutenant Gable 0565390 then learned that General Arnold required his services to make a propaganda film in order to boost aerial gunner recruitment, which was flagging due to heavy casualties. Along with Andy McIntyre he proceeded via Gunnery School at Tyndall Field, Florida to Fort Wright, Spokane where they underwent aerial gunnery and photographic training.

In December they went on Christmas leave. On 28 January 1943, after further training, they were assigned to the 508th Bomb Squadron of the 351st Bomb Group which was based at Pueblo, Colorado. The film was to be made around the Group's activities, and to aid the project Gable enlisted the assistance of Johnny Mahin as his writer. Mahin was in Intelligence, teaching aircraft identification. Colonel Hatcher personally flew Gable to fetch Mahin, who was based in New Mexico.

112: Captain Clark Gable with USAAF colleagues at Polebrook, 6 June 1943.

Gable, Mahin and McIntyre together with two cameramen, went to England with the vanguard of the 351st. 'The Little Hollywood Group' as they were known, set about preparing for their role.

The 'little group' was initially thought of as the glamour or glory boys, but it soon proved its worth. Lieutenant Gable, although offered special facilities, stayed in the Officers' Quarters and ate in the Officers' Mess. He went on to complete five combat missions. He participated in the raids on Antwerp, Courtrai, Gelsenkirchen, Heroya and Nantes. His first mission was flown on 4 May 1943 with the 303rd Bomb Group based at Molesworth; he flew with Captain Calhoun in the B17 'Eight Ball'.

Promoted to Captain, Clark Gable managed to secure certain concessions from the Group Commanders. Colonel Hatcher at Polebrook gave every assistance with regard to camera installation in the 351st aircraft, and allowed crew members to operate cameras to supplement the work of the two official cameramen. Permission was also given for prepared sequences to be shot in the hangars.

It took some time for local people to get used to the idea of meeting a famous Hollywood actor in the streets of a quiet market town like Oundle. But they evidently found him affable and obliging. Signing his autograph for Oundle School boys, or for the Market Place tailor who had sewn back a button on his jacket, was a gesture which the star was glad to make.

Captain Gable became a familiar visitor to the local villages which he toured on his small motorcycle, which was perhaps the only privilege he allowed himself. He drank in the local pubs and took an active part in the Group's social activities; he was a keen softball player.

113: Captain Clark Gable signing autographs at Oundle. The photograph was kindly lent by Mr Barry Smith, a former Oundle School boy, to whom it was inscribed by Gable.

Although officially a Group Operations Officer, he was allowed to pursue film making for the greater part of his time. He was also called upon to give morale boosting appearances at many bases. His combat participation was indeed a great fillip to the men, and Gable's posting gave Polebrook in particular a somewhat glamorous aura.

Princess Alice, in an interview with two Oundle School pupils in 1988, recalled how her husband had flown back on a surprise visit to Polebrook, where the Americans were unable to decode the message announcing his imminent arrival. In the ensuing excitement, the rumour spread that Prince Henry's plane was in fact carrying either Clark Gable or Cary Grant, and by the time he touched down, there were hordes of pressmen and locals waiting for this 'celebrity'. Despite his own eminence, Prince Henry was received with groans! Rather a surprising welcome for her husband, who would have been Prince Regent had the King died, reflected the Princess.

Clark Gable's periods of leave were usually spent in London, where he was in great demand. He was invited to attend functions, dinners, and all kinds of activities by the press, the military, dignitaries, other celebrities, the English aristocracy and even royalty. It was difficult for him to relax. His most restful days were spent with David Niven at his Windsor country home, or in the countryside around Polebrook.

Prior to returning to the States, Captain Gable was awarded the Air Medal. The 'little group' had shot some 50,000 feet of film, so they gathered together the material which had been accumulated over nine months with the 351st and returned to California.

A few months later and with the additional assistance of MGM's top editor Blanche Sewell, Mahin and Gable completed their task. Air Gunner recruitment had picked up, so the theme of the film was changed. It highlighted the general appeal and successes of the Army Air Force and the daytime strategic bombing policy.

On 15 February 1945 the results of some of Clark Gable's work were shown in the Mess at Polebrook in the shape of the film entitled *Combat America*.

Another film which involved local acting talent as well as Gable himself was *Friends in Wartime*, featuring two girls from Warmington, Delma Northen and Mavis Pollard.

When he was not involved in shooting films and German aircraft it seems that the local rooks on nearby farmland were a favourite target of the Hollywood star.

Lorna Sloan remembered clearly the moment when Clark Gable and his friends dropped in for tea, recording the event in her diary.

> We were sitting out on the terrace minding our own business — we'd already met his scriptwriter John Mahin and he'd said he would bring him down — and we heard a car roll up, and peeped round the corner, and saw Clark getting out of the car, and we shot back and sat down as though nothing had happened at all, and round the corner came Clark with all his buddies, the scriptwriter and the photographer from *Gone with the Wind*.

114: Hollywood star Clark Gable chats to Oundle schoolmaster Frank Spragg on Oundle School playing-fields.

FOUR ~ FRIENDS AND ALLIES

115: Star-struck: Clark Gable with local girls Delma Northen and Mavis Pollard. The latter, on Gable's right, was to become a GI bride.

After going back to Polebrook for a few hours to check on the safe return of a mission, Gable returned to the house with quite a party, including Major Richardson, Colonel Burns and some of the nurses from the American hospital at Lilford. 'There was a shortage of booze in those days, so we took Clark along to The George here on the corner,' Lorna Sloan recalled. 'We had a great big enamel jug and went to fill it up — and poor old Mrs Marriott who kept the pub opened the hatch, saw Clark Gable there and nearly passed out. So then they spent a considerable time here.'

In spite of the entry in her diary, both Lorna Sloan and her friend Pauline Ashby, whose family farmed at Armston, remembered Gable as a 'very quiet, retiring sort of a chap'. Even though he was already a well known star 'he didn't want to be recognised at all'.

However not everyone he met recognised the star. Elizabeth Berridge believed that her main claim to fame in wartime Oundle was that, as young Elizabeth Cole, she was the only girl who met Clark Gable who had never heard of him. Her father was chaplain at Oundle School and housemaster at the Berrystead boarding-house. 'I'd led a sheltered life,' she explained. On the same occasion, at a dance at Polebrook Airfield, she met Gable's fellow film star James Stewart. For her, and for many other Oundle girls at the time, life changed with the arrival of the Americans in that summer of 1942.

> There was much more hope. They seemed to be so rich and I felt very sorry for our soldiers. The Americans always had a lot of money and gave us presents. I had my very first pair of

> 116: 'A whale of a party' with Clark Gable and friends: 15-year old Lorna Sloan's diary record of an unexpected meeting on 24 August 1943.
> Her extract reads:
> 'I had Clarky! He is really very nice but by no means good! They did not leave till 2.30.'

silk stockings from an American soldier. Make-up was rationed, but Americans were loaded with it — it was wonderful. I think we thought the money was perhaps going to buy us victory.

Not all Oundle people welcomed the arrival of the Americans. 'Over-paid, over-sexed, and over here' soon became a common complaint among some of their hosts. It was true that the Americans had rations and wages which were far superior to those of the British, and jobs at local airfields were consequently highly prized.

Fun with the Yanks

Small wonder that with the presence of such internationally known stars the USAAF bases were to gain an added exciting dimension quite separate from their military function. Entertainment provided for the American forces brought a glamour to the airbases which it is hard to visualise now on the windswept tracts of concrete. Stoke Doyle's Ruth Moisey, now Ruth Keens, remembered the Americans' 'smart uniforms, wonderful generosity, handing out sweets and other goodies, holding parties for children, and dances. Buses took girls to the camp, but they were chaperoned by various ladies, including Miss Wickham from Cotterstock Hall'.

At the Red Cross Club at Polebrook, where she helped at dancing classes for the airmen, Joyce Hardick, or Joyce Gaunt as she was then, remembered Bob Hope starring in his own show in July 1943 with Frances Langford, Tony Romano and Clark Gable. A year later, Glenn Miller played at Polebrook, just months before the ill-fated flight on which he was killed in December 1944. Charity dances were a regular feature at the Red Cross Club

117: Stars at Polebrook: (l. to r.) Col. William A. Hatcher, Pepper Martin, Captain Clark Gable, Frances Langford, Bob Hope and Tony Romano at the Red Cross Club, Polebrook, 5 July 1943.

at Polebrook Airfield, where among local groups which helped with the organisation were the Oundle WI and the Oundle WVS.

Deenethorpe Airfield, the other base near Oundle, between Upper Benefield and the village of Deenethorpe, also had its own social life. Marlene Dietrich sang to over 2,000 US airmen when she visited the base, and the airmen reciprocated in their turn for the benefit of the local area when they entertained 800 children from Weldon, Deene, Deenethorpe, Corby and Benefield in December 1944.

Deenethorpe was one of the later American bases to come into use in October 1943, and was home to the 401st Bomb Group. The Group lost 94 planes during 255 missions; about 40 other aircraft were either abandoned on the continent or lost over this country or on the base.

There were plenty of opportunities for airmen to amuse themselves away from Polebrook and Deenethorpe. USAAF veteran Whitney Miller, a navigator with the 351st Bomb Group, thought that while the ground crews tended to come to Oundle a lot for their social life, the flying crews wanted the cinema, and Peterborough was consequently the main attraction: he himself knew The Bull Hotel in Westgate better than anywhere else.

Then of course there were the pubs. The King's Arms at Polebrook, and The Three Horseshoes at Ashton, now known as The Chequered Skipper, were the nearest watering-holes to the airfield. Among the many pubs in Oundle, The Rose and Crown in the market-place, run by the Norwood family, was a favourite. Carl Norwood, who now runs a taxi service in Oundle, revealed that the business was started by his father during the war,

118: The Chequered Skipper, Ashton.

largely as a service to airmen returning to their bases after a night out. There was so much more social life before the advent of television, he recalled. 'The pubs were full every night. You just couldn't get enough beer to sell.'

Proof of the affection with which the Americans held their 'local' is the postcard which a group of them sent from their prisoner of war camp in Germany to The Rose and Crown on 29 June 1944. 'Just to let you know that we are all alive and sure are missing your rations of mild, bitter and also the scotch,' was the message. 'And we all quit drinking, believe it or not. Hope to see you all very soon.'

Many of the airmen no doubt had more than their fair share of English beer. Local barmaids regularly had to hold bikes upright for unsteady airmen and give them a farewell push in the direction of Polebrook. Not surprisingly, not all the bikes reached their destination, as Bevil Allen remembered.

> I got to know some American servicemen pretty well, the ones at Polebrook mainly. My father had a shop which is now Owen & Hartley, and basically it was a cycle shop and we had at one time sixty bicycles for hiring out, and the airmen used to come and hire these bikes. Each hired bike had a label in the handlebar rolled up and we also painted a bar on the down tube. The airmen used to hire these bikes mainly to go on a ride in the countryside, but they used to go back to the base and either dump them in the ditch just outside the base, or sneak them into the base and ride about the base, and not return them when they were supposed to. So we'd have a check-up, and say, 'Oh God, that's another four bikes we've lost,' so I used to go up to the aerodrome and poke around till I found them and brought them back again. Nice little job. The man who was Provost Marshal, head of the military police up at the base was

119: Greetings from Germany: Sgt Joe Smith's postcard to friends at Oundle's Rose and Crown, letting them know that he and fellow USAAF prisoners of war were safe, following their capture while on a bombing mission in June 1944.

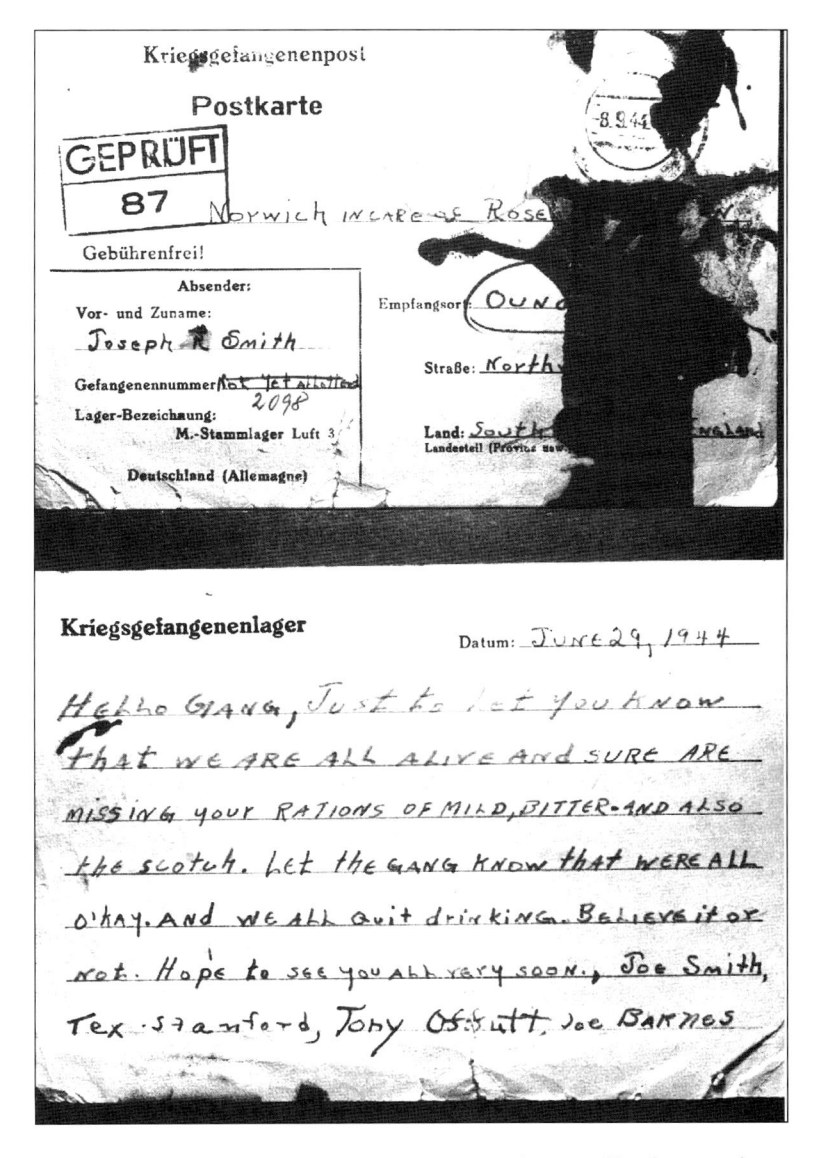

friendly with my family and he used to give me carte blanche to go up there and look around for the push-bikes, and when I found one I'd tell him and he'd find the chap who had taken it and would bawl him out for not returning it as he should have done. Then the others which were just dumped in the dyke outside the base, I'd just pick them up and bring them back. Sometimes there were chaps who'd got them and they'd try to stick me out ... 'No, no... that's my bike. I bought it from a chap in Thrapston,' and I'd have to end up cutting off the handle-grip and pulling out the bit of paper and saying, 'What about that then? It says it belongs to Allen Brothers.' 'Oh really?'

An amusing stolen-bicycle story was told by Miriam Rothschild.

The Americans were marvellously well balanced considering the strain they were under. There was frightfully little crime reported, yet there were six thousand men on my farm. In the early

120: 19-year old June Gaunt outside the cycle shop in St Osyth's Lane, Oundle, where she used to work. The shop was much used by USAAF personnel.

days the men stole bicycles because there was no other way of getting around. A military policeman came up one day and said he wanted to show me something of interest in the wood. In the centre of a dense thicket, through which we crawled on hands and knees, we reached a clearing and all around the edge were the stolen bicycles. They were being transformed with green paint, so you could not recognise your own bicycle if it was there. Hanging on one of the bushes there was a pair of silk cami-knickers, and the military policeman remarked, 'You can see they have fun here as well as dealing with the bicycles.'

Mementoes

Several talented artists on the base have left their friends in Oundle with amusing and cherished drawings as mementoes of their time here.

Jean Mabelson, who settled in Kettering, still has the cartoon drawn by airman Corporal Philip 'Red' Doucett, depicting a dance at Oundle's Victoria Hall in West Street during which, overwhelmed by their attentions, she is being carried out by two burly Americans.

Another souvenir given to their Oundle friends was a brightly coloured cartoon of three ducks delivering a flying bomb with the inscription 'Luck always, Jean'. The artist was Staff Sergeant Gene Mengee, who had worked for Disney in America, and who painted many of the striking insignia on the sides of Polebrook's warplanes.

Lorna Sloan's family still has the amusing cartoon drawn by Lester Reinke on 15 July 1943 and inscribed to her parents. It depicts a German fighter pilot getting the fright of his life on seeing the full fire power of a B17 trained on him.

FOUR ~ FRIENDS AND ALLIES

121: 'The Price of Popularity': Cpl Philip Doucett's cartoon presented to Jean Mabelson as a tribute to her effect on US airmen at dances in the Victoria Hall.

122: Flying Ducks, World War II Disney-style: a US airman's memento for his Oundle friends. Cartoon by Gene Mengee.

FOUR ~ FRIENDS AND ALLIES

123: Flying Fortress featuring Sperry Turrets,
a cartoon drawn for his Oundle friends by US airman Lester Reinke.

GIs' Girls

Not surprisingly there was the occasional troublesome incident arising from the presence of the lively new arrivals in the Oundle area. Former Oundle School boy Paul Massey remembered watching Americans fighting in the Market Place outside Bramston House, where he was a boarder, and Carl Norwood recalled the fatal stabbing which marred one evening at The Rose and Crown. The most frequent cause of the brawls was of course the shortage of female companions for the airmen. Vastly outnumbered by the Americans who descended on the town in search of fun and relaxation, Oundle wives and daughters found themselves the object of adulation. Small wonder that the female population revelled in such attention and recall their wartime days with nostalgia. With six men for every girl, they could hardly complain about a lack of social life in the town.

Dances organised by the Americans made the Victoria Hall echo and vibrate to new and exciting rhythms, recalled Elizabeth Berridge.

> We had never seen dancing like it. The craze at that time was jitter-bugging and they had dancing competitions. We were not really allowed to go, but we used to creep up onto the balcony and watch, and it was great fun. They certainly changed Oundle for ever — it never was the same after the Americans. It was a lovely, if sad time.

Margaret Hawkins and Jean Mabelson, or the Laxton girls, as they were known before they were married, have warm memories of the American friends they made. Both girls lived in Oundle Market Place, at the tailor's shop run by their father, and worked with the Women's

124: Jean Mabelson, (left), and her sister Margaret Hawkins, with their album of USAAF wartime photos.

125: Pauline Ashby (left) and Lorna Sloan revive memories of wartime Oundle with photographs of their many USAAF friends.

Land Army in the fields around Polebrook. It was a long day, with the girls setting out early from Oundle by bike to arrive by 7.00 am, counting out the B17s as the Americans set out on their bombing missions, and counting them back on the way home in the late evening. It wasn't work all the time however. 'Are you blushing or is that a tan?' is how Jean Mabelson remembered one airman's charming compliment. 'We had some very happy times, but we deserved them ... It was hard work on the land.'

Not surprisingly many local girls became GI brides. Figures released in June 1945 reveal that 250 Americans at Polebrook had married into British families, the highest number for any of the Northamptonshire airbases. Bevil Allen was well acquainted with Americans, partly because they used his father's cycle shop, but also because he had an older sister Mary. 'They used to swarm round the house after her.' Mary, together with Ella Walton, Winifred Cottingham, Margaret Goodman and Betty Lee, were just some of the Oundle girls he recalled who married Americans.

Indeed the story of the USAAF's wartime impact on the Oundle area would not be complete without mentioning in passing the living reminders of their legacy. It has been estimated that as many as 20,000 people in Britain today, aged between 40 and 50, would dearly love to make contact with their GI fathers who, for various reasons, remain elusive and shadowy figures that they have never met. They are particularly numerous in East Anglia with its high concentration of airfields. The research for *Oundle's War* inevitably resulted in pleas for help from some of these people. For years their enquiries amongst ex-GIs and Bomb Group Association officials have been met by a wall of silence. 'Usually the

American GI father will have a family of his own in the States, and it might be a traumatic and distressing experience for anyone to attempt to reunite the two sides after so long,' was a typical explanation. Two organisations have been recently set up to help searchers who for their part believe that such reunions would have a happy ending.[2]

Chewing Gum Kids

The Americans were popular with children all over Britain in the areas where they were based during the war, and Oundle children were no exception. A party was organised on a regular basis for pupils of the local schools every Christmas at Polebrook Airfield, and this was equally popular with the teachers.

Oundle children found the American airmen were a handy source of pocket money as well as sweets and chewing gum. 'The Americans were very generous, the ones that I knew,' recalled Bevil Allen. 'They were so wealthy — they used to get coins as change and just chuck it away.'

Percy Arnett, of Benefield Road, who has run a mobile grocery shop in the area for 25 years, remembers how as a schoolboy he would be paid for looking after the airmen's bikes as they visited Oundle's pubs, particularly The Rose and Crown, and The Nag's Head in West Street.

But Stewart Laxton, now living in New Road, had an experience which must have beaten any adventure of his schoolmates hands down.

126: Members of the USAAF aircrew on Stewart Laxton's Yeovil flight:
Rear (l. to r.): M. Marshall, E. J. Falcey, J. D. Carwile, C. H. Davis, P. J. Schultz;
Front: J. Harper, C. 'Pat' Harrison, J. H. Edwards.

In 1944 Stewart Laxton was a 16-year old pupil at Laxton School in Oundle. The headmaster, Sidney Leech, had declared Polebrook out of bounds to all pupils, but this did not deter Stewart from visiting the airfield most weekends with his friends.

The tailor's shop run by Stewart's father's was in part of what is now Oundle School's Bramston House in the Market Place. His mother worked in the WVS canteen in the present-day Crown Court, and Stewart often came home to find up to 13 American servicemen, invited to the house by his mother. The servicemen got to know him quite well, and he was able to visit them in their billets at Polebrook Airfield. 'Anyone in a uniform was allowed into the aerodrome, and as I was a keen member of the town's cadet force the sentry allowed me free access. The Americans were very friendly, and would buy you Pepsi and chewing gum from their canteen,' he recalled. He also experienced sad moments, such as witnessing men who would return from missions to see rows of empty beds: close friends had died, or been taken prisoner in enemy territory.

Among the former Laxton School boy's most vivid memories were the flights which he made in the American bombers. He would often go with the B17 crews on training flights over the North Sea. One day, the flight engineer whom Stewart and his family knew as Pat, asked him if he would take his place on a flight to Yeovil, where a repaired plane needed bringing back. Pat had a date he did not want to miss! Stewart accepted with alacrity, but when the B17 arrived at Yeovil they were met by thick fog. 'We were very low on fuel, so we had to be talked in onto the grass runway by the flight controller,' he recalled. 'Because of the fog it was not safe for us to land on wheels — the pilot had to belly-land.' The crew got into the middle of the aircraft and, on landing, the schoolboy saw the ball turret ripped out of the plane. The panic-stricken Stewart was the first out of the escape hatch, believing that the plane was about to explode. It was three days before he was able to get a flight home, to face a fuming mother!

Bombing Hitler's Germany

Of course life at the bases both for the aircrews and for their friends in the area was far from being one long round of parties and pub crawls. The Americans had come for a serious purpose, to bring an end to the war and to destroy the dictators.

The threat of disaster, both in the air and on the ground, was a constant one. USAAF veteran Whitney Miller, on a visit to the Oundle area in October 1994, graphically described the hardships faced by him and his colleagues. Leaving High School in 1943 to follow an aviation cadet programme he arrived in England the following year at the age of 19. His father had advised him to become an officer to avoid death in action. Trained as a navigator, he reached the rank of Second Lieutenant, and within a week of arriving at Polebrook was assigned to a crew; the oldest crew member was 21 years old. The Commanding Officer, Colonel Burns, was 24.

Whitney Miller flew a total of 30 missions on bombing raids to German cities such as Leipzig, Berlin and Dresden, each mission lasting between nine and eleven hours. While the RAF bombed Germany by night the Americans took on the daytime bombing raids. This meant an early departure, waking up at 3.00 am, before breakfast and a briefing at 4.00 am. Weather conditions were frequently appalling: within a fortnight he saw two planes collide with each other in the fog. In fact, lack of certainty about the weather was in his view the most worrying aspect of the missions he flew. The air traffic patterns of the two other nearby bases at Deenethorpe and Glatton overlapped, but the British G radar system was generally found to be accurate to within 200 feet. On one occasion however, he remembered flying unintentionally between two factory chimneys at the Peterborough brickworks. He was grateful to the radar system for a rather different reason as well: its operation generated a certain amount of heat, which he found useful in preparing his late breakfast. 'Before every mission I used to make a great thick sandwich, with a mixture of spam and scrambled egg, made with powdered eggs, and I'd leave it in place on the radar machine until the right moment,' he explained. He described the hardships of the early morning missions:

> A truck took us to the aircraft. It was usually very cold on board — the heating system didn't work and the higher you went the colder it got, sometimes down to 50 degrees below zero — so you had to wear lots of clothing. You'd put on an electric suit which you plugged in to keep warm, then a flying suit, then a Mae West, and finally a parachute. Taxiing into position took

127: Former USAAF navigator Whitney Miller on a return visit to Oundle in 1994.

about twenty minutes, and then the planes would take off at 15 second intervals. There were 36 aircraft per mission. The plane always felt heavy and overloaded on take-off. We carried a 10,000 lb bomb load, and with the armour plating the whole aircraft weighed 62,000 lbs. Our take-off speed was supposed to be 120 mph, but often planes just didn't make it. As we took off we sometimes heard the sound of an explosion up ahead and saw the flash, and guessed what had happened.

Whitney Miller described how, just before getting up into the air he would look round and see other members of the crew rocking backwards and forwards in their seats in the hope that they might raise the speed of the lumbering aircraft. Once aloft the plane would turn right, joining a circle of other craft on the same mission.

I was always nervous — a 'bandits in the air' call would give me a real sinking feeling in the stomach. At 10,000 feet you needed oxygen. Things froze very quickly in the intense cold, and it was very difficult to write. Your hands stuck to bare metal, so you had to wear gloves. You felt in a strange world at 30,000 feet. After four to five hours in the air we arrived in the target area.

The flak was usually very intense. Some target areas were protected by 5,000 anti-aircraft guns, and some of these were radar guided. You had a flak suit to protect you, which was very heavy, and you wore goggles, so you ended up looking like a man from Mars. The lead aircraft bombardier would open the bomb bay doors. If a bomb got hung up, you had a problem. It wasn't safe to close the doors, but the draught from the opening sometimes set the

128: B-17G (43-38465 TU-A) 'Favorite Lady' of the 510th Bomb Squadron from Polebrook over Kassel, Germany: the target was the Bottenhausen ordnance plant. 'Favorite Lady' was one of 35 aircraft from Polebrook on this mission.

propellers on the bombs turning, and that was how they became armed. So the bombardier's job was to stop this happening by pushing a wire into place to obstruct the propeller before getting rid of the bomb.

Completion of the bombing meant an enormous release of tension for all the crew. 'You took off your oxygen mask, because you'd got ravenously hungry. Now was the moment when my radar system proved its usefulness, and I found that my sandwich had heated up just right. There was coffee, and RAF candy, which was awful and had no flavour, but it was supposed to be high-energy.' Sometimes they brought oranges with them, but these would freeze if they were not protected.

Flying in a good formation reduced the risk of attack. If an aircraft was separated from the group it became very vulnerable to enemy fighters. And flak was always a danger. On one occasion Whitney Miller's plane was hit by anti-aircraft fire, putting one of the engines out of action after it caught fire, so that they had to fly back on only three engines. The exhausting and stressful nature of the bombing missions seems almost unbelievable, and aircrews found themselves trapped in a nightmarish cycle when the bombardment of Germany was at its height. 'When we landed at Polebrook, the crews were interrogated, and we then had a medicinal shot of cognac — I think it was to stimulate our appetites. Then it was bed at 9.00 pm, getting up again as usual at 3.00 am, sometimes for six consecutive days. On one occasion my crew flew eight days in a row until we went to the Flight Surgeon to complain about the fatigue factor.' High altitude flying caused the 'bends' — it was known as 'flak suit cramp'. After one mission they discovered that theirs was the only plane which had returned safely to Polebrook — the others in their group had landed elsewhere, some of them in France.

The destructive effects of the war in the air were horrendous for both sides, but there was no time for questions. Getting on with the job was a philosophy which was common to both civilians and military personnel during the war, and which in the case of the latter was essential if they were not to be mentally deranged by the suffering which they inflicted on the enemy. 'You never thought about the German fighter pilots personally', explained Whitney Miller. 'You targeted civilian areas on the bombing raids, but you didn't think about the people who were down there. There's no such thing as partial war. It's like going into a boxing match — if you hesitate, you're finished.'

A Dangerous Job

Local residents in the area of the airfields were only too aware of the dangers faced by the flight crews. There are still vivid memories of the near misses witnessed in the vicinity of Polebrook and Deenethorpe.

Former USAAF tail gunner Bob Kerr, from Escadido, California, returned to the Oundle area recently along with a fellow-veteran, Ben Musser, of Tuson, Arizona. They revisited a spot in the village of Deenethorpe which they would remember for the rest of their lives. Both were members of a ten-man bomber crew that cheated death half a century before, just after 8.30 am on 5 December 1943, when their Flying Fortress crashed on top of a cottage with a 6,000 bomb load and caught fire.

Mercifully, the cottage was unoccupied and the crew — three of them slightly injured — managed to scramble clear and rush through the village and warn the residents.

Bob Kerr can clearly remember Fortress 9825's last moments.

Initially there was an impact and when I looked out one of the wing tips was scraping the ground with sparks everywhere. I thought about jumping, but at that speed, decided to stay put, protecting my head and leaning against the bulging door.

Then the belly of the plane began to bulge upwards. I remember looking at the bombs we had on board and thought, 'This is it!' I crawled forward and the tailplane had gone but as we slowed I thought, 'We may have a chance!'

I didn't wait and was out of the plane in seconds. I ran so far and looked back, decided I was not far enough, ran again and cleared the cottage wall like a deer, and glancing back ran some more!

Ben Musser credits the pilot for saving their lives. 'He managed to somehow keep the nose up, despite losing the tailplane, and I am sure this is what saved us.'

The crew of 9825 then managed to get all but one of the villagers out in the fields to lie flat, shelter behind hay stacks and mangold clamps. Only one old man refused to be moved.

The fire cart operated by Polish soldiers, stationed nearby, came rushing up the road but it was too late — Boomph! The bombs, detonated by the heat from the flames of the burning aircraft, exploded at precisely 9.04 am.

Only one villager suffered any injury, Mrs Redmond, whose face was cut by flying splintered glass. All 32 cottages were damaged. The landlord of The Cardigan Arms lost his cow house, but all his cows remained standing and not a bottle of beer was broken.[3]

The noise of the explosion was heard over a wide area: Elizabeth Berridge, in bed at home in Oundle, remembered the whole house shaking.

Such accidents were inevitable, and it is fortunate that there were relatively few civilian casualties in the surrounding area. Jessie Duffin remembered the hair-raising experience of bullets hitting the cow sheds at her parents' farm outside Warmington during target practice. Even more frightening was an episode described by Miriam Rothschild.

Near Tansor Grange Farm there was a low altitude practice bombing range. The bombs made a nasty screeching noise like the tearing of calico, and penetrated the ground for about two to three feet, but carried no explosives. Quite often, however, the aircraft dropped their bombs from a high altitude and missed the target. Three hundred and seventy bombs were dropped on the surrounding land during the war. One set fire to a field of corn, which was completely burnt out, and another went through my garage roof. One day, when the bombing was very persistent I hid in a ditch for three hours, hoping not to be killed by my own side. Finally, I crawled out of the ditch and managed to ring up the Commanding Officer at the base and said, 'Can't you stop them bombing us, the aircraft have mistaken the low altitude bombing range and are missing the target because they are flying so high.' The Commanding Officer replied, 'Mrs Rothschild, I have been trying to stop them for hours but they aren't taking any notice and we can't get them to stop.' I don't know which airfield they had come from but they were flying at such a high altitude that the aircraft were invisible. All you could hear were the screaming noises as the bombs came whistling down.

HRH Princess Alice in her *Memories of Ninety Years*, recalled the terrifying moment she experienced while watching her son William rolling about on a rug on the lawn at Barnwell Manor. An American Flying Fortress bomber, limping back towards a nearby airfield swooped and dived between the Manor and a large sycamore sixty yards away, clipping its branches. Miraculously it managed to climb again and continue its run.[4]

Tragedies

More than 46,000 members of the US Eighth Air Force lost their lives between July 1942 and April 1945.

Whitney Miller revealed that during the 311 missions which were flown from Polebrook 175 aircraft were lost along with their crews. The official loss rate of 5% which the authorities maintained in order to encourage the airmen on their missions was a gross distortion of the real figure, which, he said, was nearer 46%. On one mission to Munich his group lost six aircraft, with a couple crashing in Switzerland.

When wartime tragedy did occur, it was felt that much more intensely for Oundle people who had built up friendships with Americans. In spite of the fun, the dances, and the glamour and novelty of this strange encounter in a rural setting between two very different cultures, there was an underlying tension. The war was a serious business, and the signs of the life-and-death struggle in the skies over Oundle were obvious to those who watched for them. Ruth Keens in the village of Stoke Doyle, a few miles from Polebrook, was one of the many who felt involved in this way:

> Many nights I would be wakened by the noise of aircraft and from my bedroom window I could see the lights moving across the airfield as the planes were manoeuvred ready, so I knew in advance when a raid would take place. Cycling in to work I would count the planes as they circled round as they formed up. Later on in the early afternoon we would count them back home; watching as the Very lights were set off signalling wounded aboard and often the planes crashed on landing they were so badly damaged by anti-aircraft fire. Another way of foretelling a raid into Germany was the arrival about 10 pm of pick-up trucks to take the aircrews back to base to prepare for the next day's raid.

Valerie Carpenter, of North Street, recalled watching the planes going over her parents' house in South Road and wondering about the fate of aircrew members whom she might have met. The airmen didn't say much about their missions, although once, when she asked if they were afraid, she was told that 'nine out of ten men are afraid, and the tenth man is a liar'. She regularly worked at the Red Cross Club organising the charity dances. 'You could guess when one of them was on a mission the following day when you heard him say, "I've got to get some sack early," most of the missions taking place before dawn.' When the mission returned the news could be bad for friends of the aircrews. 'We used to go to parties expecting to be with a certain person, or you'd go in the mess and there was no sign of whoever it was you were meeting,' said Lorna Sloan. 'One of the friends would come up and tell you that he'd gone down that day.' But life had to go on. 'It was an atmosphere where everybody got on with it. For the other chaps' sakes you made the best of it.'

When a crash occurred near the airfields local residents were only too well aware of what had happened. HRH Princess Alice, who lived at Barnwell for most of the war, recalled the day when she was in her sitting-room and an aeroplane passed over very low, making a dreadful noise and trailing smoke and flames. Her son William was asleep in his pram on the lawn. 'I rushed out and reached him just as the explosion from the crash shook the air. It must have been about a mile away, but the pram still leapt out of my hands. It remained upright and William appeared not to wake up; however, when Nanny Lightbody fetched him later he asked, "Is aeroplane all right?"'[5]

William Wagstaff, who grew up in the Oundle area, was living at North Lodge on the outskirts of Barnwell when he had a frightening experience involving an American plane.

I was out in the fields setting snares for rabbits, and the farmer, old man Berridge, came running over shouting, 'Get down! Get down!' and just a few seconds later this plane came down in the field. So we started running over to help, and the crew saw us — they'd all got out — and were yelling 'Go back!' They ran off Hemington way, and we charged off in the other direction and hid in the dyke, and there was the most awful bang. When we looked there was nothing left of the plane, just a damned great hole. Some of the metal from that plane, great lumps of iron, ended up on the Thrapston road. That'll give you an idea about how big the explosion was.

Some of the worst tragedies occurred not as a result of enemy action but of human error. Three weeks after the 351st Bomb Group's arrival at Polebrook, during the completion of a practice bombing mission on 7 May 1943, tragedy struck. Two of the best crews were lost when two B17s collided over the airfield. A total of 19 men were killed, including the 508th Squadron's Commanding Officer, Major Keith Birlem.[6]

For Margaret Hawkins and her sister Jean Mabelson a similar collision which they witnessed while working in the fields near Polebrook was one of the most awful experiences of the war. All the members of both aircrews were killed. The two women remembered the visit which they made with their mother to Brookwood Cemetery in Surrey to see the graves. What made the event more poignant was that the Laxton girls knew one of the casualties, Carl Jorgensen. Only the night before, he had been with his girlfriend Margaret Nobbs, of Southwick, at the Laxton family's home at 24 Market Place, in Oundle. The crash occurred, so they were told, because one of the pilots involved, who had been flying fighters, had attempted to do an aerial loop.

Touching proof of the affection and sense of loss felt by Oundle families when they heard tragic news of their American friends, is this letter sent by Mrs Laxton on 27 August 1943 to the mother of Jimmy McCurdy after her son had died on 31 July from wounds received in action.

Dear Mrs Stover,
     I have been trying for several weeks to get your address from the American Red Cross and yesterday I got it. I wanted to write and let you know that your lovely son Jimmy McCurdy was a great friend of ours and we are all so very sad at the news of his death in action — with all his pals he came to our house about three days after he arrived in Britain, and since then he came in every time he was allowed to leave the base — with the result my husband and I, our two daughters and three sons grew to love him and look upon him as one of our happy family. We all send you our deepest sympathy in the loss of such a fine son. I don't know if he ever told you about us — but he loved coming to see us and spent hours among us. I used to get his washing done for him — I did any sewing he wanted me to do and often gave him a nice meal about 8.30 to 9 in the evening. He was one of the finest fellows we have ever had the privilege to know and we miss him more than words can tell. He died the death he would have chosen — a grand and brave airman and America ought to be proud of him. I hope it will help you to know he had true friends here in Britain, friends who admired his strong personality and who will remember him for many years to come. Goodbye dear Mrs Stover — our thoughts and prayers are with you in your grief.

     Yours very sincerely,
     Gertrude E. Laxton.

The Tragedy of 'Ten Horsepower'

Another notable tragedy which upset local people was the crash of the B17 42-31763, known as 'Ten Horsepower', in countryside near Polebrook on 20 February 1944. USAAF historian and former Laxton School boy Ken Harbour gives a graphic account of the incident in his book on the 351st Bomb Group at Polebrook:

> The target was Leipzig. Sixteen planes flew the mission as high box of a First Combat Wing composite, led by Major Roper and Lieutenant Lynch, with Lieutenant Lyttle as bombardier and Captain Matthews as navigator. Seventeen planes flew the low box of the 94th Combat Wing, led by Major Stewart and Lieutenant Floden, with Lieutenant Dixey and Lieutenant Badger as navigator and Lieutenant Lee as bombardier. The low box bombed Leipzig with good results. The high box was forced to choose a target of opportunity, an industrial plant at Stazfurt.
>
> As many as 40 enemy fighters were encountered. Attacking before and after the target, they came in from all around the clock, sometimes queuing up in groups of six to twelve planes before pressing home concentrated attacks. Flak from the target was moderate and accurate. The plane piloted by Lieutenant Nelson, 42-31763, was heavily attacked. He was originally scheduled to fly right wing off the Group Leader, but the plane had run off the perimeter track and had been stuck in the mud. When they eventually became airborne they were almost an hour behind the Group. However Lieutenant Nelson managed to get close to the Group, but was still some way behind, flying 'tail-end Charlie'. Just as they were approaching the IP a fighter appeared from head-on. A 20mm cannon shell came through the co-pilot's window. It just about decapitated Lieutenant Bartley, and then ricocheted off the armour plate behind him into Lieutenant Nelson, taking away a good portion of his right jaw. Somehow Lieutenant Nelson managed to hit the alarm bell. Upon hearing this Lieutenant Martin, the bombardier, salvoed the bombs and called for the rest of the crew to abandon the aircraft, then immediately bailed out.
>
> At that point the plane went into a spin. Technical/Sergeant Carl Moore, top-turret gunner, somehow managed to get to the controls and pull the plane out of the spin, but not before it had dropped some 15,000 feet. As soon as the plane came out of the spin and was under control, Sergeant Archie Mathies moved quickly to the front of the plane and immediately asked for help in moving Lieutenant Bartley's body. Sergeant Joe Rex, the radio operator, helped drag Lieutenant Bartley to the bomb bay. Sergeant Mathies then sat in the co-pilot's seat and started to fly the plane back to England. From time to time he had to call back to ask for help in flying the plane. One person could not stand the cold from the wind coming in the completely broken windshield. Fortunately Lieutenant Nelson had insisted, during training, that each crew member should have at least two hours' experience of flying the plane, just in case they were ever forced to do so.
>
> During the attack the command radio had been destroyed, so Sergeant Rex had to rig the high power radio to send out SOS signals. As he did so the German fighters came in to attack again, hitting the plane with 20mm shells in the radio room, and injuring Sergeant Rex with shell fragments. However the fighters were driven off by the power of the gunners. Against all the odds, late in the afternoon, 42-31763 'Ten Horsepower' appeared over Polebrook. Sergeant Mathies radioed the tower, expressing his predicament, but emphasizing his intention to get the plane down as Lieutenant Nelson's injuries were such as to prevent him from bailing out.
>
> Major LeDoux, Tower Officer of the Day, immediately summoned the CO, Colonel Romig, who, when presented with the facts and the knowledge that neither Lieutenant Truemper or Sergeant Mathies had ever effected a landing, ordered Mathies to head the ship for the coast and bail out. However Sergeant Mathies's resolve forced a compromise: the remaining

FOUR ~ FRIENDS AND ALLIES

129: Three Polebrook USAAF officers: l. to r.
Lieutenant Colonel Elzia LeDoux, Colonel Eugene Romig, Lieutenant Colonel Robert Bowles.
Colonel Romig was Group Commanding Officer at Polebrook from 3 January to 12 October 1944.
Both he and Major LeDoux played a part in the tragic episode of 'Ten Horsepower'.

five gunners, Sergeants Carl Moore, Joseph Rex, Russel Robinson and Thomas Sowell bailed out over the field whilst he and Lieutenant Truemper listened to landing instructions and advice being transmitted from the tower. Colonel Romig and Major LeDoux decided to lend some comfort by taking another B17 in an attempt to 'talk them down', whilst giving instruction, and hopefully confidence, by flying alongside. This however, proved to be more of a problem than a help as the damaged aircraft was flying a very erratic course and collision was more of a probability than a possibility.

Therefore from a comfortable distance in the aircraft flown by Major LeDoux, Colonel Romig talked them through two approaches to the field. Both were too high and too fast. Another attempt was made at Molesworth, set in differing terrain, but again without success. The decision was then made to try and set the aircraft down in the countryside near Polebrook. A large rolling field to the east of the aircraft was selected. This time the approach was more purposeful, but they chose, probably without thought as they fought the controls, the up gradient rather than the down; the result was that the nose dug in, the ship disintegrated and burnt. Lt Truemper and Sgt Mathies died instantly.

The first rescue services on the scene retrieved Lt Nelson alive from the wreckage, but mortally wounded; he died later that day. On 4 July 1944, on the lawn of their home at 807 North Avenue, Ill. Mrs Henry E. Truemper received the Congressional Medal of Honor awarded to her son from Brig. General R. E. O'Neill.

A similar ceremony took place on 23 July at the Finleyville Presbyterian Church when Mrs Mary Mathies received her son's award from Major General A. Craig.[7]

130: 'Valor at Polebrook', American artist David Poole's painting of the tragic episode of 'Ten Horsepower'.

Memories of such tragedies, and even the ghosts of the heroes of Polebrook live on today in the minds of those Oundle people who were so deeply affected by them. Princess Alice, in her *Memories of Ninety Years*, told the story of how, walking in her garden, she heard the voice of one of the young American pilots who used to come regularly to Barnwell Manor for its peace and charm as an escape from the hell of the bombing missions.

> Americans from the local aerodromes so enjoyed visiting the garden that soon we left it open for anyone to come and wander around. One fair-haired young airman particularly liked it and over the months earned some privileges like helping himself to fruit. He used to come regularly, so when one evening as I was hurrying back to the house to give William his bath I thought nothing of it when I heard his voice asking, 'Can I look around again?' Not even when I turned to reply and could see no one there. Afterwards I learned that approximately the time I 'heard' him he had been shot down and killed in a bombing-raid over Germany.[8]

FOUR ~ FRIENDS AND ALLIES

131: United States airmen from local airfields being welcomed at Barnwell Manor. HRH Princess Alice and the young Prince William are in the centre. Prince Henry is fifth from the right.

Operation 'Home Run' in 1945 marked the departure of the US forces from most of the British airbases, including those in the Oundle area. During the two years that the Group occupied Polebrook, 7,000 airmen passed through the base. Some were there for the duration, others for just a few days before they were shot down. In addition to the air and ground crews of the four squadrons that comprised the 351st Bomb Group, there were support functions based at Polebrook. These included units such as the 201st Finance Company, 1206th Quarter Masters Company, 11th Station Complement, 1629th Ordnance Company, 2098th Fire Fighting Platoon, 1061st Military Police Company, 854th Chemical Company, 252nd Medical Dispensary and the 447th Sub Depot.

The return flight to the USA was an immense feat of organisation. Polebrook veteran Whitney Miller remembers it as the best piece of navigation he ever performed.

By 5 June 1945, just three years after the first arrived, the last of the American airmen had left Polebrook. Not surprisingly, it was a tearful occasion.

132: Operation 'Home Run', June 1945:
USAAF aircraft lined up for the return journey from Deenethorpe to the USA.

Enduring Links

However, the Americans were never to forget their stay in England, and many links have been maintained with the individuals and families who befriended them, quite apart from the Englishwomen who became GI brides. Their hosts, like Miriam Rothschild, have always recognised the decisive contribution which they made in the fight against Nazism.

> I don't think we realised how much we owed the Americans. They were incredibly brave, incredibly tough, incredibly dedicated, and I don't know what would have happened here if we hadn't had the American Air Force stationed at Polebrook and the various other places from where they operated. We must always be deeply grateful.

Most of the airmen stationed in Britain have formed associations to organize visits to Europe as well as reunions between themselves, and with their British friends. Over 20,000 veterans returned to areas where they were stationed all over England during 1992 as part of the USAAF Fiftieth Anniversary Reunion celebrations.

Nearly 30 years after leaving Polebrook, in 1974, five men who had served with the 351st met at an Eighth Air Force reunion in St. Louis. They decided to form a 351st Bomb Group Association. The organisation now has a membership in excess of 1,500. In 1980 it decided that a memorial should be erected at Polebrook. Between 1943 and 1945, 175 planes and their crews had been lost from Polebrook Airfield. Many aircrew were lucky enough to survive, either as prisoners-of-war, or as internees in neutral countries such as

Sweden and Switzerland. But the total number of killed or missing in action from Polebrook alone had come to 405.

133: The USAAF memorial at Polebrook Airfield.

With the assistance of Miriam Rothschild, who leased the site for a peppercorn rent for 999 years, the memorial to the American airmen of Polebrook who lost their lives now stands at the eastern end of what was the main runway on the old airfield.

A similar memorial was erected on the main Oundle to Corby road at Upper Benefield, to commemorate all those who served at Deenethorpe. The monuments are fitting tributes to the brave men whom many local people remember with affection, and well worth a visit. Worthy of note also are the memorials commissioned by Lutton USAAF historian David Clark on display in Polebrook and Lutton churches to commemorate some of the air crashes which affected the 351st Bomb Group. Cast out of aluminium from the wreckage, each one is a detailed model of the aircraft involved.

Polebrook's special relationship with the USA was celebrated again on Wednesday 29 April 1992 to mark the fiftieth anniversary of the Eighth Air Force's arrival in Britain, with an evening service in the village church attended by 13 ex-servicemen and their wives, including the president of the Polebrook Airfield Association, Clay Snedegar. For many years now the church has been a place of pilgrimage to veterans, housing as it does the memorial register of members of the Association. Recently the Association donated £1,000 to the Polebrook church organ fund. A thriving organisation, it even publishes its own newspaper, the *Polebrook Post*.

134: David Clark's memorial to 'Ten Horsepower' in Polebrook Church.

The day after their service in Polebrook church, the 13 ex-servicemen and their wives, with Clay Snedegar, attended a dinner at Oundle School's Tuckshop, offered by the Headmaster David McMurray. Local restaurateurs stepped in to make the dinner more than just another school meal. Scottish smoked salmon was provided by Elton's Loch Fyne Oyster Bar and Seafood Restaurant. Oundle's West Street restaurant Fitzgerald's served the dessert, an Old English syllabub topped with little chocolate B17s. The Talbot Hotel in Oundle, where many of the veterans stay when they revisit the area, donated a case of wine. Pupils acted as hosts to show the veterans round their school, and learnt at first-hand about some of the wartime exploits in which the American airmen had been involved.

New Bikes for Polebrook

One of the most publicised links recently concerned the visit made by American veteran Roger Johnson to repay a half-century old debt. A former bombardier based at Polebrook during the war, Mr Johnson returned on 9 May 1992 to present 94 new bicycles to the children of Polebrook and three other nearby villages.

In spite of the publicity which his visit attracted, including a long meditation on his action by Bernard Levin in *The Times* of 2 July 1992, Roger Johnson's visit and presentation was concerned with a totally personal matter. In 1944, he had been stationed at Polebrook Airfield as part of a B-17 Flying Fortress crew assigned to the 508th Squadron of the 351st Bomb Group. He recounted in his own words the events of an episode which had been on his mind for 48 years:

FOUR ~ FRIENDS AND ALLIES

135: Peter Brookes' cartoon from *The Times* of 2 July 1992, inspired by Bernard Levin's article about Roger Johnson.
© Times Newspapers 1992.

The story to follow is about an English bicycle and a 'hair-raising' World War II combat aerial mission, and a true debt owed to the citizens of the Polebrook and Oundle areas of England for the past half-century. The story can only be appreciated if the reader learns of the events and attitudes that precede the War years.

My dear Father died a month after my eighth birthday. Times were not easy in those days and my Mother counselled me, that I either roll up my sleeves and do everything possible to acquire a good education in life, or life would not be very rewarding for me. These were the depression years in America and funds were hard to acquire. Money for college had to be earned and saved. I accepted any and all work available for a youngster. When aged 12 years, I was old enough to be a magazine salesman. I sold Liberty magazine, a weekly five cent publication that netted me a half cent's profit for each one sold. I hustled and soon had a customer clientele of 35. This meant I earned slightly more than 50 cents each week.

However it was difficult to service 35 customers spread out over a large area, and it was soon evident that I needed a bicycle. My Mother understood my problem, and wanted to help, but was unable to provide the required funds. However she escorted me to a large department store where my situation was described to the manager of the bicycle department. He consented to sell me a brand new bicycle for 25 US dollars, with a down payment of eight dollars, with the balance to be paid in 50 cent weekly instalments.

I was extremely proud to be the owner of that bike — it really helped me in the sales and delivery of the weekly magazines. My bike represented my total net worth at that time. My Mother recommended that I always apply a lock whenever I left the bike unattended.

On a Friday evening I was delivering the Liberty magazines to the law students at

Hamline University in St Paul, Minnesota. They were wonderful chaps and I looked forward to my visits with these law students. So much so that I neglected to lock my bike. When I emerged from the dormitory, my bike was not where I had placed it. Clearly, someone had stolen my only means of transport.

It was a shocking experience to realise that I would no longer be able to be service my magazine customers without great difficulty. It would be difficult to continue earning my 50 cents each week. I had mixed emotions of depression to think that someone would steal and deprive me of my bike, and I also experienced feelings of guilt because of my lack of responsibility in failing to lock my bicycle. I defiantly told my Mother that I wasn't going to pay the six dollars debt that remained on the bike that I no longer had. My dear Mother patiently explained that it wasn't the fault of the bicycle sales manager at the department store that caused the bike to be stolen. She explained further that it was my duty to pay off the contracted debt that remained. A day later, she and I took the trolley to the department store and she explained to the manager that I no longer had the bike, but I would indeed pay off the debt as promised.

The manager listened to the entire story, and expressed his sorrow that the bike had been stolen. He then made a wonderful proposition. If I promised to make all repayments on the bike that was stolen, he would sell me another at the store's wholesale cost with the same instalment payment schedule. My faith in people was immediately restored. My love and respect for my Mother immediately multiplied, in that she did her very best to teach me, as a young lad, the ingredients of honour and responsibility.

Six years passed until I volunteered and enlisted as an aviation cadet in the US Army Air Corps. Great Britain had won the Battle of Britain with those marvellous RAF pilots and the anti-aircraft batteries. The Eighth Air Force had begun to coordinate efforts with the British to bring an end to a disastrous war as soon as possible. The American airmen were received with open arms at the various bases provided for them in England. As a youngster of age 18, I could hardly wait to get into the fray.

After the required training of an aerial gunner, bombardier and navigator, I began flying my missions during the summer months of 1944, assigned to the 508th squadron of the 351st Bomb Group (1st Division). We flew Flying Fortresses from the airfield at Polebrook near Oundle and Peterborough. I eventually finished a tour of 35 missions, many of which were real thrillers. There were plenty of close calls, considerable excitement, and the witness of many airmen meeting their fate. I finished my 35 missions at age 20, which at that period of time excluded me from the right to vote. The transition from boyhood to manhood was quick indeed.

This dissertation is not intended to be a review of my 35 missions. Rather, it is about a bicycle and the wonderful English people, to whom I have owed a debt for over 50 years. Occasionally bomber crewmen would be given a pass for a few days so that they could 'let off some steam'. On one such occasion, I chose to visit London by myself. While there I was introduced to some fine English folks who went out of their way to see that I was royally entertained while in London. They invited me to their home, and following this, I was then introduced to the wartime entertainment that prevailed in London and even through the bombing by the V-1 and V-2 weapons which continued unrelenting. Our English friends just never did give up. They knew that life had to go on, and they saw to it that it did. They shared their meagre wartime rations with me, and I was served with real milk and ice-cream (not the powdered kind that we had on our air bases). Real hens' eggs too, and other foods not tasted since leaving the United States. Those Britishers were totally unselfish and were generally gracious hosts. They asked nothing in return. They merely expressed their appreciation that the US airmen were over there in their country trying to win the war.

The partying had to end as I needed to return to my own base.

Transportation was via the railroad system and I began my planned journey back to my base in Polebrook late in the evening with the knowledge that I would have to make some transfers. When I arrived at my final transfer point just before midnight, I was told that no more trains would be running until the following morning. I could not wait until morning as I was not certain whether or not I was assigned to fly the next day. There were no taxi-cabs available. The blackouts were in effect, and the communities were dark and sleepy, with no apparent movements by anyone. The prevailing fog made the darkness even more ominous.

I had no choice but to walk the 18 miles back to my airbase. I alternated running and walking, but at 3.00 am was still several miles from my base. Preparations for missions often began between 3.00 and 4.00 am, and I was panic stricken with the realization that I might be the cause of messing up an aircrew that depended on me. Crews performed best as a team, and the entire scheme of operations was one of teamwork in the aircraft crews and the whole squadron and group. An airman absolutely could not be a 'no-show'.

I had to get to my base! No police officers were in sight. In fact no one was up and about in sight. There were no lights in any of the buildings or dwellings that I passed. I saw a bicycle leaning against a fence. It was not locked and there was no way I could learn anything regarding the ownership, as I could not relate it to any nearby building. My immediate thought was that I could 'borrow' this bicycle, get to my base on time, fly my mission if I were assigned to go that day, and whether or not I flew, to return the bike later that day with an explanation, an apology, and a substantial 'rental fee'. My anxiety to get to the airfield allowed me to rationalize and prevented me from realizing that I was actually stealing a bicycle, an act that I would never have dreamt as possible after my own experience with my bike as a 12-year old, and the pain and suffering that it caused me then.

Upon returning quickly to my base I left the bicycle in a place I thought to be safe as I enquired as to my flight status. Yes indeed, I was scheduled to fly that morning, and with a 'mixed' crew.

This occurred occasionally when, for one reason or another, a 'regular' crew could not fly on a particular day. Fliers did not like to go on missions without those whom they knew well, and with whom they had trained and flown in combat before. But assignments were exactly that, and we all made the best of the situation. I was assigned to fly as navigator that day. The target was strictly military, and we were able to pin-point the target and bomb with accuracy. As usual the flak was frightening, and all did not make it back home to England.

Shortly after 'bombs away' I received a message that two bombs were 'hung up' in the upper portion of the right bomb bay. It was not known whether or not they were armed, but we could not gamble on the odds. We had to get those bombs out of the airplane. As it turned out, the Toggalier (substitute bombardier) flying that day was not acquainted with the bomb rack mechanism, and stated that he could not release the bombs when I requested him to do so. In fact, no one on that plane knew how to carry out that task. I was reluctant to leave my navigation post — but there was no other choice.

I knew that the catwalk in the bomb bay was only eight inches or so wide, and the bomb bay doors would of course have to remain open. Also, we were at 23,500 feet altitude, and oxygen would be absolutely essential. I clamped on my chest parachute, my special 'escape harness and pouch' containing shoes, maps, civilian passport photos, and candy, and I clutched an oxygen 'walk-around' bottle under my left arm. This left my right arm and hand free to manipulate a screwdriver on the bomb rack. My plan came to an abrupt halt however, as I could not enter the small passageway door to get into the bomb bay with all of my equipment attached. Something had to go!

It was anything but a pleasant choice. I hated to part with anything — but I disregarded the parachute and the escape harness, opting for the oxygen necessary to keep me conscious for a matter of minutes at that high altitude. I then made it through the door, and found myself on the narrow catwalk with a fantastic view of the ground nearly five miles below. I wedged myself tightly between the racks, hung on to the 'walk-around' bottle, and manipulated the screwdriver in the racks. Out dropped the bombs, causing the plane to momentarily lurch upward. I dropped the screwdriver, and hung on for dear life, then made a dash for the door leading to safety. The gauge on the oxygen bottle was now near the zero mark.

Settling down from this excitement I returned to my navigation duties, and we made it safely home to our airbase in England. As soon as we had landed, replaced our equipment and had been 'de-briefed' I went to the location where I had left the bicycle. To my horror it was not there. I searched frantically for it for hours to no avail. I felt absolutely sick, realizing that I had stolen someone's bike, and now I would not be able to return it. Here I was, a guest in England, helping to fight a war a long way from the shores of the United States, with wonderful people who went out of their way to make all of us feel most welcome in their country. I remembered the wonderful time I had experienced just that day before with my English hosts in London. It made me feel all the sicker.

I soon finished my tour of 35 missions and returned to America. I was never able to locate that bicycle. I had returned to the general area several miles from the airbase where I originally 'borrowed' it, but the surroundings did not even seem familiar. I recalled the dark foggy night when I began riding the bicycle.

For nearly 50 years I have regretted taking that bike that night. It is only now that I am able to come up with a plan that will 'soften the blow' of what happened, at least to some extent. The person who owned that bicycle might not even be alive at this time, but whoever he was, there must be grandchildren, great-grandchildren, neighbours or friends that possibly have fallen on hard times, and cannot now see their way clear to purchase a bicycle.

136: A kiss for the Major: Eight-year old Jodie Richardson, a pupil at Polebrook School, thanks Roger Johnson for his gift of a new bike.

I have purchased from the Raleigh Bicycle Establishment a number of brand new bikes to be given to any boy or girl in the Polebrook and Oundle surrounding areas that would like a bicycle and has none at the present time because of economic reasons. Hopefully this will bring joy and happiness to many British youngsters, and, in a small way, will approach evening the score for my theft of that bicycle almost 50 years ago during World War II. I can only hope that the English people will forgive me for taking that bike that day. May the friendships between the citizens of our two countries exist forever.

The Poles

If the Americans were the largest foreign group which played a part in Oundle's wartime history, the Poles were the smallest, and yet they were the most tragic in view of the poignant fate of their homeland. Poland had after all been the most notable of the European victims of Nazi aggression in that its invasion at 5.30 am on 1 September 1939 had started the Second World War. On 31 March, Britain and France had given guarantees of military aid to Poland in case of German aggression, and the Allies' declaration of war was therefore inevitable. The German conquest of Poland was completed within a fortnight except for Warsaw, which held out until 27 September. The Polish tragedy was compounded by an unexpected and crushing blow from the east: Soviet troops marched in on 17 September, and the scene was set for yet another partition of Poland. Russia and Germany signed an agreement to divide the spoils on 28 September.

No country suffered more than Poland under the Nazi occupation. Hundreds of thousands of her people were dispersed throughout Europe to work as slave labourers. Many of the country's leaders were interned in concentration camps and executed. It is estimated that more than two million Polish Jews and hundreds of thousands of Catholics were killed by the Nazis.

Among the many victims of Nazi aggression who fled to England from the European continent, the Poles stand out as a major group who did their best to keep their national identity while fighting with the Allies. A Polish government-in-exile was set up in London at the beginning of the war and was recognised by the Western allies. However in 1944 the Russian Government ceased to recognise the exiled Polish Government because of the latter's refusal to agree to Soviet proposals for the re-adjustment of Poland's frontiers. In July a puppet Lublin Government was set up in Poland by Russia after its expulsion of the Nazis, and this was recognised by Britain and the United States. The general election held in 1947 resulted in the formation of a Communist-dominated Government which suppressed all opposition political parties and supported close ties with the Soviet Union.

Polish patriots who had fled their homeland had fought on the western fronts, and after VE Day could have gone back to Poland. Instead, due mainly to the drastic change in the Polish political situation they settled here in the West, many of them in England.

It seemed appropriate that 17-year old Przemystaw Kordos, a visitor from Poland studying in Oundle in 1995, should have the opportunity of meeting some of the Poles who have settled in Oundle, and of telling their story in his own words.

> The Polish community in Oundle is not big — no more than a dozen people. But still they have preserved the living language and rich memories. I'd like to present their experiences from the war and descriptions of their wartime journeys to England.
>
> John Czwortek, who lives at Cotterstock Avenue, and is an organist in the local Catholic church, came to Oundle more than 40 years ago. He started the war as a voluntary soldier in

the Polish infantry garrison, based in Warsaw. During the German Blitzkrieg he had to leave the capital, was pursued to the East, and after heavy fighting was taken prisoner along with his unit by the Germans. He arrived at the *stalag*, but as he was very young (16 years old) and only a volunteer, he was soon set free.

He came back to his family town, Lubliniec, in southern Poland, which was annexed by the Third Reich. He stayed there under the occupation for two years, and then he was forced to join the Wehrmacht. The Germans had an excellent reason for blackmailing him — as long as he stayed obedient to orders, they would not punish his father for taking part in the Insurrection of 1920 against German rule in Silesia. And there was only one punishment — a concentration camp. So John Czwortek had to spend three years as a soldier under the German command — mainly in France — trying to do his worst.

As soon as it was possible, without risking the safety of his family, he changed sides and in October 1944 he surrendered to the Americans, being stationed in a small town in the Vosges mountains in Eastern France. After the necessary interrogations, and having successfully dispelled all suspicions, he finally rejoined the Caparthian Fusiliers Division of the Polish Army in 1945, with the rank of Lance Corporal. He fought in the battles of Ancona and Bologna.

137: A wartime exile in Oundle: John Czwortek.

Soon the war was over. Now he had a choice of where to go. He abandoned the idea of going back to the homeland because of the Soviet occupation, and was faced with a choice between Canada, Australia, America and England. He decided on coming to England due to the European position of Britain, and arrived here, still as a soldier, in 1946.

For several years he was stationed in different military sites, including Amersham and Lilford. After his demobilisation he worked for the Lilford Timber Company, married a girl from Peterborough, and settled in Oundle. Since then his connections with the town have grown in many ways.

~ ✧✧✧ ~

Paul Francis Cichon is also a Polish-born resident of Oundle, who settled here just after the war. He lives in Lime Avenue, close to John Czwortek.

His journey to England was however totally different.

Born just before World War I in Silesia, he entered the brand new school for pilots in 1930 and became a mechanic. When war broke out, he was stationed with his squadron in Krakow, and after several days was mobilised for the defence of the besieged capital Warsaw. The old-fashioned Polish planes, built according to 1933 standards were no match for the German Luftwaffe, and the losses of his group were extremely high — no less than 75%. Because of this they were ordered to evacuate, the flying personnel being given the highest priority, and escaped to the East. Following the Soviet invasion they fled to Romania. Because of the treaty of mutual cooperation in the case of invasion between this country and Poland, Paul Cichon's group felt relatively safe when they had crossed the border. They were however disarmed and put into a camp for refugees. Thanks to inattentive guards they escaped several months later, making their way via the Polish Embassy in Bucharest, where having obtained new documents and civil clothes they arrived at Baltchik, a small coastal town on the Black Sea.

From here they were evacuated to France. As only injured people had a right to leave Romania, they pretended serious wounds and scorches. Stopping in Beirut for a month and after a journey rich in adventures, including a violent storm during their sea-journey, they reached France at the beginning of 1940. Here, Paul Cichon worked in a secret factory for plane engines in Limoges until the fall of France.

He was successful in being evacuated with the rest of the Polish personnel to England and entered 308th Polish Squadron as a Fitter 1. At the end of 1941 he started fighting with his squadron. In fact the first German plane was shot down by them just before Christmas 1941. Then the typical wandering of the flying squadron began. They changed airfields at least once a year, being based at Exeter, Northolt, and Coventry. They also changed planes: from Hurricanes, through Spitfires Mk V, and finally to Mustangs in 1943. Because of the long range of his squadron they were not moved to the Continent after D-Day, but stayed in England. As well as flying auxiliary missions in Europe, they took part in interceptions of V-1 rockets. As the squadron had very good results, the King himself came to visit them, awarding some of the pilots the Distinguished Flying Cross.

Paul Cichon was demobilized by the RAF in 1948 with the rank of Sergeant, and lived for some time in Portsmouth, finally coming to Oundle, where he was married. He worked in manufacturing, at Perkins Engines, taking retirement in 1978.

~ ✧✧✧ ~

Emil Skiba is a local clockmaker with a shop on West Street, with over 50 years of experience in the business.

He was not as lucky as his two fellow Poles. He was born and lived in a town not far away from Lvov, now in the Ukraine. As he was too young to fight in 1939, being aged 16, he stayed there with his family, and was captured by Russian occupying forces on 17 September. A mass migration then began, with the whole town's population forced to leave and move to Siberia, 100 miles east of Kazakhstan. The journey by train lasted for three weeks. Children and old people died because of the cold and starvation. The survivors arrived at the camp in a forest, and worked cutting trees and throwing them into the river, which was a means of transport. They were guarded by militia.

After two years, during the winter of 1942 Emil Skiba decided to escape. He went on foot to the nearest station. Nobody searched for him because his family claimed that he was absent through illness. In fluent Russian he said he wanted to join the army. There was no suspicion on the Russian NKVD side, for many criminals and prisoners were released from the camps to join the army. Again he took the train, this time to Novosybirsk, but a document control in the middle of the journey made him jump off. Alone in the snow, armed only with a small compass, he went on foot for three months, travelling 1600 miles, moving only at night, starving and sleeping amongst the trees. In April he reached Novosybirsk, where he obtained new documents from the Polish Embassy. He was only just in time because the militia had started searching for him, armed with his photograph.

Emil Skiba joined the Polish Army and left Russia, crossing the border to Persia. At the end of 1942 he entered the Polish army of General Wladyslaw Anders, the man who was

138: The end of an odyssey: Emil Skiba outside his West Street shop.

to lead the final assault on Monte Cassino in Italy. He then travelled through Syria and Palestine. In Tel-Aviv he met a Jewish friend of his father, who taught him his clockmaking skills. In 1943 he reached Egypt, and in the following year he was moved to Sicily. He fought in the Battles of Monte Cassino (where he was seriously injured), Ancona and Bologna. When the war ended, he was given the choice of where to go. Although he had a family in America he chose England, for it was the best country for people not fully recovered from war wounds.

He reached this country in 1945, being stationed at Thetford in Norfolk, and Lilford before being demobilised. He lived for some time in London, but as his wife came from Oundle, they came back to the town, where he opened his clockmaker's shop on West Street.

More than 300,000 Polish soldiers fought on the Western Front. Most of them settled in England, but a few went back to Poland.

In this section of *Oundle's War* I wanted to pay a small tribute to those emigrants, who lost their country many years ago with the end of World War II.

Notes
1. Much of the historical detail about the 351st Bomb Group in this chapter is based on Ken Harbour and Peter Harris' book.
2. See Michael Gibson's *Aviation in Northamptonshire*, p.221 for the information on GI Brides. The organisations WAR BABES and TRACE are listed in two recently published books, *Daddy, where are you?* by Shirley McGlade and Mary McCormack, and *Bye Bye Baby,* by Pamela Winfield. See *Oundle Chronicle*, Summer 1992, p.vii.
3. See Bob Howe's account, *Oundle Chronicle*, Summer 1994, p.4.
4. HRH Princess Alice, *Memories of Ninety Years*, p.148.
5. *Ibid*
6. See Ken Harbour and Peter Harris, *The 351st Bomb Group*, p.100.
7. *Ibid*, pp.33-34.
8. HRH Princess Alice, *Memories of Ninety Years*, p.148.

CHAPTER FIVE

Captives in a Distant Land

Prisoners in Europe

The rapid progress of German forces across Europe in the early stages of the war inevitably resulted in the capture of British servicemen with Oundle connections.

Many of them gave detailed information about the conditions in which they were held.

Former Oundle School pupil Alec Brown, who had left Crosby House in 1938 before joining up, was captured on 27 May 1940 in Belgium, and a letter from his sister to the Editor of his old school's magazine gave details of his life as British Prisoner of War No. 221 in Germany's Oflag VII C/H:

> There are 86 officers living in a room 40'x20'x12'. They have 6' long wooden beds with nine four and a half inch slats across, and a straw mattress and straw pillow. Their sheets and pillowcases are changed once a month and they have two blankets. There is one small stove in the room, on which they can cook for half an hour a week. There is a courtyard to exercise in, but it is very small, and they get two meals a day of soup and potato. Up to this date, 12 November, he had not had any food from England, but had just received one clothes parcel. He is buying himself two parcels of food a week from Jugoslavia and Switzerland. The camp is run like a university and they have plenty of entertainment. Alec belongs to a choir and choral society. There are about 1,400 officers in the camp.

The letter ended with a plea common to almost all prisoners: 'I should be so grateful if any one could find time to write to Alec, as they live for their letters.'[1]

Lovel Garrett, as we have seen in an earlier chapter, had the honour to be captured by Rommel during the disastrous 1940 campaign in Northern France, and spent the rest of the war as a POW in Oflag VIIB camp at Eichstätt, near Ingolstadt in the western German province of Franconia. A selection of his letters written during his captivity were edited by former Oundle School master Dennis Ford.

139: Former Oundle School boy Lovel Garrett, in happier times after his years as a POW in Oflag VIIB.

Although he complained of the monotony of camp routine, he provided a picture of busy activity organised by enterprising, resilient men determined to entertain each other and to keep fit. At Oundle, Lovel Garrett had been a distinguished games player, and despite the shortage of equipment there was rugby and cricket to play: the standard of hockey was particularly high as the camp was bursting with internationals, Blues and county players. Inter-service tournaments were held and the number of colonials was large enough for them to form their own national teams. Nor was there any shortage of interesting people to talk to. Besides old friends, amongst 3,000 officers Lovel Garrett found that he was always meeting new people from practically every country in the world, from whom he learnt a great deal: a practically professional orchestra, two dance bands, a cast of West End actors, several dons and innumerable schoolmasters on the intellectual side. So with this wealth of talent there were concerts, lectures, even a pantomime. To keep his brain active he read a lot of history, thanking his luck there was a good library, as private books in parcels arrived but rarely; he urgently requested Trevelyan's *History of England* and a copy of 1942 *Wisden,* and noted the arrival of books from the New Bodleian. He had a number of pupils working for private exams, began to write a novel and announced that he had completed two thirds of his own *History of England.*

More mundane tasks helped to fill the time and Lovel Garrett wrote with gentle humour of his successes and discoveries.

> We have our midday meal in the dining room, but the rest in our own rooms. There are ten people in my room and we have all food in common. This week it is my turn to room-cook and I thoroughly enjoy it, next week I am 'washer up' — not so good. ... thanks for the darning needles etc. I have no particular talent and wish I'd been taught at school, it should be made compulsory! By the way, please send me a cookery book.
>
> November 1942:
> News from you is rather scarce and as our life is rather monotonous it is difficult to find much to say, needless to say I think of you often. I work in the canteen kitchen here and find it amusing and interesting. Have you ever tried roast bully with a few prunes and fried onions; it is excellent, basting helps. I have made some very successful pie crusts out of crushed biscuits. When you buy tinned food get Armour's 'La Blanca'. Infinitely superior to any other brand. I have decided we don't at home use enough fruit and cheese in cooking meats.

In one camp the prisoners were allowed to grow their own vegetables and the following recipe was based on the first fruits of that garden.

> June 1942:
> Here is a recipe for a savoury: take two onions and a dozen radishes, toast some pieces of bread, fry the onions, then stew into a sauce, thickening with groats and milk powder, a dash of pepper and, at the last moment the radishes chopped up small, spread potted meat on the toast and pour the sauce over it. I have invented a number of recipes.

The tone of the letters is invariably good humoured but neutral and noncommittal about their captors; all outgoing letters were scrutinised by the authorities; occasionally a thick black line obliterates some comment considered unwelcome or useful to the enemy. Overall, conditions in the camps appeared tolerable, but perhaps Lovel Garrett tactfully stayed within the imposed guidelines. He reported one clash between the prisoners and the authorities.

> We had no sooner completed our swimming pool than all walks and visits to the sports platz were forbidden by the German High Command on the grounds that an English Officer had broken his parole, the General has registered a protest to the protecting power. So for the present we are confined to a space 100 yds x 40 approx including three large buildings, somewhat restricted for 150 officers. I hope we go to a big camp as more faces make life less monotonous.

There was ample time to reflect on his own future after the war; he contemplated a change of career and was pungently outspoken on English politics. He managed to follow the debate on education, reading both the Fleming and Norwood reports but voiced his doubts about the future of independent public schools. He considered reading for the Bar, entering local government or launching into politics.

> June 1942:
> I should very much like to go in for Parliament, but I am the sworn foe of the big financial interests which control the Conservatives. Labour's 'little Englanders' or the stupid tyranny of the trades unionists are equally repellent and I detest communism, the only hope is a new party and who is there to lead it? What we need is more discipline, less talk of the rights of man and more of his duties. I advise you to read Peasant Europe by Teltman if you can get hold of it. Keep smiling.

The exchange of ideas and long conversations with men from such different backgrounds altered his own view of society as they set the world to rights and looked forward to resuming a full life after the boredom, lack of privacy and frustrations of prison life. His letters talk of the eagerly awaited parcels from family or friends, requests for tobacco, gym shoes, tooth powder or razor blades, for news of casualties from *The Laxtonian* or of fellow officers, friends and above all his family, separation from which was painful, especially when he heard of the death of his father. His philosophic outlook on life had helped Lovel Garrett to accept the present with resignation but retain his confidence in the ultimate outcome. Hence the constant affectionate exhortations that they are not to worry; he is very fit, cheerful and in excellent form. His collection of letters is a remarkable tribute

140: Elliott Viney, DSO, MBE, TD, photographed during a return visit to Oundle in 1995. The MBE was awarded for his educational work in POW camps.

to sustained hope in adversity and the determination to enjoy life whatever the limitations and privations imposed by five years of the loss of freedom, family and country.[2]

Another resident of Oflag VIIB with an Oundle School connection was Elliott Viney, who had left New Street's School House in 1932, had also been captured in 1940 and spent the rest of the war as a prisoner. He remembered the occasional meetings which the Oflag's Old Oundelians used to hold, as well as a rugby match — 'about 15 minutes each way — we couldn't take more on our rations.' Elliott Viney was rewarded with an MBE for his work in maintaining morale among his fellow prisoners. His five years of captivity had kept him fully occupied as Camp Librarian, running an education service, and editing and printing a camp magazine.

An Epic Tale: the Wooden Horse from Oundle

There were many escape stories featuring prisoners of war who had spent time at Oundle. Roger Maw, a former pupil at the School, played a part in one of the most famous.

In August 1942, as Commanding Officer of No. 108 Squadron in the Western Desert, Roger Maw bailed out of his aircraft after it had been shot down, and crawled towards the German lines, his leg badly injured. His wartime career — he had won a Distinguished Flying Cross in 1941 — had come to an end, and the rest of the war was spent as a prisoner in Germany.

It was Roger Maw, during his time as a POW, who designed and built the wooden vaulting horse, the 'Trojan Horse', which made possible one of the most daring prisoner-of-war escapes. The story of the escape from Stalag Luft III was immortalised when Eric Williams later published *The Wooden Horse*, a book describing how British airman Peter Howard and his friends escaped from Stalag Luft III in Sagan, Upper Silesia, with Roger Maw's help.

Their inspiration was the epic tale of Troy. First they built a vaulting horse, then recruited keep-fit fanatics for ceaseless exercise, tunnelling all the while from under the horse to the camp perimeter. Finally they concealed themselves inside the horse and wriggled their way to freedom.

That was the splendid conception. But it had to be sold to the handymen of the camp. The prisoners' theatre boasted an excellent carpenter, but he was unwilling to participate in the scheme: his tools were, he explained to Peter Howard, 'on parole' for the dramatic productions so essential to morale.

'Why not go along and see 'Wings' Maw?' he suggested. 'He's got a few tools, and he'll lend a hand.'

Roger Maw inhabited a small room at the end of block 64 — the privilege of a Wing Commander.

A small man with a large moustache, he received Peter Howard in the casual wear in which he had been shot down. His Egyptian sandals, pink socks, bright yellow shirt, large red neckerchief and worn grey flannel trousers hardly befitted the former Commander of No. 108, a bomber squadron operating against targets in Libya and Greece.

> 'Thought I'd dress like a foreigner,' he explained later, 'then I shouldn't be noticed if I had to bail out. But I must have dressed as the wrong sort of foreigner, because I was arrested quite soon.'

The room was twelve feet by six feet. Across the narrowness of it, at the end farthest from the door, stood a two-tier bunk. The bottom bunk was made up for sleeping. The top bunk was a confusion of old Klim tins, bits of wire, bedboards, the pieces of a broken-down cast-iron stove, and the remains of a wooden bicycle that 'Wings' had started to make and never finished. Klim tins stood on the table and on the chairs. Klim tins overflowed all these and stood in serried ranks under the bunks. The tins were filled with nails, bits of string, screws, nuts and bolts, small pieces of glass, odds and ends of paint from the theatre. Everything that 'Wings' had acquired from years of diligent scrounging.

Along one wall, under the window, were fixed a drawing board and a work bench. On the drawing board was pinned a scale drawing of a sailing yacht. On the work bench lay another confusion of odds and ends, a vice made by 'Wings' out of the parts of an old bed and a model steam engine constructed from Klim tins and a German water bottle.

As Peter entered the room, the Wing Commander was nailing a wooden batten to the floor. The batten formed a frame round a large square hole he had cut in the floor.

'What's that for?' Peter asked.

'To stop me falling down the hole,' the Wing Commander replied without looking up from his work.

'No, I don't mean the piece of wood. I mean the hole itself.'

'Oh, that!' He straightened himself. 'That's part of an air-conditioning plant I'm fitting.'

'How will it work?'

'I'm fitting a fan under the floor. I've got the parts of it here.' He pointed to a wheel with propeller-like blades cut from plywood. 'The fan is driven by a belt and pulley from a large wheel under the floor. A shaft runs from the wheel up through the floor to the top of the work bench. I shall have this old gramophone turntable mounted on the top of the shaft. The winding-handle of the gramophone will be fixed to the turntable as a crank. When the room gets too hot I merely turn the handle and cold air is driven up through the hole in the floor. The hot air leaves through another hole I'm going to cut near the ceiling.'

'Why don't you use the gramophone motor to drive the fan?' Peter asked.

'Oh, the motor's broken. I used the parts to make a clock.'

'Wait till the goons see it. They'll be after you for damage to Reich property.'

'They have.' The Wing Commander said it with satisfaction. 'The Feldwebel came round this morning and started screaming at me in German. I told him to push off and bring someone who spoke English. Then a Gefreiter came crawling under the hut and tried to nail the hole up from underneath. I pranced around stamping on his fingers. He went away after a bit and came back with a Lager Offizier. I'm going into the cooler for fourteen days.'

'It's a wonder they don't take your tools away.'

The Wing Commander looked cunning. 'Look at this.' He pointed to a tool-rack fixed to the wall over the work-bench. 'Have a look at these tools.'

Peter examined the tools. Every one was phoney. It must have taken 'Wings' weeks to fashion the hacksaw blades and wicked-looking knives from pieces of rolled-out Klim tins. There were chisels too, made of wood and painted to look like steel.

'They do a swoop now and again, but all they find is this. All my real tools are hidden behind the panelling of the wall. They think I'm mad, but quite harmless, really.'

Peter laughed. 'I expect they think most of us are round the bend. I want to make a vaulting-horse and I came along to ask your advice and see if you could let me have a bit of plywood and some nails.'

'Yes, I think so.' To him a vaulting-horse was a problem in terms of materials available.

Peter explained about the tunnel. He did not want the Wing Commander to be working in the dark. 'Wings' was at once enthusiastic.

'We must set it out first,' he said. He unpinned the drawing of the sailing yacht and replaced it with a sheet of clean paper. 'It will have to be light and strong,' he said. 'Strong both ways. Both for vaulting and for carrying you inside it.' He took up a scale rule and bent over the drawing board.

Thus did Roger Maw put to good effect the knowledge of carpentry which he had gained in Oundle School Workshops. When his wooden horse was ready it stood 4ft 6in high. The base covered an area of 5ft x 3ft, and the sides were made from plywood sheets from Red Cross packing cases, stolen from the German store. The scheme worked brilliantly, allowing Eric Williams and his friends Oliver Philpot and Michael Codner to escape from Stalag Luft III on the night of 29 October 1943. His book *The Wooden Horse* became a best-seller, and the basis for film and television productions.[3]

The following year saw another famous bid for freedom from the same camp, also the subject of a book and a well-known film, *The Great Escape*. This time it was a mass break-out which the camp escape committee had planned, using 'Harry', a tunnel 120 metres long. The tunnel was equipped with rails to bring out trolley-loads of earth, was ventilated with pipes made of dried milk cans and bellows made from kitbags, and was lit using the camp's electricity supply. On 24 March 1944, 79 inmates passed through the tunnel. Three were seized near the exit, but three managed to return to England. Of the remainder who were recaptured, 50 were shot without trial, apparently on Hitler's orders. Paul Brickhill's book *The Great Escape* mentions another former Oundle School boy, Squadron Leader Denys Maw, a distant relative of the builder of the Wooden Horse, and brother of Wing Commander Michael Maw who died heroically in September 1944. A Stirling bomber pilot awarded the Air Force Cross before being shot down over Holland in 1943, Denys Maw was number 81 in the queue of prisoners waiting to escape. Just as he was about to crawl into the exit shaft he heard the crack of a rifle. 'The bastards!' he thought. 'They've known all along, and they're plugging each bloke as he crawls out.' He turned back along the tunnel to warn the others, and the would-be escapers succeeded in reaching the safety of their prison huts. They had failed in their bid for freedom, but at least they were not going to be shot in cold blood like the unfortunate fifty.[4]

Further south in Europe a successful escape from captivity was made by former Oundle School boy Ian English, a POW in Italy's Camp PG49 at Fontanellato near Parma. Captured at the Battle of Mareth in 1943, he had been transported by sea from Tunis to Naples before spending five months as a prisoner in Italy. Following the signing of the Armistice with Italy on 8 September the Allied prisoners marched out of the camp, breaking up into small groups. Ian English and two fellow prisoners made for the hills, keeping to the high Appennines while they marched the 500 miles south to the British lines. Encounters with Germans were a daily occurrence; the three men would be forever grateful to the *contadini*, the Italian country people who gave them food and shelter at the risk of their own lives, and to whom Ian English dedicated the story of his escape. Only 50 of the 500 POWs who had marched out of Fontanellato managed to rejoin the British forces.[5]

Another escape with an Oundle connection had a tragic end. Major James Syme, who had left Oundle School's New House in 1930, found himself 13 years later in enemy territory, talking by a strange coincidence to another former Oundle pupil from New House, Robert Fieldhouse. Both were in Prisoner of War Camp 29 in Italy. With a small group of others they escaped from the camp in September 1943, hiding in the Gran Sasso Mountains on their way towards Allied lines. On 1 January 1944 disaster struck: an avalanche hit the party and James Syme was killed.[6]

Close contact with the enemy in a new, non-combat situation gave some British soldiers who now found themselves as prisoners a different insight into the business of war. Oundle veteran of the North African campaign Ralph Leigh, living in East Road, was captured in June in 1942, and spent five months in a prison camp at Benghazi before being shipped across the Mediterranean to Taranto in Italy, from where he was eventually transferred to a POW camp in Germany, outside Dresden.

He recalled the moments of the day of his capture by the Germans at the fall of Tobruk on 20 June. Wounded during the attack, he had walked out of the hospital to find himself faced with a German tank.

> It was a very uncanny, unreal situation to find you were in the hands of the enemy. When this tank arrived, a German officer got out, quite a young man, spoke in perfect English. There were about ten or a dozen of us gathered together. He said, 'Just walk down the road 200 yards, you'll find some more of your friends. You'll be looked after.' He said to me, 'You're wounded, you'll be picked up.' I said, 'I'm not.' He said, 'Look at you.' Of course I was a mass of blood and flesh, I must have been a horrible sight. I told him what had happened, and he said, 'Well if you can get there you walk.' And then I thought, 'Surely this is not the ruthless cold-blooded German that we're supposed to be fighting against?'
>
> Two days later we were taken into a huge compound in the desert. All we got was a bottle of water that night. Some lorries came and took us away, and we were packed into these three-ton lorries. There must have been a couple of hundred of us, and we were poked inside by guards at bayonet point. That was the only ill-treatment I had in three years as a prisoner of war. They weren't unduly harsh, they were just making sure that we didn't make any argument. I finished up the last one on, with my legs hanging outside the door.
>
> After about a couple of hours the lorry stopped and a young German got out, a typical German, big, blond, handsome man. He too spoke perfect English, he'd just come from college. He said, 'If any of you want to ride with me you're welcome.' So I got out for a bit of comfort, and sat with him. The first thing he did, he shook hands, and said, 'Three days ago you'd have shot my head off and I'd have shot yours. You've no need for that now.' He shared his coffee and his sandwiches. And I sat there in the cab and I began to think, 'What on earth am I doing here. What's it all about?' I'd probably been responsible for the deaths of several enemy, because I was a gun layer, which meant that it was my responsibility to make sure that the shells landed where

141: Ralph Leigh, a Lance-Bombardier with the Royal Artillery, before his capture at Tobruk.

they were supposed to land, so, as much as anyone in the gun crew, I was responsible for the deaths of probably a lot of people whom, had I met in different circumstances, I would have shared their coffee and their sandwiches, and I began to think, 'What on earth am I doing here?' That's when I started to think about the futility and the stupidity of war. We were sitting there talking about our own lifestyles. We were just sharing life as ordinary everyday people. We could have been the best of friends, and, as he quite rightly said, three days ago we'd have shot each other. For what? That's what I used to ask myself. What for? And I still ask it, fifty years later.

The eight-day journey to a prison camp at Benghazi, along with 30,000 other British soldiers who had been captured at the fall of Tobruk, was marked by other memorable incidents during the journey which made a deep impression on the young Oundle man.

On about the third day, we were put into a compound at a place called Badia. There were Italian guards. Nobody had any respect for the Italians. Even the Germans detested them. The first night we were captured, everyone was longing for a drink of water. The Italians came up with lorries, and they had dirty water that they'd got in diesel cans, and they were showing you this water, and they'd let you have a bottle of water provided you gave them your watch, a ring, or a good pen. You had to give them something valuable. I'd got nothing. All I'd got was a pair of shorts and a ring that my wife gave me on our engagement, so I wouldn't part with that. The Germans came on the scene. They stood and watched a few minutes all that was happening, and they really personally set about these Italians, pulled them away, and in one or two cases they punched them. They took the water away from them. If it wasn't fit to give they threw it away, and got some more, and just gave it to everybody that was there. That's the difference in the type of people. I'm not being pro-German or anti-Italian. I'm just stating facts as they happened.

The second incident also made him think.

We were right on the beach looking out onto the Mediterranean. We were just lying about on the sand, and all of a sudden the guards went absolutely berserk. 'Il Duce! Il Duce!' shouting and screaming and waving their rifles. We looked out to sea and there was a big white yacht coming on the scene. Mussolini. Supposed to be a very ruthless, hard man. A couple of motorboats brought him in just up the road from where we were. Ten minutes later we saw them all walking down the road, and I always imagined Mussolini to be a big-shouldered man. His photographs always made him look huge, with a prominent chin. In fact he was only about 5ft 2 or 3. He walked into the camp. Of course the guards all went absolutely spare, and we were still laying on the sand. The guards came over and started prodding us with their bayonets to make us stand up to attention to him, and we weren't in the mood to be respectful to anyone at that time, having had no food for possibly two or three days. And he came over and saw what the guards were doing, and he pulled them away, and he just told us to stay there. And then, instinctively, we all stood up. I can't tell you why. But we all did. Whether it was a sort of spontaneous respect for him... And I thought, 'Who's been filling us with all these stories about the people we're supposed to be fighting?' From that time on, the guards all treated us with far greater respect than they had before.

The shortage of food was what Ralph Leigh found the hardest aspect of his captivity.

The period at Benghazi was the worst five months of my life. We were in groups of 50 in a huge compound in the desert. The temperature was 120 degrees+ every day, our food ration

FIVE ~ CAPTIVES IN A DISTANT LAND

was one army mug, which was just under half a pint, of boiled rice. Nothing in it, just rice. A little bread roll, and a small tin of very inferior meat. And that was our daily ration for five months. I was about 30 at that time, and was part of a gun-crew. It was hard work, hard exercise, and you could watch the young men grow physically. I was weighed a couple of months before I was captured, and I weighed 14 stone 2. When I arrived in Taranto at the end of November I was 9st 10. And I was pretty fit. I didn't smoke. The people that smoked were very badly affected. Although I didn't smoke, never had done, I had a longing for a cigarette. We had five cigarettes every two days, and I would have loved to have smoked them because I think you needed something to pass through your body and your lungs. But I was able to withstand the urge. We used to sell our cigarette ration for the smokers' rice ration. So for about three months they had one mug of rice for about two days, and I could understand the way they felt. At first I used to think how mad they must be. Then I began to get this urge to smoke, and I could realise then... and consequently a lot of them of them got dysentery and were too weak to get through it.

Ralph Leigh and his fellow-prisoners left Benghazi for the Italian port of Taranto on 10 November 1942, hearing afterwards that they had narrowly missed being rescued. British troops were to recapture Tobruk only a few days later, on 12 November, and to arrive at Benghazi on 20 November.

His journey from the port of Benghazi to Taranto was a frightening experience.

It took thirteen days and thirteen nights to cross the Mediterranean by boat, from Benghazi to Piraeus, through the Corinth Canal to Taranto. We only anchored once. That was at Piraeus in Greece. The only time I saw the Mediterranean was the time when we were on shore at Piraeus. The prison ship was a cargo ship. There were 1,200 people on the cargo ship. It took 13 days to avoid British submarines. Our big fear was that we would be torpedoed. The whole five months was unbearable. How we survived I just don't know.

Life in a camp in Italy was not much of an improvement on Benghazi as far as prison rations were concerned, but Ralph Leigh will always be grateful to the Red Cross for the extra food which he is sure made a vital difference.

The one feeling of gratitude which has never left me and never will was the fact that the British Red Cross, or rather the British contingent of the Red Cross based in Geneva, sent us parcels, when we got to Italy, every week. There wasn't a lot of bulk in it, but they were all vital foods to keep you going. And I'm certain that thousands of us would never have survived. I don't think I would have done. Going from 14 stone to 10 stone in five months, you can imagine, we'd got little or no strength left. The food that we got in Italy wasn't much better than that we got in Benghazi, still the same, still rice every day. The only time we knew it was Sunday was when the rice had some shreds of meat in it — there was about half the amount of rice, water and shreds of meat — it was just like a brown thin soup with no taste. We didn't like Sundays, because we liked the bulk, and the solid rice. That was our ration for every day of the week until we got to Germany.

Conditions for the British prisoners improved considerably when they left Italy.

When we got to Germany we were sent to a big camp near Leipzig, and then everyone below the rank of sergeant was ordered to go to a working-camp. We were sent to a suburb of Dresden. There were 84 of us in the camp, quite good conditions. We were billeted in a school gymnasium, which was absolute luxury. It was like living in the Hilton Hotel after living in a farm cottage. And we were ordered to go to work at different factories in the town.

With the improvement in living conditions for prisoners, it was emotional hardship and particularly the silence from loved ones at home which became the hardest to bear: friendship within the camp became vital for a POW's sanity.

> When we had the Red Cross parcels we split them up and shared them with a close friend — a friend I had turned out to be a most marvellous friend any man could have, which was a tremendous help for me. It was hard when I went at one time 13 months without a letter from home... didn't even know if my family were still alive, but he turned out to be a tremendous friend.

While at Dresden Ralph Leigh made friends with a German, and no doubt this played a part in the feelings of revulsion and anger which he has felt since the night of 13 February 1945. A total of 796 Lancasters and nine Mosquitos dropped 1,478 tons of high explosive and 1,182 tons of incendiary bombs, creating a firestorm which destroyed the city.

> I had the good fortune one day, that in the factory I was working at, the German lorry driver — he doubled as lorry driver and carpenter — had made very good friends of us because he liked his cigarettes, and towards the end of the war we were the only people in Germany that got cigarettes. We had 50 a week from the Red Cross. And one of the schoolmasters at Oundle, a music master who used to know me before the war, he used to send me 200 most months, so consequently cigarettes were a source of currency. Money was nothing to you. And one day this man pulled out a wad of 1,000 mark notes. He said, 'I'll give a 1,000 marks for 100 cigarettes.' I said, 'What do I do with 1,000 marks? Give me a loaf of bread and we'll talk business.' And that was the system that existed in the country. And one day — he knew that I'd have cigarettes with me — I didn't smoke, but I carried them around with me for bartering purposes — he'd got to go into Dresden. He drove a Ford truck, and he took me into Dresden. Believe me, it was the most marvellous city in the world, what I saw of it in about four or five hours. He took me to all the best places. On 6 February 1945 there was an air-raid, there were quite a lot of planes around. The Germans said it was a leaflet raid. At that time the German forces were coming back from the Russian front, and there were a lot of German troops there. Most of them were sick and wounded. And the leaflet said that if the troops hadn't left Dresden within seven days it would be destroyed. So the next Saturday night, seven days later, at 8.00 pm we heard the planes coming over. And we were allowed, because the guards knew this was happening, we gave an undertaking not to escape during the raid. It was a very hilly area and we could look right down onto the centre of Dresden. And in four hours 225,000 people were burnt to death. The stories we get here now are 35,000 — well I've got the book of the history of Dresden. We left Dresden about five weeks later and the official figures then were given at twenty odd thousand. It took three years to ascertain the death toll. Everybody was burnt. I've got a friend who lives in Oundle, who had been left behind at the camp in Leipzig because he was a sergeant, and that's something like 40-45 miles from Dresden and he told me after the war, that night, it was wintertime, they could stand outside and read a letter, read a paper in the light from Dresden fire. The whole place was ablaze. It was unbelievable. In the four hours from 8.00 till midnight there seemed never less than 1,000 planes in the air at one time. And they started off by dropping — I'd never seen them before or since — what they call candelabra bombs — they came down very gradually like a circle of lights and lit the whole place up. To me it was almost unbelievable. I sometimes think it couldn't have happened.

FIVE ~ CAPTIVES IN A DISTANT LAND

142: Oundle veteran Ralph Leigh: 'Having seen Dresden as it was, and then its destruction, made me a complete pacifist.'

> We went to work on the Monday morning feeling very very guilty. Right, it's all right, they'd bombed England. I suffered the bombing in London. But at that time the war was virtually over. It didn't shorten the war by 24 hours. The majority of people who died were people like us, prisoners of war, slave workers... there were hundreds of thousands of them... old people, old women, and boys your age, brought in from Russia, Poland, and all over the place to do the work, because the men had all gone in the forces. Having seen Dresden as it was, and then its destruction, made me a complete pacifist. And I don't mind if you quote that. I'm not at all unhappy to be a pacifist.[7]

Ralph Leigh was marched with his fellow prisoners out of the camp towards Czechoslovakia, where they spent three weeks in a disused tin mine, and released in March 1945 by the Russians. His return home to England in 1945 was to inspire him with further thoughts on the absurdity and the injustices of war, particularly when he was able to contrast his relations with the Germans he had met with the attitude of the authorities back at home. His anger at what he saw as betrayal of the common soldier by the British government almost led him to desert, when he finally returned to England.

> We'd finished up in East Germany in working camps, so consequently we were in contact with German guards and German people every day of the week. When you work with people for several months together you cease to treat them as enemies, and they ceased to treat us as enemies. We were equals. We had our meals with them. Before the war, before we met them, we always spoke of Germans as the enemy. The only good German, they used to say, is a dead one. People often said to me, 'How did the Germans treat you?' I said, 'Well in some cases, better than the English.' And they used to take offence at that. Then I used to explain. When

I was taken prisoner in 1942 my pay was five shillings and ninepence a day, and my wife with two children received about 32 or 33 shillings a week. When we got to Italy of course, we were under the direction of the Red Cross, and after a time we were told that we could send money home — of course we hadn't drawn any money all the time we were in the desert. So I did that, and in reply I got a statement from the Pay Office to say from the day I was captured one and ninepence was stopped, for the rest of the time I was in a prisoner of war camp. That made us very very bitter.

There was another item which made me almost feel a bit like deserting. When we came home from Germany in June '45 we had ten weeks' leave at home. Then I was sent back to Sussex for three weeks' preliminary training. At the end of the three weeks we were interviewed by an officer who asked all the details of my previous service, how long abroad, were you married, how many children. And he said, 'Oh you've only got five months to do. You're certain to get a home posting, somewhere near home.' And the next day the postings were put up: Lance Bombardier Leigh, from Oundle was sent to Belfast, Northern Ireland. A Gunner Davis from Belfast was sent to Market Harborough. Just imagine how I felt. My daughters didn't know me when I came home. I'd missed six years of their young life, and they'd just begun to accept me, and then I was sent out to Ireland. And then I often regretted that I didn't desert to bring it out into the open. I even went into the office and quite politely said, 'Look, you've got a Gunner Davis from Belfast going to 18 miles from my home, I'm going to where he lives. Can't we swap them over?' And they laughed at me. Then I used language which I've never used before or since to officers. And I was pleased to do it. I felt so bitter. I had to do something serious. Anyway I still had to go. That night I nearly came home. I think I should have done. It would have brought it out into the open. Because when I got to Ireland there was nothing for us to do. Anyway I got to Belfast, and went straight to the office. And here's the difference between some types of people and others. I met a little Irish Second Lieutenant, and I was still feeling very bitter — with three years as a prisoner of war you don't realise what that can do to a person — and I started tearing a strip off to him. And he said, 'Sit down, Bombardier. Tell me all about it.' I told him the whole story. And he said, 'Well, I can well imagine how you felt. I think I would have done a murder if that had happened to me.' He said, 'Leave it to me and I guarantee I'll get you home as soon as possible.' He did it in ten days. That was the way you were treated by different people.

Another graphic account of the emotional hardships endured by Allied prisoners in Europe is given by ex-RAF Intelligence officer Robin Miller, who described what he thought was his most moving wartime experience:

The European war was really over, and I was at my last RAF station before moving off to the Far East. It was at a place called Wing, in Buckinghamshire. The Allies were charging then across Germany and opening up the various prisoner of war camps, and also catching up with all sorts of our escapers who were at large all over the place. They were being picked up and flown to England, and our station was one of the places they were flown to, before being sorted out and sent on to other Reception Areas. There was a steady stream of Dakota transport aircraft coming in, and it was terribly moving to see them arriving in England after up to five years of deprivation in prison camps. Many of them looked pale and starved, and in all sorts of uniform, or no uniform at all. As they came down the ramp from the aircraft there were queues of volunteer WAAFs waiting to take each by the arm and lead them into the hangar where everything was laid on for them — a band playing, café tables with cups of tea and so forth. Many of them, as they stepped off the aircraft, knelt down and kissed the ground — or the WAAFs! We wandered around and chatted with them. I remember one who had a German

Army belt with the motto 'Gott mit uns', and he attempted to give this to the Padre who was standing with me. He refused it. There were quite a lot of Americans among them, and it was interesting to note how much iller they seemed to be. They can't have been in captivity nearly as long as some of the British, but the contrast in their case with the British way of life at the time was much more marked. It was strange at this time to go into the Mess, and hang up your cap next to a German Luftwaffe cap — the uniform of that enemy we had been fighting against for so long.

Oundle's prisoners in Germany seem generally to have been well treated. Elliott Viney did not find his overall view of Germans much altered by his five years there. 'Their general rigid observance of the Geneva Convention (which covers the treatment of prisoners of war) was impressive. This obedience to orders from above had its down-side, as we know; as individuals, many were friendly, though as in any nation there were repellent exceptions.'

While the ordeal of prison life took its toll among the older inmates, younger and fitter POWs found themselves better equipped to deal with their changed circumstances. Public schoolboys like Robert Aitken, captured after the attack on the *Tirpitz* in 1943, were even grateful for the hardships they had endured while at school. 'Oundle's pre-war moderately spartan style minimised the transition to naval and POW life. But being young was the major advantage, although that was what probably got most of us into the situation in the first place.'

Prisoners in Asia

The story in the Far East was of course horrifyingly different. The rapid advance of the Japanese through Asia meant that thousands of British men, women and children were trapped and spent the rest of the war in prison camps, often in appalling conditions. About 18,000 British civilians were interned in the Far East. There were 50,000 British prisoners of war: at least a quarter of them perished in the harsh conditions. Understandably, many of the victims of the camps in the Far East have never talked about their experiences. Those who have described their experience of captivity under the Japanese can help us understand the silence of the others.

Dr Elsie Crowe, who lived in Oundle for many years, was one of the civilians trapped by brutal events in the Far East when the Japanese armies swept down from Burma into Singapore in early 1942. She recalled her experiences both before and after her capture and internment by the Japanese in a prisoner of war camp on the island of Sumatra.

Together with several other doctors and nurses, Dr Crowe tried to leave Singapore courtesy of the Royal Navy. Unfortunately they did not get very far. Their ship was bombed in the Straits of Malacca, just to the north of Sumatra. 'The Japanese fighters came back in full force and bombed us to bits — there was a terrible slaughter there. We got the wounded into lifeboats and everyone who could swim was told to make for one of the many islands nearby known as 'Pom-Pom'.'

Before they reached the island, however, the Japanese returned and attacked the sinking ship. Dr Crowe sustained a fractured skull and spent the next five days in a semi-conscious state with the other survivors on the island, living off a meagre diet of tinned milk and biscuits.

Eventually they were picked up by a flotilla of small fishing boats and deposited on the coast of Sumatra. Even at this stage, they lost no hope of reaching freedom.

'Our instructions were to get help from the local people, cross Sumatra, get to the port of Pedang and hopefully get picked up by a British cruiser,' recalled Elsie Crowe. Even the most casual glance at the map of south-east Asia will give some idea of the sheer distance and terrain involved in such a journey. Miraculously some of the group managed to cross to Pedang, but found on their arrival that the Japanese had driven the British away. There was no option but to surrender.

To begin with the women and children were housed in the local convent, where they were fed and reasonably well looked after.

> The Reverend Mother of the convent had a sewing room and gave us some white cotton sheets, from which one of the nurses made us each two dresses and two pairs of pants. We lived in these clothes for three and a half years.
>
> We were all terribly conscious that we were British and of course anti-Japanese, so we all made small Union Jack brooches which we attached to our tunics.

Dr Crowe kept this badge throughout her captivity, showing it after the war to visitors at her Oundle home. It was intricately stitched, its colours darkened only slightly by dirt and the passage of time.

After six months in the convent, armed Japanese guards forced Dr Crowe and her fellow prisoners out of the building and into trucks which took them into the local town. Here they were locked up in the gaol. Conditions were appalling. 'The gaol was built for 600 people and we were 3,000 odd. It was unbelievably filthy: bugs, fleas, rats, everything you can imagine. It was standing room only.'

Six weeks later, the women were moved up into the mountains. After a day and a half driving, they finally came to a halt, to be confronted by what became their home for the next three years. The camp had high wooden walls with a sentry box and an armed guard in each corner, with barbed wire all around. Inside there were five wooden huts, and in the middle a row of concrete basins for cooking. A small stream ran through the camp and this, Dr Crowe believed, was what saved the lives of her and many other prisoners. It meant that they could keep relatively clean and halt the spread of disease. However, the supply of food in the camp was far from adequate. 'Food rations were so poor and so small that people got weaker and weaker. After about a year, beri-beri began to set in. All we got was a small cup of rice, some sago flour (which tastes disgusting) and a vegetable called can-can.'

Aided by a friend, Dr Crowe managed to commandeer all the tinned milk owned by the women (of whom there were about 2,000) in order to supplement the diets of the children (of whom there were about 900). Unfortunately, the Japanese did not conform to the Western idea that growing children need more food than adults, and gave them only half rations. The women were therefore forced to give a further quarter of their daily ration to feed the children.

By this time, the death rate, particularly among the older women, was steadily increasing.

> Things seemed to get worse and worse rather than better. We used one of the huts as a hospital, but of course we had no drugs. It was only after a year, when the situation was getting really bad, that a Japanese doctor came to inspect the camp. He spoke good English (with an American accent) and questioned us about our food and medical supplies. Well, if a Japanese face can look ashamed, I believe his did.

So horrified was the doctor at the women's condition that he gave them large quantities of drugs — insulin, morphine and magnesium sulphate — which lasted until the end of their captivity.

Besides boredom and the intense heat during the daytime, rats were a constant enemy for the women prisoners. Dr Crowe remembers one particular incident:

> There was one little Dutch girl who had long plaits of beautiful dark hair trailing down her back. When she woke up one morning she found that the rats had gnawed it right across. They were really dreadful. We had an awful problem when anyone died, especially at night. It was very difficult to keep the rats away from them. We had to have someone with a stick, guarding the corpse.

Elsie Crowe believes that she and the other prisoners were treated reasonably well by the Japanese and unlike several other camps they were not tortured or beaten. 'They were nice to the children and used to talk and even joke with them.'

Those not working in the hospital with the doctor had to go out into the surrounding jungle and clear it for the cultivation of sweet potatoes. Meanwhile, Elsie Crowe and her nurses had to try to scrape together a meal. 'We even tried fermenting the rice in order to make alcohol, but of course, it didn't work. Much of the time was spent lying down reminiscing about food.'

Only twice in those three and a half years did some of the women receive postcards from home. The only postcard Dr Crowe received was to inform her of her father's death. 'I had an awful feeling that they only gave you the postcards which had bad news. Once we were allowed to write home, but many people never got a word. There were no food parcels either.'

Despair and hopelessness were amongst the most demoralising effects of not knowing when the war would end. Bit by bit, however, the prisoners learned of the Allied advances in Europe and the Far East. 'We knew the Allies were approaching Berlin, and we heard about D-Day — I think someone in the camp had a secret radio.'

Real confirmation of Allied victory came when the Japanese suddenly started to treat the prisoners well. This began with the provision of much improved food rations.

> Instead of the normal sago flour, rice and vegetables being wheeled in, a big cartload of fresh fish arrived. The following day we were given pounds and pounds of rice. Then on the third day the prisoners were called up in front of the camp commandant. He said simply 'The war is over. You may sing your National Anthem.' It all seemed too good to be true after so many months' captivity. At that point everybody burst into tears. That was about a week after the bombing of Nagasaki and Hiroshima.

Having formally recognised defeat, the Japanese were at pains to be seen as friendly towards their prisoners as they dared. The women were reunited with their husbands, who had been kept in a separate camp, and everyone was taken back to Pedang where they were eventually shipped home to England.

There was one particular incident which Dr Crowe brought to mind. With the nearby airfield heavily bombed, the British parachuted in four engineers to repair the damage.

'It was an incredible sight,' she recalled. 'The four soldiers started repairing the airstrip whilst 60,000 armed Japanese soldiers bowed to them, obeyed their every command and let them get on with it.'

It was evident that throughout the three and a half years' captivity Dr Crowe, aged 90 when she was interviewed, kept a lively sense of humour and an unfailing trust in the eventual victory of the Allies. The fact that she returned to Singapore, having been almost crippled by beri-beri and dysentery, is perhaps a reminder of the remarkable courage shown by many of the men and women interned in the Japanese prisoner of war camps during the Second World War.[8]

A large force of Allied servicemen had been caught by the swift Japanese advance in the Far East. From Oundle School alone, at least twenty former pupils spent time as prisoners of the Japanese and were released only at the end of the war. Most of the servicemen, used as slave labour for military purposes, had harrowing tales to tell of the harshness of their captors.

The discovery of what had been happening in the camps during the war years made an indelible impression on Robin Miller, giving him a shocking insight into the evil of which human beings are capable.

> After the war ended I went to interrogate people who had been in Japanese prison camps. As you know, the Japs had no regard for human life. Eventually I was in a huge hospital compound in Bangalore, India. These were mainly used to help prisoners of war recover. We used to say that our job was to sit on their beds and take down their atrocities for the War Crimes trials. It was a very harrowing experience, and it got to the stage when my feelings for the Japs have never really recovered. People had often lost all their sense of values — they had come to view their treatment as perfectly normal. They got used to it.
>
> I actually had a fascinating interview with a chap who had been in Changi Jail. He pretended he was mad, and that his madness took the form of continuously writing music. I had a look at it, and it was not music at all! It was a code by which he had recorded all the details of what happened in the camp.
>
> In Singapore I managed to sit in on some trials of Japanese guards, which was absolutely extraordinary. They just gave evidence against themselves! One even went beyond the question of did he know who was responsible for a kill, and told the judge several times that 'Corporal Yamamoto and I killed him'. It was quite uncanny; they were just totally different.

Later on Robin Miller was posted to the Cocos Islands, mid-way between Colombo and Singapore.

> The base was used to drop supplies by parachute to the prison camps in Malaysia, Java and Sumatra. And also as a staging-post for some ex-prisoners of war on their way back to India, and home. I found myself Officer Commanding the 'Transit Camp', which was like being a sort of hotel manager. A strange sort of hotel of course, consisting only of rows of tents — there were in fact no buildings of any sort on the island — just lots of tents and marquees. I would meet incoming people with my Jeep on the airstrip, and look after them if they were VIPs. Among the VIPs I had was the Bishop of Singapore, who had been captured, and was on his way out to be looked after medically. Shortly after, he went back again to minister to his 'flock'. Soon after this I met a Colonel Cyril Wild, who had also been a prisoner of war. This man had lived in Japan and spoke Japanese. He was therefore used by the Japs as an interpreter when they were 'interrogating' our POWs. He was present at the interrogation of the Bishop, and described the scene to me and some others. After considerable starvation and

many other deprivations, the Bishop was paraded, stark naked, in front of a table behind which sat the interrogation officer. On the table was a collection of bamboo rods, coshes and leather straps. The Jap officer first lashed out at his naked body and hit him all over, and then the 'interrogation' began. Apparently the Bishop simply took all this, unflinching, and asked Colonel Wild to tell them that he forgave them for what they were doing, for he realised that 'they knew not what they did'. As a Christian, he said, he absolved them from blame. The interpreter said that he couldn't actually put this just like that into Japanese, but modified it somewhat.

Many years later, that man, when he was Bishop of Birmingham, preached at Oundle. To the boys, I suppose, he was just another fat, bearded old man in a surplice, holding forth from the pulpit and soon forgotten. I wondered at that time what they would really think if they had known what he had been through when he was a prisoner.

Coincidentally, Colonel Wild was to play a heroic part in saving the life of a fellow British officer threatened with a death sentence by the Japanese. This was the former Oundle School boy James Bradley, who, as has been seen in an earlier chapter, had been captured in Singapore and described his experiences in his book *Towards the Setting Sun*.

Following his capture James Bradley was forced to march the 17 miles to the former British military base of Changi in north east Singapore, where he arrived on 20 February 1942, and where he spent the next 14 months along with 47,000 British and Australian troops. Morale was low, the prisoners were kept in overcrowded conditions, and there were major epidemics of dysentery. The prisoners did their best to keep their spirits up. The poor diet, based mainly on rice, was supplemented with vegetables which they were allowed to grow. Soap was produced from wood ash and palm oil, and thousands of clogs were manufactured from old tyres. Concert parties were organised to raise morale, and there were even cricket and hockey matches. Books were few and far between, but a small library was set up and James Bradley joined the other students of 'Changi University', developing an interest in yacht design.

Along with a few other bold or desperate prisoners James Bradley even set up his own distillery, in spite of the considerable dangers involved: the Imperial Japanese Army had expressly forbidden this activity. But the scientific challenge was obvious from his description.

> I found a supply of overripe pineapples, which I cut up and put in a five-gallon drum, with water. To this I added some bruised bean-sprouts, which some expert informed me would act as a diastase, and then allowed it all to ferment. From the copper brake tubes of blown-up lorries I produced a coil condenser, and attached it to the lid of the five-gallon drum, under which I built a fire, and cooled the condenser by trickling water over it, being careful to catch the waste in order to use it again. It was terribly exciting when a clear liquid started to drip from the end of the condenser pipe. We were still able to find a few limes growing in the area, and on Sunday mornings we drank our neat alcohol and lime cocktails! After a time I gave this up, as it became too dangerous when too many people knew about it.[9]

Another former Oundle School boy, the future journalist Rawle Knox, captured like James Bradley in Singapore in 1942, was later to claim that his 'hooch', made from home-grown bean-sprouts helped him to survive life as a prisoner of the Japanese. A secondary benefit was that it helped him to develop a palate that stood up to all the liquor which he had to imbibe later during his career as a foreign correspondent.[10]

In spite of the poor state of health and low vitality of the prisoners, and the depressing inability to communicate with family and friends in the outside world, James Bradley found moments which sustained him. A sense of humour was vital, he recalled. Strangely, there was also comfort to be found in the surroundings. 'There were things of great beauty as well as appalling horror. As in life, the mediocre does not live long.' He was fascinated by the streams of bats which poured out of the palm trees at dusk, the agile little lizards known as geckoes, the wonderful sights of orchids and exotic shrubs in flower, the brilliant sunsets and the nights which he spent, quietly but illegally, on the roof of the prison in contemplation of the brilliance of the night sky.

> I think I shall always remember those peaceful hours on the roof at night, sometimes by myself and sometimes with others. It was a time when one thought about home, 'above' the realities of the prison camp.[11]

Things changed in August 1942 with the arrival of the Japanese Major General Fukuei. All the Allied prisoners were asked to make an illegal agreement not to escape. Their refusal was followed by the confinement of some 17,000 prisoners to Selarang Barracks on 2 September, amidst horrendously overcrowded and unhygienic conditions. Rations were cut to a third, and four recaptured escapees were shot by a cruelly inefficient firing squad. 'It has been said that this was the closest concentration of human beings since the Black Hole of Calcutta,' commented James Bradley.[12]

Worse was to come. Parties of prisoners had been moving out of Changi during 1942 to work on projects connected with the Japanese war effort. 'We were an enormous fund of cheap labour for them, always available, to be used for whatever project they had in mind, and they certainly made the most of exploiting us to the full.'[13]

In April 1943 James Bradley found himself in the 7,000 strong group known as 'F' Force who were sent north from Singapore. Their destination was unknown.

> At the station we were crowded into steel rice trucks, which were totally enclosed and unventilated apart from double sliding doors in the centre of one side. Thirty-one men were allocated to each truck, and we were packed like sardines; the only way that we could all sit was with our legs tightly drawn in.
>
> We had no form of sanitation, apart from making use of the sliding door, which had a chain stretched across the opening, and on which we used to hang precariously as the train went along. Many of our numbers had acute dysentery and were passing up to 20 or more motions a day. Gradually, they became too weak to hang out of the door unaided, and I think many would have fallen out, had they not been helped by others.[14]

The Japanese had promised the prisoners that they were being moved to a better camp. After three days' rail travel from Singapore to Thailand in stifling conditions, followed by a short march from the station, James Bradley's heart sank as his eyes took in the new surroundings:

> The camp lay on both sides of a road, and all accommodation consisted of crude bamboo-framed huts, roofed with attap (plaited palm leaves). Down the centre of each was a gangway, flanked on both sides by raised bamboo platforms about six to seven feet wide, and on these we had to live and sleep, almost touching each other. The huts were crawling with bed bugs,

FIVE ~ CAPTIVES IN A DISTANT LAND

143: James Bradley MBE, a survivor of Japanese cruelty on the Thailand-Burma railway. The photograph was taken in 1940 before he went overseas.

and the whole camp was inches deep in black mud. Flies were everywhere, and the approach to the latrines was a morass, with the trenches of the latrines overflowing and alive with dirty grey-white maggots.[15]

They had arrived at Ban Pong, some 60 kilometres west of Bangkok, and a base camp for all parties going to work on the infamous Thailand-Burma Railway.

Some years before, German experts had decided that the construction of such a railway was not feasible because of the mountainous jungle terrain through which machinery would have to be transported. But the Japanese had realised that they did not need machinery. 'They had a vast source of slave labour at their disposal, that they could drive on until they dropped in their tracks, and when the numbers dwindled through disease and starvation, they brought in more.' They were also in a hurry to push on towards the ultimate goal, the invasion of India. More than 16,000 Allied prisoners of the Japanese, and 100,000 Asian forced labourers, were to die constructing the 258-mile railway — one for each 13 ft of track.

After only one night at Ban Pong, 'F' Force set out on a 300 kilometre march lasting two and a half weeks. Travelling at night because of the intense heat during the day, the prisoners were marched in appalling conditions. The monsoon had broken, and the route was through wild and mountainous country. Sick men were kicked and beaten on by their guards, being allowed to remain at staging-camps only when it was clear that they were dying. The criminal negligence of the Japanese had allowed cholera to spread like wildfire through the ranks of the prisoners, and by May 1943 the disease was endemic in all five labour camps along the route.

Conditions at Sonkurai, 'F' Force's destination, were as bad if not worse than at Ban Pong. The camp was a sea of mud because of the monsoon, and many of the huts were roofless. 'The sanitation was indescribable', recalled James Bradley. 'The latrine pits were overflowing, because of the constant use and the now almost permanent rains, and the approach to them from the huts was fouled by men whose dysentery was so intense that they just could not reach the latrines in time.'[16]

'F' Force had been given the task of completing a stretch of 37 kilometres of railway under the supervision of Japanese engineers who showed themselves to be as savage as any of the guards.

> There were daily beatings of officers and men at work, sometimes even into unconsciousness. The object of these was to urge sick and weak men to physical efforts far beyond their remaining strength. Kicks and slaps were commonplace, and men were driven with wire whips and bamboo sticks throughout the day. If anyone worked badly, or appeared to be slacking, they were sometimes made to stand holding a rock or large piece of wood above their heads. If they let it drop, they were beaten.[17]

Injuries and ulcers, often resulting in amputations carried out with little anaesthetic, took a constant toll of the prisoners, but it was cholera and above all dysentery, aggravated by under-nourishment, which was the main threat. The news that he had been diagnosed as a carrier of cholera came as a shock to James Bradley, and led to an even grimmer stage in the hell of his captivity. As the only officer diagnosed to be a carrier he was given the task of cremating the bodies of cholera victims, being condemned to live in a separate isolation camp. 'This is a part of my life I have never been able to forget and, indeed, I can hardly write about it,' he confessed. Death came so quickly to the sick that those who were cutting wood to build the funeral pyres were themselves being cremated that same evening. 'It was frightful to see their charred and blackened bodies moving in the flames, as their muscles were affected by the heat.'[18] The Japanese, Colonel Wild recorded, displayed a mixture of callous indifference and active spite towards the sick. James Bradley survived only through the generosity of those men who risked their lives by bringing their rice rations to the cholera victims in their isolation camp, and because of his determination.

It was the latter quality which prompted him to join a group of nine prisoners in their plans for escape from the hell of Sonkurai Camp. He himself was determined, at any cost, to return to the family he had left behind in England, his wife Lindsay, and his son Roger. But the group was also united in its resolve to reveal to the outside world the inhuman conditions under which the Japanese were forcing Allied prisoners to build the Thailand-Burma Railway. They knew that recapture would mean death at the hands of the Japanese, either by firing squad or by decapitation.

The group had accumulated sufficient rations and medical supplies to enable them to reach the coast in three weeks. On 5 July 1943 they set out just before dawn. Their path westwards was through dense leech-infested jungle, and on some of the uphill stretches their rate of progress was no more than half a kilometre a day. Deadly black tree snakes were a constant hazard, but it was illness and exhaustion which were to prove their worst enemies. On the morning of 29 July they awoke to find that one of their number, Corporal Brown, was missing. He had been suffering from ulcers and gangrene, and had bravely abandoned the group so as not to slow down the others' progress.

Four more were either to die or chose to be left behind, before they arrived at the Ye River on 14 August. Here they decided to build a raft, and entrust themselves to the mercy of the current. By now they were feeling desperate. 'We must have been very near the end of our stamina and would have perished anyway. The fact that we might be shot or recaptured was something we would almost have welcomed.'[19]

The five survivors, including James Bradley, were in fact recaptured after their raft broke up on rapids. The Burmese villagers whom they met and who appeared to be befriending them had sold the escapees to the Imperial Japanese Army.

Re-arrest by Japanese soldiers on 21 August was followed by an interrogation which James Bradley described as 'civilised questioning'. This was in contrast to the treatment which the escapees underwent later at the hands of the Kempei-Tai (Japanese Military Police). Kicks and beatings alternated with news of their imminent execution, followed by the announcement that their lives were to be spared. James Bradley was puzzled by this: the only two other escape attempts of which he heard both ended in execution, with two men being returned to their camp where they were made to dig their own graves before being bayoneted to death. 'I think, in a way, we owe our lives to the fact that the Japanese admired us for having beaten the jungle for eight weeks,' he recorded.[20]

Later he was to realise that he and his fellow escapees owed their lives to the efforts of all the senior British officers who had been brought to Nieke, the Administrative Headquarters of their section of the Thailand-Burma Railway, to witness their execution on 9 October. In particular, he felt a debt of gratitude to the Japanese-speaking Colonel Cyril Wild, who was acting as interpreter. The latter's pleas for mercy had been expressed so fluently that Colonel Banno, the senior Japanese officer, had been reduced to tears when it was impressed on him that the execution of 'these brave men' would bring disgrace and shame upon the Emperor and the Imperial Japanese Army.

James Bradley spent most of the rest of 1943 at the notorious Outram Road Gaol in Singapore until his beri-beri, from which he had suffered for a long time, resulted in his transfer to Changi Hospital, and then to Changi Gaol. Then on 26 June 1944, almost ten months after his recapture, Japanese guards took him and his fellow escapees for a trial by court martial. The verdict was a formality; the sentence of solitary confinement and eight years' hard labour which he received was not unexpected. He was, however, surprised when the Presiding Judge gave each of the defendants a small bag of sweets telling them to take 'the greatest care' of their health. His days as a prisoner of the Japanese finally came to an end with the news of the Japanese surrender in August 1945.

While a prisoner at Changi, James Bradley had come into contact with another Oundle School boy with whom he had been in the same form. This was Lord De Ramsey, who had also been captured after the fall of Singapore, and who managed to use his time profitably while in the camp. Following the end of the war, he was appointed to the Pig Reorganisation Committee, set up in 1955 to look at the British bacon market. He was also awarded a bronze medal by the RSPCA after rescuing a litter of pigs from a burning barn on his estate at Abbots Ripton near Huntingdon only seconds before the flaming thatched roof collapsed. His love of the animals and expertise on their subject had dated from his time in Changi Jail in Singapore, where he had been appointed head pigman by his captors.

Both James Bradley and Lord De Ramsey were convinced that the dropping of the atomic bomb saved their lives, so poor were the conditions under which they were kept and under which they would have survived for no more than two or three weeks.[21] Later they were to become aware, as James Bradley points out, that POWs were made to dig large trenches — mass graves — for themselves.

Had an Allied landing on Japan taken place, believed James Bradley, there would have been a total massacre of all surviving prisoners-of-war and civilian internees, including women and children, not just at Changi, but at all Japanese internment camps throughout the Far East. Instructions to commandants were that no traces should remain.[22]

The news of the end of the war was received rapidly by Allied prisoners thanks to the illicit radios which many had bravely manufactured. British POWs in Asia showed the same ingenuity as their counterparts in Europe in devising methods to keep up their morale and at the same time trick their Japanese guards, but the danger was extreme: 'These men who risked their lives to get news of the war did more good for morale than anyone else, and were, to my mind, the bravest of all prisoners,' believed James Bradley. 'Some were discovered and subsequently beaten to death.'[23]

Lieutenant Colonel C. M. 'Boy' Young, a former Oundle School boy who had left School House in 1932, had joined the Indian Army and was taken prisoner in Malaya, where his unit was stationed in 1942. His main activity during captivity was to establish and maintain radio receiving stations in order to keep his fellow prisoners up to date with the news: he would walk around on crutches with a home-made radio concealed in one crutch and the batteries concealed in the other. One receiving set was made and concealed by him in a fence post in the camp compound, and this is now in the museum at the Royal Military Academy.[24]

The Japanese attack on Sumatra had been accompanied by a similar attack on Java, which fell in March 1942.

Brought up in Upper Benefield, Aubrey Clarke moved to Essex, but returned to live in Oundle. He had his own remarkable story of life in prison-camps under the Japanese. His first three months of captivity were spent in Java, where he had been caught along with 500 other British troops.

Aubrey Clarke is remarkable among the Oundle's Far East veterans for his lack of ill-feeling today towards his Japanese captors. He remembered clearly the details of his experience as a prisoner, from the first days of captivity in Java, as related in an earlier chapter. 'Conditions there weren't too bad at all. It was originally a native prison, but it was quite decent really.' Overcrowding was the chief problem — the prison had been built for 30 prisoners instead of 250.

Set to work by his captors on factory work, he and his fellows took advantage of the situation to sabotage the Japanese war effort.

> I was lucky because I was a motor mechanic by trade, and I was able to go out with a group under guard and we went to various places where they had got British and American transport. We had to take them to pieces and mark the gearboxes, engine parts, pistons and the rest of it, and they were sent then to Japan, and fortunately we were in a position to put in a few spare bolts where they were not supposed to be, so, when they got to Japan they wouldn't be much good.

His relationship with some of his guards was an unexpected contrast to the horror stories which most Allied prisoners of war in Asia have to tell:

> The Nip guard in charge was quite a decent bloke. He used to hand me his rifle while he got into the lorry with us, and I could have used it on him, but I would have only got shot anyway. He said to me one day in Japanese, '49, have you got any cigarettes?' and I said, 'No.' So then he said, 'Have you got any money?' and I said, 'No,' and he said he would get me some tobacco, and he went missing for a bit and came back with a great bundle of tobacco for 15 sens. There was 100 to a yen, and a yen in those days was about one and sixpence, so you can tell it wasn't much money. I didn't know what to do with it as I didn't smoke anyway, so I took it back to the camp and I divided it up into little packets and gave it out to blokes who hadn't got any.
>
> It was not a holiday camp but we were treated as well as could be expected. The Nips used to come round, say, in the middle of the night to see whether you were covered up properly, because although the temperature in the day was nearly up to 100, at night it got down to nearly freezing and I've seen Nips with bayonets attached to their rifles covering up blokes with blankets, which tells you they weren't as heartless as some people might imagine.

There were some moments of the cruelty which has been traditionally associated with the stereotyped Japanese prison guard, but these alternated with instances of kindness.

> We ran out of lorries and motorbikes to take to pieces, and I had an accident at the camp HQ and got my hand all tore up. We had to go to an aerodrome, which had been Dutch. The Nips had cut up all the hangars and there were all jagged edges. The commandant was there, and the Nip soldiers got a bit excited, and we had to lift these hangar pieces to be taken away. There were quite a lot of us and a Nip soldier was hitting us with sticks, and I couldn't let go because my hand was caught on this metal, and my poor fingers, you could see the bones hanging out. The Nip commandant took me back to the camp, and they bathed my poor hand in salt water which was chronic, but it saved it.

The incident is remembered by Aubrey Clarke for another reason. The wound to his hand was a blessing in disguise: while he was away, the other prisoners were put on board ship to go and work on the island of Sumatra. 'My mates who went over all lost their lives and got drowned, and my poor hand getting damaged probably saved my life because I would have gone with them.'

There were even moments during his time in Java which he sees as highly comic in hindsight.

> We had a couple of good boxers in our lot and the Nips decided we ought to have a boxing competition. Our chaps went in and thought if we beat them they'll knock the living daylights out of us, but it wasn't like that at all. When our chaps were beating the Nips up, the other Nips cheered and clapped because we were winning. It was bit ridiculous really.

He then spent four years as a POW in Japan.

The journey from Java to Japan was an experience which left him with long-term health problems.

> From Java to Japan, we went from Java to Singapore in the usual ferry, about 200 miles I suppose, and then we stayed on the beach and we were checked to see that we hadn't any diseases to carry to Japan, and we boarded a ship which was condemned by Lloyds in 1905. We were battened down in the holds and never saw daylight for about six or eight weeks

144: Oundle resident Aubrey Clarke, a prisoner of the Japanese.

because it was ever so slow getting there. Eventually we did get there, and we had tropical clothes on, and we arrived in Japan in the middle of their so called winter, so you can tell we weren't very comfortable. Being in the dark, they used to let us up for a little while at night, but on the whole we were in the dark, and it affected my sight, so ever since then I've been partially sighted.

Aubrey Clarke thought that he and the other prisoners were kept in the dark because the Japanese were afraid that the ship would attract unwelcome attention from Allied vessels.

He spent time in two camps in the south-west of Japan, both situated fairly near the coast. Conditions in the first, on arrival in Japan, were an improvement on Java if anything.

Well, they were quite good really, considering. There was slightly more space, for a start. The camp was pretty big, seven big buildings, all made of wood, and windows with see-through stuff, not glass, and about ten rooms along the bottom and ten along the top. On the floor, in each compartment there was a room which held four men. We had to sleep on the floor of course, they don't have beds in Japan, and they had carpets about six feet long and three foot wide, and that was just enough space to take four men.

There was a big cupboard which in the daytime you could put your blankets and things, and I had £3.10.0 in English money. I thought the Nips would come and pinch it, but I had some wool for darning socks and I wrapped the money in that and put it in the cupboard, so when I was liberated I had £3.10.0 in English money. I had some tools, and there were one or two of my favourites, and I buried them so the Nips wouldn't get them, and when I dug them up they were in quite good condition, and I brought them home and gave one to my wife, a little adjustable, and as far as I know she's still got it.

FIVE ~ CAPTIVES IN A DISTANT LAND

The spartan conditions made him appreciate what luxuries they did enjoy.

> Don't get me wrong, I mean it is still a prison camp, with prisoners of war, but you don't expect the Ritz do you? We had a gramophone, and a Nip officer who could speak a little English, told us we had to change the needle every three times we played a record. We used to have in there fires with charcoal which you could sit round and tell yarns. We had a charcoal burner in each of the rooms, containing four men, but unfortunately one of the men set fire to his blankets, so the Nip officer told us we had to go to the dining room afterwards to get warm there as we couldn't look after things properly.

The British prisoners were also allowed to worship in their own way. 'Our padre used to give services, and they used to sing *Land of Hope and Glory*, but we weren't allowed to sing *God Save the King*.'

Security at the camp was in evidence without being oppressive.

> Each corner of the camp had a machine gun posted, though they never used them. One day, we had to dig some trenches around the perimeter fence, and the Nips in charge said we were digging our own graves, which didn't go down well with some of the men, but they wouldn't have taken the trouble of moving us from Java to Japan just to shoot us would they?

The prisoners were made to work in a coal mine in Japan, and this experience was a further aggravation for Aubrey Clarke's health.

> Going down the coal mine, if you were on the night shift you were not too bad, but the day shift you wouldn't see daylight for about ten days. That didn't do people's eyesight much good, and the food that we had as well, because we only had rice. On the Japanese rest day, they used to try and bring us in a bit of fish or something like that to make a bit of a change, but it wasn't much, so we had to do the best we could.

The mine was about two miles from the camp. 'We used to walk, but we were getting pretty weak by that time, and when we got down there we had to do PT before we went down the mine, and also we had to bow to the East, because they worship the sun.' The prisoners received a small amount of money for their work. 'When we were in Japan working down the coal mine, every public holiday we used to have a packet of cigarettes, and a cigar, and a packet of tobacco, and we used to get about 3 yens a month. We had a little shop, but you couldn't buy much apart from curry powder, razor blades and soap. By the time we were liberated we had some Japanese money.'

Each shift in the mine lasted for two weeks, from 3.30 in the morning to 5.00 at night, with an hour's rest for dinner. It was hard work which took its toll of some of the prisoners.

> As time went by the chaps were getting thinner. It was so easy to die, but a lot of people with will power kept going. After a day in the mine, you can imagine, having to climb the stairs to your room, you had to crawl up as you hadn't enough strength in your legs. The walk back from the mine was two miles uphill. When we came up from the coal mine, we had a beautiful bath, with beautiful hot water and had a bath every day, and I think that was one of our saving graces.

The Japanese were also careful employers, in a way which was in marked contrast to the barbaric treatment of workers on the Thailand-Burma Railway.

> When we went down the coal mine, the night shift drilled the holes to put the explosives in, and before the day shift came on to get the coal up to the surface on the conveyor belt, the Nips used to go round and they would knock all the loose coal down so it wouldn't fall on us, and for three years this went on, and we never had one accident.

Sometimes Aubrey Clarke and his fellow prisoners were able to work above ground, giving a variety to the routine which he welcomed.

> Me being in charge of a squad, sometimes instead of going down the coal mine we had to make marmitans, like coal blocks, little duck eggs, for a couple of days, then we would go down the mine again, and other times we would be making charcoal, putting down wood in a big heap, covering it with soil having set fire to it, then after three days we would take the soil off and get the charcoal out.

Jobs above ground allowed them an occasional glimpse of civilian life in a Japanese village.

> There used to be a big store there and people used to listen to the announcements going on, which would probably tell them that susuki was in: that meant that the fish had come in, and we would see the Nip women going to this shop to get their rations, rice and fish and vegetables, not all that many vegetables but certainly some. The lorries that used to deliver supplies into our camp used to run on acetylene gas not petrol, and they were not very reliable, they'd be half-way to the camp and they would run out of gas, and they had to recharge the generators of the carbine to get the gas up again.

Food for the prisoners in his camp was clearly better in some cases than that which many prisoners in Europe enjoyed.

> We used to collect green stuff because we had rabbits in cages and they were going to be a stew for us later on. Unfortunately, the Nips were as hard up for food as we were, and they used to pinch some of our rabbits. We knew they wouldn't eat anything that had died, so we used to wring one or two of their necks so when the Nips came round, they saw these dead ones and thought they must have a disease or something, and said, 'We're not going to eat them', so we saved our stew-pot for later on.

Rice was a major ingredient of their diet. 'We had a big canteen or kitchen, where the men had their rice and it was cooked for us by our own men. They put a bucketful of rice in a big copper full of water and let it boil away and the rice swelled, and round the outside there used to be a burnt portion of rice, but we didn't eat that.' The prisoners were also able to provide their own food. Between the prison buildings there was enough space to grow vegetables. 'A couple of chaps used to do that without going down the coal mines. In Japan the climate is such they can grow two crops a year on the same ground, barley say followed by rice. Sometimes they'd have digones (vegetables), root crops; the climate was similar to the South of France.' The prisoners even had the opportunity to rear animals to supplement their diet. 'We had a poor little pig, and it was supposed to live on scraps but we never left any scraps so it didn't get fat, and when we were liberated they killed it to put it out of its misery.'

There were some items on the menu which he had never tasted before, and which he would not want to try again.

> One public holiday, we had a bit of shark each, and the next day the Nip guard came along and it appeared that this shark had given me a rash, and after that I dared not eat shark so I would trade my shark for a bit of rice. The Nips sent in a horse's head and hooves, one or two of them with a shoe still on, and we were supposed to make this into soup. So there was this soup with the horse's head floating about in it in a great big copper, and the hooves went down to the bottom.

Like Ralph Leigh during his time as a prisoner in Europe, Aubrey found that those prisoners who neglected their diet fell victim to illness. 'One boy, he was a hobo in America, he liked saki and cigarettes, and he used to trade his rice for cigarettes. That poor chap got thinner and thinner until he died.' The Japanese provided some medical care for their prisoners, but years of hardship proved too much in many cases. 'They put cough mixture on the window-sill for us, and they had a hospital in the camp, but if you went in there you were unlikely to come out.'

Also like Ralph Leigh, Aubrey Clarke looked forward to receiving presents from the outside world.

> On rare occasions we had Red Cross parcels, but unfortunately the Nips helped themselves, and there was only one tin per person left, and my tin was of rice. But it tasted a treat. The next time you might get a tin of bully, or bar of chocolate. I remember on one occasion I got a beautiful woollen pullover and I got some wool and embroidered on the top ABC for Aubrey Brian Clarke.

Unfortunately, it was not just the Japanese guards whom one could not trust in a prisoner of war camp, as Aubrey Clarke had discovered back in Java, at his first camp. His tobacco trading came to an abrupt end when he discovered that his fellow Britons were also capable of dishonesty.

'I got various other things like bananas, and I was told that while I was out at work on the machines some other bloke back at the camp was taking these packets of tobacco out of my kit bag and selling them to other people in the camp. I thought, "I'm not having that", so I stopped doing it.' In the new camp in Japan he experienced the same selfishness in some of his fellow-prisoners. 'We used to do our washing. That was a problem with chaps in a prison camp: if they saw something they wanted they were likely to pinch it. That was one of the things you had to guard against — "I'll watch your clothes if you watch mine."'

Not all the prisoners in his camp were British of course.

> The people I joined up with in Clacton were still together in the prison camp, not all of them, but nearly all, but a number of our troops had died and they brought in about another 250 to help keep our supplies going down the coal mine. Down the mine we had some people who the Nips had commandeered, not prisoners, who came from Korea, and they were owned by the Japanese and they were brought in and quite a lot of them could speak English and we got on with them quite well. These Koreans used to get saki and get drunk, and take the guards away from our camp to restore order up there.

While many Allied POWs heard news of Japan's surrender on their illicit radios Aubrey Clarke is probably unique in Oundle in that he heard the event which precipitated it. His camp was 30 miles away from Nagasaki.

> On this particular day, in August 1945, in the middle of the morning we heard a tremendous bombardment as we thought, because we used to hear them, but this was an exceptional one. We didn't know anything about atomic bombs; we heard all this palaver going on; we tried to get information from the Nips but nobody seemed to know what was going on or they wouldn't tell us anyway, and that went on for a week, ten days. Then all of a sudden we went on parade to go down the coal mine, which we did every morning about eight or nine o'clock and the Nip officer in charge of the parade informed us that we had to stay in the camp for the day, and then later in the day some American B29s flew over dropping leaflets to say that the war was finished.

Neither the British prisoners nor their Japanese guards knew what had happened at Hiroshima and Nagasaki. 'We had lost track of time, and discovered later that it was on 9 August 1945.'

Further drops by the B29s caused some unexpected problems for the prisoners.

> They dropped a radio so we could communicate with the pilots. We had to draw a circle in the parade ground, and they were supposed to drop supplies by parachute, and these drums full of clothes and shoes broke up on the way down and they were coming down like bombs. We had to radio them to stop because they were doing more damage, so we had to draw another circle in the paddy field and if they did break away they wouldn't do any damage, so that was better.

The period following the dropping of the two atomic bombs, including Japan's signing of the 'instrument of surrender' on 2 September 1945, was as odd for him as it was for Elsie Crowe, a prisoner in Sumatra at this time. 'We were our own bosses; the Nips used to organise parties for us to go out.'

On his way back home Aubrey Clarke saw at first hand the evidence of the destruction caused by the overwhelming power of the new weapon. 'When we were on our way home, we stopped at this particular place, and had a meal on the railway siding in Nagasaki where the bomb was dropped, and the round chimneys were standing but all the others were just flattened.'

His journey back home was not uneventful.

> We were going to the other island, where the Americans had taken, and we were on our way home from there, via the Philippines. I had a couple of kitbags, and we had to go to Ontu, on an invasion barge to this ship which was going to take us to our destination, and unfortunately, I hurt my leg jumping from the invasion barge to the ship, and I got phlebitis later on which nearly did me in. The people in charge said it was beri-beri, but I knew it wasn't, that was a disease brought on by eating too much rice. Anyway I got over it and finished up in Canada, in Victoria, and I was in hospital there for several weeks. Then we went right across Canada to the Atlantic side, 3,500 miles by train, through the Rockies, and the Great Lakes, and the Prairies, and there we stayed for about a fortnight, trying to get a bit of strength back. In Vancouver Island when I had phlebitis badly the doctor asked me if I would like to go with my mates to Halifax, the doctor advised that I stayed a bit longer and go on a special hospital

ship to Kingston Jamaica, and then we went to Southampton. There was a vicar in Kingston, who used to take us round in his car. It rained when we left England on 8 December, and four years later when we returned it was still raining.

The extraordinary thing about Aubrey Clarke's story, apart from his memory, is his insistence that 'up to a point' he missed the Japanese people on his return to freedom, and would love to go back to Japan. He remembers some of his guards with affection.

> There was a man in charge of us, we called him Pop. He was a kind old fellow, and about half a dozen of us, when we were liberated, he took us to his house and gave us a meal, and then when we were coming home, he came to see us off at the railway station. Poor old boy he was so upset because we were going. He stood on the platform and cried.

Aubrey recognised that he was lucky in having been a prisoner of the Japanese in their homeland. 'We as prisoners of war in Japan were treated very fairly, not like the prisoners on the railway line in Burma.' So how did he account for the apparent discrepancy between the treatment he received and that meted out to the majority of Allied prisoners? His explanation was twofold.

Firstly, he and his fellow prisoners were of use to the Japanese in their war effort. 'We were doing something useful for them in Japan, because they needed the coal for fuel, ground into a powder, so we were doing something important. Going on short rations for food was one thing, but we weren't tortured in the way they were in Burma.'

Secondly, he believes that the stress under which the Japanese found themselves fighting in the foreign countries which they invaded, was a major factor in the savagery with which they treated their prisoners.

> People get the wrong idea thinking Japan is a tropical hot country, but it isn't. In Burma they were working under conditions they weren't used to, and short of food as well, and pushed to get these bridges built, and had to knock our men around to get the work done. The prisoners of war on the Burma railway, every sleeper that was laid there was a dead man, quite a lot went from Singapore to the Burma road.

The stress-factor contributing to the barbaric treatment of enemies in occupied countries by normally civilized people is indeed a valid consideration. The world would in due course be shocked on hearing of atrocities committed in the Far East by Western soldiers during the post-World War II era. This consideration is something which had struck James Bradley during his time as a victim of the Japanese:

> I have always felt that the Japanese were very susceptible to their environment. Immediately after hostilities, when we were at Changi camp on Singapore Island in more or less civilized surroundings, they behaved towards us in a civilized manner. At the jungle camps along the railway they appeared to lose this veneer of civilization, and almost revert to the laws of the jungle, where they became totally unpredictable and ruthless, although of course there were always exceptions to the rule. The Allies, in some cases, were by no means perfect.[25]

There are however many instances of atrocities committed by the Japanese in POW camps on mainland Japan.

Horrific though the treatment of western prisoners by the Japanese was, it was no worse than the way in which the other Asian nations were treated by their captors. The Japanese massacres of Chinese, for example, rivalled the horrors of the Holocaust.[26]

It should also be noted that the Japanese displayed a remarkable lack of humanity in dealing with their own sick or wounded troops. James Bradley quotes an instance of this remarked on by a fellow-prisoner G. P. Adams, who was also working on the Thailand-Burma Railway:

> Immediately after our return to Konkuita trainloads of men would stop in the siding there — some were westbound Jap reinforcements, in good spirits, and excellent health. The eastbound trains were almost too disgusting to describe.
>
> The first one I saw was filled with Japanese sick and wounded; they had been shut up in those steel 10-ton trucks for many hours, without food or water, and their wounds, all serious, untended since boarding. The POWs were moved to pity, and many went forward to offer them water and even a cigarette in some cases. The now useless warriors of the Emperor lay in their own filth, and all were nauseated by the stench of their foul matted bloody dressings. Little wonder that the Japanese High Command were callous to us POWs if they could treat their own kith and kin thus.[27]

Of course, during the Second World War there were other nationals who were no less to be blamed for their monstrous treatment of prisoners. While it is true that 25% of western POWs died in Japanese captivity, the survival rate of Soviets in German camps, Germans in Soviet camps and Japanese in Soviet camps after the war, was less than a quarter: the conclusion is that the Japanese were not uniquely savage or more savage than the Germans.[28]

Prisoners in Britain

As the war progressed, enemy prisoners began to make their appearance in Britain, and they were by no means confined to the distant corners of the British Isles. It is perhaps surprising to find that the enemy was accommodated in the region, given the strategic importance of the neighbouring airfields.

However the lack of agricultural workers who had left to join the armed forces led to the setting up of several prisoner of war camps in the Oundle area to supply the necessary labour for food production. One of the biggest was at King's Cliffe.

At the start of the war Italians predominated. Bevil Allen remembered them working on his uncle's farm at Stoke Doyle, where they were taken and collected by lorry. Ruth Keens recalled them as 'cheerful, happy men, though I was told they had only dry bread for their lunch. I felt sorry for them so far away from their sunny land, but no doubt our men in their hands fared no better'. Warmington farmer John Simpson remembers meeting many of the prisoners, and playing chess regularly with an Italian, even though neither could understand the other's language. Along with other farmers in the area he maintained that one Austrian prisoner was worth three Germans who was worth nine Italians in terms of the work they did. Stewart Laxton remembered the trusted German prisoners working on the harvest. 'I saw some at Mr Horsford's farm at Oundle Lodge. They were the same sort of people as us. Most of them were relieved to be out of the war, and in England — they did not want to fight.'

Barnwell saw a number of German prisoners who did various jobs in the village. Most of the able-bodied house staff at Barnwell Manor having been called up for National Service, the gap that they left was partially filled by two German prisoners as housemaids. Their carpentry skills were much admired in the neighbourhood: the toys that they made for the young Prince William were remembered by Princess Alice many years later.[29] Oundle resident Gertrude Brown kept the carved wooden box given to her as a present by a German POW, and Tim Elcock, son of Barnwell's stationmaster, remembered learning the art of fretwork during his visits to the POWs in the house where they lived in the village. A nightly check by Barnwell's policeman was virtually the only sign that the Germans were prisoners: most of them were happy to stay as guests of the Government in what is still one of Northamptonshire's most picturesque villages. One of them even made a name for himself as goalkeeper for Barnwell's football team.

Not surprisingly, the relationship between captors and captives grew into friendship in many cases. Ruth Keens' memory of prisoners of war is typical. 'Two young German lads who must have been captured as soon as they enlisted were allowed to lodge in a private house in the village. My father, who had served in the Great War and on the Rhine afterwards, still mourned his brother, killed in 1918, but he made great friends with one lad who was always willing to give a hand with odd jobs.' This German was later to marry a friend of hers and settle in Oundle.

Indeed many of the enemy prisoners of war stayed on in England and have settled in the Oundle community, finding it preferable to the land of their birth for one reason or another. Sheila Sharman and Joyce Gaunt were just two of the local girls who befriended German POWs and eventually married them.

Karl 'Charlie' Schoenrock, who worked in Oundle School workshops, revealed how he had come to live in the area.

He was born on 3 April 1926 in the town of Kustrin, which lay on the Oder river in eastern Germany, although now it is on the Polish side of the border.

Charlie Schoenrock was the youngest of five boys and had one sister. When the war came, he was 13, and therefore too young to fight, but when he was 17, two months before his 18th birthday, he was conscripted into the German Infantry in February 1944. He was sent to fight in France against the invading Allied armies. Posted to La Rochelle after three months' training in Germany, he was sent further north ready for D-Day, and was captured by the British troops in August of the same year. German morale at this point was fairly low in his opinion, and along with four others he saw no point in resisting. 'Someone standing in front of you with a rifle and someone standing behind... What would you do? You knew your war days were up, or you'd have got your head shot off — I couldn't do anything else. We were all just walking in a field like lost sheep.'

He was well treated and stayed two weeks in a camp in France, before being sent to England and then on to America. His only complaint about his treatment related to the loss of some treasured personal possessions. 'I'd got my wallet and all my family photos with me but the Americans wouldn't let me keep them, they just took them out of my pocket and threw them on the floor and told me that's where they're staying.' He stayed in camps in America for 16 months, even though the war had ended in Europe in August the previous year; when he returned to England in January 1946 the authorities had no idea when he, or the rest of the 500 prisoners with him would have the chance to return to Germany.

145: Karl 'Charlie' Schoenrock, one of Oundle's former German POWs.

He was then shifted from camp to camp in England, staying in Liverpool, Scotland, Lincoln, at an RAF base at Cranwell, Bayfield for six months and finally staying near Towcester for a year. Life in the camps was not particularly hard, he recalled. He and the other prisoners worked as farm hands to earn money and to ease the otherwise relentless boredom. 'They left us alone to do our job, it was perfect really. We got up at six, washed and shaved and then you'd go out. The farmer was ready with his trucks and 20 of us piled into each one. Then we were out in the fields picking fruit and vegetables until 4.00 pm and then after tea we were free to do what we liked.'

Finally at the end of 1947 he was asked whether he wanted to return to Germany by the Red Cross. He decided to stay in England because he had no relatives left that he knew of, as three of his brothers had been killed in Russia, and he did not know whether his other brother and sister were alive or dead. He also did not want to go back to a Federal Republic of Germany living off Marshall Aid with food shortages, and he was not allowed to return to Kustrin as it was now part of Poland.

Coping with a new language was his major obstacle to a new life in England, but he overcame it by his own efforts.

> I'd never learnt English, so that was a problem. We all spoke our own languages in the camps, so when I stayed in England I picked up the language on the streets. There were no real anti-German feelings but as I was staying with a friend in Towcester I wouldn't really have noticed it. During my time as a prisoner of war we weren't allowed to go out anywhere, but after that you could do what you liked. Some people went back to Germany but I had got used to it here in England and the farmer let me stay, so I did. Then I went out more, made more friends and got used to being a new Englishman.

FIVE ~ CAPTIVES IN A DISTANT LAND

In 1952 he married in Warmington Church a girl he had met in Towcester. His new wife Hilda persuaded him to stay in Warmington in 1954 and so he started working at a series of jobs before settling down in a job at Anglian Water in Oundle, and then finally working for Oundle School.

Sadly Charlie Schoenrock was widowed after a happy marriage of 38 years, but with a daughter and a son born in 1954 and 1967 he is well settled in his new home country. Asked if he would ever return to live in Germany he looked up, smiled and replied, 'No, I am a naturalised Englishman.'[30]

Notes

1. *The Laxtonian*, vol. XV, no.4, April 1941, pp.209-10.
2. *The Old Oundelian*, 1993-94, pp.29-30.
3. *The Old Oundelian*, 1992-93, pp.88-89. Roger Maw features in Williams' story as 'Wings' Cameron. See *The Wooden Horse*, pp.42-8.
4. I am indebted to his brother David J. Maw, a fellow former Oundle School boy for this information. See Paul Brickhill, *The Great Escape*, p.197.
5. Ian English tells his story in *Assisted Passage — Walking to Freedom — Italy 1943*, Privately published, 1995.
6. *The Laxtonian*, vol. XVI, no.6, December 1945, pp.237-8.
7. Ralph Leigh was speaking to a small group of 13-year old Oundle School boys. Estimates vary as to the final death toll for the bombing of Dresden, from the 250,000 claimed by the Nazis, to 135,000 put forward by the British historian David Irving. The latest estimate by the German historian Friedrich Reichert, writing in 1995, is 25,000.
8. I have based Dr Crowe's account of her captivity on the article written by former Oundle School boy Nick Squires in *The Laxtonian*, 1986, pp.102-4.
9. James Bradley, *Towards the setting sun*, pp.28-9.
10. *The Old Oundelian*, 1994-95, p.89.
11. J. Bradley, *Towards the setting sun*, p.30.
12. *Ibid.* p.33.
13. *Ibid.* pp.23-4.
14. *Ibid.* pp.41-2.
15. *Ibid.* p.43.
16. *Ibid.* p.52.
17. *Ibid.* p.53.
18. *Ibid.* pp.57-8.
19. *Ibid.* p.81.
20. *Ibid.* p.97.
21. *The Old Oundelian*, 1993-94, pp.88-89.
22. J. Bradley, *Towards the setting sun*, p.129.
23. *Ibid.* p.96.
24. *The Old Oundelian*, 1965-66, pp.58-9.
25. J. Bradley, *Towards the setting sun*, p.117.
26. See Buruma, *The Wages of Guilt: Memories of War in Germany and Japan*, London, 1991.
27. J. Bradley, *Towards the setting sun*, p.99.
28. See Buruma, *op.cit.*
29. *The Lady of the Manor*, in *The Laxtonian*, Summer 1984, p.3.
30. Charlie Schoenrock's account of his captivity is based on an article by Oliver Sharp in *The Laxtonian*, 1991, p.69, with additional material from Gary Bosworth.

CHAPTER SIX

The End

Celebrations

Victory in Europe Day, on Tuesday 8 May 1945, was marked by celebrations in Oundle as in thousands of communities all over Britain.

It was a memorable affair, recalled Elizabeth Berridge.

> I was at College and we were allowed to go home. I got on the train in Birmingham and it was packed with Canadian Air Force men. It was hard to get on and we all stood in the corridors, singing songs all the way to London. When I got to London, I danced the hokey-cokey outside Buckingham Palace in a huge crowd. I got a train back to Peterborough and hitch-hiked back to Oundle. My parents were absolutely horrified because they thought this was dangerous — not at all, everybody was in such a good mood! Everybody danced and went mad. There was dancing in the streets — so much happiness. The School all joined in. My husband-to-be was home then and he was determined not to go back as he said the war was over. We all danced in the big bus shelter where the bus depot near Pick Arthey's is — this was a shelter for double-decker buses. It was wonderful — totally spontaneous.

True, the schoolboys did celebrate. Former Oundle School pupil Patrick Lane recorded his memories.

> The Allies had linked up with the Russians and with the Italian front. Four days later it was all over and VE Day was announced with two days' national holiday. We heard Winston Churchill and the King on study radio. I did a war dance in my gas mask as army lorries roared into the town and gave us rides to the station and back. The Yanks arrived from Polebrook Aerodrome laden with chewing-gum. In the Market Place, a huge snaking line danced the Conga. On the second day I got buried in a good book and walked into the Chapel Thanksgiving Service halfway through. Yet it all seemed dazing and unreal. The blackout curtains went for six, but other restrictions remained for many years.

But Bevil Allen, then aged 17, remembered the celebrations in the pubs rather than the chapel.

> We went mad. I can remember one experience... we were all so hyped up by the end of the war that I can remember Oundle schoolboys going in the pubs, and the pubs were full of schoolboys celebrating, and there were masters chasing them out of the backs of the pubs and they were coming in the front again.

In fact it was young people who were responsible for some of the crazier stunts, as Bevil Allen remembered. 'There were some schoolboys who piled into the bus going to Peterborough and one of them drove it into Peterborough and all the way back again, celebrating — everybody thought it was a great game.'

146: VE Day outside The Nag's Head in West Street:
(l. to r.) Ella Walton, Susan Walton, June Gaunt, Joyce Gaunt, with the landlord and his daughter.

Even the 12-year old Michael Pickard, who had just joined Oundle School's Berrystead House as a new boy, later to become Chairman of the London Docklands Development Corporation and Master of the Worshipful Company of Grocers, had only hazy memories of how he ended up on a brewery lorry miles away from Oundle following the general celebrations of VE Day.

Another well-known and respected Oundle resident, John Cunnington, recalled how with friends, Jack Cotton and he set fire to a haystack in the field which is now the Recreation Ground on New Road. Subsequently he joined the Oundle Fire Brigade.

VJ Day on 15 August was also celebrated, but it was a quieter affair, taking place as it did during the school holidays.

Oundle's Gratitude

Almost everyone in the town had come into contact with the suffering caused by the loss of loved ones in war, even if they had not been of an age to take an active part. Schoolboys like Bevil Allen remembered boys who had been in the Sixth Form when he started at Laxton School, who had gone into the Forces and had been killed.

A total of 18 former pupils from Laxton School died in action. A memorial to those of Laxton School who had served in both world wars was unveiled in the Laxton School Long Room on 20 May 1950, bearing the names of 50 pupils.

The 27 names of those from Oundle town who died in the Second World War were added to the town's War Memorial as follows:

SIX ~ THE END

Corporal D. A. Ashby
Warrant Officer D. F. Barber
Private L. E. Barber
Corporal R. E. Black
BSM F. W. Briggs
Lieutenant J. A. Brittain
Gunner A. J. S. Burdett
Major A. L. Butcher
Lieutenant D. H. E. Collier
Sergeant L. E. Cottingham
Lance Corporal H. G. Dew
Private L. E. Fox
Sergeant N. A. Hill
Flight Sergeant J. Horsford DFM
Sergeant T. W. Hughes
Captain C. F. King
Lieutenant J. M. H. King
Sergeant J. L. Marlow
Gunner W. H. Marshall
Private W. A. J. Martin
Pilot Officer J. H. Mason DFC
Captain C. M. Osman
Flight Sergeant P. Richardson
Gunner J. W. Roughton
Corporal G. C. Smith
Sergeant Pilot A. W. Taney
Flight Lieutenant N. C. Tatam

147: Remembrance Sunday, 1994, at Oundle's War Memorial.

The list includes all those who died on active service, whatever the circumstances. William Marshall, for example, had been a Gunner with the 155/94th Anti-tank Regiment of the Royal Artillery for only twelve months when he died of complications caused by peritonitis at the Conway Valley hospital in Wales. An Oundle man, he had worked for the School as a gardener after leaving the secondary school in West Street. He was only 19 years old.

Apart from the names of fallen servicemen on the town's war memorial, other tributes to their sacrifice have been made.

Oundle Middle School has Houses named after four men from the town — Barber, Marlow, Mason and Richardson — men who in fact were hardly more than boys when they perished. Another War Memorial in the town was designated in the form of the Recreation Ground on New Road.

A total of 252 former Oundle School boys, along with the 18 former Laxton School boys, had lost their lives while on active service in the Second World War. Two former members of staff, Lieutenant John Brittain, and Captain Charles Osman also died in action, both in the Battle for France in 1940. The final figure for those serving in the armed forces during the war was to reach 2,480, after all available information had been received in September 1947. Of these, 392 received decorations, and 372 were mentioned in despatches.

To commemorate these men, the volume *Oundle Memorials of the Second World War 1939-1945* was published. It consists of a list of all those who served in the war, along with short biographies of those who had lost their lives, including photographs. In 1950 the ambulatory of Oundle School chapel was made into a shrine for the memories of all the Old Boys who had fallen in both wars.

There is one memorial worn by Oundle's Mayor, the origins of which are not widely known. In 1957 the Oundle School Memorial Trust presented a chain of office to the Chairman of the Council commemorating those former pupils of Oundle and Laxton Schools who had died during the War.

Eight years later, following an approach to the School made by the family of John Heron Rogers, who had died on active service in 1942, a further memorial was established. The area of conifers north of Benefield Road known as Heron Rogers Wood is a living reminder of the ultimate sacrifice made by the School's former pupils. A stone cairn was erected in a clearing. It bears these words:

> Heron Rogers Wood
> This woodland was planted in 1965
> In Memory of John Heron Rogers, Lieutenant, RNVR, and all his
> fellow Oundelians who lost their lives 1939-45.

Many families no doubt felt that their greatest cause for celebration was not so much victory for the nation as relief that they had survived the war years unscathed. Lewis Keens, of Herne Road, counted himself particularly fortunate. A picture on the front page of the *Daily Sketch* of Saturday 4 November had featured his mother with the caption 'Mother holds "review" of eight enlisted sons'. She had been shown contemplating photographs of all eight at her cottage in Hampshire, evidently pondering their likely fate in the world

SIX ~ THE END

148: The Heron Rogers Wood Memorial to Old Oundelians who died on active service during World War Two.

149: A photograph showing all ten sons of the Keens family who served in the Forces during World War Two, along with their sister. Lewis Keens is standing, third from the right.

conflict that had begun a month earlier. Now, in 1945, all were back safely, along with two more who had joined up in the course of the war, and Lewis's sister Florence, who had served as a nurse.

For some Oundle people the end of the war was marked by a feeling of exhilaration about the future which they feel has not been matched by events. Alec Payne's view was typical:

> Immediately after the war, there was a sense of expectation and urgency, which was symbolised by a festival down in Battersea, where people were still optimistic that this country was going to change: there were not going to be the same social barriers, and we were going to see our way through to the top of the world. If you went on holiday in Europe at that time, you were treated as kings of the world. They thought that we had done very well, and they treated you as if you had. Now in fact, they would wonder what you were up to. So in that sense, there was a sense of anticipation and optimism that something good had been done, and something good was going to come out of it. And gradually bit by bit, it disappeared.[1]

Picking up the Pieces

Most of those who had been on active service were overjoyed to be returning home, and felt a sense of elation as they discovered new and fulfilling careers for themselves. 'When I got home it was incredible,' recalled Robin Miller. 'I was planning to return to America, but my parents persuaded me to stay in England and I found a job teaching music at Tonbridge School. I then had to get out of the RAF, which I did, and then realised that teaching was what I really wanted to do. So it was very exciting, and also very profitable, as I was also being paid for being a Flight Lieutenant for the first term! Life for me was very good at that time, and I thoroughly enjoyed it.' He felt that the war had intruded for long enough. 'It was a sort of unreal interlude to my life and I consequently did not join any of these RAF organisations. It was marvellous to get back to reality.'

Others were lucky enough to have already chosen a profession which had a clear career path, and were able to throw themselves into this. Ben Grantham remembered one difficulty. 'I had of course no clothes I could wear, as I had left behind clothes I had long ago outgrown, and found the clothes ration difficult.' But this was a minor problem. 'I was soon absorbed back into medical studies, and had very little time to think too much of my difficulties outside exams.'

Staying on in the services provided one answer for those who felt at a loss. 'Adjusting to being at home was quite difficult and took some time, but I carried on in the army after the war so it was not that different,' recalled Charles Tod.

For some servicemen there were still vital jobs to be done. Life at sea continued to be almost as hazardous as it had been in wartime because of the problem of the vast numbers of mines which had been laid. Kenneth Gadd was one of those who carried on in active service to do the vital work of restoring peace to the sea. He was still sweeping mines when the war ended, and the Royal Navy's task in this area continued until the 1960s. 'Everyone, all the battleships and all that, packed up, but because there were so many mines we had to carry on. In fact there are still some in various parts of the world now.'

Kenneth Gadd found it equally easy to adapt to civilian life, becoming a Trinity House pilot and taking ships in and out of Southampton. 'I really just went back to sea again.'

Post-War Problems

But for many, understandably, the end of the war was a traumatic experience as they tried to readjust to civilian life. Not everyone was as lucky as the doctors, teachers and regular soldiers who managed to rediscover the normality of everyday existence.

The problem of ex-prisoners of war like Aubrey Clarke and Ralph Leigh was a particularly difficult one, in view of the poor health of so many of these former servicemen. Aubrey Clarke, in spite of his relatively humane treatment at the hands of the Japanese, was 35 years old, suffering from poor eyesight, and had lost a considerable amount of weight. 'They wanted to get rid of us, but they couldn't turn us out until we were fit. It took six months for me to get back what I had lost.'

It was not just his physical health which had been damaged by his wartime experience. 'When I got to King's Cross station to come to Peterborough I had never felt so lonely in my life. I'd lost all my mates,' he recalled.

Some people took one look at post-war England and fled. Returning to a cold and miserable English climate was an unattractive prospect for Tom Fiddick who had spent much of his wartime in exotic postings. 'My initial reaction was to get back into the sun as soon as I could, and my one idea was to go abroad again and to get a job. I had no job, you see. I went straight from school into the Navy, and life in England in 1947 was very hard for everybody, severe rationing, coldest winter on record.'

The psychological problems caused by years of stress in often terrifying situations were one difficulty that servicemen had to face. USAAF veteran Whitney Miller recalled the nightmares from which he suffered in the post-war years. Ex-Merchant Navy man George Bristow admitted that he was one among thousands of ex-servicemen in Britain for whom barbiturates were the only form of help offered by a medical profession which did not at that time realise the value of counselling as it does today. Witnessing the death and suffering of both friends and enemies at close quarters had often been a daily occurrence; the consequences would be far-reaching, and largely unsuspected by the next generation. 'Of course you felt guilt... guilt at feeling relief that it was your mates, and not you, that had gone down in another ship.'

Half a century after the end of hostilities, surveys of Second World War veterans have shown that one in five still have major psychological problems relating to their war experience, with the proportion rising even higher among those who spent time in prisoner of war camps.

The strain of running Oundle School during these dark years would take its toll on Dr Fisher, who was to die on 2 October 1945, scarcely a month after he had retired as Headmaster. The School appreciated what he had been through. 'Known as "Bud" or "Boodle", he was much mimicked by the boys, but there was genuine affection for the great man,' believed Robin Paterson. 'It cannot have been easy running a boarding school for some 620 boys in the midst of a war.'

For ex-Bramston boy John Keene, 'There is one memory of Kenneth Fisher which endures, and that was at the end of term when he retired. Instead of going back to our Houses immediately after the film as one was supposed to do, the whole School lined the path from the Great Hall to the right hand entrance of School House, and cheered the old man to the echo. He had to take several encores before finally retiring for the night. It was sad that he died so soon afterwards.'

Kenneth Fisher is buried at nearby Achurch. The Bishop of Peterborough, in his Address, recalled a meeting with him in the School Chapel on the occasion of his visit for a confirmation, when the Headmaster had shown him where it was hoped to place a War Memorial for those former pupils who had fallen in the conflict. 'Little did I think as he talked to me then that he himself was to be a casualty of the war. And yet there can be no doubt that he was.'[2]

Feelings for the Enemy

Naturally enough, Oundle people felt as bitter as anyone else in Britain whose life had been damaged by the war. For Miriam Rothschild in Ashton, the Nazi threat had represented something particularly evil and terrifying. Her Jewish connection had given her an involvement in European affairs which had gone beyond any perspective seen by most Oundle people, and which had given the conflict a deeper meaning.

> The war was the most appalling thing. When it was over, every morning for months I woke up saying, 'Thank God the war's over.' It was the first thought that came into my mind. But it was a doubly terrible experience for Jews, because our entire family was annihilated: my husband's family, and all my mother's family. About two escaped. The Russians rescued one, but everyone else went into gas chambers and we knew perfectly well that was happening, because it had started before the war, and the war was the climax. Everyone we liked or cared for was annihilated. My mother-in-law, my father-in-law, my husband's brothers, everybody was killed. It was not like here, when it was someone from this family and someone from another family. By the end of the war, we had no family left abroad at all.

For Bevil Allen, Germany and all Germans were a target of resentment, and it was only gradually that a more reflective view began to make itself felt.

> At the time of course every German was a German whether he was a Nazi or not, and we thought all Germans were bad, naturally, because we were at war with them. But we realised afterwards it was the Nazis we were bitter against, for the people that we knew and were killed and would never come back, and I would not forgive Hitler in any way.

The true realisation of the suffering inflicted on the inhabitants of Hiroshima and Nagasaki also took time to sink in. Like those on active service in the Far East who had greeted the news of the destruction of Hiroshima with elation, Bevil Allen had no idea of the real nature of the new and horrific weapon. 'We heard on the news that they had dropped an atom bomb on the Japanese and it had created an immense amount of devastation. You then got to know what the atom bomb was, what it had done and what the after-effects would be, which were pretty horrendous.'

At Oundle School, a debate on 13 October 1945, reflected the lack of awareness of the implications of the new weapon for world peace. The motion, that 'This House believes that the use of the atomic bomb makes the political unity of the world an immediate necessity,' was defeated by 111 votes to 27.[3]

As time went by there were those who were conscious of the suffering being endured by Germans as a result of the war. Autumn 1947 saw a meeting of Oundle School Senior Modern Languages Society at which a pupil, Charles Delamain, stressed the appalling havoc wrought by the RAF and the shortage of food which was prevalent all over Germany. Another pupil, Michael Jackson, wrote in the same vein in *The Laxtonian* of December 1950, after a visit that he had made. 'We do not realise in England what bombing is really like, and to see its consequences is a real education.'[4]

150: The hero of El Alamein at Oundle in 1947.

Yet Monty's visit to Oundle in 1947, following an invitation from the headmaster Graham Stainforth, proved that the vast majority of young people were far from discovering the pacifism of the anti-nuclear '60s. Former Oundle School pupil Patrick Lane remembered the talk that the hero of Alamein gave about the battle in the Great Hall, using blackboards and coloured chalk. 'He said he'd pose for photos on the lawn outside, only to find himself confronted, outflanked and finally encircled by a galaxy of Brownie box cameras. Stainforth was grimacing fiercely at several boys and whispering, "It just isn't done!" as they surged about like a football crowd.' Even in 1961, another wartime 'star', air-ace Group Captain Douglas Bader was fêted as a celebrity visitor to the School.

Fifty years later, feelings have mellowed. Many of Oundle's Second World War veterans feel a comradeship-in-arms which extends to their former enemies. 'The Germans ought to have been invited to the D-Day celebrations,' believes Barnwell's Donald Akroyd. 'There was never any great hatred between the British and Germans and indeed British soldiers in North Africa ostensibly afforded a greater respect for Rommel than they did for their own officers.' For John Robinson, the German regulars were 'just as honourable and decent as the rest of us'.

151: Group Captain Douglas Bader (right) meets a CCF cadet during his 1961 visit to Oundle, accompanied by Headmaster R. J. Knight (centre) and David Anderson, in charge of the School's CCF.

There are signs that one day will see a similar mutual respect grow out of our relationship with Japan. Even among those Japanese guilty of the most cruel atrocities towards prisoners of war in the Far East there are some who have taken the lead in expressing feelings of remorse.

In the run-up to the fiftieth anniversary of VJ Day a television programme featured one of the heroes of *Oundle's War*. Central Television's *Tokyo Encounter* focused on the meeting between ex-Oundle School boy and POW James Bradley and his former guard on the Thailand-Burma railway. Hiroshi Abe, an engineer lieutenant in charge of working parties at Sonkurai Camp, served 11 years imprisonment as a war criminal after being found guilty of maltreating British prisoners of war. 'I can never forget the suffering of your men when you had to burn and bury your dead,' he told James Bradley. 'I must take a large part of the blame for what happened.' His words, evoking the former POW's most horrifying memories, brought tears to the eyes of the two men and their interpreter. Less than a fortnight later, on 6 August 1995, during the commemoration in Japan of the fiftieth anniversary of the dropping of the atomic bomb on Hiroshima, a remarkable lead was given by its Mayor. Takashi Hiraoka told the 13,000 guests gathered at the ceremony to remember the victims of the world's first atomic bomb: 'With the suffering of all the war's victims indelibly etched in our hearts, we want to apologise for the unbearable suffering that Japanese colonial domination and war inflicted on so many people.' It was a moving statement. Three days later, Nagasaki's Mayor Itcho Ito echoed these feelings at the ceremony marking the fiftieth anniversary of his city's destruction.

SIX ~ THE END

152 : (L. to r.) Hiroshi Abe, former Oundle School boy James Bradley and fellow POW Douglas Weir at the Commonwealth War Graves Cemetery in Yokahama.
Photograph from Big Story © Carlton UK Television.

The Lessons of War

Fifty years of peace have enabled many veterans of the 1939-45 conflict to evaluate their experience. Some of them whose stories have been used in *Oundle's War* were invited to explain how the war had changed their view of life, and to say whether their wartime experience had been a positive or a negative one in terms of dealing with life's problems.

All were agreed that the levelling factor had been the war's most valuable aspect for them, particularly if they had come from what they saw as a socially sheltered background. 'I think it did me a lot of good,' believed Robin Miller. 'Knocked a lot of veneer off, although as I said earlier it was sort of unreal — I was not destined to do that at all. I mixed with a lot of people that I would never have had anything to do with before. I mean, going into the RAF at the very bottom, I found a whole lot of people that had a completely different set of values to me, who spoke a different language from myself, mostly consisting of one word with four letters!' Charles Tod's experience as a soldier was similar.

> I think it made me grow up very quickly and it broadened my horizons. I had a public school education, so it knocked any corners off and made me more tolerant... It gave me a wider knowledge of men than I had when it started... It was very positive. I was taught a lot about fellow man in the war. It was definitely positive.

Retired GP Ben Grantham saw educational benefits in his war experience which would help him in his profession.

> I suddenly found myself having to grow up fast. I realised that I was in a position in which it was likely that I personally would soon be asked to be responsible for others rather than a child depending on everyone else. I also came from a family where there was a very strong tradition of leading and fighting for 'the right'. Wartime experience was without a doubt a very positive experience for me. I learned to live with my fellow man. I learned to understand him better. My experiences in dealing with men were of untold value in my profession.

What valuable lessons therefore had they learnt, that another generation, raised in comfort far from the horrors of war would never learn? What have today's young people both gained and lost by not sharing the experience of their grandparents? 'A quite impossible question to answer,' believed Ben Grantham.

> Different times and situations pertain today. For us we lost valuable time in settling to our chosen careers. We lost many friends. We had to watch the destruction of many things we held dear. We emerged after the war into a world which had been completely altered, and whether we approved of that lost world or not it was certain we should never see it again. I think it is possible that we learned a lot about the value of the contributions that other people were making. And realised that there was a togetherness and brotherhood in combatting evil, and we needed everybody's contribution, and we ourselves had to make our contribution too. Selfishness would get no one anywhere.

For Kenneth Gadd such togetherness was a fundamental requirement if his ship was not to go down with all hands, providing a lesson for life in general. 'The most important thing is the question of discipline. You had to be very disciplined in war and I think it's very difficult today for young people to appreciate the restrictions of the war conditions, how you all had to toe the line, as it were. Because you could not run a ship or something like that unless there was strict discipline. There's a limit to what you can do in a very tight society, as the world is, with your neighbour alongside you — so you've got to have discipline otherwise you're going to fall out with one another.'

The camaraderie of war is also seen by Oundle's veterans as a positive aspect whose intensity has been denied to a peacetime generation. 'Today's younger generation have gained a longer life span, as war is such a waste of lives, in particular for the young, but they may have missed out on the comradeship that we all had,' believes Charles Tod. 'The best experience was definitely all the friendship.'

Such a view was echoed by American airman Whitney Miller. His wartime experience made a big impression on him. 'It was a vast plus in my life. The camaraderie was one thing... It was very strong. The war also taught me that I was able to handle anything that life could throw at me.'

But the former USAAF navigator expressed better than anyone the truth about the lessons of war which he had discovered during those murderous flights over Europe. 'Nothing could be worse than that Polebrook experience. It was a great adventure... It was the most important thing that happened to me... but it was bad... it was scary... and I wouldn't do it again.'

Former Oundle GP Michael Lewis, who served in Normandy with the Royal Army Medical Corps, also recognised that there were some positive aspects. 'One dealt with a lot of commonplace problems apart from merely medical, in the army — problems that the men had with their families, advice they wanted, so that was all valuable experience.' But

SIX ~ THE END

he was unequivocal in his rejection of war as a formative experience. Today's young people have gained a chance to live a normal life without their future and careers being interrupted. 'I don't think they have lost anything, war is a total disaster and just has to be endured.' And yet the disaster of war had to be faced to avoid the even greater evil of the dictatorships. 'We felt that the Germans, who had distinguished themselves in the past in a clever and civilised country, had slipped back, as I said, into a ruthless and barbaric outlook on the rest of the world.'

~ ✧✧✧ ~

Half a century after the end of World War Two, the relationship between the major European powers bears thankfully little resemblance to the one which was so damaged by the ambitions of the dictators of 1939. But the sacrifice of so many of Oundle's youth in the cause of freedom has not been forgotten. As another school year drew to a close in the summer of 1995, Oundle's headmasters addressed pupils, parents and teachers, many of whom had attended the fiftieth anniversary celebrations just one month before.

'Political considerations in a modern united Europe dictated that the VE Day commemoration should celebrate peace rather than sound a note of triumphalism,' reflected Laxton School's headmaster Bob Briggs. 'Yet it would be wrong for us to forget that the War was certainly a triumph over evil.' Or, as Oundle's David McMurray put it the following

153: Gerald Touch's widow Phyllis in front of the plaque which she unveiled in Laxton School Cloisters commemorating her husband's achievements, with (left) C. Holdsworth Hunt, Master of The Worshipful Company of Grocers, and Bob Briggs, Headmaster of Laxton School.

day on 1 July in his Speech Day address to 3,000, quoting Old Oundelian Cecil Lewis: 'In 1939 there was no doubt that the world had an enemy, and it was plain to everyone what sort of society would ensue under the thumb of men entirely devoid of conscience.'

That weekend saw the unveiling of a plaque in Laxton School Cloisters to commemorate the wartime technological achievements of Gerald Touch. Oundle welcomed back as heroes Robert Aitken, Robert Butler, Lucian Ercolani, Norman Jewell and Elliott Viney. We were doing something, tiny though it was, to recognise the debt that we owe to them and their generation for the freedom that we have enjoyed in Europe since 1945. And if, fifty years on, the news from the former Yugoslavia was more appalling than usual today, it merely emphasizes that the freedom for which so many sacrifices were made, in the struggle against régimes founded on ancient prejudice and appalling cruelty, is a fragile, as well as a precious thing.

154: Some of the heroes of *Oundle's War* with its author:
(l. to r. Lieutenant Colonel Robert Butler MBE, MC, Lucian Ercolani DSO, DFC, the author, Michael Downes, Robert Aitken DSO, Captain Norman Jewell DSC, MBE, Elliott Viney DSO, MBE, TD.

Notes
1 Alec Payne would like to point out that he believed that extracts from his interview would be rewritten in a more formal style.
2 *The Laxtonian,* vol.XVI, no.6, December 1945, p.209.
3 *The Laxtonian,* vol.XVI, no.6, December 1945, p.212.
4 *The Laxtonian*, vol.XVI, no.12, December 1947, p.509; vol.XVII, no.9, December 1950, pp.575-76.

SIX ~ THE END

~ Postscript ~

The idea of a book about Oundle at war had been at the back of my mind for some time when I rediscovered history master Dudley Heesom's eight-page article *Oundle in wartime*. Half inclined to forget the project I had been about to dismiss it altogether. After all, I had been told by many people that 'nothing happened in Oundle during the war'. And Dudley Heesom's article was of course right in stating that real danger hardly arrived in the town.

But I could not help thinking that further pages needed to be written, if only to satisfy my own curiosity.

What were the stories behind the names on the War Memorials in both the schools and the town? And was it really true that the chief interest of Polebrook was in allowing Clark Gable to walk the streets of Oundle?

Hearing Ralph Leigh's horrific account of his experiences in North Africa, and discovering in back numbers of school archives incredible tales of heroic exploits and tragic losses made me want to bring Oundle's wartime story properly to light. Reading the 16-year old Patrick Duerden's school project on life in the town during the war, and his account of Oundle's amazing fund-raising efforts, was a further source of inspiration to which I am greatly indebted.

Meeting the veterans of the 351st Bomb Group and listening to their fascinating and harrowing stories convinced me that further efforts were needed to highlight their achievements after fifty years. 'Oh yes, there was an airfield there Sir, wasn't there?' heard as a comment from the occasional pupil did not seem to me to be a sufficient obituary for the 405 American airmen from Polebrook Airfield alone, killed or missing in action between 1943 and 1945, and the many hundreds more who were appallingly injured, physically and mentally. Listening to the Oundle taxi-driver telling how he still takes their surviving comrades to the memorial on what remains of the airfield, and watches them weeping on the windswept concrete made me certain that their story should be included.

So *Oundle's War* would attempt to be an expression of sympathy and gratitude, as well an evocation of a world at war, in all its aspects — atrocious, bizarre and amusing as well as glorious and heroic. Sympathy for those who declined to collaborate on the project because it would have evoked memories too painful for them to recall, as well as gratitude for the sacrifice made in the cause of freedom. By involving Oundle grandchildren of the wartime generation in the book's preparation, using them to interview some of the veterans of the conflict, I would be doing something to make them aware of the sacrifice that had been made, a sacrifice which had saved us from invasion, and which finally brought to an end those monstrous dictatorships with their slave-labour camps and their programme of systematic genocide. It seemed only natural to make The Royal British Legion the sole beneficiary of all sales proceeds from the book.

There would never be enough time to ensure that the research for *Oundle's War* was done as thoroughly as it should have been, and I apologise for the many gaps, and no doubt the many errors in what is bound to be an imperfect chronicle of an age which I did not know. Limitations of space and time, for example, meant that I was unable to treat more than one of Oundle's airfields in sufficient depth. There are however excellent specialist publications on this subject, and I am indebted to their authors for allowing me to draw on their material.

It would have been an impossible task to track down all the Oundle-born survivors of the conflict. Equally it would have been churlish to exclude those present members of the Oundle community who have been welcomed into it even if they were born outside the area, particularly if their contribution to the book was to be a part of what is in effect a historical mosaic. For just this reason I included the tales and adventures of those who received their education in the town and no longer live here, but who view Oundle with continuing affection.

Of course there will be flaws in this chronicle which will contain contradictions and unanswered questions, just as war itself in so many ways is irrational and often inconclusive. But as an Oundle resident I felt it was important for the town to do something to commemorate the fiftieth anniversary of one of the most momentous events of the 20th century, and something which would be a lasting tribute and testimonial to the efforts of a generation. And to show that things did happen in Oundle during World War II, as of course they did to a greater or to a lesser extent in every town, every village and every home in Britain during those six terrible years.

Oundle, August 1995

155: Oundle War Memorial, a drawing by local artist Diana Leigh.

TEXT AND PICTURE CREDITS

Grateful acknowledgement is made to the publishers and copyright holders for permission to reproduce previously published material from the following:

Text

Memories of Ninety Years, by HRH Princess Alice, Duchess of Gloucester, Collins & Brown, London, 1991

There Shall be Wings The RAF: 1918 to the Present, by Max Arthur, Hodder & Stoughton, London, 1993

Towards the setting sun, by James Bradley, J. M. L. Fuller, 1984

The Great Escape, by Paul Brickhill, Faber and Faber, 1951

Nine Lives, Through Laughing Eyes, by Lt. Col. Robert Butler MBE, MC, Invicta Publishing, 1993 (obtainable from Invicta Publishing, 21 Manor Road, Milford on Sea, Lymington, Hants SO41 0RG)

The Second World War, by Winston S. Churchill, Cassell & Co Ltd. Reproduced with permission of Curtis Brown Ltd, London, on behalf of the Estate of Sir Winston S. Churchill. Copyright the Estate of Sir Winston S. Churchill

The Daily Telegraph (Obituaries for Patrick Beesly, 22 August 1986, © The Telegraph plc, London, 1986; Dr Charles Newman, 2 September 1989, © The Telegraph plc, London, 1989; Rear Admiral Ben Bryant, 25 November 1994, © The Telegraph plc, London, 1994)

Oundle and the English Public School, by Raymond Flower, Stacey International, 1989

Fifty years on — life in the Oflag, by D. H. Ford, *The Old Oundelian*, 1993-4

Battle of Britain, by Norman Franks, Bison Books, 1981

Aviation in Northamptonshire, by Michael L. Gibson, Northamptonshire Libraries, 1982

When the skies were full, by Peter Green, *FlyPast Magazine*, 1993

The Lady of the Manor, by Jonathan Hand & Angus Piper, *The Laxtonian*, Summer 1984

A Chronicle of the 351st Bomb Group (H), by Ken Harbour & Peter Harris, Byron Kennedy and Company, Revised 1985

The Challenge of War — Scientific and engineering contributions to World War Two, by Guy Hartcup, David & Charles, Newton Abbot, 1970

Oundle in Wartime, by Dudley Heesom,*The Laxtonian*, Michaelmas Term, 1980

The Thirties at Oundle, by Dudley Heesom,*The Laxtonian*, Michaelmas Term, 1979

What did you do in the War, Auntie? The BBC at War 1939-45, by Tom Hickman, published by BBC Books at £15.99 in hardback, 1995

The Laxtonian

All my Yesterdays: an autobiography, by Cecil Lewis, Element Books Limited, 1993

Sagittarius Surviving, by Cecil Lewis, Leo Cooper, 1991

Wellington — Pillar of State, by Elizabeth Longford, London, 1972, Weidenfeld & Nicolson

Wellington — The Years of the Sword, by Elizabeth Longford, London, 1969, Weidenfeld & Nicolson

We'll Meet Again, by Vera Lynn (with Robin Cross and Jenny de Gex), Sidgwick & Jackson, London, 1989, and Macmillan General Books Ltd

The Newmans of Barnsley, by John Newman Ward, Ashgrove Press Ltd, Bath, 1986.

Northamptonshire at war, A selection of photographs, Northamptonshire Libraries, 1979

The Old Oundelian

The Ousel, Bedford School's magazine

Peterborough Evening Telegraph, (1 June 1994) for permission to quote extracts from Rex Milborne's account of the Normandy landings.

The Country House in Wartime 1945-1939, by Caroline Seebohm, Weidenfeld & Nicolson, London 1989

Karl 'Charlie' Schoenrock, by Oliver Sharp, *The Laxtonian*, 1991

A prisoner in Sumatra, by Nick Squires, *The Laxtonian*, 1986

A History of the SAS, by John Strawson, Secker & Warburg, London

The Times, (Obituaries for the Right Hon. Sir Rodger Winn, © Times Newspapers Limited, 1972; Gerald Touch, 6 December 1994, © Times Newspapers Limited 1994).

The Wooden Horse, by Eric Williams, 1949, HarperCollins Publishers Limited

Pictures

Photograph of Miriam Rothschild by Robert Barber: 1; Photograph of Dr V. A. Grantham by Aspect Photography, Water Newton: 2; Mrs E. Berridge: 4, 40, 107, 131; Mrs P. Cawdell: 6, 7; Mr H. J. Matthews: 8, 68; Mrs J. Hardick: 10, 38, 111, 112, 115, 117, 120, 146; Mr J. Hinman: 14, 29, 30; Mr D. Ford: 16, 21, 22, 23, 39, 41, 44, 45, 60; Mrs G. Ashby: 17, 18, 19, 20; Mrs N. Blunt: 24; The Rotary Club of Oundle: 25; Mr W. J. Irving: 27; Mrs P. Gidley: 32, 33, 34, 49, 104; The Laxtonian: 36, 47, 57, 114; Mr P. Duerden: 37; The Old Oundelian: 46, 64, 110, 139; Oundle School Photographic Society: 48, 81, 150, 151; Mr W. Monk: 50; Cdre K. A. Gadd CBE, DSC: 51, 52, 53; Mrs P. Hunter-Gordon: 54; Mr G. Potts: 55, 56; Oundle School Memorial Trust: 58, 63, 65, 83; Mrs L. Fallace: 59; Mr C. A. Lewis: 61; Mrs J. Stevens: 62; Mr P. Burdett: 66; Mr P. Kelham: 67; Capt. N. A. Jewell MBE, DSC: 69; Mr G. Bristow: 70; Mrs M. Burr: 72; Mr L. Ercolani DSO, DFC: 73; Mrs A. Hudson: 74; Miss A. M. Roughton: 75; Mrs G. M. Measures: 76; Mr R. Aitken DSO: 77, 78; Imperial War Museum: 79, 108; Photographs by Chris Lowndes: 80, 82, 93, 100, 140, 153, 154; Lt Col R. Butler MBE, MC: 84; Mrs D. Marlow: 85, 86, 87, 88, 89; Mr D. Eadie MC: 90; Mr E. Maslen-Jones MC, DFC: 91, 92; Dr M. Lewis: 94; Mr N. C. Graesser: 96; Mr A. Spring: 97, 98; Mr A. Hayward: 99; Mrs W. Fitzjohn: 101, 102; Mr D. Maw: 103; Mr R. Gent: 105, 106; Mr R. B. Miller: 109; Mr B. Smith: 113; Mrs L. Sloan: 116, 123; Mr K. Harbour: 119, 126, 129; Mr K. Harbour and Mr N. Ham: 128; Mrs J. Mabelson and Mrs M. Hawkins: 121, 122; Mr and Mrs R. School, and David Poole: 130; Mr R. Sismey: 132; Peter Brookes' cartoon of 2 July 1992, © Times Newspapers Limited 1992: 135; Mr R. Leigh: 141; Mr J. Bradley MBE: 143; Mr N. Carpanini and Grapevine: 148; Mrs R. Keens: 149; Carlton UK Television: 152; Mrs D. Leigh: 155. The remaining photographs were taken by the author.

SELECTED BIBLIOGRAPHY

In addition to specific material for which copyright permission was sought, and which are listed separately, the following works have been consulted and may be of interest.

Bullock, Alan — *Hitler A Study in Tyranny*, London, 1954

Buruma, Ian — *The Wages of Guilt: Memories of War in Germany and Japan*, London, Cape, 1991

David, Saul — *Churchill's Sacrifice of the Highland Division,* Brassey's, 1995

English, Ian — *Assisted Passage — Walking to Freedom — Italy 1943*, Privately published, 1995 (Obtainable from the author, Dale Cottage, Preston-under-Scar, Leyburn, North Yorkshire DL8 4AH)

Holloway, B. G. & Banks, H. — *The Northamptonshire Home Guard 1940-1945,* published by The Northamptonshire Home Guard, 1945

Irving, David — *The War between the Generals*, Allen Lane, London 1981

B. H. Liddell Hart, *The Second World War,* Cassell & Co, 1970

McGlade, Shirley & McCormack, Mary — *Daddy, where are you?* Smith Gryphon, 1992

Montagu, Ewen — *The Man Who Never Was*, Evans Brothers Limited, London, 1953

Northamptonshire County Council — *Air Raid and other War Incidents in Northamptonshire* 1939-1945, 19 July 1945, Appendix to report of the Emergency Committee

Oundle Memorials of the Second World War 1939-1945 published by the Oundle School Memorial Trust

Salmond, J. B. — *The History of the 51st Highland Division*, The Pentland Press, 1995

Tinsley, Terence — *Stick and String*, Buckland Publications Ltd., London, 1992

Walker, W.G. — *History of the Oundle Schools*, The Grocers' Company, London, 1956

Winfield, Pamela — *Bye Bye Baby*, Bloomsbury Publishing Ltd., London, 1992

Wright, Michael (ed.) — *The World at Arms: The Reader's Digest Illustrated History of World War II*, London 1989

Every effort has been made to trace the copyright holders of material quoted in this book, and the publishers will be happy to deal retrospectively with this matter if any copyright has inadvertently been breached.

INDEX OF NAMES

Abe, Hiroshi 304-5
Adams, G. P. 290
Aitken, Sub-Lieutenant Robert 141-3, 146-9, 273, 308
Akroyd, Donald 179, 303
Alexander, General Sir Harold 117, 125, 155, 201
Alexander, James 70, 74
Allen, Bevil 1, 11, 18, 25, 27, 35, 37, 46, 48-9, 51, 62, 230, 237-8, 290, 295-6, 302
Allen, Mary 237
Alms, Brigadier James 187
Anders, General Wladyslaw 259
Anderson, David 304
Anderson, Sir John 46
Armstrong, Colonel Frank 221
Armstrong, Lieutenant Colonel John 176
Arnett, Percy 238
Arnold, Lieutenant General H. H. 223
Ashby, Corporal D. A. 297
Ashby, Gladys 29-30
Ashby, Pauline 227, 237
Atcherley, Air Marshal Sir Richard 101
Atcherley, Air Vice Marshal David 101, 210
Auchinleck, General Sir Claude 109, 125

Bader, Group Captain Douglas 303-4
Badger, Lieutenant William 246
Baines, Frank 176
Baker, N. I. 205
Bamford, Mrs Win 39
Bamford Snr., Mrs 39
Banks, Monty 217
Banno, Colonel 281
Barber, Mrs Murray 106
Barber, Private Leslie 211, 297
Barber, Rolf 73
Barber, Warrant Officer Donald 211, 297
Barker, Hugh 14
Barnes, Captain E. A. 56-7
Bartley, Lieutenant Ronald 246
Beaufoy, G. Maurice 75
Beaumont, Group Captain Stephen 82
Beesly, Lieutenant Commander Patrick 132
Bennett, F. 52
Berridge, Elizabeth 9, 25, 35-6, 50-1, 62, 64, 76, 82, 222, 227, 236, 243, 295 (see also *Cole, Elizabeth*)
Berridge, Lieutenant Colonel F. R. 55-6, 208-9, 245
Berridge, Lieutenant David 208-9, 211
Berridge, Lieutenant Richard 209

Berridge, Michael 50
Berridge, Miss Anne 38
Berridge, Mrs Dorothy 38
Bingham, Charles 27
Birdsall, Flying Officer William 161
Birkbeck, Lieutenant Colonel Alexander 140
Birlem, Major Keith 245
Black, Alma 110
Black, Corporal Reginald 110, 297
Black, Councillor Harry 110
Black, Dorothy 110
Blackwell, Mr 53
Blunt, Nora 25, 76
Blythe, Major Kenneth 176
Bond, Captain G. D. (Christopher) 182-5
Bowden, Lord Vivian 14-5
Bowen-Davies, Flight Lieutenant Caradoc 83
Bowles, Lieutenant Colonel Robert 222, 247
Bradley, James 116, 277-82, 289-90, 304-5
Bradley, Lindsay 116, 280
Bradley, Roger 116, 280
Branfoot, Captain J. M. 57
Brassey, Lord 32
Brickhill, Paul 266
Briggs, Battery Sergeant Major Frank 96, 297
Briggs, Bob 307
Briggs, Sir George 12
Brindsley, Ernie 53
Brinson, Major William L. 193
Bristow, George 128-30, 178, 301
Brittain, Lieutenant John 65, 91, 297-8
Brodie, Air Commodore Ian 98-9
Brookes, Peter 253
Brown, Alec 261
Brown, Corporal 280
Brown, Flight Sergeant Edward 202-3
Brown, Gertrude 291
Brown, Lieutenant Commander Anthony 154
Brown, Reverend M. 154
Brown, Sub-Lieutenant Peter 114
Brunt, Trooper 155
Bryant, Rear Admiral Ben 132-4
Bugatti, Ettore 98
Bull, Corporal Frederick 186
Bullock, Alan 83
Burdett, Gunner Avery John 108, 297
Burns, Colonel Robert 227, 239
Burns, Mr 47
Butcher, Lieutenant Colonel Alfred 65, 297
Butler, Captain John David 174-6
Butler, Christopher 119-20

Butler, Lieutenant Colonel Robert 85, 118-23, 156-60, 196-8, 215, 308
Butler, Phoebe 118-21, 160
Butt, Mrs 39

Caborn, Miss 39
Calhoun, Captain 224
Cameron, Lieutenant Donald 146
Campbell, Donald 98
Carne Rasch, Brigadier Guy E. 38
Carpenter, Valerie 244
Carter, Bill 36, 53
Carter, Fred 53
Carwile, Technical Sergeant John 238
Case, Lieutenant Herbert 56
Cichon, Paul 258-9
Clark, David 251-2
Clark, General Mark 128
Clarke, Aubrey 116-7, 282-9, 301
Clarke, Gordon 53
Clarke, Ruff 53
Clipston, Mrs 39
Cockburn, Brigadier John 109
Codner, Michael 266
Colbourne, Private Philip 194
Cole, Elizabeth 227 (see also *Berridge, Elizabeth*)
Cole, Reverend Wilfred 9, 62
Collier, Lieutenant D. H. E. 297
Collier, Mrs 39
Colson, Captain Alec 128
Cooke, Lieutenant Geoffrey 185
Coombs, Captain Philip 57, 221
Coombs, Sybil 222
Cooper, Sergeant Navigator Alan 161
Cottingham, Sergeant L. E. 297
Cottingham, Winifred 237
Cotton, Jack 296
Cotton, Philip 9, 52
Cox, Ernie 24
Craig, Major General A. 247
Crawley, Mrs 39
Cropper, Donald 158
Crowe, Dr Elsie 273-6, 288
Cullingford, Mr 38-9
Cunnington, John 296
Cutcliffe, Alan 32, 57
Czernin, Squadron Leader Count Manfred 100, 187
Czwortek, John 257-8

Daniell, Lieutenant Colonel K. F. 169
Davies, Lord 182
Davis, Gunner 272
Davis, Technical Sergeant Cleo 238
Dawson, Air Vice Marshal Graham 115
De la Bere, Brigadier Ivan 120

De Ramsey, Lord 281
de Ville, Eric 93
Delamain, Charles 302
Dew, Lance Corporal H. G. 297
Dietrich, Marlene 17, 229
Dixey, Lieutenant Joseph 246
Dodsworth, Bert 53
Donegani, Joan 18
Dönitz, Admiral Karl 84, 132, 154
Doucett, Corporal Philip 'Red' 232-3
Douglas, Mrs 39
Downes, Michael 308
Downes, Rosie 41
Dudgeon, Captain Patrick 154-5
Duerden, Patrick 309
Duffin, Jessie 1, 50, 243 (see also *Northen, Jessie*)
Dunkley, Brennie 85

Eadie, Major Denis 168-9, 213
Earnshaw-Smith, Rev. Harold 49
Eckhard, Captain Basil 128
Edwards, Mrs 39
Edwards, Sergeant Junior 238
Eisenhower, General 178, 187, 202
Elcock, Tim 291
Elliott, Major Russell 154, 180
Elson, Inspector 'Grip' 196-8
Embry, Air Marshal Sir Basil 101, 210
English, Ian 139, 266
Ercolani, Barry 174
Ercolani, Wing Commander Lucian 112-4, 135-7, 171-4, 308
Evans, Charles 165
Evans, Sergeant Denis 89-90

Fairclough, Second Lieutenant Wilfrid 108
Falcey, Sergeant Edward 238
Fallace, Lucy 95-6, 104-5
Fallace, Tom 104
Ferguson, Brigadier General A. F. H. 56
Ferris, Jamie 169
Fforde, John 198
Fiddick, Tom 83, 214, 301
Fieldhouse, Major Robert 266
Fields, Gracie 217
Finnegan, Jack 76
Fisher, Dr Kenneth 6, 23, 33, 62, 67, 73, 75, 91, 170, 301-2
Fisher, Margery 65
Fisher, Miss 34
Floden, Captain Donald 246
Flower, Raymond 6
Ford, Dennis 261
Formby, Ella 18
Formby, George 18

INDEX OF NAMES

Foster, Charles 20
Foster-Anderson, Lieutenant Donald 140
Fox, Mrs 42
Fox, Private L. E. 297
Francis, Gunner Arthur 180
Freeman, Captain Derrick 128
Frodsham, Sub-Lieutenant Neville 106
Fukuei, Major General 278
Fulmer, Lieutenant 193

Gable, Captain Clark 222-9, 309
Gadd, Commodore Kenneth 2, 84, 86-9, 92, 141, 199, 300, 306
Gainer, Captain E. St. C. 58
Gale, Margaret 24, 41
Galland, Adolf 100, 187
Game, Philip 36
Garrett, Lovel 94-5, 261-3
Garrett, Syd 53
Gaunt, Frank 53
Gaunt, Joyce 228, 291, 296 (see also *Hardick, Joyce*)
Gaunt, June 18, 232, 296
Gautier, Kurt Theo 93
Gibson, Mick 108
Gibson, Wing Commander Guy 167
Gidley, Mrs Peggy 46 (see also *Wade, Peggy*)
Giraud, General Henri 128
Gloucester, Prince Henry, Duke of 55, 63, 225, 249
Gloucester, Prince William of 243-4, 248-9, 291
Gloucester, Princess Alice, Duchess of 21, 26, 36, 38-9, 45, 50, 55, 63-4, 225, 243-4, 248, 291
Goddard, Major Peter 187
Goodman, Margaret 237
Gordon, Captain Richard 216
Gort, General Lord 92
Graesser, Colonel Sir Alastair 186-7, 209
Graesser, Rhidian 24, 27, 49, 56, 65-6
Grant, Ian 10
Grant-Taylor, Major 157
Grantham, Dr V. A. (Ben) 1, 3-4, 70, 82-3, 111, 118, 300, 305-6
Green, Peter 20
Greenyer, Corporal 119
Grimshaw, Bill 158-9

Hancock, Bob 53
Harbour, Ken 246
Hardick, Joyce 18, 228 (see also *Gaunt, Joyce*)
Hardwick, Sub-Lieutenant William 134
Harper, J. 238
Harris, Air Marshal A. T. 'Bomber' 135
Harrison, Sergeant C. 'Pat' 238
Hart, Liddell 83, 109
Harvey, Captain C. E. 56

Hatcher, Colonel William A. 222-4, 229
Hawkins, Margaret 236, 245 (see also *Laxton, Margaret*)
Hayward, Tony 190, 194-5
Healey, Bob 195
Heard, Captain J. H. 57
Heesom, Dudley 4-6, 15, 23, 27, 31, 54, 57, 68-70, 132, 309
Hellier, Lieutenant Colonel Francis 178
Helms, Erwin 4
Heron Rogers, Sub-Lieutenant John 106, 298
Hewett, Major H. P. 31, 39, 57-8
Hewett, Second Lieutenant 156
Higson-Smith, Peter 11
Hill, Jack 53
Hill, Sergeant N. A. 297
Hinman, John 2, 21
Hiraoka, Takashi 304
Hodgson, Colonel Ralph 137-8, 213-4
Hodgson, Lindsay 48-9
Holdsworth Hunt, C. 307
Hollis, Corporal William T. 192-3
Hope, Bob 17, 228-9
Horn, Joe 53
Horn, Mrs 39
Horsford, Flight Sergeant John 205, 207, 297
Horsford, Mr 290
Houghton, Tom 53
Howard, Peter 264-5
Howitt, Lieutenant Peter 185
Hudson, Ted 18
Hughes, Sergeant T. W. 297
Hugill, Lieutenant Commander Tony 190
Hunt, Vivian 85
Hunter-Gordon, Major Patrick 89-90
Hyne, Flight Lieutenant Gerald 161

Illius, Flying Officer Andrew 161
Ismay, Lord 154
Ito, Mayor Itcho 304

Jackson, Arthur 67
Jackson, Michael 303
Jerrard, Alan 97
Jewell, Captain Norman 127-8, 150, 152-3, 308
Johnson, Fred 53
Johnson, H. 52
Johnson, Major Roger 252-6
Jolowicz, Tony 58
Jorgensen, Carl 245

Keene, John 12, 69, 301
Keens, Florence 300
Keens, Lewis 92, 298-9

317

Keens, Ruth 1, 9, 17-20, 26-7, 33, 36, 40, 49-50, 64, 76, 180, 228, 244, 290-1 (see also *Moisey, Ruth*)
Kelham, Flying Officer John 124
Kenrick, Dorothy 204
Kent, Duke of 112
Kerr, Bob 242
Kimura, Lieutenant General Hyotaro 214
King, Captain Christopher 139, 297
King, Henry 139
King, Lieutenant John 139, 297
King, Olive 139
Knight, Richard 304
Knox, Rawle 277
Kordos, Przemystaw 257

Lake, Denis 66
Lakeman, Maurice 65-6
Lamb, Henry 83
Lane, Captain George 177-8
Lane, Mrs George 2 (see also *Rothschild, Miriam*)
Lane, Patrick 20, 70, 75, 295, 303
Lane, Wing Commander S. A. 163
Langford, Frances 228-9
Laski, Professor 4
Lassen, Herr W. 182
Lawrence, T. E. 98 (see also *Shaw, T. E.*)
Laxton, A. 52
Laxton, Gertrude E. 245
Laxton, Jean 28 (see also *Mabelson, Jean*)
Laxton, Margaret 28 (see also *Hawkins, Margaret*)
Laxton, Mrs A. 39
Laxton, Stewart 238-9, 290
Leayton, V. 52
LeDoux, Major Elzia 246-7
Lee, Betty 237
Lee, Captain Robert 246
Lee, Walter 53
Leech, Sidney 239
Leeper, Sir Rex 200
Leigh, Diana 310
Leigh, Lance-Bombardier Ralph 96-7, 124-5, 210, 267-72, 287, 301, 309
Levin, Bernard 252-3
Lewington, H. 52
Lewis, Cecil 97-9, 198-201, 308
Lewis, Dr Michael 180-2, 186, 191, 306-7
Lewis, Ivor 198
Lightbody, Nanny 244
Lilford, Baron 64
Lombard, Carole 222
Lovibond, Major Thomas 186
Ludlow, G. 52
Lumley, Major Heaton 106
Lynch, Lieutenant 246

Lyttle, Lieutenant 246

Mabelson, Jean 232-3, 236, 245 (see also *Laxton, Jean*)
Macmillan, Harold 200
Mahin, Johnny 223-4, 226
Malan, Monsieur 6
Maltby, Major General Christopher 116
Markham, Mrs 37
Marks, Mara 96
Marlow, Mrs D. E. 163, 165
Marlow, Sergeant John 161-7, 297
Marment, Major Arthur 168-9, 214
Marriott, Mrs 227
Marshall, General George C. 177
Marshall, Gunner William 297-8
Marshall, Lieutenant Colonel Arthur 92-3
Marshall, Sergeant Maurice 238
Martin, Lieutenant 246
Martin, Pepper 229
Martin, Private W. A. J. 297
Maslen-Jones, Captain Edward 169-71, 212, 214-5
Maslen-Jones, Captain Robert 214
Mason, Lottie 44-5
Mason, Miss 34
Mason, Pilot Officer John 205-6, 297
Massey, Paul 75, 236
Mast, General 128
Mathies, Mrs Mary 247
Mathies, Sergeant Archie 246-7
Matthews, Captain H. J. (John) 15, 49, 64, 125
Matthews, Captain Nelson E. 246
Maw, David 204-5
Maw, Squadron Leader Denys 204, 266
Maw, Wing Commander Michael 203-5, 266
Maw, Wing Commander Roger 203, 264-6
Mays, Raymond 98
McComish, Roy 212
McCurdy, Jimmy 245
McIntyre, Lieutenant Andrew 223-4
McMurray, David 252, 307-8
McPherson, Lance-Bombardier 90
Meadwell, Flight Sergeant Edward 161
Measures, Captain Benjamin Guy 139-40
Measures, Mr and Mrs Benjamin 139
Melton, Molly 179
Mengee, Staff Sergeant Gene 232, 234
Messervy, Major General Frank 168
Milborne, Rex 176-7
Miller, Flight Lieutenant Robin 6-8, 80-1, 178, 210, 215-7, 272, 276, 300, 305
Miller, Glenn 17, 228
Miller, Second Lieutenant Whitney 229, 239-42, 244, 249, 301, 306
Milliken, Captain George 185

INDEX OF NAMES

Mills, Freddie 118
Mills, Michael 6, 73-4
Milton, Major 222
Mitchell, R. 52
Moisey, Ruth 1, 180, 228 (see also *Keens, Ruth*)
Monk, Flight Lieutenant Bill 79-80
Monk, Gordon 79
Monk, John 80
Montagu, Lieutenant Commander Ewen 151-3
Montgomery, Field Marshal Viscount Montgomery of Alamein 70, 125-6, 139, 180, 182, 185-6, 303
Moore, Technical/Sergeant Carl 246-7
Morgan, Lieutenant General F. E. 187
Morshead, Lieutenant General Sir Leslie 213
Moss, Pilot Officer Frank 108
Mowbray, H. 52
Muntz, Major R. A. 56
Muspratt, Richard 102
Musser, Ben 242-3
Mutaguchi, Lieutenant General Renya 168
Mycock, David 56, 65
Mycroft, Mrs 34

Nelson, George (Lord Nelson of Stafford) 12-3
Nelson, Lieutenant Clarence 246-7
Newman, Arnold Charles 12
Newman, Dr Charles 12, 36
Newsome, Noel 83
Newton, Chris 53
Niven, David 226
Nobbs, Margaret 245
Northen, Delma 226-7
Northen, Jessie 1 (see also *Duffin, Jessie*)
Norwood, Carl 229, 236

O'Connor, Lieutenant General Sir Richard 182
O'Neill, Brigadier General R. E. 247
Orchard, Lieutenant Antony 169
Ordish, Flight Lieutenant Charles 134
Osman, Captain Charles 15, 65, 91, 297-8
Owen, Sir Alfred 12
Owen, Vic 41

Paget, General Sir Bernard 196
Palmer, Herbert 12, 46, 68
Parker, Miss Connie 38
Parker, Miss Ethel 38
Parkinson, Sub-Lieutenant Robert 134, 149
Parnell, Mrs 39
Paterson, Robin 33, 75, 301
Paxman, Edward 12, 134
Payne, Captain Alec 76, 81, 188-9, 208, 300

Pearce, Frances 28
Penwell, Private 192
Perry, Lieutenant Peter 59
Philpot, Oliver 266
Pickard, Michael 296
Pike, Blondie 195
Pinckney, Captain 155
Place, Charles 149
Place, Rear Admiral Godfrey 144, 149
Pollard, Flight Sergeant Thomas 211
Pollard, Mavis 226-7
Poole, David 248
Portal, Air Marshal Sir Charles 135
Potter, Company Sergeant Major John 115
Potts, Captain Michael 90-1
Potts, Lieutenant Gordon 90-1
Priest, Mrs 47
Priestman, Major P. 57
Prior, Corporal 109
Pye, Harold 13

Rahmann, K. 6
Reading, Stella, Marchioness of 28, 40
Reddaway, Lieutenant Colonel Norman 93, 139
Redhead, L. 52
Redmond, Mrs 243
Rees, Griffith 27, 49
Reinke, Lester 232, 235
Rex, Sergeant Joe 246-7
Ribbentrop, Joachim von 9
Richardson, Flight Engineer Sergeant Peter 137, 297
Richardson, J. 52
Richardson, Jodie 256
Richardson, Major Franklin 227
Richardson, Mrs 34
Richmond, Jessie 25, 50
Riddell, Lieutenant Colonel Duncan 179
Riddle, Arthur 53
Rob, Captain Charles 139
Roberts, General 'Pip' 182-4, 211
Robinson, John 190, 303
Robinson, Miss Dora 38
Robinson, Sergeant Russel 247
Robson, Mrs 38
Romano, Tony 228-9
Romig, Colonel Eugene 222, 246-7
Rommel, Field Marshal Erwin 94, 106-10, 117, 124-5, 139, 154, 161, 182-3, 196, 261, 303
Roper, Major Leonard 246
Rosebery, Lord 20, 63
Roskelly, Mrs 1
Rothschild, Miriam 2-3, 8-9, 19-20, 28, 47, 49, 61-62, 111-2, 177-8, 222, 231, 243, 250-1, 302 (see also *Lane, Mrs George*)

Roughton, Gunner James 138, 297

Sanderson, Frederick 12, 65, 97
Saunders, Reggie 12
Sauntson, Keith 12
Sauntson, Margaret 12
Schoenrock, Hilda 293
Schoenrock, Karl 'Charlie' 37, 291-3
Schofield, Ted 170
Schultz, Technical Sergeant Peter 238
Schuschnigg, Dr 100
Scobie, General Ronald 200
Scotland, Colonel 189
Scott, Major John 222
Seebohm, Caroline 61
Selangor, Sultan of 217
Sewell, Blanche 226
Shallard, Wing Commander H. P. 210
Sharman, Captain John 111, 126, 140
Sharman, Sheila 291
Shaw, Aircraftsman T. E. 98 (see also *Lawrence, T. E.*)
Shaw, George Bernard 97-8
Shaw, Lawrence 'Tub' 34
Shepley, Flight Lieutenant George Rex 93-4, 99-100
Shepley, Jeanne 100
Shepley, Pilot Officer Douglas 93, 99-100
Shepley, Seymour 100
Short, Mrs 38
Shurrock, Captain Teddy 216
Sikkenga, Lieutenant Albert 205
Simmons, Wing Commander Donald 135
Simpson, John 290
Skiba, Emil 260
Slim, Field Marshal Sir William 139, 168, 171, 212
Sloan, Lorna 221-2, 226-8, 232, 237, 244
Smart, Ruth 50
Smith, Barry 225
Smith, Corporal G. C. 297
Smith, Corporal Russell M. 193
Smith, G. L. 14
Smith, Mrs Winifred 29
Smith, Sergeant Joe 231
Snedegar, Captain Clay 251-2
Sowell, Sergeant Thomas 247
Speer, Albert 135
Spooner, Company Sergeant Major 156
Spragg, Major Frank 57, 226
Spriggs, Percy 53
Spring, Albert 191-4
Spurrier, Lieutenant 193
St John Booth, Second Lieutenant Michael 185
St Leger, Flying Officer Charles 161
Stainforth, Graham 303

Steele, Air Marshal Sir Charles 208
Stevens, Brigadier 212
Stewart, James 227
Stewart, Lieutenant Colonel James 246
Stirling, Captain David 115
Stokes, Mrs 48
Stopford, General Montagu 212
Stover, Mrs 245
Straight, Air Commodore Witney 198
Stretton, F. 9, 52
Schuschnigg — *see Schuschnigg*
Swithinbank, Lieutenant Denis 149
Syme, Major James 266-7

Taney, Sergeant Pilot Alfred 137, 297
Tarleton, Ben 157-8
Tatam, Flight Lieutenant Noel 205, 297
Taussig, Heinz Wolfgang 8 (see also *Tyrrell, Henry William*)
Tedder, Sir Arthur 202
Thompson, P. 52
Thomson, Lieutenant 134
Thorington, Vic 2, 84, 106-7, 109, 179
Thring, Commander 131
Tibbets, Major Paul W. 221
Tinsley, Major Terence 139
Tod, Major Charles 1, 84, 118, 300, 305-6
Touch, Gerald 13-4, 307-8
Touch, J. 52
Touch, Phyllis 14, 307
Truemper, Lieutenant 246-7
Truemper, Mrs Henry E. 247
Tuffs, Mrs Peggy 29
Turner, Squadron Leader Rodney 85, 107, 114
Turnill, Willoughby 86
Tuttle, Air Commodore Geoffrey 200
Tyrrell, Henry William 8 (see also *Taussig, Heinz Wolfgang*)

van Zanten, Johan 192-4
Venning, Lieutenant D. L. 57
Vessey, C. 52
Vickers, Sir Geoffrey 12
Villiers, Amherst 98
Viney, Major Elliott 95, 263-4, 273, 308

Waddams, F. C. 15
Wade, Peggy 46 (see also *Gidley, Peggy*)
Wagstaff, William 244
Waite, Mrs 38
Walker, W. G. 'Willie' 20, 57
Walker, Wing Commander Donald 167
Walton, Ella 237, 296
Walton, Susan 296
Warr, Lance Corporal John 70
Watkinson, Richard 75

INDEX OF NAMES

Watson-Watt, Professor Robert 13
Watts, Drum Major 121
Wavell, Field Marshal Sir Archibald 107, 109, 138, 196
Weir, Douglas 305
White, Flying Officer David 161
Whitwell, Douglas 45-6
Whitworth, Air Commodore John 167
Wickham, Lady Ethel 221
Wickham, Molly 45, 228
Wild, Colonel Cyril 276-7, 280-1
Williams, Eric 264, 266
Williams, Mr 48
Williamson, Major Andrew 110
Williamson, Major William 127
Wills, C. 52
Wilson, Graham 53
Wingate, Major General Orde 174
Winn, Right Hon. Sir Rodger 131-2
Winser, George 195
Winterton, Major General Sir John 93, 117
Wood, Miss A. M. 39
Wood, Sir Kingsley 42
Wright, A. 52
Wykeham-Barnes, Group Captain P. G. 210

Yamamoto, Corporal 276
Yandell, G. 36
Yeld, Lieutenant R. K. 57
York, Duchess of 56
Young, Edward 133
Young, Lieutenant Colonel C. M. 'Boy' 282
Younger, Bill 107